MAIN STREET AMUSEMENTS

MAIN STREET AMUSEMENTS

Movies and
Commercial Entertainment
in a Southern City,
1896–1930

Gregory A. Waller

Smithsonian Institution Press

Washington and London

Editor: Fran Kianka
Production editor: Jack Kirshbaum
Designer: Alan Carter

Library of Congress Cataloging-in-Publication Data

Waller, Gregory A. (Gregory Albert), 1950–
    Main Street amusements : movies and commercial entertainment in a Southern
city, 1896–1930 / Gregory A. Waller.
        p.   cm.
    Includes bibliographical references and index.
    ISBN 1-56098-504-6 (alk. paper)
    1. Motion pictures—Kentucky—Lexington—History.   2. Performing
arts—Kentucky—Lexington—History—20th century.   I. Title.
PN1993.5.U743W36   1995
791.43′09769′47—dc20   94-43157

British Library Cataloging-in-Publication data available

Manufactured in the United States of America
00   99   98   97   96   95   5   4   3   2   1

⊗ The paper used in this publication meets the minimum requirements of the American National
Standard for Permanence of Paper for Printed Library Materials Z39.48–1984.

For permission to reproduce any of the illustrations, please correspond directly with the sources.
The Smithsonian Institution Press does not retain reproduction rights for these illustrations individually or maintain a file of addresses for photo sources.

Cover illustration: Detail of the auditorium of the Kentucky Theatre. Photo courtesy University of
Kentucky Photo Archives

For my father

and the memory of my mother

CONTENTS

FOREWORD

In the last twenty years, the study of American film history has emerged from the doldrums to become a dynamic area of inquiry and a significant contributor to the broader fields of cultural history and American studies. One important strand in this renaissance has been a growing recognition of the importance of film exhibition and moviegoing itself as historical phenomena. There has been a new sensitivity not only to this historical evolution but also to geographic particularity and to the cinema's concrete interaction with, and relationship to, other forms of commercial entertainment and popular culture. Gregory Waller's *Main Street Amusements* represents a compelling culmination of these trends. The rigorous case study of moviegoing and popular amusements in Lexington, Kentucky, demonstrates the broad insights that can be gained through close examinations of a single community—insights that help us understand the extraordinary transformation of daily life that has occurred in twentieth-century America.

Movies were once largely seen as a form of undifferentiated mass communication that offered the same experience to people in Peoria and Manhattan, Pensacola and Spokane. Such consensus history has lost its force as feminists such as Elizabeth Ewen, Judith Mayne, and Miriam Hansen examined ways

in which moviegoing was an activity of special significance to women. Robert
Sklar and Roy Rosenzweig have likewise considered the experience of film
viewing from the perspectives of working-class immigrants. Focusing on the
eastern industrial city of Worcester, Massachusetts, in his book *Eight Hours
for What We Will,* Rosenzweig has shown the many ways in which movies
differed from previous and contemporaneous leisure-time activities. In focusing on Lexington, Waller's study expands upon and further illuminates Rosenzweig's analysis. Unlike Worcester, Lexington had a relatively small
industrial base and served as a regional commercial center. Most residents
were native-born Americans rather than immigrants. The sharp divisions
were racial, not ethnic. Located in a border state, Lexington residents often
behaved like their neighbors further to the south and occasionally like their
compatriots to the north. Reading Waller's story, one periodically realizes that
some version of the Civil War was still being fought in the arena of culture;
at other times, the very issues that beset film practices in the North—Sunday
closings, the gradual development of regional chains, and so forth—were
evident in Lexington. Because Waller has chosen a region that has received
little previous attention from film scholars, he has been able to raise new and
important issues about cultural formation.

The history of American cinema cannot be written without a well-
grounded understanding of exhibition patterns in the nation's cities and
towns. After cranking through many hundreds of reels of microfilm in an attempt to establish such patterns over relatively brief periods of time, and
after avidly reading and making use of numerous local accounts, typically
presented in article form, I have become acutely aware of the difficulty of
undertaking such studies, and the potential dangers if they are not ade-
quately realized. These studies are only as valuable as the historian's
research, ingenuity, and analytic skills. One frequently cited study of pre–
World War I exhibition in Austin, Texas, concludes that the moviegoing habit
came later to that part of the nation, and perhaps to many other areas as well:
according to this scholar, the first film exhibition came in 1900, with regular
film exhibitions only occurring about 1910 and then in small-time vaudeville
houses. I have never examined the Austin newspapers, the principal source
for this author's survey, but trade journals for the amusement industry indicate that a theatrical company showed films of a bullfight to residents of the
Texas capital in December 1896 and that nickelodeons (modest storefront
motion picture theaters that typically charged patrons five cents for admission) were booming by the spring of 1907 (four in March and nine in May).

Instead of a puzzling, if intriguing lag of four to five years in comparison to eastern cities, we encounter a more typical and understandable one of six to nine months, similar in many respects to the situation in Lexington.

Film historians sometimes function like astrophysicists trying to ascertain the amount of matter in the universe. In seeking to grasp the actual scope and depth of motion picture practice, one survey of New York City nickelodeons, for example, found few such theaters in Italian neighborhoods and concluded that Italians, in contrast to Jews, did not go to the movies. Yet trade journals from the early nickelodeon period provide descriptions of moviegoing along the major thoroughfares (the Bowery and Park Row); these emphasize that Italians were not only a presence in these theaters but a presence comparable to that of Jews. The position of Italian immigrants in New York City thus parallels, rather than contradicts, the information that Rosenzweig provided in the study of Worcester. The point is that revisions in the history of pre-1920 cinema will be founded on quicksand unless these case studies are grounded in thorough and thoughtful research into primary sources and then judged in relationship to each other.

There have been reliable histories of local exhibition—one of the first and one of the best was George Pratt's study of Rochester, New York—but Waller demonstrates that there is no substitute for a book-length examination such as this one. The longer form provides the scope and requires the sustained attention that gives this project unprecedented maturity and value. It allows him to examine the community's response to cinema and specific kinds of film through sermons, proposed ordinance, and newspaper reviews. He is able to relate this to Lexington's long-standing role as an entertainment center that fostered, or at least tolerated, a range of activities from roller skating to prostitution. In *Film History: Theory and Practice* (1985), Robert C. Allen and Douglas Gomery called for a new generation of film scholars to investigate the history of moviegoing in their local communities, using the selected community's newspapers as a principal resource. Waller provides a model, albeit a somewhat daunting one, of how this can and should be achieved. He has made a close, exhaustive study of available resources but is also careful to acknowledge the areas in which key research materials have been lost. In the case of Lexington, Kentucky, African American newspapers have not been preserved. But as Waller makes clear, the comparative lack of information about moviegoing in the black community does not mean that African Americans avoided the cinema. Rather he finds ingenious ways to compensate, at least partially, for the loss of essential sources.

In its current state, the history of American film now features *Shared Plea-sures*, Douglas Gomery's overview of motion picture exhibition in North America, on one hand, and more narrowly and systematically focused studies such as *Main Street Amusements*, on the other. From both we have much to learn. Waller's achievement, however, underscores the serious need for simi-lar endeavors if we are ever to understand fully the history of cinema and moviegoing in the United States. Waller's book not only makes fascinating reading in and of itself, it provides a framework within which other, often more fragmentary studies—past and future—can be situated and judged.

Charles Musser
Yale University

PREFACE

Main Street Amusements views the history of film and commercial entertainment in America during the silent era from the bottom up. It is concerned with exhibition practices and programming strategies, ticket prices and seating arrangements, promotional schemes and attempts at legitimation, reform campaigns and moviegoing habits—all seen from a quite precise local, rather than national, perspective. The locality in question is not the Lower East Side of Manhattan, Chicago, or Worcester, Massachusetts, but Lexington, Kentucky, then a small city with little heavy industry, few first-generation immigrants, a substantial African-American community, a preponderance of native Kentuckians, and a sense of itself as being southern. Even with the impressive body of research during the past fifteen years that has reshaped our understanding of film history, there has been relatively little scholarly attention devoted to how commercial entertainment was packaged, promoted, and consumed locally, especially outside major metropolitan areas.[1] Lexington's size, location, and biracialism make it a particularly apt subject for a case study.

As something of a regional marketing center whose population grew from about 26,000 in 1900 to 45,000 by 1930, Lexington was large enough to

have two daily newspapers, a park and playground system, its own anti-vice
campaigns and high-culture concert series, a long-standing reputation as a
profitable one-night stand for touring theatrical productions, and a range of
public amusement ventures: skating rinks, amusement parks, vaudeville
houses, and storefront picture shows, as well as palatial movie theaters. At
the same time, Lexington was small enough so that it is possible to chart in
depth the growth and transformation of commercial entertainment in the city
over a more than thirty-year period.

In the make-up as well as the size of its population, Lexington differed
substantially from those urban centers that figure so prominently in both traditional and revisionist histories of film. This Kentucky city simply was not
home to identifiably ethnic, immigrant working-class communities. What it
did have were strong economic and social ties to the small towns and agricultural heartland of central Kentucky. And like the South as a whole, Lexington
had a large black population, upwards of 39 percent in 1900. To insist on
these characteristics is not to suggest that Lexington can somehow stand in
for all of Kentucky, much less for the entire South. (In fact, I will indicate,
usually in notes, just how much the exhibition and reception of the movies
varied even in as relatively homogeneous a state as Kentucky.) We can, however, think of Lexington as regional without insisting that it is some Dixie-
styled Middletown. Studying it provides us with a position outside the
metropolis from which to reconsider certain guiding assumptions about, say,
moviegoing in the nickelodeon era, demands for censorship in the 1910s,
and film exhibition during the age of the picture palace. Most important, examining Lexington underscores just how deeply race (in addition to gender
and class) figured in the workings of commercial entertainment as business
venture, social occasion, and public leisure-time activity.

"Commercial entertainment"—not simply the movies. I have kept film
exhibition and moviegoing at the center of this book, in part because the
movies did "have the day" in Lexington by 1915, if not earlier. But from the
outset my ambition has been to remain attentive both to the specifics of theater design, programming policy, and marketing schemes, and also to more
general questions about the fear of amusement, the filling of leisure time, the
uses of high and low culture, and the public articulation of values and goals
as Lexington moved into the twentieth century. This aspiration toward social
history requires that the movies be seen in the context of other cheap amusements, special events, and public recreational occasions. As with all contex-

Commercial Entertainment in
Downtown Lexington, 1896-1930

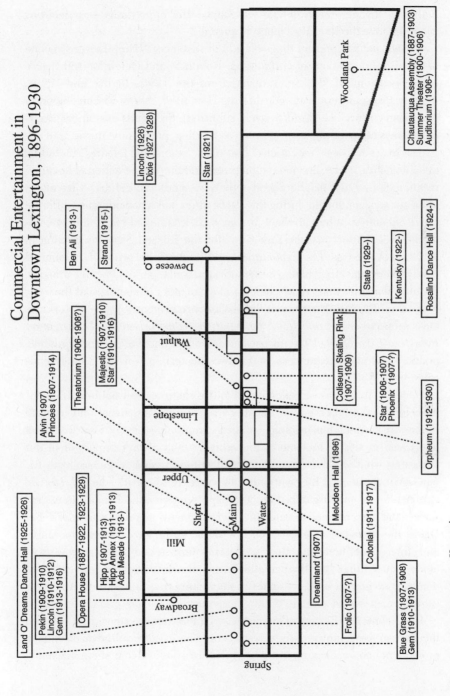

Land O' Dreams Dance Hall (1925-1926)

Pekin (1909-1910)
Lincoln (1910-1912)
Gem (1913-1916)

Opera House (1887-1922, 1923-1929)

Hipp (1907-1913)
Hipp Annex (1911-1913)
Ada Meade (1913-)

Alvin (1907)
Princess (1907-1914)

Theatorium (1906-1908?)

Majestic (1907-1910)
Star (1910-1916)

Ben Ali (1913-)

Strand (1915-)

Lincoln (1926)
Dixie (1927-1928)

Star (1921)

Deweese

Woodland Park

Chautauqua Assembly (1887-1903)
Summer Theater (1900-1906)
Auditorium (1906-)

State (1929-)

Kentucky (1922-)

Rosalind Dance Hall (1924-)

Coliseum Skating Rink (1907-1909)

Star (1906-1907)
Phoenix (1907-?)

Orpheum (1912-1930)

Melodeon Hall (1896)

Colonial (1911-1917)

Dreamland (1907)

Frolic (1907-?)

Blue Grass (1907-1908)
Gem (1910-1913)

Walnut

Limestone

Upper

Short

Main

Water

Mill

Broadway

Spring

Downtown Lexington, Kentucky.

tualizing, though, the problem—or maybe the opportunity—is deciding where to draw the line. How much is enough?

Various models present themselves. For instance, "Using Leisure" is one of the six main sections of *Middletown*, Robert S. and Helen Merrell Lynd's classic account of Muncie, Indiana, from the 1890s to the mid-1920s, roughly the same era I am considering. For their "study in contemporary American culture" (as *Middletown* is subtitled), the Lynds examined "traditional ways of spending leisure," such as reading, performing music, and engaging in art activity; "inventions" that were "re-making leisure," including the automobile, radio, and motion pictures; and the "organization of leisure," meaning family and neighborhood activities, sports, and clubs.[2] City recreation surveys conducted during the 1910s often had a considerably different sense of context. When Michael M. Davis, Jr. conducted his "study of commercial recreations in New York City" for the Russell Sage Foundation in 1911 (published as *The Exploitation of Pleasure*), he primarily examined candy shops, meeting halls, ice cream and soda parlors, penny arcades, dancing academies and dance halls, and all manner of commercial theaters. More recently, Roy Rosenzweig, in his important contribution to working-class social history, *Eight Hours for What We Will: Workers and Leisure in an Industrial City, 1870–1920*, focuses on saloons, Fourth of July celebrations, public parks and playgrounds, and movie theaters in Worcester, Massachusetts.

In these three cases, reflective of quite distinct twentieth-century approaches to the "problem" of locality and leisure, the social and cultural frame within which moviegoing is placed varies considerably. How we adjust this frame is always to some extent arbitrary and always important in determining what we end up saying about entertainment in general and the movies in particular. By positioning moviegoing alongside the increase in automobile use and organized club and sport activity, the Lynds can underscore "the decentralizing tendency of the movies upon the family."[3] For Davis, the notion of neighborhood is crucial, so he surveys soda fountains and street corner hangouts. Rosenzweig, in contrast, demonstrates how nickelodeons and other "public recreation" sites like the saloon and the Independence Day picnic reflect "some of the distinctive features of American working-class development."[4]

In my contextualization of movie theaters, I have for the most part followed the lead of Lexington's daily newspapers, which gathered advertisements, promotional notices, reviews, and brief feature articles in one section, usually called something like "Amusements." Motion pictures took their place here, along with touring exhibitions, legitimate theater, vaudeville, minstrel shows, fairs, carnivals, amusement parks, concerts, skating rinks, dance halls, and even the occasional lecture or benefit show. This quite inclusive field of "amusement" I take to be the prime context for the movies in Lexington. The city's park and playground system and those events and enterprises that specifically sought out a "colored" audience also figure prominently in my study. Since I am most interested in public activities that were—generally— commercial, scheduled, and announced as such, I pay virtually no attention to saloons or to certain topics that are central in *Middletown:* social and ser- vice club activity, leisure within the home or the neighborhood, reading hab- its, and the role of the automobile.

The meaning and scope of what constituted "amusement" varied some- what with the locality and the region, but to what extent does the "local" or the "regional" figure at all in an era often said to be characterized by what Bruce A. Austin calls the "standardization of recreation"?[5] George T. Blakely, for example, matter-of-factly begins *Hard Times and New Deal in Kentucky, 1929–1939* by asserting that the popularity of automobiles, radio, and Hollywood "transcended state borders and aided in the breakdown of provincialism and the homogenization of culture."[6] *Main Street Amusements* seeks to test this notion of standardization against the specific conditions in Lexington, in the process paying due heed to how provincialism and homoge- nization entered into local discourse about the movies and commercial enter- tainment. I have learned much in this regard from an important trend in American social history, which has, in Miriam Hansen's words, examined how "older forms of working-class and ethnic culture" resisted or were co- opted or gave way to "cultural homogenization."[7] Does the absence of "ethnic culture" in Lexington necessarily mean that "standardization" ruled the day? Precisely what entertainment was made available to Lexington audiences and under what conditions was it received? We can, I will argue, acknowledge the importance of local and regional variation and negotiation of mass culture without falling prey to problems that often beset local history: naive boost- erism or the yearning for a supposedly more autonomous provinciality.

Yet before making any claims about the capacity of local communities to resist or customize mass culture, we need to find out much more about the uses theaters like the Lexington Opera House were put to, the programming strategies they employed, the way they were perceived in the community, and the people who determined operating policies. Thus what Rosenzweig calls "entrepreneurs of leisure" figure prominently in my account: Lexington's theater owners and operators, would-be moguls, private investors, and expansion-minded amusement corporations.[8] What they booked into their venues and how they spoke of and managed their enterprises reveal much about the Lexington market, the variable limits of local prerogative, the appeal of "un-provincial" product, and the status of commercial entertainment as a business.

In gathering such information for one place between 1896 and 1930, I was struck by the wealth of material available and also by Lexington's ambivalent desire for and fear of "imported" entertainment and a national (mass) culture in the making. This ambivalence is part of what I consider to be the city's "reception" of commercial entertainment in general and motion pictures in particular. Taking reception as well as exhibition into account is one of the things that separates the sort of local history I have in mind from uncritical (if still useful) antiquarianism.

It is simple enough to agree that reception is important; documenting historical instances of reception is another matter. There is, for example, the occasional newspaper editorial or review and the inevitably scanty, piecemeal evidence about the behavior and response of actual audiences watching specific shows. This material does not provide much of a handle on what Lawrence W. Levine calls the too easily forgotten "truth that precisely the same forms of culture can perform markedly distinct functions in different periods or among different groups. It is in the ways they receive and utilize culture that people exert far more control over their lives and their societies than historians often acknowledge."[9] Of course, determining people's capacity for "exertion" and the degree and effect of their "control" is a difficult task indeed, and while I will offer some speculation on that score, I will be more concerned with the way one community—or, rather, the set of communities that made up Lexington—received the movies and other forms of commercial entertainment. What sort of public conversation and power struggles did the movies generate or exacerbate among business interests, city officials, churches, and reform movements, both white and African American? Of particular interest in this light are well-documented moments of heightened conflict: debates over the need for local or state censorship, sabbatarian campaigns to end Sunday film screenings, and efforts to prevent *The Birth of a Nation* from being shown at the Lexington Opera House.

Reception can also be approached from a quite different angle, as a matter less of exertion than of representation. How were audiences depicted in sermons, for example, or cartoons or editorials? What sort of customers were hailed by advertisements? What made the crowds drawn to amusements a dangerous threat or a token of utopian possibility? What anecdotal stories were most likely to be told about moviegoing? This information together comprises a sort of history of representations of reception, a barometer of local anxieties and aspirations as "modernity" loomed over or beckoned to Lexington.

Obviously, newspapers are a crucial resource in getting any handle on reception so understood. Lexington's two daily papers—the Republican *Leader* and the Democratic *Herald*—quite comprehensively covered not only municipal elections and four-star events, but also school, church, playground, and club activities, city government deliberations, retail business dealings, and all sorts of public leisure-time pursuits. I do not assume that this coverage was politically nonpartisan or not in some fundamental way in service to the status quo. Nor do I assume that these two daily newspapers fully and accurately spoke for and to and about all people in the community. Nonetheless, between the amusement section, the editorial page, and the regular columns in the *Herald* and the *Leader* devoted to society events, police court proceedings, "colored notes," and church activity, I found a great deal of information about how commercial entertainment figured in the social history of Lexington during this period. Quite often these newspapers printed in full material that could be considered "primary" historical documents: city ordinances, Sunday sermons, letters to the editor, legal texts (for example, articles of incorporation), public resolutions issued by reform groups, detailed theater schedules, and the like.

Supplementing and sometimes correcting the information I culled from a day-by-day, page-by-page examination of the *Herald* and the *Leader* is material drawn from archival holdings at the University of Kentucky and other area sites, city directories, oral history interviews, motion picture trade magazines, and black weekly newspapers like the Indianapolis *Freeman*. However, certain information that would have been invaluable is simply not available. For example, no copies remain of central Kentucky's black newspapers during this period, and business records do not exist for any local theater. Since there is no tradition of social science research on Lexington, I could not draw on formal recreation surveys comparable to the ones conducted during the 1910s in, for example, Milwaukee, Portland, and Springfield, Illinois; nor could I tap the sort of interviews, social work reports, welfare conference records, and extensive contemporary literature that Kathy

Peiss so effectively draws on in *Cheap Amusements: Working Women and Leisure in Turn-of-the-Century New York*. For the first decades of the twentieth century (and, in large measure, up to the present), there simply was almost no interest in the social history of Lexington, which was neither Appalachia nor the teeming metropolis and so did not seem to merit academic attention. I hope that *Main Street Amusements* prompts further study of this particular locality.

My findings are organized into a roughly chronological narrative. Though some Lexington residents during this period indulged in nostalgia, championed progressive causes, and feared the effects of imported amusement, *Main Street Amusements* is no more intended as a tragedy of nineteenth-century innocence lost than as a paean to the progressive defeat of provincialism or an ironic vision of hegemonic standardization triumphant. I begin with an overview of turn-of-the-century Lexington. Chapters 2–5 proceed from the so-called "novelty year" of 1896–97 when motion pictures premiered locally, through the pre-nickelodeon period (1897–1905) when they became regular attractions at several quite distinct local sites, to the establishment of storefront picture shows (along with vaudeville theaters and skating rinks) in the nickelodeon era, and the increasing dominance of film exhibition in an expanding commercial entertainment market between 1912 and 1916. Chapter 6 examines reform efforts and protest campaigns through 1916, most notably concerning theater safety codes, Sunday film showings, local censorship initiatives, and the Lexington screening of *The Birth of a Nation*. Chapter 7 reviews the same period, this time from the perspective of black theatergoers and the variable terms and conditions of segregation in a biracial society. Chapters 8–11 take the local exhibition and reception of the movies from World War I through the 1920s, when more elaborate programs became the norm, the "jazz environment" made its mark on Lexington, and city theaters were wired for sound. *Main Street Amusements,* in other words, moves from the premiere of the vitascope to the installation of Vitaphone, screening the silent film era in terms of its impact on one locality and viewing Lexington by the light of the movies.

ACKNOWLEDGMENTS

Thanks for help, advice, and encouragement from a host of people along the way, in and out of academia, in and out of Lexington: John G. Cawelti, Richard deCordova, Thomas Cripps, Joe DeSpain, David Durant, Nancy Dye, Lucy Fischer, Jane Gaines, Brenda Ijams, Mary Kay King, James Klotter, Richard Koszarski, Armando Prats, Judy Rogers, Dan Streible, Nikki Swingle, and George C. Wright. And, more generally, thanks also to those organizations that work to support local history research in Kentucky: the Oral History Commission, the Kentucky Humanities Council, and the Kentucky Historical Society.

Conversations with Richard Angelo have helped to shape this book, and so have the invaluable comments of Charles Musser and Douglas Gomery and the advice and support of Mark G. Hirsch, editor for the Smithsonian Institution Press. Being welcomed so graciously into the quite different communities of Campbellsville, Kentucky, and Hamilton, New Zealand, put me in the right frame of mind and spirit for rethinking my research on Lexington.

Without the ongoing assistance of the University of Kentucky's Special Collections and Archives, especially Tom House, this project simply would not have been done. Brenda Ghaelian of the UK FACTS Center guided me through the creation of the two maps, and along with Dave Hart, gave me valuable computer advice. As usual, Walter Foreman was always willing to put his expertise and his printer at my disposal. The University of Kentucky Graduate School provided funds for the production of illustrations and for a microfilm reader. Interlibrary Loan and Periodicals at the M. I. King Library fulfilled request after request. Elvis Costello and Emmylou Harris and a host of other artists provided the music that kept me sane through many long hours spent scanning microfilm.

Elvis and Emmylou are a tough act to follow, but for long-term help and hospitality way beyond the call of duty, special thanks to my sisters, Andrea and Beth, to my in-laws, Belle and Harold Barnett, and most of all, again, to Robin, Moby, and Graham for living with this project (and Lexington) and me these many years.

Different versions of Chapter 2 appeared in *Film History* 3, no. 3 (1989), Chapter 3 in *Velvet Light Trap* 25 (Spring 1990), and Chapter 7 in *Cinema Journal* 31, no. 2 (Winter 1992).

MAIN STREET
AMUSEMENTS

ONE

Lexington
at the
Turn of the Century

Motion pictures premiered in Lexington on the evening of Tuesday, 15 December 1896, at the Lexington Opera House, when a touring theatrical troupe, the Holmes & Wolford Company, presented about a dozen "views" between the acts of their featured stage production, a "sensational melodrama" entitled *The Smugglers*. This particular strategy for exhibiting motion pictures, as we will soon see, was fairly typical. But from a distance the Holmes & Wolford stage/screen performance looks like a strange, even estranging, experience indeed: action-packed, highly emotive, and conventionalized "scenic" melodrama combined with (or interrupted by) black-and-white, silent, and yet nonetheless "lifelike" moving pictures of a Parisian street, a seaside beach, and "pickaninnies" in a public bathing pool.

Adding to the incongruity, the site for this joint display of live actors caught up once more in the vicissitudes of melodrama and anonymous pedestrians and bathers captured on film was the Lexington Opera House, which had in the summer of 1896 undergone a "grand transformation," with an eye toward increased elegance and refinement. The lobby walls of the refurbished Opera House, wrote the society columnist for the Lexington *Herald*, "are of a changeable rosy and green hue, fading into the same tints of the frescoed

3

ceiling," around which circled two rows of incandescent lights. A "glorious red carpet" guided patrons into the auditorium, with its "handsomely decorated" walls and eight exclusive theater boxes draped in pale green and gold. Overhead, the "rounded ceiling tinted in the palest pink fad[es] into the most delicate blue, until it loses itself into space." The Lexington *Leader* declared: "The general effect is simply gorgeous . . . the greatest surprise of all that will greet the patron's eye is the brilliantly beautiful and dazzling new curtain" on which was painted a "home scene in Italy," complete with "figures perfectly natural," drawn in "delicate and lovely colors" and set off by a picture frame-styled border.[1] All in all, the Opera House's new curtain epitomized a certain ideal of refined, pleasing, and delicate art. On December 15, this curtain rose to reveal *The Smugglers,* which then paused in mid-action to give way to images of "pickaninnies," waves, and Parisian streetcars moving across a makeshift screen.

Commercial Entertainment and Public Recreation

I will return in Chapter 2 to the Holmes & Wolford engagement and the initial exhibition and reception of motion pictures in Lexington. First, however, I will briefly survey the sort of commercial entertainment and public recreational activities available in Lexington in 1896. Just how did a program like that presented by the Holmes & Wolford Company fit into the booking schedule of the Opera House and, more generally, into the range of amusements offered to and chosen by the city's residents at this time? Establishing this larger context will help characterize Lexington as it approached the turn of the century, allowing us better to gauge subsequent changes in the leisure life of the city.

Unquestionably, the Lexington Opera House—"an object of cherished pride in the community"—was the preeminent permanent venue for commercial entertainment in Lexington.[2] Built in 1887 by the locally based Broadway Realty Company, after the destruction of the city's original opera house by fire, the new building was designed by Chicago theater architect Oscar Cobb to be a large, modern venue, ushering in a new era in what was perceived to be Lexington's rich theatrical heritage.[3] This theater had seating for approximately 1,250 patrons in its gallery, balcony, first floor, and box seats. In size, elegance, and prestige the Opera House far surpassed the city's other public halls and auditoriums, as well as the theaters and opera houses

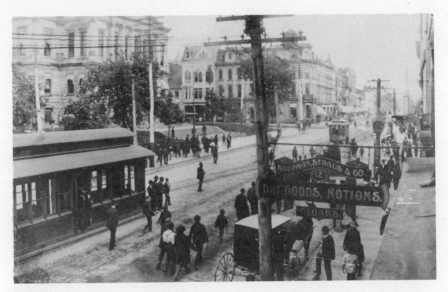

Downtown Lexington at the turn of the century. Photo courtesy University of Kentucky
Photo Archives.

in surrounding Central Kentucky towns. Appropriately, it was located on
Broadway, though the Opera House shared a block not with other theaters
but with millinery, wallpaper, and carpet shops, a drugstore, a grocery, and
several saloons, while across the street was the Centenarian Methodist
Church and a bicycle shop. From its opening it was leased and managed by
Charles Scott, a Kentucky native, active member of the Elks and the Knights
of Pythias, and a graduate of Kentucky University in Lexington, whom a local
newspaper described in 1900 as a "widely known and highly esteemed citizen" of the city.[4] Even as late as 1924, well after he had moved from Lexington, the *Herald* could still praise Scott as "one of the safest, sanest and most
reliable managers in America," under whose guidance the Opera House
functioned as a local "institution of great cultural value."[5]

Scott's theater was not literally an *opera* house, though during 1896 he
did book several self-styled "comic opera" companies. These and other road
shows, often routed through Cincinnati or Louisville, were the mainstay attractions at the Opera House, during a season that began in September and
wound down by mid-April or early May. The touring productions that appeared locally in 1896 included, for example, *Hamlet* and *Faust*, in addition

The Lexington Opera House, "object of cherished pride in the community." Photo courtesy Transylvania University, Lexington, Kentucky.

to contemporary well-made plays (*Madame sans Gens*), spectacular melodramas (*The Great Train Robbery*), homespun comedies of rural Americana (*Si Plunkard*), and farces built around Irish or German comedians. These one-night stands together comprised about half of Scott's total play dates. Also booked into the Opera House that same year were eight musical recitals and concerts, six minstrel shows, four lectures, four benefit theatricals with local amateur talent, and four appearances by mind readers and magicians. In other words, Lexington's sole permanent site for theatrical entertainment could in the same season be home to a sentimental reading of "negro dialect stories" and to a magician said to be capable of "theosophic projection of astral bodies"; a minstrel show complete with "camp meeting shouters, mobile buck and wing dancers, creole beauties [and] hoodoo charm workers," as well as a local production of *Ben Hur* for the benefit of the Protestant Infirmary.

The Holmes & Wolford Company's screening of motion pictures was but one in a series of novel visual attractions during 1896 at the Opera House: the "trick pantomime," *Humpty Dumpty*, for instance, included a live four-round "scientific" boxing exhibition; Primrose & West's Big Minstrels offered the "incomparable mechanical scenic marvels" of a large-scale diorama; and Hi Henry's Minstrels closed their show with "a shadowgraph spectacular," entitled "Around the World in Ten Minutes." Robert C. Allen notes that during this period, "among the novelties desperately sought by vaudeville managers to enhance their competitive positions were visual spectacles of one sort or another."[6] Judging from the touring companies that played Lexington, minstrel shows were equally drawn to visual novelties that could, perhaps incongruously, share the stage with traditional entertainment turns.

During the season, Scott managed to book the Opera House for about half the available play dates, not counting those "dark" days when the theater was used for political rallies or meetings sponsored by civic or church groups. His multipurpose (and multi-audience) theater was absolutely central to the city's cultural life, particularly because there were no other permanent theaters or dime museums in Lexington. The relatively few public performances staged at the city's smaller halls were limited primarily to musical recitals and amateur shows—usually "benefits" presented under the auspices of quite respectable local institutions. Thus variety shows were sponsored by the Central Labor Council and the National Fraternal Union, and the YMCA attempted to attract new members by staging a performance that included vocal quartets, a banjo soloist, and a "graphophone demonstration."[7]

Churches, too, sometimes arranged for inexpensive entertainments, such as an evening of vocal and instrumental music presented to raise funds for a "colored" Episcopal church. For my purposes, the most noteworthy of these benefit shows was that held in March 1896 under the auspices of the Central Christian Church's Young People's Societies of Christian Endeavor. According to promotional notices, tickets to this event cost twenty-five and thirty-five cents, and the main attraction was "Edison's electric concert and exhibition." Twenty-one selections were on the bill, including "such novelties as storms at sea, scenes during railroad wrecks, part of a sermon by Sam Jones, etc., everything illustrated," as well as "the great bands, singers, orators, chimes, etc. faithfully reproduced upon the new electric phonograph and correctly pictured on canvas in life-like motion. The audience not only hears Holding's great band play the 'Night Alarm,' but sees a fire in New York City with flames arising and little children rescued from a burning building, with firemen and engines all at work in motion."[8] The date of the showing, as well as the site and the type of "views" offered, all indicate that this was not a motion picture exhibition. Yet this multimedia, electrically powered program—lifelike, thrilling, informative—definitely looks forward to the sort of touring motion picture shows Lexington would often see in the following years.

While "Edison's electric concert and exhibition" had obvious affinities with the spectacular visual novelties featured in minstrel shows, it also shared much with a quite different sort of program: the public lecture which sought to be as entertaining as it was edifying. Among the touring speakers who visited Lexington in 1896 were a southern humorist who delighted audiences with "stories and plantation melodies";[9] the Reverend Thomas Dixon (later the author of *The Clansman*), who lectured at Kentucky University on "Backbone"; and missionaries who often used stereopticon slides to illustrate their accounts of work among, for example, the "bloody Turks" and other "savages of the East."[10] Individual distinctions notwithstanding, in terms of content as well as local sponsorship, virtually all these nonprofit, nontheatrical events could be said to occupy a sort of perfectly legitimate cultural middle ground, well above what might have been labeled cheap amusement.

Quite the opposite was true of commercial "exhibitions" that arrived from outside Lexington.[11] That these shows were regarded as being by definition suspect is proven by the fact that the city had an ordinance specifically designed to discourage and carefully monitor the activities of traveling "exhibitions" or "museums." Whereas Lexington's yearly license fee was $150 for any opera house or theater where shows were given and admission charged, and $50 for any hall used for dances or other "paying amusements," the fee for temporary exhibitions was $5 a day or $25 a week. Furthermore, any would-be exhibitor was required to submit a written application to the city clerk, "stating the character of the entertainment he desires to give and the prices of admission to the same." If this official found the exhibition "not immoral or hurtful," it would be granted a license. Yet any such license could be immediately revoked if the mayor deemed the exhibition "to have become a nuisance, or in any way hurtful or offensive to public morals."[12]

In spite of this prohibitive ordinance, several exhibitions did play Lexington in 1896, offering entertainment billed as exotic and sensational, and therefore quite distinct from the supposedly refined, accomplished displays of talent featured in most local recitals and benefit performances. Exhibitions could, however, forestall fears of impropriety by advertising themselves as unique educational opportunities. This tactic was apparent, for example, when a self-styled explorer and scientist put several Eskimo "natives" (including, quite prominently, twin five-year-old girls) on display in a former church turned public auditorium. Schoolchildren were especially encouraged to attend what was billed as an "object lesson in the habits, implements, kinks, strange manners, native songs, dances and ceremonies of the Eskimo."[13]

It was but a short step from displaying Eskimos to setting up an "impromptu museum" in a Main Street building formerly used by a laundry. On exhibition here was Minnie, the Australian "Wind Girl," said to be "a very wonderful creature [who] comes nearer to supplying Darwin's 'missing link' than anything else in this country."[14] Like the Eskimos, Minnie proved to be a good draw. The *Leader* reported that "the crowds were so great that at times it would seem impossible to crowd another person into the store room, and that the ladies were more than pleased could be told by their pleasant countenances and the length of time they tarried enjoying the cute ways of the girl."[15] No less an example of marvelous nature than the "missing link" was a fifty-foot embalmed whale that could be seen in a special railway car for a mere ten cents. Even though this exhibition was beset by "mischievous boys" armed with firecrackers, it still managed to run for two weeks during the same month in which motion pictures were introduced in Lexington.

Other traveling exhibitors were more closely allied to skilled circus performers who could make extraordinary use of merely ordinary nature. For example, a "Professor Berry" set up a tent downtown to demonstrate his techniques for training horses, while under electric lights at a local park, another "professor" conducted sharpshooting displays and built a show around two horses trained to dive off towers into the water far below. It is not difficult to imagine these two equestrian attractions, along with the Eskimos, the missing link, and the embalmed whale, all being part of one large carnival, sent out piecemeal to arrive at different times and to set up activity at various locations around the city. Actually, these exhibitions were independent entrepreneurial operations, connected only by the fact that they arrived from outside Lexington, bearing attractions that were worth paying to see precisely because they were so far removed from what was held to be familiar, home-grown, and/or natural.

One series of exhibitions was, however, an exception to this general rule. When two professors at Kentucky State College early in 1896 began what were said to be the first experiments south of the Mason-Dixon line with "wonderful X rays" and a "fluorescent screen," public interest was immediately stirred, and throughout the spring, these "exhibitions and experiments" were opened to the community at large. They soon became a much-discussed source of "pleasure and instruction," and the *Herald*'s society column even mentions "theater parties, so to speak," arranged to see "the wonders of the X ray."[16] As Charles Musser notes, in the second half of the nineteenth century, "demonstrations of new scientific and technological knowledge were popular cultural events."[17] Unlike many larger cities, however, Lexington had no arcade or phonograph parlor ready to make commercial use of X-ray machines. Yet the drawing power of the State College exhibitions did attest to a fascination with seeing the visible world in a new way and with innovative technologies for the mechanical production of images, a fascination soon to be focused on the "scientific marvel" of motion pictures.

Like these X-ray experiments, certain store window displays also had exhibition value in turn-of-the-century Lexington. "Artistic window decoration," particularly the sort of "extravagant display" to be found in large cities, was, according to the *Leader* in March 1896, still "something of a novelty" locally. But "show windows" increasingly came to feature colored electric lights and moving parts, since "a well-lighted store window . . . never fails to attract attention."[18] Interestingly, the most "attractive" window displays often were not explicitly tied to particular purchasable products or services. These show windows were, in fact, small-scale exhibitions, sometimes as simple as a model of a steamship or a set of photographs of prominent stage celebrities. The Christmas shopping season occasioned more elaborate windows. One major retail store, for example, featured a meticulously detailed miniature Swiss village, complete with working water wheel and electric lights, that was patterned after the Electric Scenic Theatre at the Chicago World's Columbian Exposition. The possibilities were quite varied: a bicycle shop exhibited photographs and native "curios" gathered during the owner's recent trip to South Africa; a cigar store put X-rays on display; and a prominent clothing store offered an "old log cabin scene" à la *Uncle Tom's Cabin*, complete with "a pleasant looking old Negress," who "worked away at the spinning wheel," pausing at times to sing a "plaintive old Southern melody suggestive of the ante-bellum days."[19] These particular displays were eye-catching enough to warrant mention in local newspapers, and, along with the ephemeral products of the bill poster, these quasi-scientific, folkloric, ethnographic, or artistic window displays hint at the extent to which exhibitionism infiltrated day-to-day life in Lexington's central business district.

As novel visual attractions, Lexington's store window displays form part of an exhibition continuum that in 1896 included traveling museums, onstage dioramas, and motion pictures of bathers and Parisian streets. Similarly, a performance continuum stretched from *Uncle Tom's Cabin* troupes to small-scale animal acts to itinerant street performers who worked the crowds around Lexington's city hall, including a trick bicyclist, a pair of African-American minstrels in the employ of "Quaker medicine vendors," or a female "snake charmer," whose act consisted of allowing herself to be bitten by rattlers and to have nails inserted into her muscles. Like the display windows in downtown stores, these street performers provided interludes or fragments of diversion and entertainment that was available to all passersby, and so was quite distinct from the amusement offered inside traditional male enclaves like the saloon, shooting gallery, and poolroom.

With the Opera House for all purposes closed from mid-May to the end of September, and with children out of school and days long and hot, leisure-time pursuits available in Lexington necessarily differed in the summer from the rest of the year. As would be expected, warm weather encouraged more outdoor activities. By the spring of 1896, the bicycle craze in Lexington was "growing like a conflagration,"[20] indicative of what John Higham describes as a national trend during the 1890s, particularly among the urbanized middle class, to embrace the values of "dynamism," athletics, and the "outdoor movement."[21] Somewhat more loosely connected with this trend was the Lexington Railway Company's successful attempt to market trolley riding on summer evenings and weekends as a "delightful and pleasant" pastime. Usually as part of a specially organized "trolley party" (filled with "laughing, happy children and fond mothers and fathers"), riders paid five cents each to be transported by brightly lit electric railway cars for one or two loops around Lexington's "belt-line" track system.[22] These "electrical excursions" were a recreational activity both dynamic and passive, novel and convenient, inexpensive and in no way "offensive to public morals." In effect, the Railway Company had turned the horse-and-buggy outing into more of a mass entertainment, the first of several attempts by this company to attract riders during off-work hours with the promise of "delight."

Unlike trolley riding, cycling, when organized into a day of competitive races at the fairgrounds, also counted as one of an increasing array of spectator sports made available to area consumers. The Bluegrass region of Kentucky had long been known for its horse farms and racing facilities, and major thoroughbred and trotting horse meets were held in the spring and fall, attracting much out-of-town revenue. During the summer of 1896, the Lexington Athletic Club sponsored professional boxing matches, and the city fielded a semi-pro baseball team in the newly organized Blue Grass League. Plans were even announced for the Kentucky Trotting Horse Breeders Association to purchase the city's privately owned fairgrounds and build "an attractive park and music hall, summer theater, bowling alley and other buildings."[23]

Such a project, which did not come to fruition, no doubt looked potentially lucrative because local people made much of fair-weather public recreational opportunities. During the summer months, Lexington's black citizens, for example, regularly held cakewalk competitions, and the newly reformed Colored A & M Association, financed locally by the sale of a hundred $25 shares of capital stock, staged a fair in early September that drew a reported crowd of twelve thousand on its busiest day.[24] Other well-attended outings involving picnicking, dancing, and athletic competitions were organized in late May by the city's firemen and on July 4 by the Young Men's Institute (a Catholic organization comparable to the YMCA). The largest of these events was the Labor Day picnic and parade, when, according to the *Herald*, "all classes of people came out, residents and people from the neighboring towns," giving Lexington the look and feel of "circus day in a country village."[25]

An actual "circus day" had occurred on April 29, when the Adams, Forepaugh and Sells Circus staged a street parade and then two performances at a lot some distance from downtown. This top-flight circus attracted, the *Leader*'s society columnist noted, enough "belles and beaux"—in addition to the "hoi poi loi"—to "almost be regarded as a society event."[26] (Surprisingly, there was only one other notable traveling show that played Lexington during the summer of 1896, a tent show production of *Uncle Tom's Cabin*, which offered but one performance.)

April 29, the date of the Adams, Forepaugh and Sells visit, was in fact a red-letter day for public entertainment in Lexington, at least according to the *Herald*, which, without a trace of irony, commented that "three big-star events" were slated for the city on that date: the circus, the spring horse racing meet, and the execution of Henry Mitchell Smith, a black man convicted of raping an elderly white woman.[27] Fifteen minutes before the execution, the governor granted a temporary stay. But Smith was hanged on June 2, and though the execution was technically closed to the public, "neighboring house tops, windows, fire-escapes, telegraph and telephone poles were thickly lined with a crowd of idle curiosity seekers" numbering at least five hundred.[28] I cite this horrific spectacle in part to dispel any nostalgic aura lingering around summertime trolley parties and cakewalk contests. Furthermore, the very fact that an execution could be referred to as a "big-star event" underscores an all-important point: both the audience's "curiosity" and the object of that curiosity (the show, the event, the exhibition) have social and ideological implications, telling us much about daily life in a particular place at a particular time.

Population, Race, and Economics

The preceding survey of what Lexington residents were offered and what they chose in the way of commercial entertainment and public leisure-time pursuits during 1896 is intended to do more than enumerate the sort of amusements that early motion pictures coexisted with and competed against. The particular mix of entrepreneurial exhibitions and nonprofit entertainments, the varied schedule at the Opera House, and the array of summertime recreational activities together help to define and situate Lexington. So, too, does the fact that this small city in 1896 had no arcade, dime museum, amusement park, burlesque house, or vaudeville theater. In this way Lexington—which most often thought of itself as southern or at least as non-northern—differed substantially from the great metropolitan centers of the Northeast and Midwest.

Census data underscores the extent of this difference. According to the 1900 census, Lexington ranked as the 153rd largest city in the United States.

Between 1890 and 1900 it had grown by the rather modest figure of 22.3 percent, reaching a population of 26,369. (It had been ranked 110th in 1880, but had dropped to 139th in 1890.)[29] Local newspapers put Lexington's actual population—and therefore its likely market for goods and services—at closer to 30,000, including many people who lived in suburban areas immediately outside the city limits or in more rural sections of Fayette County, for which Lexington served as the county seat.[30] The 1902 city directory made a similar point by including listings for over 3,700 county residents.

At the turn of century, the rest of Fayette County, exclusive of Lexington, had a population of 15,702. Somewhat further from the city, but still accessible by road, train, and, beginning in 1901, interurban railways, were several towns (including Georgetown, Paris, Winchester, Versailles, and Nicholasville) with a combined total of about 15,000 residents.[31] By taking these small towns into account, the *Herald* was able to describe Lexington as "the center of a large city with a radius of from twenty-five to thirty miles."[32] Lexington's role as an urban center for this part of central Kentucky directly affected the commercial entertainment business in the city. For example, certain of the Opera House's attractions needed to draw, in addition to city residents, either rural folks or "society" theatergoers from outlying towns. Thus, when renowned actor Richard Mansfield performed locally in 1903, he was greeted by a "large and cultured audience" representing "nearly every town in the Blue Grass."[33] Later, during and after the nickelodeon period, Lexington-based amusement companies frequently operated theaters in nearby towns. It also seems likely that the way controversies over film censorship and sabbatarianism were resolved in Lexington was dictated in part by the more conservative attitudes that dominated the surrounding area.

In Lexington proper, 924 (or 3.5 percent) of the population was foreign born, and over half of these people had lived in the United States for more than fifteen years, while only 39 had arrived during the previous five years.[34] This first-generation immigrant population contained no more than a few people born in Asia, Eastern Europe, Scandinavia, or the Mediterranean region (aside from Italy). Lexington's foreign-born population principally came from Ireland (428) and Germany (181) and, to a lesser extent, from England (88) and Italy (50).[35] Though the Irish and Germans had been in the late nineteenth century and continued to be by 1900 the only substantial white ethnic groups in the city, they accounted for only a small part of the total population, and neither constituted an insular or ghettoized subculture.[36]

Whatever formal ethnic ties they maintained were connected with specific churches (German Lutheran and German Evangelical churches, for example, offered "preaching in German") and with the limited activities of social groups like the Friendly Sons of St. Patrick or the German Enjoyment Club, which sponsored occasional picnics or dances.[37]

All told, some 3,160 (or 12 percent) of Lexington's residents were classified as being of "foreign parentage" (meaning that one or both parents were foreign born). To put this figure in some perspective, consider that in 1900 almost 38 percent of Louisville's population was of foreign parentage, while this group constituted 49 percent of the residents of Covington, a good-sized northern Kentucky city near Cincinnati.[38] Among U.S. cities in the 25,000–30,000 population range, Lexington, in the size of its first- and second-generation immigrant population, was most comparable to Joplin, Missouri, and to southern cities like Jacksonville, Florida; Fort Worth, Texas; Montgomery, Alabama; and Chattanooga, Tennessee. It was quite different in this regard from other cities with a similar total population, such as Bay City, Michigan; Cedar Rapids, Iowa; Gloucester, Massachusetts; Joliet, Illinois; Racine, Wisconsin; and Sacramento, California.[39]

Census data, of course, can tell us little about attitudes and day-to-day relations among the various population groups in Lexington. Perhaps because first-generation immigrants numbered less than a thousand, and most of them were from Germany and Ireland, the "foreign" presence was rarely deemed noteworthy by the local press. One remarkably revealing exception occurred in January 1896, when a streetcar accident took the life of a small Syrian child whose family lived with several other families in crowded rooms downtown. After making a charitable visit to the girl's home, the *Herald*'s usually cheerful and proper society columnist was prompted to see the arrival of these "Arabs" as a harbinger of more "sinister" and "hideous" changes:

> Lexington is an easy going old town. It isn't much in the way of manu-
> factories, but it has the best of everything else. It has always had its poor,
> and its evil quarters, but they have never been the poor and evil quarters
> of a great city. . . . It has even always had its tenement houses, but they
> have been Lexington tenement houses, in some indescribable way perme-
> ated with the shiftlessness and good nature of the South. They have not
> been the cut-throat dens lost in the darkness of a great city. But now this
> more innocent phase of squalor—if I may use the term—is undergoing a
> sinister change. Immigration is overflowing its murky reservoirs in the

great cities and settling in doubtful pools among our streets. It is hideous
to think of the cancer of such old world wretchedness fastening upon the
conservative poverty-principles of old Lexington.

For this columnist, the question became: can "old Lexington" protect itself
against the changes which flow from the urban North to pollute "a unique
and somewhat aristocratic community" and infect its good-natured poor? It
is not difficult to see how the anxiety so manifest here might also be triggered
by commercial entertainment that could bring the (old and new) world to
Lexington. In fact, the moral of this particular column had to do with the eye-
catching appeal and hidden costs of cheap amusement, and what began as
defensive abhorrence of the immigrants shows its other face as dangerous
attraction: "It is pleasant on a sunshiny day to hear the hand organ in the
street, to give the dancing bear a wide berth and drop a penny in the mum-
mingish [sic] palm of a wizened monkey. But when one reflects how and
where these Arabs are lodged during the nights of frost and bitterness, the
'foreign' atmosphere lent our thoroughfare loses some of its gaiety."[40] In contrast to the "Arabs," the crucial benefit of traveling exhibitions or minstrel
shows or circuses was precisely that these commercial entertainments were
not "lodged" in Lexington. Yet the problem of providing cheap (and often
"foreign") amusement without somehow corrupting the local environment
inevitably arose when vaudeville theaters and nickelodeons began to open
locally.

Perhaps occasional wafts of a "'foreign' atmosphere" could make its presence felt so palpably in Lexington because the city's comparatively small
immigrant population and its below-average rate of growth between 1890 and
1900 made it a relatively stable community. Equally telling is another statis-
tic, concerning in-migration rather than immigration: 86.1 percent of the
city's population had been born in Kentucky.[41] Regardless of whether Lexington was actually heir to a "unique and somewhat aristocratic" southern heritage, it was roughly representative of the South in terms of the nativity and
mobility of its populace.

And Lexington in 1900 was decidedly southern in that its 10,132 black
residents accounted for approximately 39 percent of the total population.
This was a substantially higher figure than any other city in Kentucky: African Americans comprised 19 percent of Louisville's population, for example,
and only 0.5 percent of Covington's. Much more comparable to Lexington
were Nashville (37 percent black), Chattanooga (43 percent black), and Bir-

mingham (43 percent black).[42] Like these southern cities, Lexington was unquestionably a biracial society, with well-established black residential areas,
churches, and service organizations, a segregated public school system, and
a striking inequity between the large size of the local black population and
the small role it played in the city's business and political life.[43] Some whites
undoubtedly rued the vanishing of the "Southern darkey," a figure of "unal-
loyed simplicity and lovableness."[44] But with a sense of self-congratulatory
civic pride, the *Leader* in 1901 reprinted an article from *Leslie's Weekly* written by a black professor from Alabama, who claimed that in Lexington "the
race problem is completely solved, and the Negro and white population are
as distinct in their social relations as the stars in the heavens."[45] As we will
see, Jim Crow "solutions" were also extended to cover new commercial entertainments and other leisure-time activities—crucial sites for the ongoing negotiation of racial relations.

In general, then, turn-of-the-century Lexington was demographically of a
piece with the cities that Lawrence H. Larsen studies in *The Rise of the Urban
South*. Like Lexington in 1900, in 1880 the urban South at large was home
to a substantial black population, very few "migrants" from other states, and
a small number of foreign-born immigrants (preponderantly Irish, German,
and British). "These figures," Larsen concludes, "reinforced the insular nature of southern life" and testified to "a direct connection between the Old
South and the New South."[46] Here, then, are specifically regional factors that
would seem to have inevitably come into play as the United States entered
the age of mechanical reproduction and mass entertainment. Once Lexington
moved into the twentieth century, what effect did this southern heritage of
insularity and traditionalism have on the local business of commercial entertainment and the city's response to motion pictures?

The amusement business depended not just on regional preconceptions
and prejudices but on local economic conditions. The society columnist troubled by the presence of "Arabs" took Lexington's lack of "manufactories" as
proof that it is an "easy going old town," though the *Herald* on other occasions
in 1896 was quick to point out that "Lexington in the past few years has
been making rapid strides toward the assumption of metropolitan airs and
manners," meaning, among other things, that the city's first bona fide department store had opened in September 1896, a modern "ornament to business
in Lexington and the town's enterprise."[47] From this perspective, Lexington's
economic prospects were bright, what with several thriving "manufactories,"
including four cooper factories, two brick companies, the Lexington Stove

Company, and the Blue Grass Tobacco Company, which together employed some 450 men.[48] The 1900 census identified 272 "manufacturing and mechanical industries" in Lexington, employing 1,464 wage earners and collectively worth only $3 million.[49] Thus, even following the government's broad definition of "industry," it is apparent that Lexington did not approach the industrialization of small-sized cities in the Northeast and Midwest.

Nonetheless, the Chamber of Commerce and local newspapers consistently promoted Lexington's "constant march of progress."[50] Among the most prominent signs of the city's "boom" were the seven railroads that served Lexington and facilitated its role as a regional marketing center; the Lexington Railway Company, which had almost fifteen miles of track in the city, and which would participate in the construction of permanent summertime amusement facilities; the Lexington Brewery Company, the first of several enterprises to be financed by "foreign" (i. e., nonlocal) capital; the Kentucky Trotting Horse Breeders Association, whose track seated five thousand and was used for various public events; and several new warehouses and plants, including a "branch house" of Armour's wholesale meat company.[51] Clearly, what Lexington lacked, and would continue to lack, according to a 1903 editorial, was "the busy hum of factory wheels," a sound the *Leader* felt would be "more soul-satisfying than Wagnerian opera."[52]

Along with the absence of large-scale factories, there was also virtually no labor unrest in the city, until unionized streetcar operators and conductors battled with strikebreakers in July 1913. Local skilled-trade unions (carpenters, typographers, electricians, printers, and so on) were prominent only during the yearly Labor Day parade and picnic. The largest percentage of Lexington's work force of 11,508 (one-third of whom were women) was grouped under what the census referred to as "Domestic and Personal Service" and "Trade and Transportation."[53] The former category included servants, nurses, barbers, employees of hotels and restaurants, and "unspecified" laborers—comprising some 40 percent of the city's wage earners. "Trade and Transportation" included employees of banks, offices, railroads, and retail and wholesale businesses—comprising about 25 percent of the wage earners.[54] Given that there were no large factories in the city, 77 percent of Lexington's predominantly black, female work force were servants, laundresses, and seamstresses, supporting historian David R. Goldfield's contention that "it was rare" in the South of the 1890s "to find an urban black who was not a laundress, domestic, or unskilled laborer."[55]

Lexington's biracial system, of course, required black ministers and teachers, and there were, according to the 1902 city directory, four black attorneys and five black physicians practicing locally. All told, the 1900 census count of Lexington's professionals included 266 teachers and professors, employed in public schools, private academies, Kentucky University (later Transylvania University), and Kentucky State College (later the University of Kentucky). In the years to come, college faculty members and administrators often spoke out publicly on matters pertaining to commercial entertainment, while college students would constitute an important market for vaudeville and motion picture theaters. Lexington also had 101 clergymen, 83 lawyers, and 81 physicians and surgeons.[56] There were, in fact, about the same number of professionals as there were people classified as agricultural laborers or farmers, though Lexington's 1898 police report notes that the greatest number of people arrested were farmers, laborers, those with "no occupation," and "loafers."[57]

With a well-developed professional class and a large low-income laboring class, Lexington's economy primarily involved service and trade, and its commercial life ultimately depended on its position as the "heart" of an agricultural region whose principal crops were tobacco and hemp. The turnpikes and railway lines that radiated out like arteries from Lexington graphically illustrate this well-worn metaphor.

At the center of the city, and therefore of the surrounding region, was Lexington's downtown business district, which was concentrated in a four-by-six block area. The city's lumber mills, processing plants, and small manufacturing concerns were located on the edges of this clearly demarcated area, which contained Lexington's banks, hotels, and newspapers, virtually all of its law firms and doctor's offices, the Opera House, the county courthouse, the meeting rooms and halls of fraternal organizations, and—in 1902, for example— more than half of the city's 152 licensed saloons. At the turn of the century the central business district of a small city like Lexington also included wholesale and retail grocers, photographers, clothing stores, restaurants and sidewalk stands, livery stables, dry goods stores, furniture dealers, printers, hardware and paint stores, and the small shops of tradesmen and milliners. The largest and most prestigious stores were located on Main Street, later the site of the city's Union Station and the motion picture "palaces" built in the 1910s and 1920s. A block south of Main Street, near the police station, was what was known as Lexington's "colored main street." Traversed by railroad tracks, this two-block stretch housed a few retail stores, the Colored Odd Fellows Hall, small shops of black barbers and tradesmen, and several res-

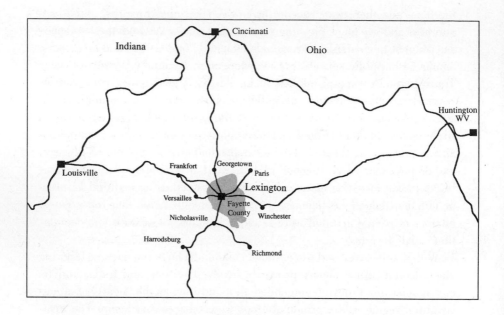

Central Kentucky.

taurants and saloons. As would be expected, the central business district, with its day and night life, was the obvious site for commercial entertainment ventures, including bowling alleys built in 1898–99 and vaudeville theaters and nickelodeons opened in 1906–7.

Close to the central business district were the campuses of Kentucky University and the State College, and approximately a mile from downtown were the fairgrounds and two north-end lots where tent shows were staged. Like the downtown area, these locations were readily accessible by streetcar, as was Woodland Park, a twenty-acre site just east of the city that would soon be purchased for a municipal park.

A few boardinghouses and small dwellings were located in the central business district, but the major residential areas of the city were elsewhere, as geographer John Kellogg convincingly demonstrates in his study of the formation of black neighborhoods in Lexington. Kellogg notes that, by the end of the nineteenth century, a "visitor traveling the main streets through Lexington might wonder where the houses of the many blacks he saw working all over town were to be found," for "Negro residences were hidden from view." While the most expensive white-owned, single-family homes were concentrated on large avenues surrounding the central business district, black "urban clusters," mainly established between the 1860s and the 1880s, tended to be located on the outskirts of the city on poor quality bottom land abutting railroad tracks or in side street enclaves in predominantly white areas. According to Kellogg, a "rising demand for white working-class housing" in the 1880s led to the growth of two "poor white areas," one of which, Irishtown, would come to be known as the "tenement" section of Lexington.[58]

After the turn of the century, real estate developers opened new upper middle-class white suburban subdivisions with full utility services and good schools about a mile from downtown on the east side of Lexington. The growth of the city's electric street railway system went hand in hand with this increasing suburbanization.[59] Yet while certain white residential areas and black urban clusters contained grocery stores, churches, schools, or saloons, the downtown business district unquestionably remained the commercial center of the city. And Lexington, proclaimed local boosters, was "the railway, commercial, financial, educational, social and political center of the far-famed and fertile Blue Grass Region."[60]

What the Chamber of Commerce did not tout or even publicly admit was that part of Lexington's prosperity and centrality stemmed from its being more "wide open" (or more "corrupt" or "cosmopolitan," depending on your point of view) than adjacent small towns. Lexington's infamous red light district prospered well into the late 1910s, regardless of anti-vice crusades, and the city regularly licensed more than 120 saloons annually, many of which contained slot machines and ignored Sunday closing laws. Judging from grand jury indictments, gambling was common, particularly in downtown "pool halls" that handled wagers on horse races. To such places, wrote one outraged critic, "men and boys go with visions of moment-made fortunes floating through disordered brains, to spend an entire afternoon in feverish excitement, and leave with less than nothing, depressed and disheartened."[61] Such excesses and such "disorder" raised the ire of ministers and members of civic organizations like the Central Kentucky Women's Club, giving impetus to a series of local reform campaigns conducted precisely during those years when motion pictures and vaudeville were introduced in Lexington. As we will see, for certain members of the local community, these new venues for commercial entertainment, which dispensed pleasure for profit and courted a "habitual" clientele, were simply one more means of promoting and purveying vice. Yet film exhibitors and vaudeville theater owners were also able to profit from this situation by clearly separating their businesses from saloons and pool halls, thereby gaining an important measure of legitimacy.

Local conditions in Lexington did not, strictly speaking, determine what commercial entertainment (almost always from *outside* the city) was available for the city's residents. Neither did these conditions somehow remain static while commercial entertainments came and went. If it is impossible to do little more than speculate on the larger ideological changes wrought on one small city by motion pictures, vaudeville, and other amusements, we can at least lay the groundwork for such speculations by examining how local exhibitors ran their operations, how motion pictures were programmed and marketed in the city, and how Lexington's various communities and constituencies took in and took to commercial entertainment.

TWO

Introducing the
"Marvelous Invention"

During December 1896, some eight months after the much-publicized premiere of Edison's vitascope at Koster & Bial's Music Hall in New York City, four different motion picture projection systems arrived almost simultaneously in Lexington. This situation reflects above all a predictable, if somewhat belated, attempt to gain the maximum short-term profit from what one local newspaper advertisement hyperbolically touted as "the most marvelous invention of the nineteenth century."[1] "Inventions" would have been more accurate, for in Lexington the cineomatragraphe (sic), phantoscope, vitascope, and Amet magniscope all vied for the title of *the* invention—the *most* marvelous. The situation in this relatively open market mirrors in small scale that brief period in motion picture history before the apparatus for projecting moving film images became standardized and taken for granted by the public, a "ruthless period" that first-generation film historian Terry Ramsaye dubs the era of the "lawless" film "frontier," during which "a new set of commercial conventions had to be evolved and established."[2] If nothing else, as Charles Musser proves, the motion picture "novelty year" of 1896–97 offered a "rich diversity of exhibition circumstances" for the new medium.[3] These circumstances depended on the local market, but they were hardly unique to Lexington.

The Phantoscope and Cineomatragraph

By the end of 1896, the "marvelous invention" itself was so obviously newsworthy that the local press lauded the arrival of the "wonderful Phantoscope" in Lexington, even though this projector was never actually used for a public screening in the city. Thomas Armat and C. Francis Jenkins had premiered what they would call the phantoscope at the Cotton States Exposition in Atlanta in October 1895, and thus can be credited with one of the first "public showings of projected movies for a paid admission."[4] They did not achieve any significant commercial success in Atlanta and were soon challenging each other in court over patent rights. Armat entered into an agreement with Thomas Edison and the distribution company of Raff & Gammon, and the phantoscope, with minor modifications, was redubbed "Edison's vitascope," so as to benefit from the inventor's fame. Jenkins, meanwhile, began to market the phantoscope through the Columbia Phonograph Company.[5] Ramsaye notes that by November 1896 a few phantoscopes had found their way to Chicago, Philadelphia, and New Orleans.[6]

A month later, one of Jenkins' machines appeared in Lexington through the efforts of Charles Scott. On several occasions during November 1896, the *Leader* reported on Scott's plans to go to Chicago to investigate firsthand Edison's "wonderful vitascope" and book a motion picture exhibition for the Opera House. He returned to Lexington, having secured a phantoscope, which he described as "the latest scientific invention," capable of "throwing views on canvas" that were far clearer and more distinct than those projected by Edison's machine.[7] On December 9 the phantoscope and some twenty "views" arrived. Scott arranged a private test run, which apparently was a disappointment, since he did not schedule any public screenings of this much-awaited novelty.

Within a week, however, Scott's newly redecorated theater did have the distinction of introducing motion pictures to Lexington. On the evening of Tuesday, December 16, and the matinee and evening of the following day, the Holmes & Wolford repertoire company offered what their advertisement called a "special attraction"—the "Cineomatragraph" (sic) "showing moving pictures life size and very natural between acts of the performances" of three

Interior of Lexington Opera House (1898). Photo courtesy University of Kentucky Photo Archives.

"stupendous, scenic productions." A "rep" company like Holmes & Wolford performed several different plays on each (usually) week-long stop on its tour.[8] Such troupes (commonly called "10–20–30's") offered the cheapest theatrical amusement then available at the Opera House. For the price of a ten-, twenty-, or thirty-cent ticket, the audience got a performance that included not only a familiar melodrama, farce, or romantic comedy, but also "specialties" between the acts: illustrated songs, comedy routines, jugglers, dancers, and other vaudeville turns.

On their December go-round, Holmes & Wolford's sole specialty was the cineomatragraph, which was given an unusually prominent place in their newspaper advertisements. To exploit the "marvelous invention" in this manner was perfectly in keeping with the efforts of rep companies to drum up business, since they could not rely on the drawing power of stage stars. It was also in keeping with the late nineteenth-century popular theater's capacity for incorporating visual novelties. (Recall the minstrel shows mentioned in Chapter 1, which featured dioramas and shadowgraphs when they played the Opera House in 1896.) Perhaps that is why both Lexington newspapers found nothing whatsoever troubling (or even noteworthy) about Holmes & Wolford's combination of live-action melodrama and "real life" views. The local press simply ignored *The Smugglers* in their reviews and deemed the cineomatragraph a "great hit" that was "alone worth the price of admission," even if there had been "vexing but unaccountable delays" during the "mechanical" part of the program.[9]

Melodeon Hall: A Vitascope Theater

Holmes & Wolford was the first of several rep companies during the next decade that offered motion pictures to patrons of the Opera House, though after the "novelty year," most 10–20–30 companies relegated motion pictures to the same secondary status as other specialties. Within a week of the premiere of the cineomatragraph, a quite different strategy for marketing and exhibiting motion pictures sought to capture a larger share of the Lexington audience. On 20 December 1896, a large advertisement in both Sunday newspapers announced the December 23 premiere of the Edison Company's vitascope at Melodeon Hall, a 350-seat second-floor site that had earlier in the 1890s housed the Commercial College of Kentucky University.[10] Located at 36½ East Main Street, Melodeon Hall was near the center of Lexington's business district, directly across from the county courthouse. Guiding this enterprise was W. A. ("Colonel Billy") Thompson of Cincinnati, a manager of boxers and wrestlers, who was well known in Lexington as a real "hustler" and "one of the best-posted sporting men of the country."[11] The Melodeon Hall vitascope theater was one of several entertainment ventures Thompson had promoted locally. During the fall race meet in October 1896, for example, he had arranged with Charles Scott to book a mind reader and an evening of boxing and wrestling matches at the Opera House.

With Edison's vitascope, Thompson had what looked to be a surefire money-maker, at least in the short haul. The *Leader* had mentioned this invention as early as May 1896, and between May and July, the vitascope premiered in a number of eastern and midwestern cities. Its first commercial engagement in Kentucky was apparently at a Louisville vaudeville theater on 20 September 1896, and by the time it arrived in Lexington, the vitascope

OPERA HOUSE

——TWO NIGHTS——
——AND MATINEE——

Commencing

Tuesday, December 15

The Holmes & Wolford Co,,

Presenting three Stupendous
Scenic Productions.

Tuesday night, the Sensational Melodrama,
"THE SMUGGLERS."

Wednesday matinee, the romantic
drama,
"THE BRAND OF CAIN."

Wednesday night Frank Mayo's greatest success,
"THE STREETS OF NEW YORK."

10,000 pounds of special scenery carried
for these plays.

——SPECIAL ATTRACTION——
——THE   CINEOMATRAGRAPH——

The most marvelous invention of the
nineteenth century will be on exhibition showing moving pictures life size
and very natural between each act of the
performances.

PRICES—10c, 20c and 30c.

Ladies admitted free Tuesday night
when accompanied by one paid 30-cent
ticket.

The first public screening of motion pictures in Lexington. Lexington *Herald*, 15
December 1896.

```
━━MELODEON HALL━━
36 1-2 EAST MAIN STREET OPPOSITE COURT HOUSE.
SUCH INVENTIONS MAKE HISTORY.
BEGINNING WEDNESDAY, DECEMBER 23rd, AND DAILY THEREAFTER.

HOURLY PERFORMANCES          VITASCOPE          The Supreme
  Of Edison's Original and                                  Electrical Wonder
  Preternatural Invention, the                                Of the Century.
IT AMAZES, DELIGHTS AND STARTLES ONE BY TURNS.   NATURE ANIMATION.   LIFE ITSELF SEEMS TO BE PLACED BEFORE THE SPECTATOR.

AFTERNOONS AT                   PERFORMANCES                   EVENINGS AT
1, 2, 3, 4 AND 5 O'CLOCK.                                     7, 8 AND 9 O'CLOCK.
                        Admission, 10 Cents.
```

First advertisement for "Billy" Thompson's short-lived vitascope theater. Lexington *Herald*, 23 December 1896.

was beginning its "Fifteenth Triumphant Week" at Heck & Avery's Museum in Cincinnati.[12] With only the sometimes pricey Opera House dominating the local commercial entertainment scene, Lexington was a potentially lucrative market.

Thompson's short-lived enterprise in Lexington is an example of vintage turn-of-the-century showmanship in the service of selling what was quickly becoming a major American commodity—"cheap amusement." Like the front man for a Wild West show, he fed the local press a daily dose of publicity. Thompson himself as well as the vitascope made for good copy, while his impressive initial advertisement gave the Melodeon Hall engagement the stature of a history-making event. For promotional purposes, Thompson held a private screening on December 22 for the press and other specially invited guests, including the mayor and his wife, several professors, and a host of society types—precisely the sort of people who could be counted on to attend a high cultural recital or a major touring attraction at the Opera House. Significantly, this event was covered in the society columns of both newspapers, which described the audience as "delighted" and "enthusiastic," fully won over by the wizardry that was able to produce "the intense reality of these shadows" and so "invoke life from nothing."[13]

"The mere announcement of the coming of Edison's latest invention to Lexington has caused much favorable comment," wrote the *Herald*.[14] Knowing full well the commercial value of Edison's name, Thompson milked the Edison connection for all it was worth. After all, during 1896 in Lexington, as elsewhere, the American "wizard" Edison was repeatedly linked by the

press with phonographic sound reproduction, X-ray images, and new technological breakthroughs such as the "autographic telegraph," a device for
transmitting photographs by wire. The cineomatragraph might be heralded
as "the supreme electrical wonder of the century," yet only the vitascope
was, as Thompson's advertisements insisted, not some "cheap imitation" but
"Edison's Original and Preternatural Invention" that had arrived in Kentucky
"direct from Edison's laboratory in Menlo Park." And the two workmen who
accompanied Thompson to Lexington were, he declared, "expert engineers
from Edison's work shops in New York."[15]

Actually, the electricians who operated the projector had been hired by
Thompson in Cincinnati, and the machine itself had been rented from Allen
F. Rieser, who earlier in the year had paid $1,500 for the vitascope territorial
rights for Pennsylvania, exclusive of Pittsburgh and Philadelphia, and then
had purchased for $5,000 the Ohio rights. (Apparently, no vitascope rights
specifically for Kentucky were sold.) By December 1896 Rieser was sublet-
ting projectors and films.[16] Thompson may have lied about his direct conduit
to Menlo Park, but his brief sojourn in Lexington is in keeping with the overall vitascope marketing policy. Raff & Gammon, exclusive American agents
for the vitascope, sold territorial rights to lease projectors, buy Edison films,
and sell subfranchises. What they envisioned—and what, according to Robert C. Allen, quickly led to a commercial dead end for the vitascope—was
that this machine would be exhibited in "the penny arcade, or phonograph
parlor, and [in] presentations by itinerant showmen."[17] Billy Thompson was
one such "itinerant showman."

Thompson's publicity for Melodeon Hall touted not only Edison's invention but also the actual commodity, the moving pictures themselves. Befitting
the work of a wizard, the "marvelous" vitascope was deemed "preternatural"
precisely because it "portrays every figure, action, color and effect true to
nature, life-like, life size and distinctively perfect, as if [one is] looking upon
actual scenes."[18] This realism/authenticity was for Thompson the prime selling point of motion pictures. Viewing such an uncannily accurate, machine-
made simulacrum of life "amazes, delights and startles one by turns"—an
advertising claim that situates vitascope images more in the context of other
"amazing" entertainment like the sideshow and the illusionist act than
the performances of a 10–20–30 troupe or a touring company from New
York City.

Yet Melodeon Hall promised to offer *more* than delightful, amazing entertainment. To forestall the criticism that often greeted imported amuse-

ments—a deep mistrust such as was expressed in Lexington's ordinance
concerning museums and exhibitions—newspaper previews of the vitascope
performance bestowed socially redeeming value on the act of moviegoing by
declaring that this invention had been "endorsed" by journalists, clergymen,
and schoolteachers, who deemed it "a splendid educator and developer of
the mind, a broadener of one's nature, and a trainer to habits of close observa-
tion."[19] To facilitate this pedagogic function, Thompson promised that a "lecturer will be on hand at each performance to explain all views," though no
such lecturer is mentioned in descriptions of the actual screenings.[20] The
movies' promise of pleasure was thus legitimated, brought within the acceptable boundaries of pragmatic, even progressive middle-class ideals, along
with X-ray demonstrations and Eskimos on display. White women and children—clearly part of Thompson's target audience—would not be imperiled
by what they saw at Melodeon Hall. In fact, Thompson invited the children
of the Orphan's Home to be his guests on Christmas Eve, and his matinee
performances were directed specifically at "ladies and children . . . and any
lady may visit one of these performances without an escort with perfect impunity, as she will be assured of courteous treatment and every attention."[21]

Thompson's theater opened on the afternoon of December 23, with vitascope shows running hourly from 1:00 to 5:00, each costing an admission
price of ten cents. Melodeon Hall had been, Thompson insisted, "thoroughly
overhauled," fitted with comfortable seats and a good heating system, and
decorated with "evergreens, flags and bunting."[22] The projector, housed in a
small room in the back of the hall, cast "half-life size" figures on to a framed
white screen; perhaps, as Musser notes of the first vitascope screenings in
New York City, each brief film was spliced into a loop and shown several
times consecutively.[23] Thompson had promised a program filled with well-
known moving pictures (including *The Widow Jones Kiss* [aka *The May Irwin
Kiss*], *The Empire State Express,* and *Laloie Fuller's Dance*), but newspaper
accounts do not mention any of these films. Among the views that were shown
and praised were mildly exotic subjects like soldiers marching toward the
camera, a trapeze performance, and a skirt dance in "various colors." Also
featured were two films that the white Lexington audience would no doubt
have recognized as reassuringly "real-life" vignettes: African-American boys
dancing and an African-American woman washing a child.

For the twenty-five-cent evening show, Thompson hedged his bets by co-
billing the vitascope with Miss Winnie Anderson, who conducted a "seance
of Spiritualism and Theosophy." (Like Edison's machine, Miss Anderson ar-

rived with good credentials; she was said to have "received the indorsement [sic] of the Royal Society of London.") While the Holmes & Wolford Company inserted its cineomatragraph views between the acts of a sensational melodrama, Thompson elected to combine marvelous lifelike images with logic-defying illusionist tricks done "in full gas light on an open stage."[24] Would this particular exhibition strategy have tended to undercut any pretense of pedagogic purpose? Would it have underscored the technological, mechanical basis of motion picture projection? Would it have diminished or heightened the magic of the moving image?

Unfortunately, the opening night reviews do not address these questions, but they do indicate that Thompson's promotional efforts paid off, as "large crowds" flocked to Melodeon Hall. The *Leader* gave high marks to Miss Anderson's act and announced that "to say that wizard Edison's latest invention was a success, is to speak in sparing praise of the sensation it caused. Throngs of ladies and children crowded the hall at each performance, and all seemed delighted."[25] These "throngs" constituted a hitherto largely untapped audience for commercial entertainment in downtown Lexington. As of December 29, Thompson dropped the spiritualist half of the bill and added a second evening showing of the vitascope. To assure repeat patronage he promised a steady stream of "new views," including films of Niagara Falls, a New York City tenement fire, and the six-round Corbett-Courtney fight. Four days after the opening of his vitascope theater, Thompson outlined plans for the expansion of his enterprise to include a dime museum "that will cater particularly to ladies and children" and a theater featuring dramatic productions at prices "to suit all classes."[26] The good people of Lexington, he insisted, deserved the same caliber of inexpensive commercial entertainment as the residents of Cincinnati; Thompson, with the know-how and gumption of a sporting tout, would usher in a new, more cosmopolitan era in the Bluegrass.

Thompson's attempt to use moving pictures and Edison's imprimatur as a springboard for establishing an amusement complex in Lexington abruptly ended on December 31, after the two vitascope operators broke into Melodeon Hall during the night and took the machine back to Cincinnati. They claimed they had not been paid their weekly salary of $50 and feared that Thompson was about to steal the rented vitascope for which they had put up a $300 bond. Thompson, in turn, accused the men of theft and charged that Rieser had not provided him with the steady supply of new films that he had contracted for. The case of Melodeon Hall was not atypical: Allen notes that similar distribution problems wrecked the entire vitascope enterprise, and motion picture theaters set up elsewhere in the United States at this time rarely lasted more than four or five weeks.[27]

All told, Thompson's vitascope theater lasted no longer on Main Street than did the "impromptu museum" that had housed Minnie the Wind Girl. On 17 January 1897, Thompson returned to Lexington and announced that he would soon reopen Melodeon Hall with a "new and improved" vitascope. This plan never materialized, though Thompson hit town again a month later touting a new venture, a train excursion to the upcoming boxing match between Fitzsimmons and Corbett in Carson City, Nevada. Stripped of its projector, Melodeon Hall again became available for assorted local events, including a chrysanthemum show staged by the Chamber of Commerce to promote downtown shopping. Then plans were announced to transform the hall into a "first class playhouse" or into a "School of Telegraphy." Instead it became the Kimball Music Hall, where dances and recitals were held. In 1902, spurred by yet another eastern craze that swept the provinces, this hall once again became a venue for commercial entertainment, this time as a short-lived "Ping Pong Parlor." Success stories and box office hits count for much in cultural history, as well they should; failures, fly-by-night operations, and ambitious schemes often provide a no less intriguing sense of the limits of possibility.

Exhibiting the Magniscope

During the week-long run of the vitascope at Melodeon Hall, a fourth motion picture projector made its appearance in Lexington when Charles Scott returned from New York City after purchasing an Amet magniscope. Although one Lexington newspaper referred to this machine as "undoubtedly one of Edison's greatest inventions,"[28] it was actually built by Edward Amet, who, with George K. Spoor, marketed the magniscope in the Midwest. Musser notes that this projector was "portable and designed for work with touring companies" and was advertised as being for sale "outright, without restrictions, and at a reasonable price."[29] No doubt both the price and the portability of the magniscope appealed to Scott, particularly after his bad luck with the phantoscope.

Scott's method of exhibiting the magniscope between December 1896 and March 1897 was much different from Thompson's attempt to create a vitascope theater. For one thing, motion pictures were more of a sideline for Scott, who was at this date quite successfully running the Opera House, serving as the business manager of the Lexington Chautauqua Assembly, and booking tent shows during the summer season. Though somewhat pressed by Thompson's entrance into the Lexington market, Scott could afford to call his own motion picture shots, so to speak. He could also rely on the strong support of the local press. For example, the *Herald* applauded Scott's efforts at obtaining a magniscope since "he bears the entire expense; and his only aim being to give to his home patrons the latest in everything, whether it is the latest theatrical fad or the latest electrical invention."[30]

Latest is the key word here, reflecting a widespread cultural reverence for and fascination with inventors and technical progress (recall the local response to the State College X-ray experiments), and perhaps also belying the inferiority complex of a small provincial city. Indeed, one function of the Opera House (like the syndicated columns on athletics, fashion, and the legitimate stage in the Sunday newspapers) was to serve as a medium for Lexington's exposure to cosmopolitanism and the *au courant,* meaning in this case the magniscope, "the latest and most improved instrument of the kind now on exhibition."[31]

Scott premiered the magniscope on the afternoon and evening of December 26 between the acts of Slater & Martin's production of *Uncle Tom's Cabin.* There were in the 1890s well over 130 "Tom" troupes touring the United States, and Slater & Martin's ranked among the largest and most lavish, equipped with three brass bands, twenty horses and mules, eight "Man-eating Cuban and Russian Blood Hounds," and an "eight-foot" tall black teenager.[32] Tom troupes regularly fleshed out Harriet Beecher Stowe's melodrama with musical routines, visual novelties, and spectacular effects, so Scott presumably had no compunction about adding inter-act motion pictures to this performance of *Uncle Tom's Cabin.* Since this play was a perennial favorite in Lexington, a large though not necessarily "high-class" audience could be expected, attracted in part by a free street parade and outdoor band concert, as well as by the novelty of the magniscope. The matinee had a special admission price of twenty-five cents for any seat in the house, while in the evening, tickets ranged from twenty-five to seventy-five cents. At this date, the standard Opera House policy consigned African Americans to the gallery, the cheapest and least visible section of the theater. But for *Uncle Tom's Cabin,* all of the fifty-cent balcony seats were also "reserved for colored people."

It would be poetically just and ideologically apt to report that *Uncle Tom's Cabin* provided the backdrop for motion pictures of frolicking pickaninnies and mammies at work, but the newspaper accounts do not mention which films were shown to the "immense crowds" that filled the Opera House's 1,200-plus seats. The *Herald* simply declared the magniscope pictures to be "a revelation to the general public," of "such accuracy and with such magnificent effect that all were perfectly delighted." To substantiate this claim, the paper quoted a female patron who deemed these views "the finest she had ever seen."[33] Hardly a conclusive sample of opinion, but it is notable that a woman was called upon to speak as Lexington's first "expert" movie-goer. What the *Herald*'s judgment seems to imply is that Scott, the local businessman with (purportedly) only the interest of Lexington in mind, had managed to outdo Thompson, the flashy itinerant showman. A similar attitude was suggested by a *Herald* column of 2 January 1897 that took city officials to task for collecting license fees from the Opera House, but not from other entertainment-for-profit establishments, such as, presumably, Melodeon Hall.

Scott planned his next showing of the magniscope for an open matinee date on January 6, two days after veteran touring star Thomas Keene had appeared at the Opera House in *Julius Caesar*. This time Scott made use of yet another exhibition strategy. He organized an "entirely mechanical entertainment" in which motion pictures as well as some three hundred stereopticon "dissolving views" would be accompanied by "Edison's latest electrical phonograph playing the popular airs of the day." The musical portion of the program was handled by George Walker, who had previously toured the region giving phonograph concerts.[34] Contemporary accounts do not specify what role Walker played during this performance, whether any sound effects were employed, or if there was any attempt to link sound with image thematically, as had been the case with the traveling "electric concert and exhibition" mentioned in Chapter 1. However, Scott's "all-mechanical" event—combining still images, magniscope views, and recorded sound—could not help but reinforce the notion that motion pictures were the latest marvelous addition to the modern tradition of mechanical reproduction.

For this engagement, Scott targeted a youthful audience; hence the performance was set for 2:30 in the afternoon "to give school children a chance to see the pictures." Ten-cent children's tickets and twenty-cent adult tickets put this "entirely mechanical entertainment" within the reach of virtually anyone with some disposable income for commercial amusements. The press noted with approval that Professor Anderson's State College class and the student body of Professor Smith's Commercial College planned to attend the matinee. Blessed by these higher education professionals, Scott's program could only be taken as respectable and worthwhile, with no danger whatsoever that it might constitute a "nuisance, or [be] in any way hurtful or offensive to public morals," like those traveling attractions so feared by the framers of local ordinances. Indeed, quite the reverse. When Scott arranged for another magniscope exhibition in late February, the *Herald* offered an unqualified endorsement of the new medium: "this is one of the greatest of educators for the little ones and all should go and take the little ones."[35]

To assure that the magniscope would consistently generate at least some revenue without requiring a supply of new films, Scott sent his "all-mechanical" show on the road during January, February, and March to smaller central Kentucky towns such as Versailles and Mt. Sterling, and then as far south as DeFuniak Springs, Florida.[36] These magniscope tours were part of Scott's effort at this time to diversify as well as expand his field of operation beyond Lexington. During the 1895–96 season, for example, he managed Macauley's Theater in Louisville for the Klaw & Erlanger chain, and in February 1896, he closed a deal to lease the Opera House in Frankfort, the state capital. His career as a motion picture exhibitor, however, ended after he booked the magniscope for the Lexington Chautauqua Assembly in July 1897, where the half-hour moving picture program was "much enjoyed by the crowd."[37]

The only magniscope performance actually described in any detail by the Lexington press occurred on March 1 at the Opera House. Although these accounts do not explain the precise arrangement of the program or the use, if any, of sound accompaniment, they do capture some sense of a provincial motion picture exhibition circa 1897. On this occasion, moving pictures again shared the stage with a rep company, Rentfrow's Jolly Pathfinders, which specialized in "musical farce comedies." There was no place for the magniscope in a higher-priced touring production like Nat Goodwin's *An American Citizen*, which played the Opera House on March 15. But Rentfrow's type of theatrical entertainment, out to provide "mirth for the millions," was another story. These performances of unsophisticated comedies, interspersed with songs and dance routines and accompanied by the company's own musicians, provided a suitable frame for motion pictures. Call it guilt by association: if the magniscope shared the stage with the Jolly Pathfinders, were not the movies more likely to be perceived as a source of "delight" rather than of educational uplift?

On March 1 the Rentfrow troupe presented *Below Zero*—a farce about a hungry tramp—with the company's band performing marches, a xylophone solo, and other "grand, delightful, entrancing" numbers. At some point or points in the proceedings came a diverse array of magniscope films that captured "real life" as: domestic pastoral (a "lovely farmyard scene" showing a little girl feeding chickens and ducks), dangerous spectacle (footage of horses being rescued from a burning stable and of the New York City fire department responding to an alarm), and newsworthy event (films of a boxing match between Edwards and Warwick and a thoroughbred hurdle race at the Buffalo Country Club). The horse race footage, in particular, "set the house wild"— not just because these spectators were Kentuckians. It was that the camera was "so placed that the races are seen coming straight at the audience." At least part of the novelty of motion pictures arose from the new way of viewing they could provide, absolutely distinct in this case from a fixed, "theatrical" perspective. Significantly, and perhaps predictably, what truly "set the house in a roar," according to the *Herald,* was the "very funny" film of "an old colored woman washing a baby"—"real life" as social comedy, ideological reinforcement, "mirth for the millions."[38]

Several things about the introduction of motion pictures in Lexington during the "novelty year" of 1896–97 stand out: the concerted effort to draw women and children (though not in this case families per se) as spectators; the sometimes contradictory marketing of motion pictures as a scientific achievement, a visual novelty, a "preternatural" marvel, an educational medium, and a source of thrills and delight; and the various ways these new "views" were positioned as popular-price attractions at the Opera House and Melodeon Hall. Lexington newspaper accounts seem to corroborate Musser's contention that "from its outset . . . the cinema drew its audiences from across the working, middle, and elite classes."[39] By scheduling the magniscope along with *Uncle Tom's Cabin* and Rentfrow's Jolly Pathfinders, Scott made motion pictures available to at least some blacks as well as whites, some rural folk as well as city dwellers. Clearly, the reception of the "marvelous invention[s]" by local audiences—which we cannot determine in any empirical sense—was structured and at least potentially circumscribed by where these films were exhibited, what company they kept on stage, and how they were promoted and legitimated. Miriam Hansen proposes that for early cinema audiences "the meanings transacted were contingent upon *local* conditions and constellations, leaving reception at the mercy of relatively *unpredictable,* aleatory processes" (her italics).[40] But to a great extent context reined in unpredictability. Except in the case of Melodeon Hall's afternoon screenings, Lexington's first moviegoers did not solely (or simply) watch "new views." They experienced motion pictures in the company of other mechanical reproductions, or juxtaposed with other illusionist tricks, or sandwiched between the acts of *Uncle Tom's Cabin* and familiar rep troupe melodramas and comedies. Thus was "Edison's" marvel initially emplaced in the city—commercially, culturally, and ideologically—through a process that continued during the next ten years, as motion pictures were exhibited at the Opera House, Chautauqua Assemblies, churches, summertime theaters, large-scale fairs, and street carnivals in Lexington.

THREE

**Situating
Motion Pictures
in the
Pre-Nickelodeon Period**

Between the local premiere of the cineomatragraph, vitascope, and the magniscope in 1896 and the opening of Lexington's first nickelodeon in June
1906, motion pictures became for the most part simply another fixture in the
city's range of commercial entertainments. No entrepreneur attempted to set
up something along the lines of Thompson's vitascope theater. More significantly, none of the four vaudeville houses that opened downtown stayed in
business for more than a month, and so Lexington continued to lack one of
the principal turn-of-the-century outlets for exhibiting motion pictures.
There was something of a drop in the number of film screenings locally during
1901–2, in keeping with a national trend that Musser has identified.[1] Yet by
April 1904, the *Leader* could note that "moving pictures are seen almost every day in Lexington."[2]

The kind of films local audiences saw during the pre-nickelodeon period
surely helped shape their conception of the medium itself and its social and
cultural import as cheap amusement, say, or educational tool. Thus it is important to note the rise of highly topical, proto-newsreel footage and the role
of Lyman Howe's "High-Class Moving Pictures," cinematic renderings of the
Oberammergau *Passion Play*, and films of championship prizefights. Yet a

list of titles that were screened locally cannot tell the entire tale, for the place of the movies in Lexington was very much a function of the movies' place, that is, how and when they were made available, publicized, exhibited, *em-placed* in the leisure life of the city as it moved into the twentieth century.

In Lexington, as in the industrialized urban areas of the Northeast studied by social historians such as Roy Rosenzweig,[3] leisure time in the pre-nickelodeon period was increasingly seen as an aspect of daily life to be filled, regulated, and exploited for profit. For example, the city continued to experience a rise in all sorts of sports activities.[4] Horse racing, particularly at the 5,000-seat Kentucky Trotting Horse Breeders Association track, still drew large crowds, as did Sunday professional and semi-pro baseball.[5] Collegiate football attracted increased attention, along with novel(ty) sporting events such as Independence Day auto races and baseball games between area players and traveling all-female teams. Meanwhile, in an attempt to turn a profit locally from what had already proven economically viable in larger cities, Lexington's first bowling alley—appropriately called the Manhattan Cafe and Bowling Alley—opened downtown in 1898.

The Manhattan reserved half of its six lanes for women and thus promoted at least some semblance of heterosocial culture, but Lexington's interest in bowling (and other indoor commercial recreational activities) and the growing attendance for seasonal spectator sports did not cause any noticeable backlash. The pre-nickelodeon period was, however, marked by increasingly more concerted efforts at monitoring and regulating time not spent at work, church, home, or school. By 1903 the *Leader* could rather hyperbolically refer to the "reform tidal wave" that was washing over and cleansing the city.[6] Jane Addams and Carry Nation each made two local appearances between 1898 and 1904, years that also saw Lexington's Anti-Gambling League at least ostensibly rid the city of slot machines, while the Law and Order League mounted a highly publicized campaign against saloons that violated Sunday closing laws. At the same time, reform groups such as the Civic League and the Central Kentucky Women's Club, which were more inclined to promote social amelioration, directed their efforts toward the creation of a city playground system.[7] Both local newspapers strongly endorsed the "moral necessity of recreation," calling the orderly, adult-supervised playground an ideal site for the inculcation of "good morals and good manners."[8] Besides, as the *Herald* pointed out, such playgrounds were a way to keep "control" over the "worse element of city urchins."[9] In effect, the larger and more habitual the "audience" for playgrounds, the better.

Like Lexington's playgrounds, none of the four main sites where motion pictures were screened in the pre-nickelodeon period required excuses or legitimation. Yet the Lexington Opera House, the summer theater at Woodland Park, the Chautauqua Assembly, and the Elks Fair were quite distinct sites in terms of the audiences they sought to attract, the civic obligations they tried to fulfill, and the precise contextual framework they provided for motion pictures. And each of these sites, as we will see, offered its own version of "entertainment," packaged with the social and cultural needs of turn-of-the-century Lexington in mind.

Lexington Opera House

During the pre-nickelodeon period the Lexington Opera House unquestionably remained the city's preeminent permanent venue for commercial entertainment in part because Scott diligently worked to maintain his theater's image as a refined, elegant, safe, well-equipped venue. By systematically modernizing and refurbishing the Opera House, he assured that it would continue to attract premiere road shows and thus theatergoers "distinctively of the cultured class."[10] Safety and respectability required not only a new asbestos curtain and stylish green velour-covered seats in the auditorium, but, perhaps more important, a solicitous concern for the welfare of the theatergoer. Sometimes this demanded what Lawrence W. Levine calls the "taming" of audiences, as when Scott cracked down on disruptive "gallery gods" who occupied the theater's cheapest seats.[11] Or it could entail the banning of smoking in the Opera House lobby so as to prevent ashes and spit from soiling women's gowns, or it could literally involve the policing of the theater. It would seem that Scott regularly had problems with those same "urchins" whom the *Herald* hoped would somehow be controlled by a city playground system, for outside the lobby doors during evening performances "rowdy boys" "made the air resonant with their whoops and yells."[12] Indeed, this site apparently attracted a nightly "crowd of loafers," causing the mayor in September 1900 to station policemen in front of the Opera House.

The local press, too, supported Scott's efforts, lauding his initiative and acumen in arranging each Opera House season. The *Leader* found him to be the ideal manager, attentive, at home with the local and conversant with the national. With his knowledge of central Kentucky audiences, Scott could "grasp the wants of the public"; with his frequent trips to New York City and

Opera House program, 1901–2: Chas. Scott and his muse. Photo courtesy University of Kentucky Photo Archives.

Chicago, he could "keep pace with the ever-moving things theatrical."[13] Yet, in fact, for his "first-class" attractions, Scott relied on the Klaw & Erlanger booking agency and later on the Theatrical Syndicate, an extraordinarily influential monopoly formed in 1896.[14]

Key to the Theatrical Syndicate's control over the booking of touring productions was its coast-to-coast chain of metropolitan area theaters and its access to hundreds of provincial venues that could support one- or two-night stands.[15] This allowed "combination companies" (so-called because they were organized to perform a "single play for the season on a prearranged tour") to work the maximum number of road dates with the minimum amount of expensive dead time lost in transit.[16] The Lexington Opera House, by this logic, benefited from its proximity by rail to Cincinnati and Louisville and its position on the route to Nashville, Chattanooga, and points south. For a fee of from 5 to 10 percent of the gross receipts for each performance booked, the syndicate simplified scheduling problems and increased the availability of "better" products for provincial theaters.[17]

By systematically routing productions originating on the New York stage through all sections of the country, the Theatrical Syndicate fostered some degree of homogeneity, rendering the premiere commercial playhouse in a small city like Lexington into a medium for Theater, that is, for an institutionalized, national form of stage entertainment and legitimate culture.[18] However, some variation was possible since, as Alfred Bernheim notes, one selling point of the syndicate was that it "could also assure theatres a rotation of plays best suited to the taste and appetite of local theatre audiences."[19] Given that major combination companies played Lexington for one (or, rarely, two) nights, Scott had a great many dates to fill, and there were, according to the *New York Dramatic Mirror*, some 392 traveling companies on the road in December 1900, for example.[20]

I have not been able to determine exactly what type of attractions Scott had to chose from nor precisely how much freedom he had in selecting his bookings. In February 1900 Scott described his options and priorities as follows: "Lexington being on its particular Southern circuit has to take what it can get at such times as it is most convenient to the traveling companies. With that, however, it is one of the most fortunate cities of its kind in the country for first-class bookings. . . . while it is necessary to book popular price and repertoire companies to fill in from time to time, the aim of the management has always been to get the very best attractions on the road."[21] On other occasions he put the matter differently, announcing that his real

intent was to satisfy "the tastes of the many."[22] Surely a theater like the Opera
House found it economically necessary to appeal to what Scott called different "tastes"—a resonant, ambiguous word that could at times refer to social
class, educational background, age, gender, and/or race. What "tastes" did
Scott acknowledge, and how did motion pictures figure as part of the multipurpose Opera House's diverse schedule in the pre-nickelodeon period?[23]

The upper-tier attractions at the Opera House were predominantly combination companies, with tickets ranging from twenty-five or fifty cents for
gallery seats to $1.50 or $2.00 for the best box seats. These "first-class" productions differed appreciably from the uplifting, genteel high culture of musical recitals and literary societies. While there were a number of realistic
dramas, Shakespearean revivals, and well-mounted spectacles, the great percentage of combination companies offered farcical, satiric, or musical comedy.[24] The highlights of each season, however, were star vehicles. Much of
the Opera House's high standing locally stemmed from Scott's ability to book
stars of the first rank, year after year, thereby treating Lexington to the likes
of Edward H. Southern and Julia Marlowe, Maude Adams, and, most vener-
ated of all, Joseph Jefferson in *Rip Van Winkle* (for which ticket "speculators"
resold premium seats for as much as $10.00). Appearances by these actors
were invariably the most expensively priced attractions at the Opera House,
and they qualified as social events of the first order, drawing theatergoers
from throughout central Kentucky, who were typically described as "intelligent," "brilliant," "cultured," and "sophisticated." It was these performances and, to a lesser extent, the occasional concert by a classical virtuoso,
a symphony orchestra, or John Philip Sousa's band that could be taken as
evidence of Scott's desire "to elevate the stage in this city" so that it might
purvey "better and more cultured sentiment."[25]

Though Scott was inclined to play up his cultural contribution, the fact is
that 10–20–30 repertoire troupes like Rentfrow's Jolly Pathfinders filled almost as many total play dates at the Opera House in this period as the more
prestigious combination companies. Whereas a "first-class" attraction, by
virtue of its touring schedule, linked Lexington with larger cities (and ultimately with Broadway), a rep troupe such as the Van Dyke & Eaton Company
traveled a quite different route: in 1899, for instance, it went from Lexington
to Mt. Sterling and Maysville, Kentucky, then to Wheeling and Huntington,
West Virginia, then to Zanesville, Ohio.[26] If not literally working class, 10–
20–30 productions were workaday theater, we might say: time-tested plays—
or at least very familiar genres (usually melodrama and comedy)—staged

without costly sets or spectacular effects and incorporating specialties such as illustrated songs, vaudeville turns, and motion pictures between the acts.

Distinct from both rep troupes and combination companies were "popular price" attractions, usually companies that year-in and year-out traveled the provinces offering crowd-pleasing mainstays such as the "Big Melo-Dramatic" *James Boys in Missouri,* the Yankee farce, *Uncle Josh Spruceby,* and the temperance favorite, *Ten Nights in a Bar Room.* With ticket prices from twenty-five cents to $1.00, these touring productions tended to highlight spectacular scenic effects. When Charles B. Yale's *Everlasting Devil's Auction,* for instance, played the Opera House in 1903, it was in its "22nd Edition" and featured vaudeville acts, a tableau of hell, and a scenic "Tribute to Our Country."[27] Several of these durable, readily accessible popular-price productions shared a distinctively regional flavor, if only by virtue of a common nostalgic focus on nineteenth-century southern life. Such plays included *In Old Kentucky, Under Southern Skies, In Louisiana, Coon Hollow,* and *The Moonshiner's Daughter.* The "tastes" Scott sought to satisfy with this type of entertainment were most likely rural, traditional, and unsophisticated; that is, those people interested less in metropolitan airs and bravura performances than in the "big," the "melo-dramatic," and what they felt to be reassuringly constant about America. According to the *Herald,* the audience for the popular-price favorite *Way Down East* "includes the vast number of people who never go to a playhouse,"[28] quite unlike the "gallery gods" who regularly filled the cheap seats or those representatives of the "cultured class," whose frequent theater parties were duly noted in society columns.

In Lexington, *Uncle Tom's Cabin* was unquestionably the premiere popular-price attraction, often booked twice a year at the Opera House even after the local chapter of the Daughters of the Confederacy began a vigorous campaign against this play in 1902, charging that it "slurred" the "fair name" of Southerners and was likely to "inflame race prejudice among the large class of Negro citizens."[29] The controversy continued for several months, explicitly focusing on the accuracy and effect of *Uncle Tom's Cabin,* while implicitly raising broader questions about the degree to which local communities were able to control potentially dangerous popular entertainment. The Daughters of the Confederacy's protest did not gain much public support, and Scott held firm, evoking his prerogative as a businessman and deferring once more to the "tastes" of the community at large: "I wish there were no such shows [as *Uncle Tom's Cabin*], and I do not care to book them. I am a public manager, however, and manage a public institution . . . as the white people patronize the show even more so than the colored people and fill the house every time it is given and send their children as well, it means money to me, and I do not see why I should not furnish such attractions when there seems to be a demand for them."[30]

In 1905 the Daughters of the Confederacy renewed their protest and lobbied the state legislature, which passed what came to be known as the "Uncle Tom's Cabin bill." This statute prohibited the "production of theatrical performances that tend to create racial feelings and prejudice."[31] This piece of special-interest legislation could almost stand as an emblem of Lexington's biracial society: the bill assumed that "racial feelings" had yet to be "created"; that the potential "prejudice" of blacks against whites was the central issue; that only a few dangerous performances were capable of creating these "feelings"; and that "prejudice" was not somehow the goal of the entire Jim Crow system. Ironically, the "Uncle Tom's Cabin bill" would play a significant role ten years later when a campaign was mounted to prohibit the local screening of *The Birth of a Nation*, as we will see in Chapter 6.

One result of Scott's professed desire to satisfy the "demands" of a range of potential theatergoers, and thus to fill the Opera House as often as possible, was that he attempted to attract the large black population of Lexington and its rural environs without challenging the city's codes of racial segregation. His solution was typical of the region and the period: allow blacks to purchase seats in the gallery—so-called "nigger heaven," accessible by a rear entrance—or, on special occasions, to occupy the balcony. The only time this "natural" arrangement was mentioned by the local press was when a pair of white college students attempted to sneak into the Opera House by blacking their faces with cork.[32]

Scott most obviously courted black theatergoers by booking several times each season minstrel shows that would draw black (as well as white) audiences; in such cases, the Opera House newspaper ad specifically noted that the balcony would be reserved for "colored persons." Like *Uncle Tom's Cabin*, minstrel shows drew what the *Leader* described as "top-heavy" crowds, as the "galleries filled to suffocation" with "colored people who were out in force."[33] *In Darkest America* and the *Black Patti Troubadours*, however, generated no local controversy whatsoever, since they were assumed to be "merely" entertainment that provided a suitably harmless way for blacks (and whites and children) to spend their leisure time.[34]

If appearances by stars of the legitimate stage underscored the Opera House's status among society types and its connection with urban glamour and sophistication, Scott's frequent booking of blackface troupes (both "All White" companies and those that featured black casts and headliners like Bert Williams and George Walker) linked his theater with otherwise quite different venues. For example, a regular feature on the midway at the Colored A & M Fair was a tent show in which "Southern plantation scenes and life in the South is faithfully reproduced," and the 1902 Maccabee's street fair included among its attractions "The Old Plantation," a "Southern Minstrel Exhibition."[35] Thus did the Plantation survive into the twentieth century, ritualized and enacted in different sites, serving as musical accompaniment to the Jim Crow practices that pervaded all aspects of daily life in Lexington.

In addition to booking minstrel shows, Scott sought the patronage of "local colored society" at the turn of the century in other ways as well: for example, by allowing the Opera House to be used for: a reading by the African American poet Paul Dunbar and a production of Dunbar's musical comedy, *Clorinda;* two plays mounted by the Lexington-based Afro-American Comedy Company; and a lecture by Booker T. Washington in June 1902. Black charity groups raising funds for the Chandler Normal School and the Colored Widow and Orphans Home also held benefit performances at the Opera House, as did a number of white community groups, from prominent fraternal organizations and the YMCA to the city's firemen and the Brotherhood of Locomotive Engineers. And every June public schools held their commencements on Scott's stage. Such bookings testify to the fact that the Opera House played a central role in the civic affairs of the city. As a site for *Uncle Tom's Cabin* and Richard Mansfield, minstrel shows and noted lecturers like Eugene V. Debs and Carry Nation, this multipurpose venue acted as a sort of cultural forum, giving voice to many (never "all") tastes and discourses, which were legitimated by and circumscribed within a refined, respectable, safe environment.

Motion Pictures at the Opera House

Given the virtual absence of vaudeville theaters in Lexington and the range of attractions Scott booked, it is not surprising that the Opera House became one of the city's major venues for film exhibition in the pre-nickelodeon period. For one thing, motion pictures continued to be used as between-the-acts specialties by 10–20–30 rep troupes and, occasionally, by a show like Wormwood's Monkey Theater, which featured Edison's projectoscope along with some thirty monkeys, twenty-nine dogs, and assorted tropical birds. In such cases Scott contracted with the company, which supplied its own specialties. The presence of motion pictures on the bill seems to have made no difference one way or the other in terms of the audiences such shows drew or the frequency with which they played Lexington—not the movies, but monkeys or melodramas were what people paid ten, twenty, or thirty cents to see.

Yet there were a number of popular-price attractions booked into the Opera House that did rely exclusively or primarily on motion pictures. These included touring programs featuring films of prizefights or the passion play, as well as Lyman H. Howe's shows that combined newsreel footage and exotic travelogues with elaborate sound effects and musical accompaniment. Howe's exhibition, later dubbed the "Lifeorama," premiered in Lexington in 1903, a year that, according to Charles Musser, saw a "boom . . . among traveling exhibitors in the nation's opera houses."[36] As part of a route that traversed Ohio, Michigan, Illinois, West Virginia, and Kentucky, one of Howe's companies returned twice yearly to the Opera House until 1917, with heavily publicized programs that consistently drew good crowds. In effect, Howe's exhibition became a popular-price staple, like the annual appearance of Al G. Fields' Minstrels.

The single motion picture exhibition in the pre-nickelodeon period that drew the most attention from the Lexington press, however, was a benefit for the fire department that was presented in February 1903 by "Professors" Gorman and Swanson.[37] These two traveling "moving picture men" banked on the novelty of locally filmed pictures, a strategy that had earlier proved successful for companies like Biograph and Selig.[38] (Appendix 1 lists all local productions mentioned in Lexington newspapers between 1896 and 1930.) After waiting for a sufficiently sunny day, Gorman and Swanson staged for their polyscope camera a full-speed race down Broadway, featuring all the horse-drawn and steam vehicles of the fire department. A cloud blocked the sun, causing them to shoot a second take in which, fortuitously enough, a stray dog was trampled by the fire chief's buggy, adding to the desired spectacular effect. Plans were then announced for the filming of a panoramic view of downtown Lexington from the rear of a moving streetcar, though this seems not to have taken place. The fire department "race" scene, along with closer shots of prominent firemen and policemen, was shown ten days later as the centerpiece of a benefit program, which also included exotic dancers and local singers performing live, as well as additional comic motion pictures of, for example, a Henderson, Kentucky, audience "laughing at the moving pictures" (meta-film of the first order!). This benefit packed the Opera House

with what the *Herald* called "its largest and most appreciative audience"—
well over 1,800 spectators—and an extra matinee performance was added.[39]

In Lexington, at least, Gorman and Swanson's successful exploitation of
local views was not repeated in the pre-nickelodeon period. The lengthy films
of heavyweight championship fights screened at the Opera House in September 1897, August 1899, and January 1900 represented a quite different use
of the new medium and a quite different strategy for exhibiting motion pictures.[40] Booking these programs attested to Scott's policy of bringing to Lexington the latest metropolitan attractions. But fight films were hardly a risky
venture, since prizefighting was widely covered in the local press, and live
bouts were held at various halls in the city, including the Opera House itself,
which had hosted a winner-take-all "Battle Royale" in May 1897. Furthermore, each of these films, whatever their distinctively cinematic qualities,
was packaged very much like a self-contained theatrical touring show and so
could readily be slotted into the conventional booking format of the Opera
House, which depended on a steady stream of different and somewhat diverse product.

From the first, however, fight films looked likely to be as controversial
as they were lucrative.[41] The veriscope filming of the Corbett-Fitzsimmons
championship fight in March 1897 sparked the first major outcry specifically
focusing on the pernicious possibilities of motion pictures as a *mass* medium.
A week after the fight, the leader of the Women's Christian Temperance Union
(WCTU) called upon President William McKinley and state government officials to prohibit "the reproduction, by means of the kinetoscope, or kindred
instruments, of the Corbett-Fitzsimmons fight, or any like exhibition at any
future time." The potentially widespread, insidious influence of this new mechanical means of "lifelike" reproduction demanded the strictest of measures. "We believe," the WCTU announced, "that in making this request we
are seeking the best welfare of the citizens, especially the youth of our land,
who could not but be brutalized by such life like presentations of these degrading spectacles. We learn that preparations upon the largest scale are being made for invading not alone our great cities, but every village and hamlet
with this spectacular performance, so that, bad as was the influence of the
fight upon the comparative few who witnessed it in person, it would be infi-
nitely worse because so much more far-reaching if thus produced."[42]

The *Herald* gave front-page coverage to this "Knock Out . . . Planned by
Women," and in May 1897 the Second Presbyterian Church in Lexington

unsuccessfully requested the board of aldermen to "pass at once an ordinance prohibiting the exhibition in our city of any picture, however made, or representation of such fights."[43] So the invasion proceeded as scheduled, with Scott booking one of the eleven companies touring with the *Corbett-Fitzsimmons Fight* for three matinee and evening showings on 30 September–2 October 1897, with tickets set at twenty-five and fifty cents for the matinee and from twenty-five cents to $1.00 for the evenings. Publicity material promised an experience "as real, and live and actual" as the original event, capturing not just the action within the ring but also the reactions of "every famous character who was at the ring side"—the "perfect realism" of cinema here being in the service of the historic rather than the quotidian (as in Gorman and Swanson's local views).[44] Though attendance was generally "fair," the *Leader* was more than satisfied on all counts, noting in particular the wealth of detail provided by the veriscope images. Motion pictures were apparently still enough of a novelty in the fall of 1897 that this review also felt compelled to describe the workings of the projector, which was mounted in the rear of the Opera House's first floor and cast pictures "about 28 by 15 feet upon the curtain." Sound accompaniment was limited to a bell struck whenever the timekeeper signaled the beginning and end of each round.[45]

Terry Ramsaye argues that until the Corbett-Fitzsimmons film, "the social status of the screen had been uncertain. It now became definitely low-brow, an entertainment of the great unwashed commonalty [sic]."[46] But this was not the case in Lexington. Seeking more than only "low-brow," male fight fans, Scott took pains to attract a somewhat genteel heterosocial audience, "those thousands of ladies and gentlemen who, in a quiet way, take keen interest in sporting matters."[47] (In promoting, say, *Rip Van Winkle* or *Uncle Tom's Cabin*, Scott made no effort to enlarge and redefine the potential audience.) A promotional article that appeared a week before the scheduled screenings claimed that "one of the most remarkable features of the veriscope pictures of the contest is the great interest shown in the exhibition by women."[48] True or false, this "fact" established a precedent, and by scheduling matinee showings "especially for ladies," Scott provided a "perfectly proper" opportunity for women to take in the *Corbett-Fitzsimmons Fight*.[49] Moviegoing in this particular instance was rather rigidly segregated along gender and perhaps class lines. The *Leader* reported that the opening day matinee audience "was only a fair one in size, and was largely made of ladies," while the crowd for the evening show "was much larger and more enthusiastic."[50]

—THREE DAYS BEGINNING—
—MATINEES DAILY—

**Thurdsay,
Friday,
Saturday** Jan. 25

THE GREATEST MOTION
    PICTURES EVER TAKEN.
—THE—

Jeffries-Sharkey
BIOGRAPH.

Direction of W. A. Brady and Thos.
O'Rourke.

The largest and most marvelous ever
known in the history of Moving Pho-
tographs. 216,000 DISTINCT PICTURES.
TIME IN REPRESENTATION, 2½
HOURS. Showing every move from
start to finish of the greatest Battle of
Modern Times. Every Detail complete.
The Marvel of a Progressive Age.

——PRICES——

Parquet and Fauteuils........... 50c
Dress Circle.... ....35c
Balcony.. ....25c
Gallery...... ....15c

—MATINEE PRICES—
Children 10c, Adults 25c.

Fight films at the Opera House.
Lexington *Herald*, 25 January
1900.

In contrast to the veriscope production, the International Cineograph film of the eleven-round Jeffries-Fitzsimmons fight was not accorded any special treatment when it played the Opera House in late August 1899. Scott scheduled only one matinee, added a "live wire walker" to the bill, and set prices at ten, twenty, and thirty cents.[51] Though the *Leader* described this show as being "well received" and "very interesting," the *Jeffries-Fitzsimmons Fight* apparently did rather poorly since, for the Saturday performances, all seats were reduced to ten cents.[52] Biograph's *Jeffries-Sharkey Contest* fared some-

FRIDAY AND SATURDAY,
APRIL 21 AND 22.

The Famous
Passion Play

MATINEE SATURDAY.
MOVING PICTURES,
      DESCRIPTIVE LECTURE,
SACRED MUSIC,
      ILLUSTRATED SONGS.

PRICES—15, 25 and 35 cents.

Matinee—Children 10c, adults 20c.

The first of several local screenings of *The Passion Play*. Lexington *Herald*, 21 April 1899.

what better during its three-day run in January 1900. While Scott again made no special effort to entice genteel theatergoers, his matinee shows were in part aimed at children, who could get in for only ten cents. The *Jeffries-Sharkey Contest* was a "wonderful show," the *Leader* declared, "just like being at ringside."[53] This comment gets at the basic appeal of turn-of-the-century fight films: they offered the opportunity to see (and judge) for yourself a sporting event of national significance from a ringside seat all for no more than the cost of a standard popular-price attraction.

The only other motion picture exhibition in this period that was distributed in basically the same fashion as a theatrical touring production was *The Passion Play*, which did not require much in the way of cultural/social legitimation.[54] In April 1899 Scott scheduled *The Famous Passion Play* between *Nathan Hale*, "the fashionable event of the season," and the popular-priced *Coon Town 400*, "the newest and funniest Colored Show on Earth." This particular version of *The Passion Play* combined moving pictures, illustrated songs, and a "descriptive lecture," with Lexington's Central Christian Church choir on hand to provide "sacred music." The *Herald*'s society column fully recommended the program as "an exceedingly valuable lesson to children, especially those who are interested in Sunday-school."[55] Tickets were priced accordingly: fifteen, twenty-five, or thirty-five cents for the evening shows; ten cents for children and twenty cents for adults at the Saturday matinee.

Exhibitions like *The Famous Passion Play* have a particularly interesting place in the pre-nickelodeon period because, as Musser notes, "many exhibitors showed passion-play films, but no two programs were exactly alike. Showmen exercised a fundamental, creative role."[56] Even if we are not out to make a case for the "creativity" of exhibitors, we still need to pay attention to where and how "primitive" cinema was exhibited.[57] The various Lexington screenings of passion-play films are a revealing case in point. After its local premiere, *The Passion Play* returned to the Opera House in October 1899, not as part of a unified "sacred" program but as the "prelude" to *The South before the War*, a nostalgic mainstay filled with "old Southern plantation festivities." This odd juxtaposition of film and live theater created an ideologically charged fantasy of the first order. A year later, *The Passion Play* was rescued from the commercial theater, as it were, when it was shown at St. Paul's Catholic Church. As far as I have been able to determine, this was the first motion picture screening in a Lexington church. A spokesman for St. Paul's understood the politics of emplacement: "the Oberammergau Passion Play," he declared, "is too sacred to be shown in theaters or halls; the church is the only place."[58] How different the reception of *The Passion Play* (and motion pictures in general) must have been at St. Paul's than at the Opera House when this film opened for *The South before the War*, or later, in October 1902, when some version of *The Passion Play* filled two matinee performances in a rep company's week-long engagement, taking a slot usually occupied by a melodrama or farce. Its reception must also have been different in April 1903, when Professor J. V. Snow, a black traveling motion picture exhibitor, screened *The Passion Play* at three of Lexington's black churches, in shows that also featured comic motion pictures and newsreel-styled footage, with Snow himself providing vocal, cornet, and graphophone accompaniment. These five exhibitions of *The Passion Play* in Lexington demonstrate the sort of diversity that Musser describes, a diversity that extended not only to how these films were programmed, but also to what audiences they were directed toward and to where and under whose auspices they were exhibited.

Woodland Park Summer Theater

During the off-season, Charles Scott booked an occasional local benefit show
or 10–20–30 company at the Opera House, but he made no concerted effort
to take advantage of the market for summertime commercial entertainment.
The Lexington Railway Company, in contrast, continued to court this market
actively during the pre-nickelodeon period, most notably by funding a summer theater in Woodland Park, a wooded, twenty-acre site abutting potentially prime residential land, located about a mile from downtown but easily
accessible by streetcar. This tract was owned by the Lexington Chautauqua,
which used it for two weeks in midsummer for an assembly. In the late 1890s,
the park's semi-enclosed auditorium was sometimes booked for band concerts and traveling shows. Newspaper editorials and community leaders repeatedly called for the city to purchase this land for Lexington's first large
public park, arguing that "all classes" of local residents need "a breathing
space . . . during the oppressive months of the year."[59] (As later events would
bear out, "all classes" in this context meant white people. After Woodland
Park was opened to the public on a regular basis, the newly constituted Park
Commission refused to grant permits for black revivals and picnics.)

The economic rationale for this civic initiative was that a park with regularly scheduled amusements would attract out-of-town visitors and keep at
home money that was being spent on Saturday and Sunday railroad excursions to Louisville, Cincinnati, and regional spots like the Natural Bridge. In
1902 voters passed, by almost a three-to-one margin, a bond issue to purchase Woodland Park for $38,000. The transaction was formally completed
in April 1904. That fall, a second bond issue to fund the construction of a
permanent 2,500-seat indoor auditorium passed, and the Park Commission
hired Frederick Law Olmsted's renowned Boston architectural firm to pre-
pare a master plan for a city park system, featuring Woodland Park as its
centerpiece.

The development of Woodland Park was directly linked to the Lexington
Railway Company, which by 1902 controlled not only the streetcar system
but also Lexington's ice manufactories, electric light plant, and gas company.[60] In promoting Woodland Park as a summertime site for working- and
middle-class recreation, the Railway Company sought to increase off-hour
streetcar use since a major line ran from downtown to the park. The lure of
free or very inexpensive entertainment at Woodland Park perhaps also en-

couraged local residents to become accustomed to traveling by streetcar some distance from their homes (and neighborhood saloons) in search of leisure-time diversion.[61]

Whereas in the summer of 1896 the belt-line trolley ride itself had been marketed as inexpensive entertainment for summer evenings and weekends, now the destination had assumed primary significance. But even in 1896, the Lexington Railway Company had looked into the possibility of establishing "an amusement enterprise of an extensive nature in Lexington during the summer months . . . either at the Fair Grounds or Woodland Park where people can go and enjoy themselves in summer as in other cities."[62] It opted instead to sponsor novel attractions like parachute jumps and the launching of what was billed as the "largest balloon on Earth." Then, in 1900, the Railway Company became committed to promoting "most wholesome entertainment" on a regular basis at Woodland Park, including dancing, vaudeville acts, and, quite prominently, motion pictures, such as the *Jeffries-Sharkey Contest*. Admission was free to streetcar patrons, who were assured that the auditorium was "well-officered," so they should not fear being accosted by "objectionable characters."[63] Crowds that first summer were as large as 1,500 people.

The following year what was dubbed the "Woodland Park Summer Theater" operated in a similar manner from mid-May to mid-August, except for the two weeks that the Chautauqua Assembly utilized the grounds. The newspaper notices for 1901, however, make no mention of motion pictures; the bills tended to feature "lady contortionists," ethnic comedians, singers, trapeze artists, and the like. Under the management of a local musician hired by the Railway Company, the Summer Theater in 1902 began to charge ten cents for reserved seats and instituted a Saturday children's matinee. More important, in July 1902 the Lexington Chautauqua agreed to "open" Woodland Park to the public, with the city providing uniformed policemen to insure law and order and the Railway Company paying for tennis courts and swing sets, as well as continuing to sponsor theatrical attractions and nightly dances. At least 2,000 people attended the grand opening of the park.

No summer theater was scheduled at Woodland in 1903, but after the city purchased the park in April 1904, it opened a playground, where children could be "surrounded with the most wholesome influences" and be "taught the lessons of usefulness and patriotism."[64] (That same summer the Park Commission tried to crack down on "youngsters using cigarettes and playing cards" at the park, another instance of that vaguely defined hooliganism that

The multipurpose auditorium at Woodland Park. Photo courtesy Transylvania University, Lexington, Kentucky.

so troubled the powers-that-be.) The Railway Company also resumed its sponsorship of free entertainment, with vitascope films and illustrated songs as the prime attraction.

By May 1906 the improvements at Woodland Park were finished, and the city had a permanent facility that surpassed the Opera House in size, if not in elegance. The Lexington Railway Company immediately booked into the new auditorium a prestige production of the very first rank: Sarah Bernhardt in *Camille,* with tickets at $1.00, $2.00, and $3.00. The Civic League then organized a weekly series of Sunday afternoon band concerts—"moral amusement" suitable for the Sabbath—with $15 of the $35 weekly cost borne by the Railway Company. These attractions might be seen as an attempt to redefine the role of the park by reserving part of its "breathing space" for the cultured classes. Yet the daily fare remained resolutely popular. In June 1906, the same month Lexington's first nickelodeon opened for business, the Woodland Park auditorium was leased for the summer season by D. J. McNamara, then also manager of the Capitol Theater in Frankfort,

Kentucky. McNamara's stock company began the summer by offering melodramas and comedies with moving pictures and illustrated songs as specialty
items. After several weeks, he shifted to a vaudeville format that included
motion pictures as the final act. By August a "Professor" Murdockio was
presenting daily free film screenings as an adjunct to the ten- and twenty-
cent vaudeville performances.

Woodland Park was not simply a natural "breathing space." It was, from
the perspective of the Lexington Railway Company, an indirect source of
profit. It was also a public recreation area—complete with sports fields, playground equipment, and police supervision—in which the leisure life of white
children, working men and women, and families was provided for and, if not
completely dictated, then surely circumscribed. It was a heterogeneous site,
hosting dances, playground activities, motion pictures, and live theater, and
offering an opportunity for strolling, roller skating, playing tennis, or having
a picnic. But it was at the same time a regular, mundane, everyday site; going
to Woodland Park did not constitute an event like a railroad excursion or a
trip to the Elk's Fair or even a night at the Opera House. By making movies a
well-nigh daily attraction at Woodland Park, the Lexington Railway Company
helped create the audience that would soon frequent downtown moving picture shows.

Lexington Chautauqua Assembly

The Lexington Chautauqua Assembly, a yearly event running for ten to fourteen days during the end of June and the beginning of July, may have occupied the same physical space as the Woodland Park Summer Theater, but
in their functions and aspirations these two summertime enterprises were
thoroughly distinct. Founded in 1887, the Lexington Chautauqua was one of
a large number of "independent assemblies"—there were 150 such assemblies by 1904—that were established after the success of the original Chautauqua in upstate New York and the Chautauqua Literary and Scientific Circle,
a four-year educational correspondence program that had some 180,000 participants across the country by 1891.[65] Begun in 1874 as a Sunday School
teachers assembly, Chautauqua's nonsectarian, though still broadly Christian, agenda soon grew to include scientific demonstrations as well as the
study of history, literature, and foreign languages, and lectures by temperance advocates, prominent political figures, and inspirational speakers. Its

"Wholesome, restful instruction, harmless amusement and uplifting associations": the Chatauqua Assembly at Woodland Park at the turn of the century. Photo courtesy Transylvania University, Lexington, Kentucky.

goal, as one historian of the movement has put it, was "the improvement of the human condition,"[66] and by the 1890s Chautauqua had become a well-recognized exponent and embodiment of a particular progressive model of Culture and educational self-improvement.[67]

Much more than the summer theater at Woodland Park or even the Opera House, the Lexington Assembly consistently received active support from the local press, which published schedules of events, glowingly reviewed each day's activities, and encouraged attendance. For Chautauqua was deemed "a Fixture in the Educational Life of Kentucky" that provided a thoroughly "elevating" blend of "wholesome, restful instruction, harmless amusement and uplifting associations."[68]

Though the Chautauqua Assembly had a higher-minded, noncommercial, and more overtly pedagogic agenda than the Opera House, these two sites were linked by Charles Scott, who served as business manager of the Chautauqua from 1887 to 1903. And, presumably, many of the well-established middle- and upper-middle class people who frequented the more "refined" Opera House attractions also supported Chautauqua. For example, among those who rented tents at the 1904 assembly were the wives of prominent businessmen, as well as such groups as the First Presbyterian Church, the First Baptist Church, the Sons and Daughters of the American Revolution, and the WCTU.[69] Regularly scheduled events were directed specifically toward Sunday school and public school teachers, college students, young children, and temperance advocates. To say, as did one staunch proponent of Chautauqua, that the summer assemblies attracted "noble, cultured and conscientious men," "intellectual, appreciative women," and "pleasure loving young people" proves little about actual audience demographics, but it does reflect who Chautauqua supporters imagined themselves to be: neither dour teetotalers nor the crowds that needed policing the rest of the summer at Woodland Park.[70]

From 1897, when Scott's magniscope was booked, until the local Chautauqua movement ended in 1904, motion pictures became a regular feature of the Lexington assembly. So at least to some degree they accrued the cultural benefits of being associated with what the *Leader* called an "institution of intellectual and moral recreation" that "has always stood for the best and noblest in human life."[71] Printed programs for the Chautauqua invariably relegated motion pictures to the category of "Entertainments," along with magicians, band concerts, "liquid air" demonstrations, caricaturists, and illustrated songs. No plantation shows or sensational melodramas here, only decidedly wholesome attractions, well suited for the entire family and not inimical to the assembly's pedagogic/cultural aims.[72] Films were usually scheduled for three or four different dates and were screened at around 8:30 P.M. in the auditorium; they were the concluding attraction, after a highly structured day filled with instruction, oratory, and musical interludes. This might seem to be analogous to the role that motion pictures played as "chasers" in some vaudeville theaters. At the Chautauqua Assembly, however, the final entertainments were an important drawing card. And far from taking the movies as a signal to depart, the crowd "always waits for them, no matter what fears of not getting a seat in the first [street]cars to town."[73]

The most successful exhibition of motion pictures at the Lexington Chautauqua was in 1899, when the American Vitagraph Company was booked for July 3 and 4, then held over for the next two nights because its films had proved to be such a "great hit."[74] What so captivated the Chautauqua audience about the Vitagraph films? Not the sheer novelty of moving pictures, nor even the fact that Vitagraph provided unprecedentedly "clear, distinct and well-regulated pictures." It was the "new views" themselves, the *Leader* declared: panoramas of the Rocky Mountains and the Brooklyn Bridge, early "fantastic" films like *The Devil's Castle,* and, above all, the "12 minute long" *Spanish Bullfight* and a series of highly topical films of the Spanish-American War. (Bullfighting was apparently exotic and foreign enough—it was a *Spanish* bullfight, after all—to be a suitable subject, while prizefighting was not.) Safe at home, under the auspices of cultural uplift, Chautauqua's spectators could watch triumphant "history" unfold: supplies unloaded at Tampa, the American flag raised in Havana, Dewey's flagship in Manila Bay, and, most stirring of all, the Battle in the Philippines, which "was so full of action and so realistic that it aroused the audience last evening [the evening of July 4] to wild enthusiasm."[75]

A good part of the audience's enthusiasm was no doubt due to the fact that they were primed to see what they had so often read about in the front-page wire service articles and illustrated Sunday features in Lexington newspapers. The "splendid little war" of 1898 for several years provided excellent material for highly topical commercial entertainment, such as Pain's Battle of Manila, a "spectacle" combining melodramatic tableaus, acrobatic stunts, and a fireworks display, which Scott booked for three shows at Woodland Park in October 1898. While Pain packaged the war into a continuous, grand-scale extravaganza, other touring shows simply incorporated the national adventure in Cuba and the Philippines into their already diverse programs: Buffalo Bill's Wild West Show of 1901, for instance, outfitted some of its horsemen as Rough Riders; Al G. Fields Minstrels introduced "On to Cuba," a comic sketch of soldier life, for its 1898 tour; and when Wm. H. West's Big Minstrel Jubilee played the Opera House in January 1900, its grand finale was "that spectacular sensation," the "storming of San Juan Hill."

The inchoate motion picture industry could hardly have asked for a more "moving" subject: heroic patriots in action, troop and ship movements, the spectacle of battle. War films assumed a prominent place in vaudeville theaters, and Edison even "renamed his Projecting Kinetoscope the 'Wargraph' for the duration of the hostilities."[76] Professor D. E. Frontz brought his "Animated Art Tour by 'Wargraph'" to the Opera House for a two-day engagement in March 1899, featuring war films along with comedies, railroad and horse race scenes, and pictures of dancing girls and "celebrated statuary." Quite clearly, the wargraph was something of a misnomer. For Spanish-American

War films, which exemplified the impulse toward topicality, verisimilitude, and chauvinistic celebration, were packaged with other types of films that had very different preoccupations and objectives. Further, these moving picture exhibitions often took their place in the larger (and more diverse) context of a Chautauqua program or a vaudeville bill.

One indirect domestic effect of the War of 1898 was that American motion picture production and exhibition placed greater emphasis on so-called "living newspapers" that recorded news events worthy of banner headlines.[77] This genre was well suited to the Chautauqua's notion of entertainment, and Vitagraph returned to provide "scenes from the Philippines and Boer War" for the 1900 Assembly. Yet living newsreels were soon to be found in sites that did not share Chautauqua's pedagogic mission, venues like the moving picture show at the 1901 Elks Fair, which featured scenes of Carry Nation and of Queen Victoria's funeral procession.[78]

Carnivals and Fairs

According to Charlotte Herzog, "state, county, and regional fairs"—as well as "world's fairs" like the one held in St. Louis in 1904—were "popular places to exhibit cinematic apparatuses."[79] This certainly was the case in turn-of-the-century Lexington. As early as 1897, the Colored A & M Fair, the most important black fair in the region, offered "a great indoor exhibition of the latest moving picture invention, the projecting kinetoscope."[80] And for their annual "Street Fair," a four-day event usually held downtown in May, the local Maccabee lodge booked traveling carnival companies whose attractions included a ferris wheel, fireworks, blackface performers, "electrical" exhibits (erupting volcanoes, models of Jerusalem), and a motion picture show.

Central Kentucky's largest and most widely publicized fair was staged by the Elks for a week during August at Lexington's fairgrounds. The city government, area businesses, and the press all actively supported the Elks Fair, which they saw as a means of showcasing Lexington and boosting the local economy. While Woodland Park was developed as a means of filling leisure time day in and day out, the Elks Fair was designed and marketed as a special event of the first order and a break—almost a vacation—from daily affairs. The Lexington Chautauqua, too, was an event of sorts, but this testament to cultural uplift was necessarily geared toward a rather circumscribed audience. The Elks Fair, in contrast, sought immense crowds composed of all citizens, except perhaps for the highest social elite (who were not likely to be in Lexington during the dog days of August in any case). The only commercial entertainment events comparable to the Elks Fair in this respect were the two or three large-scale traveling shows that visited Lexington each year, for example, the Ringling Bros. or the Forepaugh-Sells Circus, or the Cole Younger & Frank James Historical Wild West Show, with its display of "Heroic Manhood," or John Robinson's Great World's Exposition, which brought to Lexington the "Great Biblical Spectacle" of Solomon and Sheba, as well as an aquarium, aviary, and one hundred "beautiful dancing girls."[81] These heavily promoted touring productions exemplified a remarkable capacity for organization and mobilization, all in the service of spectacular displays of "inoffensive" exoticism and orchestrated excess.

Excess was an anathema and exoticism at most a subject for instructional lectures at the Chautauqua Assembly, which relegated "Entertainment" to a separate, secondary category within a larger pedagogic agenda. The Elks, in contrast, promoted their fair as "The Greatest Amusement Program Ever Given in the South." On this program were free attractions such as the floral hall, livestock show, and college and business exhibits, which were all likely to draw quite different participants and spectators who might otherwise have little common ground. Such attractions, showcasing the local, testified to the community's commerce and its rural roots, its educational opportunities and its "feminine" accomplishments.

But it was the midway that was "the feature of the fair that draws the attention of all classes in all sections of the Blue Grass."[82] At the fair, the *Herald* wrote in vaguely Whitmanesque tones, one could join in the "commingling of great masses of the common people" with "farmers, and merchants, and mechanics, and physicians, and attorneys, and ministers."[83] Such descriptions picture the Elks Fair in general and the midway in particular as the utopian realization of the commercial and social promise of a truly mass entertainment. The fair thus became analogous with "Circus Day," an unofficial yet regularly celebrated holiday that involved "people of all ages, colors, sexes [and] previous conditions of servitude."[84] While Circus Day often seemed a nostalgic throwback to the nineteenth century, it could also mean something quite different, as when the *Herald* noted, apropos a visit in 1896 by the Adams, Sells and Forepaugh Circus: "Lexington might well have easily been mistaken for the metropolis. The mixed society which surged up and down her spotless boulevards gave them an air of exciting variety."[85]

Circus day in Lexington at the turn of the century. Photo courtesy Transylvania University, Lexington, Kentucky.

The Fourth of July in Lexington might find "everybody and his family, white and colored," enjoying themselves at several separate celebrations: in 1901, for instance, these included a Colored Odd Fellows picnic at the race track, a patriotic Chautauqua meeting at Woodland Park, and a benefit for St. Joseph's Hospital at the fairgrounds.[86] Even the largest public picnics, such as the Council of Labor's annual Labor Day celebration, were sponsored by specific organizations and so underscored racial, class, or religious affiliations. Circus Day, however, at least gave the appearance of heterogeneous masses—free from work, adult concerns, racial and class distinctions—democratized in the presence of grand-scale commercial entertainment. Comparably, the Colored A & M Fair was said to appeal to both the "little barelegged boy" and the "doctor in his comfortable gig," while a visit to the midway of the Elks Fair, according to the *Leader*, would transform even the "staid man of business" and the "gouty banker" into "great, good natured children."[87]

Just how "mixed" was "society" on Circus Day, how democratized were the crowds who attended the Elks Fair? Among all the passing references in local newspapers to the way city and country people, men and women, and children and adults together toured the midway, there is one first-person account that is particularly striking. After attending the 1899 Elks Fair, J. Alexander Chiles, a black lawyer and outspoken civil rights advocate who later served as president of the Negro Business League in Lexington, wrote a letter to the *Leader* expressing his "high appreciation and deep gratitude" for the "courteous treatment accorded me and mine" and "manifested to my race" at the fair. The very terms of Chiles' testimonial contextualize the Elks Fair, suggesting how race relations were usually experienced in Lexington at the turn of the century, on the days around Circus Day: "Never can it hereafter be said that my race at all white fairs conducted in Fayette County by white people were treated as slaves and chattel; never can it be hereafter said that we did not, at least once in our lives, in Fayette County, Kentucky, at a fair conducted by white people, have equal opportunity to see everything that we desired to see for our money and to visit any of the places on the fair grounds we desired to visit."[88]

On this occasion, "at least once" in his life, in the exception that proves the rule, had Chiles wanted to take in the movies at the Elks Fair, he could have paid a dime, entered the black tent on the midway, and seen the Corbett-Fitzsimmons fight film, now in its second Lexington run, almost two years after its local premiere at the Opera House. The following summer brought "Edison's latest vitascope" to the fair to "reproduce all of the interesting events of the day."[89] And at the 1901 fair, people who may have missed seeing Carry Nation when she lectured at the Opera House and toured Lexington saloons could watch living newspapers of her, along with Theodore Roosevelt's lion hunt and Queen Victoria's funeral procession.

While motion pictures shared the Opera House stage with rep troupes, combination companies, and minstrels, served as entertainment after Chautauqua's inspirational lectures, and became one of Woodland Park's daily offerings, at the Elks Fair motion pictures competed and were necessarily associated with other midway attractions. (If newspaper accounts and advertising are any indication, the moving picture show was never more than a minor attraction and not even a feature of the 1902 or 1903 Elks Fairs.) In

1899, for example, this meant that the moving picture tent was in the company of the Cuban midget Chiquita, "from all accounts . . . the crowning feature of the Midway," as well as such other attractions as the German beer garden, the Turkish Theater, the Gypsy Camp, the Crystal Maze, the Moulin Rouge dancers, and "Darkness and Dawn," which included a tableau of hell and a heavenly "dance of the nymphs."[90] As part of the midway, under the auspices of the Elks and with the blessing of the local powers-that-be, "realistic" motion pictures participated in a multifaceted discourse of the Other, which was "consumed" as (un)natural aberration, foreign entertainment, sexual display, and visual spectacle.

Lexington was but one stop for the touring amusement companies that the Elks hired to run the midway at their fairs, for the entertainers who appeared at the Chautauqua Assemblies, and for the itinerant showman who screened *The Passion Play* at local black churches. Similarly, the combination companies, minstrel shows, and motion picture attractions that played the Opera House and the Wild West shows and circuses that set up tents in Lexington repeated their performances in a host of other cities and towns. The pervasive phenomenon of touring underscores the homogenization of commercial entertainment, if not nationally, then at least regionally in America at the turn of the century, before the advent of what we would call the "movies." Yet any explanatory claim that ignores the local configuration of sites, sponsors, and occasions tells, at best, only part of the story of entertainment in the prenickelodeon period, which in Lexington, at least, was marked by a desire to embrace twentieth-century novelty and cosmopolitanism and, at the same time, to maintain nineteenth-century ideals of community and Culture. Was this contradictory? Yes, but it seems not to have been perceived as such, anymore than was Charles Scott's booking policy at the multipurpose Opera House, or the contradictory fact that the same site was home to the Chautauqua Assembly and the Woodland Park Summer Theater or that the Elks Fair had a floral hall as well as a midway.

FOUR

Getting the Habit:
Moving Pictures,
Vaudeville, and
Commercial Entertainment
in the Nickelodeon Period

Motion pictures may have been almost daily fare in Lexington by 1904—screened at Woodland Park and in carnival tents or occasionally slotted into the Opera House's schedule—but their everyday presence in local life became truly inescapable once permanent venues designed solely for the purpose of profiting from cheap amusement went into business downtown. Nonetheless, the opening in June 1906 of the Theatorium, Lexington's first five-cent moving picture show, was no grand, auspicious event, heralding a new epoch in commercial entertainment. Judged by contemporary newspaper accounts, this occurrence was nowhere near as significant to the community as, say, the opening of the new YMCA facility (with a gymnasium, pool, and 220-seat auditorium) in April 1905 or the new, Andrew Carnegie-endowed public library in July 1905. Maybe this picture show looked to be but one more in a string of low-rent entertainment ventures—"ping-pong parlors," "winter circuses," "foot-cycle academies," and the like. The Theatorium's premiere did, it turns out, initiate what I will refer to as Lexington's nickelodeon period, which might be something of a misnomer because this six-year span (1906–12) saw the opening of not only more than ten different picture

65

shows, but also the city's first successful vaudeville theater, amusement park, and skating rinks, all of which I will examine in this chapter.[1]

Yet even with this expanding array of commercial entertainment venues, no Lexington theater offered the sort of "small-time," combined vaudeville/ motion picture format that had proved so lucrative after 1908 for William F. Fox and other promoters in the East.[2] As a result, an account of the nickelodeon era in Lexington looks substantially different from a history based on a large eastern metropolitan area. From the perspective of social history, the differences are even more pronounced, for Lexington's first-generation picture shows were not localized in the manner of New York City's nickelodeons, which, in the words of Kathy Peiss, "took on the flavor of the surrounding [ethnic] neighborhood" and offered "a heightened version of life in the tenement districts."[3] The surrounding neighborhood for the Theatorium included the 2nd National Bank and the county courthouse.

If the premiere of the Theatorium marks the beginning of the nickelodeon period in Lexington, I take the construction of the Colonial Theater, which opened in August 1911, and the Orpheum Theater, which opened some eight months later, both as marking the culmination of this period and also ushering in an era in which the movies unquestionably became the city's most popular form of commercial entertainment. Within five years, the 70-seat Theatorium had been replaced by a 400-seat self-styled "picture palace," which itself gave way four years later to a new 1,600-seat theater expressly designed and constructed for motion pictures. The social and cultural importance of the movies grew accordingly.

Storefront Nickelodeons

Inspired, no doubt, by the nationwide spread of nickelodeons, particularly in cities like Pittsburgh and Chicago, two men from Liverpool, Ohio (near the West Virginia border) opened the Theatorium, Lexington's first storefront moving picture show, on the ground floor of a building that had formerly been occupied by the National Exchange Bank at 111–113 Cheapside, right off Main Street, across from the Fayette County courthouse. Equipped with approximately seventy chairs and a phonograph to attract the attention of passersby, the Theatorium was open from 1:00 to 10:00 every day except Sunday, with fifteen- to twenty-minute shows that were changed twice weekly. Its first and only newspaper advertisement ran for three days, promising moving pic-

SE BALL

JB STANDING.

TIONAL LEAGUE.

	Won.	Lost.	P. C.
	39	17	.696
	34	1	.667
	35	19	.648
	29	28	.509
	23	33	.411
	21	33	.389
	21	36	.368
	17	36	.321

RICAN LEAGUE.

	Won.	Lost.	P.C.
	29	18	.617
	31	20	.608
	30	20	.600
	26	22	.542
	26	25	.510
	23	25	.473
	18	32	.360
	15	36	.294

DAY'S RESULTS.

ational League.
. Brooklyn 1.
Philadelphia 0.
Incinnati 1.
2, St. Louis 1.
erican League.
, New York 2.
Washington 10.
Philadelphia 4.
t. Louis 2.
rican Association.
y 8, Louisville 4.
4, St. Paul 1.
10, Indianapolis 8.
neapolis, rain.

GRASS CHAMPIONSHIP.

f a series of six base ball
Blue Grass championship
ed Sunday afternoon be-
exington and Paris Base
the Belt Line Park. Three
nes are to be played in
he other three at Paris.
unusual interest in the
se games. In a similar
ar Paris won by a narrow
exington, with a splendid
name, is determined to
ags this year. Sunday's
be a good one. It will
lock.

HOUSE PAINTS
NTEED SATISFACTORY,
REFUNDED.   15-3

THEATORIUM.

Moving Pictures and Illustrated Songs.

Changed Twice a Week.

The Kleptomaniac

—AND—

The Miser's Daughter

—ON—

Friday, Saturday and Monday
Open 1 to 10 P. M.

ALL WELCOME.

11 Cheapside.   Admission 5c.

for. There were more than a thous-
and employes, and about four hundred horses, to say nothing of the
other animals. Everything was transported without friction or delay, so
far as the circus people were concerned, although difficulties were constantly coming up by reason of the failure
of railroad facilities. The military observers were impressed with the systematic work, which would probably
not be possible in the army, for the
reason that men must be constantly
changed, and the officer who has
charge of transportation today may be
detailed to barrack instruction next
year. This uncertainty is more pre-
valent now that most of the staff departments are made up of temporary
personnel by the detail of line officers
to four-year periods of staff duty. It
was stated that if the experience with
the circus furnished any illustration
it was to be entirely on the side of the
permanent personnel and the encouragement of specialties.

Woodland Park Auditorium

WEEK COMMENCING
MONDAY, JUNE 11,
WOODLAND STOCK CO.
PRESENTING
High-Class Royalty Plays.
BIG SPECIALTIES
5   BETWEEN ACTS   5
INCLUDING MOVING PICTURES
AND ILLUSTRATED SONGS.
OPENING BILL MONDAY NIGHT
THE BEAUTIFUL COMEDY
DRAMA
"THE SENATOR FROM
KENTUCKY."
A DOLLAR SHOW FOR
10 AND 20 CENTS.
NO EXTRA CHARGE FOR RE-
SERVED SEATS.
A car load of special scenery.

Special Excursion

TO

Natural Bridge

SUNDAY JUNE 17

$1 Round Trip; Children 50c

Train leaves 8:30 a. m. Good
music and a pleasant day in the
mountains.

LEXINGTON ENJOYMENT
CLUB

The premiere of Lexington's first storefront picture show. Lexington *Leader*, 16 June 1906.

Selling Sunday pictures at the Star. Lexington *Herald,* 21 October 1906.

tures and illustrated songs, with *The Kleptomaniac* and *The Miser's Daughter* as the premiere bill on 12 June 1906.

By December 1907, William Yent, local ticket agent for the C & O Railroad, had taken over the Theatorium. It had operating expenses of about $15 a day, while, Yent complained, "the performances are frequently to be given to less than half a dozen patrons."[4] Within six months, a bookstore had moved into the site of the now defunct theater. Still, the Theatorium managed to remain in business on a shoestring budget for almost two years, far longer than the other theaters that opened in Lexington in the fall of 1906, as "moving picture fever" struck the city. For example, a Hale's Tours exhibit, run by an erstwhile newsboy who "by industry and thrift" had risen Ben Franklin-like to "a position of trust and responsibility," lasted at best a few months.[5]

Somewhat more successful was the Star Theater, which opened on 1 October 1906 in what formerly had been a Rudolph Wurlitzer store on Main Street in the same block as the city's largest and finest hotel, the Phoenix Hotel. Hugh Ettinger, proprietor of the 300-seat Star, promoted his new enterprise with large newspaper ads that encouraged Lexingtonians to "Get the Habit," for the Star's "polite, fashionable moving pictures and illustrated songs" made it "a nice place to spend a half-hour: With the children! With your wife! With your girl!" Ettinger vowed that only the "latest and best pictures" from around the world would be featured at the Star's continuous performances from 1:00 to 5:00 and 7:00 to 10:00 P.M. Among these pictures were the tramp comedy *This Side Up* and *The Two Orphans* which, according to the *Herald,* "a large audience enjoyed as well as a real drama. Ladies and children with their handkerchiefs weeping during the sad part."[6] Children, weeping or otherwise, were targeted from the outset. This nickelodeon debuted with a "special school children's matinee," and Ettinger gave a free sack of candy to every child who attended a matinee during the Star's opening week; with any luck, these kids would habitually return not just to the theater, but to the Star's penny arcade machines. Ettinger was also the first theater proprietor in Lexington to introduce Sunday screenings, running titles like *Ben Hur* and *The Passion Play* so as not to incur the wrath of local ministers.

Two weeks after its opening, the Star survived one type of setback that continually threatened nickelodeons when a reel of film caught fire causing only minor damage. But Ettinger faced a more serious problem when he and the man who ran the Star's penny arcade were arrested in January 1907 for contributing to the delinquency of two teenage girls who had purchased at the Star certain postcards that the police deemed to be "obscene matter." The girls had nearly fifty such cards in their possession, and they admitted to "making a habit of going to the theater [the Star]."[7] The very language of Ettinger's ads had returned to haunt him, and this linking of the movie theater (rather than the films themselves) with obscenity and the corruption of youth was precisely the sort of incident that would fuel anti-nickelodeon campaigns in Chicago.[8] Surprisingly, Ettinger's arrest caused no public outcry, though it probably hastened the closing of the Star.

The fate of Hale's Tours and the Star Theater did not discourage other would-be entrepreneurs, for four nickelodeons opened in Lexington within a year and a half, as motion pictures became a daily fact of life in the city.[9] While Boston's nickelodeons, according to Russell Merritt, were clustered in "the most prosperous and most fiercely competitive theater district in town" and in the city's "skid row,"[10] Lexington's moving picture shows took their place in the central business district, alongside banks, clothing stores, restaurants, saloons, and specialty shops.

Accessibility, five-cent tickets, convenience—these were selling points of the storefront picture show, whose continuous performance format was closer to saloons and store window exhibitions than to the Opera House, perhaps allowing nickelodeons to serve as a challenge to (or respite from) what historian T. J. Jackson Lears calls "the triumph of clock time" that "seemed assured by 1890."[11] Of course, the product itself was also a selling point. Lexington's nickelodeons co-billed moving pictures produced for a broad, general market with illustrated songs—the song performed by a local (per-

haps at times amateur) singer and his or her accompanist(s) and the illustration provided by approximately twenty slides, cued to the song's lyrics.
Eileen Bowser argues that this frequently used format encouraged audience
participation, thereby contributing to the "communal factor" that was an "important element of the moviegoing experience."[12] But what about the implications of the moving picture-illustrated song exhibition strategy for the
reception of the movies? Did the "communal" interaction between singer and
audience help to determine how spectators responded to the moving pictures
on the bill? How evident was the continuity between, for example, the sentimental ballads, regional songs, and light-spirited romantic tunes (all illustrated by appropriate slides) and the split-reel or one-reel films that were
shown? How much did the presence of certain musicians work to localize a
performance in which songs, slides, and moving pictures all came from
"outside?"

The questions we ask about reception depend on our assumptions about
precisely who constituted the nickelodeon audience. As Merritt notes, early
commentators in magazines such as *Outlook* and the *Saturday Evening Post*
emphasized the importance of moving picture shows for the working-class,
immigrant residents of "urban slums" and "ghettos."[13] "Part of the success
of the movies," Roy Rosenzweig reasons, "rested on their ability to attract
the underpaid and overworked as well as those who were gaining a bit more
disposable income and a few more free hours in the early twentieth century."[14] In Lexington, where there was no substantial immigrant population
and no "hum of factory wheels," working people would have been quite distinct from the urban masses who figure so prominently in most accounts of
the nickelodeon period. And I could find no indication that middle-class families and children shunned local motion picture theaters, even after the arrest
of the Star's proprietor.[15]

Whatever the social demographics of the audience, it seems likely that in
Lexington, as in Grand Rapids, Michigan, "repeaters" afflicted with "moving
picturitis" accounted for most box office receipts.[16] Characterizing these habitual customers has from the first been a basic impulse and a common rhetorical move in public talk about the movies (suggesting how much our
conception of arts and media hangs on how we construct their audiences).
According to W. Stephen Bush of *Moving Picture World*, "everybody—that
means young and old, rich and poor, intelligent and ignorant" attends moving
pictures. A 1907 editorial in this trade magazine made an even grander
claim: "the moving picture theater is not confined to any class or clique. The

millionaire and the clerk, the laborer and the capitalist, sit side by side and both find equal enjoyment in the pictures."[17] These effusive assertions call to mind the celebratory evocations of the Circus Day crowds discussed in Chapter 3. Judging from the sparse evidence available and from the city's deep racial and class divisions, it does not seem very likely that Lexington's moviegoers in the early nickelodeon period approximated this vision of a heterogeneous, eminently satisfied audience growing progressively more good-natured and democratic with each hour spent together in the dark. Of course, discrediting or even empirically disproving *Moving Picture World*'s claims does not cancel out the historical significance of these claims as utopian, egalitarian vision, canny self-promotion, or just wishful thinking on the part of the fledgling motion picture industry.[18]

Outside the Nickelodeon

Even after the emergence of permanent shows that combined moving pictures and illustrated songs, film exhibition in Lexington was not limited to theaters like the Theatorium and the Star. For one thing, certain venues that I described in Chapter 3 continued to screen motion pictures in the nickelodeon era. The midway at the 1906 Bluegrass Fair, for instance, offered moving pictures of the San Francisco earthquake and fire, and the 1907 Maccabee's street carnival featured a Hale's Tours exhibit, which was said to provide a "perfect" illusion of riding in a train, as "magnificent scenes" of the United States and Canada passed by.[19] The Opera House also maintained its diverse schedule of attractions, including 10–20–30 companies (some of which still used moving pictures as specialties) and Lyman H. Howe's biannual appearances. Far more elaborate than standard nickelodeon fare, a typical Howe show—for example, his fall 1906 offering at the Opera House—included a full two hours of film covering newsworthy events (the Olympic Games in Rome, the wedding of King Alphonso) and scenes of "world travel" (the carnival at Nice, life in a Burmese teak forest), all accompanied by much-praised "natural and realistic" sound effects.[20] This moving picture program, so ideologically loaded in its implicit sense of what events were newsworthy and what places on earth were worth visiting, was pitched as educational entertainment that eschewed fictive narrative and drama.[21] Meanwhile, a few blocks away a nickelodeon like the Star was promising that its films would make spectators reach for a handkerchief or erupt into laughter.

In addition to the Opera House and local fairs, there were other sites for motion picture exhibition and other uses made of film in Lexington during the first years of the nickelodeon period. For example, a lecturer at the YMCA who was promoting the economic opportunities of Texas illustrated his sales pitch with motion picture scenes. Similarly, the Lexington chapter of the Civic League used films and stereopticon slides to attract "colored people" and schoolchildren in particular to its "City Beautiful" lectures, originally designed by the National Cash Register Company to explain how a city might achieve harmony among "Nature, the Home and the Factory."[22] An even more blatant use of moving pictures as come-on for the desired audience was an open-air program staged by the Brown Shoe Company in July 1906. A crowd estimated at ten thousand people filled the street and the grounds of the courthouse (across from the Theatorium) to see films of the St. Louis World's Fair, the Brown shoe factory in operation, and "the happy adventures of Buster Brown and his famous dog, 'Tige.'" These motion pictures were projected on a sheet strung across the front of a shoe store. According to the *Leader,* Professor Forrest High, the conductor of this free show, was "so tactful in the use of his advertising matter as to make one forget that it is advertising after all."[23] Surely, the Brown Shoe Company could not have asked for higher praise for its "free" show.[24]

The strongest competition to nickelodeons came not nearly as much from traveling motion picture exhibitors as from the skating rinks operated in Lexington in 1906–8. Indeed, during the first years of the nickelodeon era, when the local market for regularly scheduled, readily available cheap amusement exploded, the most profitable "fad" in the city was not moviegoing but indoor roller skating.

Lexington's first bona fide skating rink, run by Henry J. Naumann, from Detroit, opened for business in early November 1905 on the second floor of Jackson Hall, which was the city's commercial market house. Naumann scheduled band concerts and skating for two daily sessions, 2:00 to 5:30 and 7:30 to 10:30 P.M., and a matinee session on Sunday, with "the best of order assured." Admission was fifteen cents, with a twenty-five-cent charge for skate rental. Sunday afternoon skating was the "new craze," the *Herald* announced soon after the rink opened.[25] But the other tenants of Jackson Hall complained about the noise and brought a suit that led to the cancellation of weekday sessions. Then the city raised the license for skating rinks from $25 to $100 (once again, license ordinances functioned as a barely disguised means of regulating commercial entertainment), and Sunday skating was challenged because of Kentucky's Sunday closing law. In March 1906, Naumann's rink shut down for good.

The commercial potential of skating rinks was not lost on local investors, who had more capital and more inside knowledge of the Lexington market. Bishop Clay, a prominent realtor and later an unsuccessful democratic candidate for mayor, headed the Lexington Athletic and Amusement Company, which opened the Mammoth Skating Rink on Christmas Eve in 1906. This enterprise was located on West Fourth Street, in a residential area several blocks north of the central business district, and its hours of operation (2:00 to 5:00 and 7:00 to 10:00 P.M..) roughly paralleled those of the downtown moving picture shows. The Mammoth Rink accommodated up to nine hundred people and featured a Wurlitzer "Monster Military Automatic Band."[26]

Throughout 1907, what "local capitalists" called the "roller skating rink fad" attracted much more attention from the Lexington press than did the growing number of moving picture shows, no doubt in part because nickelodeons did not purchase advertising space as regularly as did the city's skating rinks.[27] Nationally syndicated comic strips referred to the craze, and a skating couple were even featured in an ad for a local haberdashery.[28] By the end of 1907, three rinks were operating in Lexington: the Mammoth Skating Rink, which had added 10:00 to 12:00 A.M. sessions, specifically for ladies and children; the Grand Colored Rink, financed and run by two black Lexington residents and situated several blocks from Main Street in a black residential area;[29] and the Coliseum Skating Rink, located on Main Street near the Phoenix Hotel, with room for six hundred skaters and one thousand spectators in the gallery.[30] The Coliseum offered skating lessons, contests for children and adults, and performances by professional skaters in an attempt to capture a regular clientele. The Grand Colored Rink staged quite similar promotional activities. During Christmas week in 1907, for example, it held a skating contest, a cakewalk on skates, a grand ball with a ten-piece orchestra, and a "Rube Carnival," in which the participants dressed as "country rubes."[31] The Grand Colored Rink also allowed in "white onlookers," a policy that occasioned an angry letter to the *Leader* from a "colored rinker," implying that the very presence of (slumming?) white spectators would make this site for "colored" leisure-time activity only one more means of keeping blacks in their place, which really wasn't *their* place after all.[32]

In effect, Lexington's skating craze was over by April 1908, when the Coliseum and the Mammoth rinks suspended operations for the summer. (The Grand Colored Rink seems to have closed for good around that time as well.)

Both venues reopened in October, yet the Coliseum was soon transformed into an automobile garage. Similar plans for the Mammoth rink fell through at the last moment, and it remained in operation into 1909, with few special promotions and virtually no advertising. Apparently the situation was the same elsewhere across the country, for *Variety* reported in March 1908 that "the craze for wooden wheels has almost subsided," as evidenced by reports "from all over the country . . . of skating rinks turning into picture show places."[33]

During the first years of the nickelodeon era, skating rinks attempted to turn a profit from recreational sport or play (not unlike bowling alleys in this regard), though in their special events, the rinks often resembled dance halls or amateur vaudeville shows, complete with a gallery of onlookers. Local newspapers invariably grouped ads for the Coliseum and the Mammoth rinks together with material for the Opera House, vaudeville theaters, traveling shows, and nickelodeons—all under the heading of "The Stage" or "Amusements." Obviously, skating rinks offered a quite different "amusement" experience to the consumer than did moving picture shows (though it is an oversimplification to call the latter experience passive and the former active). These two venues were, however, equally accessible, inexpensive, and open on a regular basis both afternoons and evenings. In this way, then, skating rinks were geared toward and helped to foster a society in which a sizable number of people had the time, money, and inclination to seek out ways to fill their leisure time, apart from the home, school, saloon, or church.[34] While the Coliseum Rink and the Star Theater competed for patrons—indeed, they were located on the same block—they both promoted attitudes toward the consumption of commercial entertainment that would, in a few years, help to create the sort of habitual moviegoers that the proprietors of the first nickelodeons could only dream of.

Failure and Success in the Picture Business: Dreamland and the Princess Theater

Neither the skating rink fad of 1907 nor the major recession that year put any damper on the burgeoning business of cheap amusements in Lexington. Whereas two years earlier the Opera House had been the only commercial showplace in the city (apart from those saloons that offered live entertainment), in December 1907 an "Italian fruit vendor" told the *Leader* that "there are now nine theaters and picture shows running in this town, and all that is needed to fill out the list of amusements is a good snake show."[35] Indeed, 1907 had seen the opening not only of the Coliseum skating rink, three different vaudeville theaters, and the city's first black-operated nickelodeon, but also of the Lexington Country Club—an exclusive site that symbolized and reaffirmed class and racial boundaries—and the new Union (train) Station on Main Street, a "democratic," efficient, Jim Crow-tailored facility that testified to the vital role of the downtown area and to the commercial progressiveness of the city.[36]

Many of these new entertainment ventures failed miserably, including, most notably, a combination arcade and moving picture show called Dreamland that opened with much ballyhoo in February 1908 and closed barely five months later.[37] Dreamland, by all appearances, had a great deal going for it: it was located in a two-story West Main Street building with over 150 penny arcade machines on the street level and a five-cent moving picture show upstairs; its hours of operation were 8:30 A.M. to 10:30 P.M., appreciably longer than any other show in town; and its style throughout was "elegant," from the multicolored electric sign on its white and gold facade to its theater "furnished in richest crimson."[38] Furthermore, the four owners of this enterprise were already successful saloon and hotel operators. This is likely why, when plans for Dreamland were announced, a Republican candidate for city office remarked that "there are so many show houses opening . . . and so many [Democratic] saloon men going into the business, they must think that the prohibition wave is going to wipe them out of existence."[39] Or perhaps the saloon men had diversification and the economic coexistence of saloons and picture shows in mind.

Two of Dreamland's financial backers, William F. (Billy) Klair and Patrick Mooney, were not only owners of saloons but also members of the Board of Aldermen. Indeed, the second-generation German immigrant Klair was, according to a recent dissertation, Lexington's political "boss," who would through the 1920s wield "immense influence in local and state politics."[40] The political clout of Klair and Mooney doubtless explains why the city commissioners took up the matter of picture show licenses for the first time in February 1908, soon after Dreamland's opening. The proposed new ordinance called for a lump sum advance payment of $250, rather than a $5 per week fee, payable weekly.[41] A lawyer representing Dreamland endorsed this change, which, he told the Ways and Means Committee, "would keep out small and transient operations." The manager of one of the "smaller shows" protested that the "little fish" simply wanted an equal chance, since "it's a case of the survival of the fittest anyhow."[42]

And so it was, apparently, for by the fall of 1908, all the arcade machines had been sent back to Chicago, and the vacant Dreamland site had been occupied by a seasonal gift shop. Yet two blocks away, one of the "smaller" moving picture shows, the Princess Theater, remained in operation and would continue to do so through three changes of ownership until 1914. Located at 271 West Main Street, right around the corner from the Theatorium, this nickelodeon (initially called the Alvin) opened sometime in early 1907. After undergoing the first of several remodelings, it was renamed the Princess in February 1908 and boasted a new white and gold stucco front with a sign "requiring six to eight hundred electric lights."[43] At this same time, Stanley Platt, its owner and manager, began to run a small newspaper advertisement and to provide the papers with promotional material that often included brief synopses of the films and the titles of the songs to be presented each day.

During the next three years, the Princess—first under Platt's management, then, after May 1910, operated by two other Lexington residents, John Elliott and E. T. Graves—was marketed as a moving picture show that set out to cater to what one of its promos called the "better class of people."[44] Thus, for example, its notices in 1909–10 claim that the Princess screens only "first run" films (prestigious "Film-de-Art" productions) and also pitch the virtues of the theater itself: its safety measures, improved ventilation system, seventy-five additional seats (for a total of approximately three hundred), and the "steady, clear bright picture" made possible by a new "silver screen" and Powers projector.[45] "The moving picture business is hardly what it once was," a Princess notice declared in October 1910, "a few years ago a man could find a vacant store, procure a few second hand opera chairs, picture machine, canvas curtain and phonograph, and be ready to start a nickelodeon." Now, as the Princess proves, money must be spent and standards are getting progressively higher, and "the best class of people in Lexington approve of the Princess policy."[46]

The Princess remained a going concern through 1911–12, still charging five-cent admission for a show that included a singer and two reels of motion pictures.[47] The Motion Picture Patents Company (MPPC) licensed films screened at the Princess changed daily, including Sunday, and each bill usually combined a comedy and a drama, romance, or western with an occasional

Crowds during the streetcar workers strike in 1913. Note the signs for the Princess and the Hipp. Photo courtesy Transylvania University, Lexington, Kentucky.

"scenic" or "industrial" split-reel (such as *Small Trades in Havana*) thrown in. During March 1912, for example, sixty-eight different films were shown at the Princess, many of which were identified in promotional notices by genre (as "western," "love story," "detective story," "comedy") and/or by starring performer (e.g., John Bunny, Mary Fuller, Maurice Costello).[48]

In August 1913 the Princess was sold to three local women, including Carrie Bean, former secretary and treasurer of the theater, and Flossie Sheriff, then the pianist at the Princess. (These women incorporated their company with a capital stock of $5,000 divided into 250 shares and a debt limit of $10,000.) They supplied "plenty of fresh paint, new paper and attractive decorating" and began to feature more multiple-reel productions, including a few three-reel films like 101 Bison's *Captain Kidd*.[49] Even with this shift toward longer films, however, the Princess could not compete with new downtown venues, and it went into receivership in April 1914. Bean and her associates received $1,000 to transfer their lease to the building, which was then razed.[50]

All told, the Princess stayed in business for almost seven years, far longer than Dreamland or any of the other storefront moving picture shows that opened in downtown Lexington in 1906–07. Did the Princess actually fill some niche in the marketplace by catering to the "better class of people?" It obviously made an effort to pull in what Merritt calls the "larger middle-class family trade,"[51] though as Musser explains in his study of Lyman H. Howe, the "middle class" is better understood as including at least three "distinct cultural clusters": genteel, "refined culture"; "morally conservative, church-oriented culture"; and "vibrant, commercial, urban, popular culture, which also attracted middle-class patrons."[52] Charles Scott managed to draw all three of these "cultural clusters" to the Opera House. But who knows if a nickelodeon like the Princess could or did attract this clientele, since target audiences are one thing and actual customers another. Perhaps it is enough to note that the Princess publicly identified its patrons as being of the "best class," a gesture of flattery or wish fulfillment that doubtless did register with at least some theatergoers. A similar strategy, as we will see, was used in the marketing of vaudeville in Lexington.

Introducing Vaudeville to Lexington

Given the popularity of vaudeville across the nation, it is somewhat surprising that Lexington's first successful vaudeville theater did not open until November 1907.[53] There were, however, several earlier, fly-by-night efforts to promote vaudeville locally, all short-lived. For example, an auditorium on East Main Street offered a "Winter Carnival" with acrobats, trick cyclists, and trained animal acts like Colonel Edgar Daniel Boone and his performing lions and wolves for a few months in 1897. The following year a promoter from Chicago did no better with a "strictly refined and moral" vaudeville theater in the same location. Then in 1904, when inexpensive, so-called "family" vaudeville was, according to the New York *Dramatic Mirror*, "crop[-ping] up all over the western part of the country,"[54] a Louisville magician opened the Unique Theatre in a vacant store a block off of Main Street on North Upper. The Unique promised to "cater to family patronage," and it prominently featured "Edison's masterpiece," *The Great Train Robbery*, on its eight-act bill. Yet even Edison's magic could not shore up the Unique, which stayed afloat for only two weeks before the manager disappeared, stranding performers and leaving behind unpaid bills.

Vaudeville-style acts still remained popular specialty items for rep troupes that played the Opera House and for the traveling amusement companies hired for local fairs and carnivals. And after the opening of Lexington's first nickelodeons, the time seemed right for an inexpensive vaudeville theater that included motion pictures on its bill. Such was the plan of Milt Davis, who came from Cincinnati to open the 450-seat Lyric Theater in what had recently been the Upper Street meeting house of the Calvary Baptist Church. In the name of respectability, Davis vowed that a policeman would be on duty at all performances; he even went so far as to apologize to the Lyric's audience after a female performer "made a remark not on the bill to a man in the audience."[55] The Lyric's moving pictures (dubbed the "Lyriccograph"), according to one of the theater's promotional notices, "take well with the audiences, and it is noticeable that the patrons of the house remain in their seats until the final curtain."[56] The problem was that not enough customers were there to begin with, and the Lyric closed after three weeks. Six months later, in September 1907, an "amusement promoter" from Ludlow, Kentucky, and then two men from Indianapolis again tried to utilize this former church for a vaudeville theater, but even with all seats priced at ten cents, both enterprises failed almost immediately.

Clearly, inexpensive tickets and promises of clean, family-oriented amusement were not enough to make vaudeville profitable in Lexington. All the unsuccessful attempts I have mentioned were promoted by out-of-towners with little capital and apparently no ties to even small-scale vaudeville circuits. This was also the case, at least at first, with yet another show business venture in 1907, the approximately 350-seat Majestic Theater, set up in a vacant store right off Main Street on North Upper. After several changes of ownership, this theater closed in August 1908.

The Majestic reopened in October 1908 as a moving picture show, under the aegis of the Majestic Amusement Company, which had been incorporated for $5,000 with one hundred shares of stock, split between H. C. Lancaster and E. T. Graves, two Lexington saloon-keepers. The Leader reported that the theater drew more than ten thousand patrons in its first week, in large part because the new management secured a quite novel attraction: Swanson's Talking Pictures. The "talking" for these pictures was provided by three actors who spoke their lines from behind the movie screen, thus giving the "moving figures on the screen . . . a life-like reality."[57] A silent motion picture and an illustrated song rounded out the Majestic's bill, which was presented five times daily. After a month during which they performed some thirteen different "talking pictures," Swanson's company moved on, and the Majestic shifted to a five-cent moving picture-and-illustrated song format. Three attempts in 1909–10 to reinstate vaudeville at the Majestic failed, though it stayed in business thanks in part to manager John Elliott's promotions, including two-for-one children's tickets, a beautiful baby contest, and sheet music giveaways.[58] In April 1910 the Majestic was leased by Stanley Platt (former owner/manager of the Princess) and renamed the Star.

L. H. Ramsey and the Hippodrome Theater

Probably the main reason why the Majestic never turned a profit as an inexpensive vaudeville house was that from the first it had competed with the Hippodrome, a 450-seat theater that gave its premiere vaudeville performance on 25 November 1907. The Hippodrome, or the Hipp as it was commonly called, was located at 325 West Main in a building formerly occupied by a large dry goods store. It scheduled daily shows at 3:00, 7:30, and 8:45 P.M., featuring an illustrated song, motion pictures, and three or four acts booked through the National Vaudeville Circuit—all for ten cents. L. H. Ramsey, manager and principal owner of the Hipp, also owned a successful sign company that specialized in bill posting, printing, and billboard painting. Lexington papers found the self-promoting Ramsey to be good copy and consistently depicted him as an example of what an enterprising local man might accomplish in the relatively new field of commercial entertainment.

For Ramsey, expansion—and, to a lesser degree, diversification—was the means to assure and to signify commercial success. With his sign company as a profitable base, he promoted Independence Day fairs and other summertime events through his Lexington Amusement Company, then launched the Hipp.[59] When vaudeville proved successful, Ramsey added one hundred seats to the Hipp and began organizing a "chain" of vaudeville houses, modeled on and sharing acts with his Lexington venue. In May 1908 he took over a theater in Huntington, West Virginia, and by the summer of 1909, Ramsey had also acquired—according to the *Herald*—vaudeville houses in Charleston, West Virginia, Portsmouth, Virginia, and Memphis and was planning to lease another in Cincinnati.[60] Meanwhile, one of his sons opened a picture show in Frankfort, Kentucky, while another son became manager of Frankfort's Capitol Theater, which Ramsey had leased. In Lexington, Ramsey backed his son-in-law Stanley Platt's purchase of the Majestic in March 1910.

As taken as Ramsey was with the possibilities that commercial entertainment offered for entrepreneurial empire building, he was equally aware of the prestige and practical benefits to be gained from cooperative business associations. Thus he served as director of the National Vaudeville Managers Association, and he maintained very close ties with Gus Sun's National Vaudeville Association. On a local level, in 1908 he organized and presided over the Theatrical Mechanical Association, which included employees and managers of Lexington's various theaters. In 1912 he chaired the inaugural convention of the Kentucky Motion Picture Exhibitors League, which will be discussed more fully later, and joined with other exhibitors in the state to form the Western Exhibition Feature Film Company to import foreign-produced motion pictures.[61] Whether or not Ramsey's business directly profited because of his connection with such organizations, these ties surely helped to legitimate his own ventures and to make the business of commercial entertainment in Lexington seem more businesslike, particularly after the string of failed vaudeville theaters the city had seen.

According to Ramsey himself, the Hipp and his other theaters were so lucrative because they offered "a moral show, by moral people, for moral people."[62] This promise of "clean shows, amusing without vulgarity, thus catering to women and children," was a standard refrain in the advertising for Lexington's previous vaudeville theaters.[63] And, as Albert F. McLean notes, the promoters of "big-time" vaudeville were no less driven by this "obsession with 'purity'."[64] What particularly stands out is Ramsey's continued insistence on this point long after the Hipp had become a going concern, as if vaudeville itself—like street carnivals and traveling exhibitions—required constant surveillance and legitimation, perhaps because of its association with the values and the inhabitants of some distant metropolis. "There is nothing," Ramsey sanctimoniously proclaimed to a *Herald* reporter in November 1909, "that requires more constant vigilance" than the vaudeville show. Hence "there is but one salvation for any vaudeville house in this community, that is, give a show at all times to which any mother feels perfectly safe in sending her girl, knowing that she will neither see nor hear anything tending to the suggestive of ill."[65] Once the popular audience is reduced to the "girl"—doubly at risk because she is both female and child—then the heroic, ever-vigilant male theater owner/censor becomes the guarantor of the safety of the (feminized) "community."[66] (Ironically, as we shall see in Chapter 6, Ramsey was not completely averse to running afoul of mothers and ministers alike in his capacity as film exhibitor.)

Ramsey's pronouncements notwithstanding, there was no single "vaudeville" show, just as there was not one version of the circus or the *Uncle Tom's Cabin* troupe. For example, McLean offers as a "typical performance" an eight-act, over two-hour bill at B. F. Keith's Boston Theatre, which included no motion pictures or illustrated songs.[67] This type of vaudeville had appeared very briefly in Lexington in October 1907, when the Opera House booked Klaw & Erlanger's Advanced Vaudeville for a week's run. But the Hipp presented a quite different version of what Robert C. Allen calls vaudeville's "modular format of presentation."[68]

Unlike the star-studded shows booked into the major vaudeville circuits, a typical Hipp show included six acts and played three hour-long performances daily for a week (excluding Sunday). Take, for instance, the week of 12 February 1909, when the Hipp advertised a bill that would not offend "the most refined taste," headlined by a one-act "romantic drama of the Napoleonic period," and also including a blackface comedian, a "comedy-musical" duo, the four "Fantastic Labelles" (acrobatic specialists in the "European Mysteries"), a local tenor performing the illustrated song, "You Have To Sing an Irish Song," and, last on the bill, motion pictures (the "Hipposcope"). Ramsey's promotional material underscored the "diversity" and sheer magnitude of the Hipp's "High Class Vaudeville," which, in this particular week, recombined elements from the legitimate theater, minstrel show, circus, recital, and nickelodeon, creating a mixed menu that served up local talent and "European" fare, ethnic sentiment and regionalist Americana, drama and comedy, and whatever happened to fill the Hipposcope part of the bill.

A program like this was unquestionably less diverse and less grand than a show touring the Keith circuit. The Hipp's offerings, however, were reasonably typical of other small houses in the Midwest and the South that booked their acts through the Gus Sun agency. According to ads in *Variety*, the Sun Circuit—based in Springfield, Ohio—had grown from 87 "first-class Family Vaudeville Theatres in Ohio and the adjoining states" in 1907 to 134 "three a day" houses in Ohio, Pennsylvania, Kentucky, Maryland, Indiana, West Virginia, and Indiana in 1908, to 250 family vaudeville theaters, including 75 "Big Houses," in 1910. The Hipp was not listed as one of these "Big

Houses," so I assume its fare was representative of the 175 smaller theaters on the Sun Circuit.[69]

With vaudeville well established, Ramsey in 1910 began offering motion pictures and illustrated songs at the Hipp on Sundays from 2:00 to 6:00 and 7:00 to 10:30 P.M. He bought out his partner in March 1911 and made public his plans to take over an adjoining building and erect a one thousand-seat vaudeville theater. Large ads in both Lexington papers sought investors who were willing to spend $10 a share to own "a piece of the new Hipp," a "real vaudeville theater, comfortable, safe, convenient."[70] Even with this unusual tactic, Ramsey failed to attract enough buyers to cover the capital stock of $35,000. So he canceled his original plans and, instead, turned the building next door into a sheet music store and a 260-seat moving picture show called the Hipp Annex, which opened for business in August 1911. Thus Ramsey could be said to have created an entertainment complex somewhat akin to the one promised by Colonel Billy Thompson back in 1896. Only in place of a dime museum, the Hipp included a soda fountain in the lobby and a sheet music store linking the vaudeville stage and the nickelodeon, both of which featured illustrated songs.

Blue Grass Park

After moving picture shows, skating rinks, and vaudeville theaters, the last addition to Lexington's commercial entertainment market in the nickelodeon era was Blue Grass Park, an amusement park built by the Lexington Railway Company in 1909 on twenty-six acres of land near Fort Springs, six miles from town. Once again, as with the "electrical excursions" by trolley in 1896 and the development of Woodland Park at the turn of the century, the Railway Company stood to gain not only prestige and gratitude, but also more tangible benefits from its investment. Admission may have been free, but virtually anyone wishing to attend the park from Lexington or the surrounding smaller communities would have to buy a twenty-cent interurban railway round-trip ticket. In addition, the Railway Company profited from rental fees and the sale of concession rights.

What the public received in exchange was a fair-weather site for family activity and clean amusement, more precisely, a dance pavilion open on Wednesday and Saturday evenings, a merry-go-round, baseball diamond, and

Amusements

OPERA HOUSE

Matinee and Night,
Saturday, April 10

Go and see the George M. Cohan
New York Song Show

"The Honeymooners"

With Willie Dunlay, the singing and dancing comedian.

Supported by a clever cast of
principals. Beauty chorus. Magnificent costumes. Special scenery.
Hear the Cohan song hits.

PRICES: Matinee 25c to $1.00,
Night .... 25c to $1.50

TUESDAY, APRIL 13,

"THE SOUTHERN CROSS"

A DRAMA OF THE
CIVIL WAR.

Benefit of Morgan Monument.
Prices 25c to $1.00.
Sale of Seats Saturday.

The Hipp

Best Show 10c
On Earth for

A clean cut vaudeville performance
lasting about an hour three times every day except Sunday.
A place where you can take your
mother, sister or sweetheart, knowing
before you go that nothing will be
said or done that could offend her in
the least, and that she will enjoy an
hour of healthful amusement.
"Trdy to get in."

MAJESTIC
.Vaudeville..
(Incorporated.)

Lexington's Splendid New
Amusement Palace

Over Sixty Minutes Delight And
Laughter at Every Performance For
10c.

Polite Service, Comfortable Seats
and a Clean Show. Seats reserved
on request. Call Home 'Phone 718.
"GO WHERE THE CROWD GOES"

BLUE GRASS THEATER.

Main and Broadway
PICTURES CHANGED DAILY
Mr. Wester sings the illustrated
songs.

The range of amusements available locally in 1909. Lexington *Herald*, 10
April 1909.

Sunday band concerts. Blue Grass Park was, a large ad explicitly announced, "for the use of white persons only. We aim to make it a family resort of the highest order." In this spirit, the Railway Company prohibited the sale and use of intoxicating beverages on park grounds and promised that the area would be "well policed so that the patrons will be protected from all rowdyism."[71] It would appear that to qualify as a "family resort," Blue Grass Park had to identify itself unmistakably as an absolutely segregated facility with no touch of the saloon and of (working-class) "rowdyism."

In preparation for the 1910 summer season, the Railway Company invested even more heavily in Blue Grass Park, adding a "scenic railroad" said to have cost $15,000, a $12,000 carousel, more sports and boating facilities, children's playgrounds, landscaped and well-lit walkways, and a shooting gallery. Motion pictures also became a regular feature, although they never figured as prominently in the park's advertising as did the nightly dances and Sunday evening "sacred concerts."[72] For the *Leader* reporter who covered the 1910 opening day festivities, however, the most commendable aspects of Blue Grass Park were the "thorough policing of all parts of the grounds" and the "excellent arrangements" made to facilitate the arrival and departure of interurban railway passengers.[73]

In the way of permanent facilities, when the dust cleared at the end of the nickelodeon era, Lexington was left with: Blue Grass Park, the Railway Company's well-established and entirely respectable site that combined features of an urban amusement park, a natural picnic spot, and a multipurpose city park; Ramsey's expanded Hippodrome, home to Gus Sun vaudeville and Sunday moving pictures; the Lexington Opera House, still booking Howe's exhibitions and theatrical touring companies, along with its first multi-reel feature film, *Dante's Inferno;*[74] the Woodland Park Auditorium, rarely used for commercial purposes, and then solely for high-art attractions like the Russian Symphony Orchestra;[75] the Princess, Star, and Hipp Annex, which shared a similar moving picture-and-illustrated song exhibition format; and two small, black owned and operated theaters which will be examined in some detail in Chapter 7.[76] Of these venues, only the Opera House had existed in 1900 (or even in 1905), and the growth of commercial entertainment had far outstripped the 33 percent increase in Lexington's population from 1900 to 1910. The role of motion pictures in this expanding market became even more prominent with the construction of two new movie theaters in 1911–12.

FORGET YOUR CARES

Come out from the grime of the city's smoke and dust, the sun's
rebounding heat. Come out to cool refreshing, pleasant—

BLUE GRASS PARK

Give the wife and the little ones the full benefit of an afternoon or a day's recreation
and pleasure. Spend your evenings at this exhilarating pleasure resort.

BOATING —— BATHING ——— MUSIC ———— DANCING

SCENIC RAILWAY —DANCING PRIZES TUESDAY and FRIDAY Evenings
20-MINUTE CAR SERVICE AFTERNOON AND EVENING

Nature, family fun, a bathing beauty: the Lexington Railway Company promotes Blue
Grass Park. Lexington *Herald,* 5 July 1920.

Colonial Theater

The Colonial Theater, which opened with much fanfare on 1 August 1911,
was not an "annex" to a preexisting theater, nor was it a refurbished vaudeville house. It was financed, planned, and operated exclusively as a motion
picture theater, in fact as a self-proclaimed "picture palace." Yet in important
ways this four hundred-seat theater was simply an extension of the storefront
nickelodeon, offering moving pictures and illustrated songs in a site previously occupied by a five-and-ten-cent store. The Colonial Amusement
Company spent some $2,500 of its $15,000 total start-up costs remodeling
the interior and erecting a new front for this 25 x 125 foot building located
at 224 West Main Street, across from the county courthouse on a block also
occupied by two shoe stores, a florist, a haberdashery, and two dry goods
stores. The most visible addition was a large electric sign, topped by a "moving" "electric dancing girl." The *Herald* noted that during hot summer nights
"many men, lying upon the lawn surrounding the courthouse, contented
themselves with watching the antics of the electric dancing girl on the Colonial Theatre."[77]

Overseen by this "little dancing lady," the Colonial was the last word in
"safety, beauty, elegance and refinement," or at least so claimed its full-page,
grand opening advertisement in both local papers. The theater was, according to this announcement, richly and carefully decorated in its tiled and

Postcard for the Colonial, soon after it opened.

mirrored lobby and throughout, veritably a "work of art in every sense of the word." It was, moreover, built to the industry's "highest standards," equipped with nineteen ventilators, five exits, "expertly" installed wiring, a screen elevated some six feet above seat level, a Powers No. 6 projector, and a completely enclosed operator's booth. These features were designed to assure the comfort, security, and satisfaction of the audience. (The moral "cleanliness" of the Colonial's show itself was not mentioned, at least not here.) The Colonial was, *Moving Picture World*'s Louisville correspondent declared, "the pinnacle of the architect's genius."[78]

Though this theater had no balcony or box seats and could hold no more than four hundred people, it was obviously promoted as a sort of opera house in miniature. No other moving picture show in Lexington could offer, for instance, two doormen (including a former policeman) and five ushers, all in uniform. This innovation was right in line with the advice that *Moving Picture World* offered to exhibitors: "if possible, a polite and uniformed attendant should always be present to . . . inspire confidence, keep order and attract women and children into the house."[79] The Colonial's opening day advertisement, however, did not feature photographs of the doorman or the ushers. In keeping with the spirit of the "electric dancing girl," this advertisement included large portraits of the young women who would be serving as cashiers, pianists, and vocalists. Their presence guaranteed that this new showplace would offer not simply order and safety but a full measure of "feminine" beauty, elegance, and refinement—for only a nickel or a dime, anytime between 10:00 A.M. and 11:00 P.M.[80]

While the Colonial's hours of operation and low admission prices remained basically the same from 1911 until the theater closed in 1917, its exhibition policy did change in response to local competition and national trends in the motion picture industry. Initially, the Colonial, like Lexington's other moving picture shows, offered two (or, rarely, three) reels of pictures changed daily, with piano accompaniment and an illustrated song. At approximately forty minutes each, a minimum of fifteen such shows could be presented per day. The Colonial's admission charge was raised from five to ten cents for more elaborately advertised special attractions like Vitagraph's three-reel *Vanity Fair*, which was booked for three days in December 1911,[81] and then in 1912 for Bison 101's three-reel *Custar's [sic] Last Fight*, a Christmas Day screening of Thanhouser's *Star of Bethlehem*, and the latest motion pictures of Teddy Roosevelt.

With the addition in March 1913 of one hundred more seats and the installation of a large mirror screen, said to have cost $1,000, and two new ozone air purifiers, the Colonial Amusement Company touted its theater as "the most beautiful and up-to-date motion picture theatre in Central Kentucky." Colonial ads also insisted that the theater's operators were all well-paid professionals and its films were absolutely unobjectionable, even for the "most fastidious taste." Doubling ticket prices from a nickel to a dime for everyone over ten years of age was justified by—and so, tautologically, affirmed—the theater's status.[82] The "new" Colonial's program expanded accordingly, to include four reels of the "latest" pictures, three singers, a pianist, and a six-piece orchestra. To encourage repeat customers and attract bargain hunters, the theater sold books of thirty five-cent tickets for $1.00.[83]

Faced with the opening of two much larger and grander theaters in downtown Lexington (to be discussed in the next chapter), the Colonial first tried to compete head-to-head: scheduling six-reel shows, then "all feature bills" with four different Alco, World, or Paramount multi-reel films per week; and enlarging its orchestra to nine (piano, bass, flute, clarinet, cornet, trombone, drums/xylophone, and two pianos) and then twelve pieces.[84] These moves were undoubtedly "progressive," but the cost of booking feature films and maintaining a good-sized orchestra was economically feasible only for those Lexington theaters that were double or triple the size of the Colonial.

From the end of 1914 on, the Colonial increasingly became a venue for one-, two-, and three-reel productions, changed daily. It capitalized on the immense popularity of Chaplin's comedies in 1915, experimented that same year with using two different orchestras performing daily, and again briefly attempted to go "all-feature" in 1916. Eventually, the Colonial came to depend more and more on serials and one-reel comedies. When it closed this theater in January 1917, the Colonial Amusement Company announced that "the increasing popularity of the motion picture and the demands of the public for more elaborate programs has made considerable inroads upon the business of the Colonial."[85] After remaining vacant for some time, this building on Main Street once topped by an electric dancing lady was leased by a store specializing in women's "ready-to-wear" clothing.

Colonial Amusement Company

The Colonial Amusement Company, whose enterprises in central Kentucky extended well beyond the Colonial Theater, was incorporated in March 1911 with a capital stock of $10,000, divided into one hundred shares.[86] (A year later, the board of directors voted to increase the company's capital stock to $30,000.) The principal investors were two men from well-established, middle-class Lexington families: George Michler, who co-owned the store the Colonial would displace and whose family ran a floral shop; and B. J. Treacy, who soon became a quite successful insurance and real estate salesman and took an active role in civic organizations such as the Board of Commerce and the "Clean City Club." Treacy and Michler were by no means silent partners, but the major figure in the Colonial Amusement Company was twenty-eight-year-old John Elliott. The son of a harness dealer, Elliott was a lifelong resident of the city who had been an insurance agent and a clerk before he began managing the Majestic Theater and oversaw its transformation from a vaudeville house to a moving picture show in 1908. He then co-owned and operated the Princess in 1910 before becoming general manager and president of the Colonial Amusement Company.[87]

The Colonial's eye-catching, electrified "moving lady." Photo courtesy University of Kentucky Photo Archives.

Four months prior to the Colonial's opening, Elliott acquired the Star, which he operated basically along the same no-frills lines as a storefront nickelodeon. In March 1913 the Colonial Amusement Company temporarily closed the Star because construction work being done on the fifteen-floor Fayette National Bank Building, Lexington's first "skyscraper," hindered access to the theater. From the time it reopened in November 1913 to its last show in January 1916, the Star had no pretensions to being anything but an inexpensive, convenient showplace, seldom advertised in the newspaper and increasingly reliant on pictures in at least their second run. (In March 1915, for example, the Star screened Griffith's *Judith of Bethulia* [1913], which had played at the Colonial eleven months earlier.)

Virtually all of Elliott's quite effective promotional efforts in the early 1910s focused on the Colonial rather than the Star. Most obviously there was the Colonial's electric sign, the dancing girl who bore no direct connection to either the theater's name or to the fare it presented. This "moving lady," presiding over the city's first self-proclaimed "picture palace," emblemizes some of the contradictory claims and attractions of moving pictures/photoplays: at once garish and classy, mechanical and lifelike; a display of "feminine" refinement and an enactment of dance hall "antics"; a flamboyant expenditure of money and energy and an exhibitionist spectacle out to capture the (masculine?) eye and turn a profit.

The electric dancing lady balanced atop the Colonial found her complement below in March 1913, when Elliott brought in Essanay leading man Francis X. Bushman for what were advertised as "lectures" at each of the Colonial's Easter Sunday shows. Bushman, the *Leader* wrote, "held his audience spellbound [with] his graphic and vivid descriptions of the different steps in making a photoplay."[88] Since Bushman was among the most popular "picture personalities" of the day, his local appearance was no doubt intended to underscore the Colonial's claim to be "Lexington's Highest Class Motion Picture House" and also to tap the public's increasing fascination with screen stars and the process of moviemaking.[89] Bushman may have been cut in the mold of a stagebound matinee idol, but by bringing him to Lexington in the flesh, the Colonial was affirming its commitment to photoplays, not spoken dramas or vaudeville.

Bushman on that Easter Sunday did not merely emote or wave to his fans, he "lectured," which must have pleased Elliott, for the legitimation of moving pictures and moviegoing was still in process (or progress, depending on one's view of cheap amusements). In fact, a sabbatarian campaign that targeted movie theaters in particular was then in full swing in Lexington. In Chapter 6, we will see how Elliott and the city's other theater owners and managers directly responded to local pressure for enforcement of blue laws and for stricter censorship practices. Two somewhat more indirect responses by the Colonial Amusement Company can be briefly noted here. These promotions involved schoolchildren—a crucial audience for any moving picture show—but more important, in terms of legitimation, they literally brought Lexington's widely respected superintendent of schools, M. A. Cassidy, into the Colonial and the Star.

In a generous civic gesture in March 1912, Elliott invited "worthy pupils" with good attendance records at one of the city's elementary schools to a free show at both of his theaters (where children from the Orphan's Home were regularly admitted for free.) Cassidy accompanied these diligent students and arranged with Elliott for a similar program citywide. The superintendent returned actually to lecture to schoolchildren at the Colonial in December 1913, in conjunction with the free screening of a "thrilling and exciting" safety film, *The Price of Thoughtlessness,* sponsored by the Lexington Railway Company. After these appearances, it would be increasingly difficult for local citizens to view the Colonial or the Star, *ipso facto,* as dens of iniquity. Cassidy's visits, like the Colonial's new ozone air purifiers or its extra exits, were a testament to the theater's safety.

As president of the Colonial Amusement Company, Elliott not only oversaw the promotion and daily operation of its two Lexington theaters, but he also expanded the company's holdings to include several other central Kentucky venues. In January 1912 the Colonial Amusement Company announced its intention to "open a string of moving picture theaters in practically all the surrounding towns adjacent to Lexington."[90] Such ambitious plans, of course, were hardly unique; witness L. H. Ramsey's "chain" of small vaudeville theaters mentioned earlier in this chapter. Elliott moved quickly, closing a deal in February 1912 with the mayor of nearby Paris, for a building that would become the 250-seat Alamo Theater. A year later, the Colonial Amusement Company purchased a similar sized theater, the Alhambra, then the "leading picture house" in Richmond. In January 1914 the company acquired the Pastime in Maysville, sixty-five miles northeast of Lexington, and took a two-year lease on the Paris Opera House, which was slated to be used for "big feature films and road shows."

Having built up a string of six houses in about two years, the Colonial Amusement Company then sought, unsuccessfully at first, to acquire or build a large motion picture theater in Lexington. Finally, in November 1916, this company purchased a substantial interest in the 1,600-seat Strand Theater, which will be discussed more fully later. The Star had become expendable and was closed by the Colonial Amusement Company in January 1916; a year later the Colonial, too, shut its doors for good. Elliott, as we will see, remained a prominent figure in the local and regional commercial entertainment business well into the 1930s.

Orpheum Theater

In contrast to John Elliott, John Stamper, Jr., the owner and manager of the Orpheum Theater, conducted his business in a manner not unlike a small-town motion picture exhibitor. That is to say, once the Orpheum was in operation, Stamper did not attempt to forge a chain of picture shows, nor did he invest in lavish renovations. Nonetheless, the Orpheum remained open from

1912 to 1930, which is all the more surprising since it was not the only show in a one-horse town or in a secluded residential neighborhood. The Orpheum was located at 100 East Main Street, in the midst of Lexington's central business district, meaning that while it profited from great foot traffic, those shoppers, out-of-town visitors, schoolchildren, and white-collar employees passing by could just as easily walk on to another theater.

Prior to opening the Orpheum, Stamper had run the Star from October 1910 to April 1911; he also owned and operated a grocery/liquor store in Pralltown, a black neighborhood near the State College campus. This business came under much fire from local "dry" forces, who accused Stamper's grocery of selling liquor on Sundays and endangering easily tempted university students. In the face of stricter city ordinances enacted in 1913, Stamper turned his grocery business over to his brother and thereafter stuck exclusively to managing the Orpheum.

Located in a former drugstore that Stamper leased from the Phoenix Hotel, the Orpheum was built and outfitted at a cost of approximately $18,000, with the actual construction work bid at $11,284.[91] This new theater was clearly intended to surpass Lexington's first-generation nickelodeons and to rival the Colonial, which was already in operation when Stamper signed his lease in November 1911. Indeed, in most respects, the Orpheum was a slightly scaled-down version of the Colonial. Built on a 25 × 68 foot site, the three hundred-seat Orpheum had an usher on duty at all times, a small "toilet room for ladies," an enclosed projection booth located above the box office, a sloped floor that allowed for better viewing, and an 11 × 16 foot screen that Stamper touted as the largest in the city. No "electric lady" danced atop the Orpheum, but a marquee with 75 twenty-five-watt bulbs ran across the entire front of the building. According to the *Leader*, this newest addition to Lexington's leisure life was a "gem of architectural beauty and attractiveness" throughout, particularly in the green-and-ivory-toned auditorium with its mahogany woodwork and brass trim.[92] What Stamper offered was an environment that aspired to be beautiful, modern, comfortable, practical, and safe— qualities and ideals that are more in keeping with the early twentieth-century department store and railroad station than with the saloon or the mom-and-pop corner grocery.[93]

Like the Colonial, the Orpheum was open from 10:00 A.M. to 11:00 P.M., with a similar moving picture-and-illustrated song format, plus the added novelty of an experienced "lady trap drummer."[94] Each day brought three or four reels of moving pictures and one or even two songs. During November

1913, for example, the Orpheum screened some fifty-five one-reel, eleven two-reel, and four longer films (including *Sapho* twice). Multiply these figures by four or five and you have some sense of just how many motion pictures each month passed through a small city like Lexington at the end of the nickelodeon era. The sheer quantity of this daily changing product itself suggests a world of variety and plentitude, novelty and productivity. However, like the modular structure of vaudeville, the daily schedule at a theater like the Orpheum followed what was by 1913 a familiar logic: songs performed between films and at least one comedy on the bill virtually every day.

This "order," such as it was, should not blind us to the randomness and dis-unity of a typical Orpheum program, for example, that of 7 November 1913, which included a one-reel comedy (*Friday, The Thirteenth*), a sentimental ballad ("The Heart of a Rose"), a two-reel romantic spy melodrama set in Japan (*The Oath of Otsuri San*), and a ragtime song ("The Puzzlin' Rag"). We can be sure that the spectators for this show did not rise in outrage as at some proto-dadaist performance; by 1913, such an audience doubtless knew what to expect of the movies and of moviegoing. In addition, Stamper, following the cue of exhibitor trade magazines and the production/distribution industry's own promotional information, was particularly diligent and detailed in his newspaper advertisements, which marketed and sorted out the mass of new product by title, studio, actor, story line, and often by genre (for example, "domestic drama," "domestic farce comedy," "conventional western drama," "typical farce comedy burlesque"). That he and virtually all of Lexington's other theater operators in this period advertised in this way suggests that at least some and probably a good percentage of the local audience comparison shopped when it came to cheap amusements, choosing how to spend their money on the basis of the specific program rather than the theater.

Like Elliott, Stamper attempted to compete with Lexington's new, large theaters by increasing the number of reels per show and by adding a small "orchestra" led by Miss Estrella Hailey, who, the *Herald* noted, had devised a unique system for cueing different sorts of music ("everything from grand opera to ragtime") "to conform to the action of the accompanying [photo]play."[95] At its most ambitious, in the fall of 1915, the Orpheum offered a five-piece "symphonic orchestra" and six reels of moving pictures. But by this date, the only way a small theater could survive in Lexington was as a second-rank house. In fact, what surely helped keep the Orpheum in business was the Colonial Amusement Company's decision to close both the Star and the Colonial, leaving Stamper with the only five-cent theater in town. For the rest of the decade and on through the 1920s, the Orpheum filled this not very prestigious but apparently profitable spot in the marketplace, bearing witness, in a fashion, to the viability of the concept of the nickelodeon.

Douglas Gomery contends that "by 1910 a permanent base for movie exhibition had been set up across the United States almost before anyone realized it."[96] Lexington, as I have suggested, lagged a bit behind in this regard, with the Colonial and the Orpheum not opening until 1911–12. But what people in Lexington surely did realize was that the face of commercial entertainment in the city had changed dramatically—and repeatedly—over a six-year period. It was not so much the presence of nickelodeons per se that increasingly separated Lexington from the small towns of central Kentucky. It was the entire range of new amusement ventures that tested the market regardless of failures like Dreamland or the deflation of the skating rink fad. Along with the sheer volume of motion picture product that passed through Lexington, there was a quite unprecedented increase in commercial entertainment options, afternoons and evenings, everyday throughout the year. These options betokened Lexington's modernity, up-to-dateness, and urbanity, to which the marketing strategies surveyed here responded in different ways: Ramsey by loudly insisting that the vaudeville at the Hipp was vigilantly overseen; the Princess by pitching for "better class" customers; Elliot and Stamper by initially selling their new theaters as comfortable, safe, and state-of-the-art venues. These strategies reflect certain anxieties fostered by the commercial entertainment environment—the fear of a certain "class"-less ness, the lack of established standards, the sense of fly-by-night impermanence—that the new theaters of the 1910s would tackle head-on.

FIVE

The Movies Have the Day:
The Business of
Film Exhibition
in the 1910s

Initially, at least, the Colonial and the Orpheum were promoted as being
closer in elegance and comfort to the Lexington Opera House than to the
city's first-generation nickelodeons. Both of these theaters, however, were unquestionably, unashamedly moving picture shows. They may have sought to
broaden the regular audience for the movies, but they had no aspirations to
forego the screen for the stage. In retrospect, it is apparent that the opening
of the Colonial and the Orpheum marked the beginning of a decade in which
the movies came to dominate the local commercial entertainment market,
which, as we will see in Chapter 6, helps account for Lexington's increasingly
heated public debates over film censorship and Sunday movie screenings.
New, larger theaters signified Lexington's "progress" in the 1910s, an era in
which the feature-film program became prominent, a two-tier system of film
exhibition developed, and the legitimate stage struggled to maintain its commercial viability. These trends are best demonstrated by a close look at the
financing, design, day-to-day operation, and precise booking policies of:

Ada Meade Theater: A renovated, expanded, and renamed version of the
Hippodrome, the Ada Meade was built by the Lexington Theatres Com-

pany and opened in October 1913. It sat 934 and was used for low-price
vaudeville Monday–Saturday and film programs on Sunday.

Ben Ali Theater: Built as a luxurious 1,411-seat multipurpose legitimate theater by the Lexington-based Berryman Realty Company, the Ben Ali
opened in September 1913. It adopted an all-motion picture format in
May 1915.

Strand Theater: This 1,600-seat theater built by the Louisville-based Phoenix Amusement Company opened in October 1915. From the first the
Strand was designed to be the city's largest movie theater.

Ada Meade

In December 1912, with the Colonial and the Orpheum well established,
L. H. Ramsey told the *Herald:* "I am not making handsome money like some
of my friends in the picture business. I am making some but not enough for
the amount of money invested and the time I am giving to the picture business."[1] Ramsey had taken a variety of measures to increase his revenues at
the Hipp Annex: he scheduled all-movie bills with "positively no picture
slides on the program";[2] distributed postcards of the most popular "Independent players";[3] even experimented with a so-called "daylight screen," which
was supposed to allow for viewing movies in a semi-lit—and therefore
"safe"—environment.

By November 1912 Ramsey was actively seeking a buyer for his Lexington
theaters through a classified ad in *Moving Picture World.* (The ad claimed
that he had over $20,000 invested in these venues.)[4] Apparently he got no
takers, for he decided instead to close the Annex and enlarge the Hipp. With
this goal in mind, Ramsey joined with several local investors to form the
Lexington Theatres Company, presided over by Bishop Clay, the realtor who
had been responsible for the Mammoth Skating Rink. Other investors and
officeholders in the company included Lexington dentist W. S. Herndon and
Frank Christian, a "prosperous farmer and cattle broker."[5] In this new corporate arrangement, Ramsey's official title was "manager," and the shift in
control over the theater was symbolically underscored when the Lexington
Theatres Company conducted a public contest to come up with a name for
the "new" Hipp. A local attorney suggested that the theater be named for
Ada Meade Saffarans, a Lexington-born actress who was then a successful
touring musical comedy performer. So when it reopened in October 1913, the

Hipp had become the Ada Meade, a unique name that, unlike the more generic "Colonial" or "Orpheum," carried a specific local connotation and linked the new theater, however tenuously, with femininity and the legitimate stage.

The Ada Meade was designed by W. H. St. Clair, said to be a renowned theater architect then residing in West Virginia. Its lobby featured a "beautiful little pagoda effect," and inside the auditorium itself, raspberry-colored carpet was coordinated with gilt-decorated boxes and ivory and apple-green walls. All in all, the Ada Meade was, in the words of the *Herald,* "airy, roomy, bright, colorful and cheerful," and it fully met "every requirement of comfort, sanitation, acoustics, [and] safety." Moreover, it featured a large 28 × 50 foot stage, eight dressing rooms, steam heating, an ozone cooling system, and a thoroughly equipped projection and lighting booth. Whereas the Hipp had sat about 550 and the Hipp Annex 260, the Ada Meade had 934 total seats: 516 on the main floor and 418 in the two balconies. One major addition was a second balcony, which opened directly onto the street, expressly designed for "colored" patrons. Another addition was twelve "beautiful boxes" (six on the first floor, six in the first balcony), which were intended to "give the Ada Meade a dignity and tone that no other house of its class in the South possesses."[6] By this logic, the more stratification within the theater, the more "dignity and tone" it exuded.

Judge James H. Mulligan provided the dedicatory speech for the Ada Meade's gala 20 October 1913 premiere. The judge praised the "wisdom and propriety of high-class, clean and proper public amusements"—including vaudeville of the sort introduced to Lexington by Ramsey.[7] The Ada Meade basically stuck to the format of the Hipp: five acts booked through the Gus Sun Agency, plus one or more Kinemacolor films (for which Ramsey was the sole local exhibitor),[8] all accompanied by an orchestra composed of piano, clarinet, cornet, violin, cello, and drums. Tickets were set at ten and twenty cents for the 2:30 matinee and from ten to fifty cents for the evening shows at 7:30 and 9:15. On Sundays, the Ada Meade offered two singing acts and six reels of motion pictures (including at least one Kinemacolor film) run continuously between 2:00 and 10:00 P.M., with children's seats at five cents and adults at ten cents.

The Ada Meade's booking policy (aside from the screening of Kinemacolor productions) remained by and large the same during the next four years, though Ramsey himself was ousted in January 1914, barely three months after the grand opening. The separation was acrimonious, with Ramsey at

The Ada Meade

Lexington's New Vaudeville Theatre Will Have Its Opening

Monday Evening,

October 20th at 7:30 P. M.

SIX BIG ACTS ! SIX

Of High Class Vaudeville Including The

Kinemacolor Motion Pictures (Natural Color Photograhy)

Prices: 10c, 20c and 30c

Box Seats 50c

OPENING PROGRAMME

EDNEY BROTHERS COMPANY
One Act Musical Comedy
"SLUMMING IN CHINATOWN."

WELTER AND CLUCAS
Comedy Conversationalists
Singing and Talking

MORTIMER SNOW & COMPANY
Presenting a Comedy
"THE DIAMOND BRACELET."

THE THREE AMERES
Comedy Acrobats

MENLO MOORES' "THE FAIR
CO-EDS."

A Merry Musical Melange of School
Days in Three Spectacular Scenes.

THE ADA MEADE
The Lexington Theatres Co.
(Incorporated)

Bishop Clay, President.
Dr. W. S. Herndon, Treasurer.
L H Ramsey, Manager.

T. C .Fuller, Vice President.
Frank Christian, Secretary
John W. Townsend, Press Representative.
Miss Margaret Ramsey, Ticket Seller.

Announcing the opening of the Ada Meade, with both the investors and the entertainers listed. Lexington *Leader*, 19 October 1913.

least looking the part of the "showman" betrayed by Clay and the other "money men," who then completed the takeover by asking for the resignations of three other Ada Meade employees, Ramsey's son, daughter, and brother. As he had done in 1911, Ramsey took out ads in local newspapers seeking public investors for his New Hippodrome Company. Once again, this tactic failed. On 5 April 1914, he filed a $15,000 suit against the Lexington Theatres Company, trying to recover his share of the Ada Meade, including $5,000 for what he called the "vaudeville franchise" itself.[9] I found no evidence concerning how this litigation was resolved, but the upshot of the controversy was that Ramsey moved to Jacksonville, Florida, where he established a hog farm, and the Lexington Theatres Company sought a lessee for the Ada Meade.

In August 1914 the Louisville-based Gurnee Amusement Company began operation of the Ada Meade, adding this house to its two theaters in Louisville and four in Ohio. Nelson van Houten Gurnee, president of this company, soon moved to Lexington and began to run the Ada Meade according to what he rather pretentiously called the "theory of scientific booking." Whereas Ramsey's public pronouncements had always stressed the inoffensiveness of the shows that he ever-vigilantly oversaw at the Hipp, for Gurnee, the manager's prime task was creatively selecting and arranging a six-act bill so that it would comprise a "well-ordered, swiftly moving panorama of pleasure."[10] Did these two "theories" of commercial entertainment translate into noticeably different types of vaudeville in Lexington? Not as far as I can tell, perhaps because both managers were limited to the range of touring acts that were then available to a small city venue.[11] Judging from the rather detailed promotional notices in Lexington newspapers, these acts did not change appreciably between 1907 and 1916. Gurnee did come to book an occasional "tabloid," which Abel Green and Joe Laurie, Jr. describe as an "abbreviated musical comedy at the vaudeville level," with "four or five principals, seven or eight chorus girls," and "one set of scenery."[12] Yet like the Hipp, the Ada Meade's mainstay was "superior vaudeville," with headliners on the order of Princess Alohikea and her hula-dancing Royal Hawaiian Serenaders and the Stan Jefferson Trio, with its "celebrated impersonation of Charlie Chaplin."[13]

In April 1916 the *Herald* reported that the Gurnee Amusement Company was very much a going concern, with four theaters in Louisville and others in Frankfort, Kentucky, Muncie, Indiana, and Kent and Columbus, Ohio. The company even announced plans to acquire two houses in New Jersey. No doubt Gurnee was as much given to press-agentry and self-promotion as

Ramsey had been. But accurate or not, the notion of the independent, ever-growing theater chain seemed to carry a particular symbolic weight during this period, perhaps as a demonstration of entrepreneurial capitalism at work (in an age of highly visible trusts and monopolies), perhaps as an indication that Lexington was on a circuit with other cities and so was more likely to get a better product. Local papers made no mention of Gurnee's theater chain when they reported in February 1918 that the Ada Meade had been sold to William James, who owned a comparable venue in Columbus, Ohio.

Ben Ali

Unlike the Ada Meade, which changed owners but consistently maintained a similar booking policy, the Ben Ali had the same owner during the 1910s but tried several different formats until it became a motion picture theater in May 1915. Yet what is of interest here is not just the Ben Ali's three-year transformation from staging combination company productions to exclusively booking motion pictures, but also the social, cultural, and economic import of this theater as an investment, a civic showplace (and showpiece), and a site that originally looked more in keeping with the end of the nineteenth century than with the second decade of the twentieth.

Built in 1912 for an amount almost ten times greater than the $18,000 start-up cost of the Orpheum, the Ben Ali was named for one of central Kentucky's richest and most well known capitalists, James Ben Ali Haggin. Haggin made his fortune from mining operations, then retired in 1897, dividing his time between New York City, Newport, Rhode Island, and his 8,000-acre Elemendorf Farm outside Lexington. In 1911 the 89-year-old Haggin decided to build a lavish new theater in Lexington, with the planning and construction to be overseen by Charles H. Berryman, the business manager of Haggin's Kentucky operations.[14]

Berryman was a Lexington native educated at Kentucky University, who had risen from being a bookkeeper and salesman to become director of the local Internal Revenue Office, and then president of the Elemendorf Coal and Feed Company and the Central Kentucky Bluegrass Seed Company. He also was appointed postmaster of Lexington for a two-year term in 1915, served on the board of directors of the Phoenix Hotel and the Burley Tobacco Company, and was an influential member of the Fayette Equal Rights Association and the Republican Party. Unlike the other local men I have mentioned who became involved in the commercial entertainment business, Berryman belonged to both the highly exclusive Lexington Club and the Lexington Country Club.[15]

Once Berryman and Haggin had picked out a site on the corner of Limestone and East Main Street, directly across from the Phoenix Hotel, they circulated a stock subscription paper soliciting investors. Their plan was to capitalize the Ben Ali at $120,000, half preferred and half common stock. While Ramsey twice failed to find public investors for the Hipp, Berryman— with Haggin's reputation and wealth behind him—readily succeeded, and the Berryman Realty Company was incorporated in February 1912. Among its publicly declared "purposes" was the erection and operation of an "opera house," an ice plant, and an automobile garage. Haggin controlled 250 shares of the corporation's common stock. Berryman, the Phoenix Hotel, and the Combs Lumber Company (which would build the Ben Ali) each controlled fifty shares of preferred stock; Desha Breckinridge, editor and publisher of the Lexington *Herald*, held twenty-five shares of preferred stock, and a host of "leading citizens and firms" also invested in the company.[16]

In its account of the Ben Ali's opening night festivities, the *Herald* published a list of stockholders, including over eighty prominent doctors, lawyers, and businessmen, as well as a good number of the city's major retail stores and wholesale suppliers. The impression given by this list was that the Ben Ali represented a grand civic gesture, jointly funded by Lexington's old money, new money, and emerging white collar elite (typified by Berryman). However, unlike the Lexington Country Club, for example, the Ben Ali symbolized a commitment to the central business district and to the servicing of a broad, if highly stratified, audience. The diverse members of this audience could find their own level in the Ben Ali's twelve boxes, the 616-seat main auditorium, the 379-seat balcony, or the 416-seat second balcony (or gallery).

The new theater's ticket prices and its physical layout were designed to reaffirm the social hierarchy—purged, of course, of anyone who could not afford a second balcony ticket. In this respect it followed the model of the Opera House, rather than the all-seats-one-price policy of Lexington's new one-floor movie theaters, the Colonial and the Orpheum. And it was obvious from the outset that this "Theatre beautiful" saw only the Opera House, not the city's picture shows or the Hipp, as its competition.[17] At last Lexington had, in the words of the *Ben Ali Theatre Magazine*, "a Theatre fully the equal of any house in the East."[18] Indeed, the Ben Ali saw part of its mission as the "winning back" to the legitimate theater of those patrons "who have within

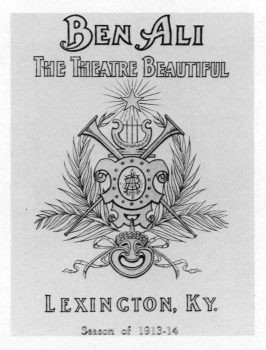

Selling elegance and class: the initial program design for the Ben Ali. Photo courtesy University of Kentucky Photo Archives.

the last few years changed their allegiance to the motion picture shows."[19] Berryman's first step in this project of cultural reclamation was aligning his new theater with the Shubert theatrical syndicate.

The eastern connection went further, however, for Manhattan architect W. H. McElfatrick had designed the Ben Ali, and the Tiffany Studios of New York City were in charge of its "entire decorative scheme." A spokesperson for Tiffany told the *Leader* that the Ben Ali, like "all the theaters, must cater to the ladies. We must arrange things so they will be benefitted, so none will be seated where there will be a harmful color effect, where every woman may feel that her own gown was thought of in arranging the lights."[20] The Ben Ali's promotional material placed much less emphasis on safety, technological sophistication, and convenience (prime selling points of the Colonial and the Orpheum) than on the new theater's spacious foyer and arcade, its top-grade, specially dyed carpeting, gold-decorated mahogany box seats, and numerous rest rooms for female patrons, even in the second balcony. Above all,

to showcase its high-class patrons, there was the Ben Ali's indirect lighting
and Tiffany's color scheme of peacock blue and gold, which gave the theater
what the *Herald* called an air of "exquisite taste and harmony," very much
"conducive to restfulness of vision."[21]

The high point in the Ben Ali's short-lived career as an eastern-styled
legitimate theater was unquestionably its opening night, 23 September 1913,
for which it booked *The Passing Show of 1912,* a comic variety revue. (As at
the Opera House, at the Ben Ali the "legitimate" was by no means synony-
mous with the high cultural.) The real show, however, was the "beautifully
dressed," "brilliant" audience, the cream of Bluegrass society, with James
Haggin occupying the right front lower box. "The elegant gowns seen in the
audience and the brilliancy of every detail made a gorgeous scene," gushed
the *Herald*'s society columnist.[22] Here was a spectacular event that no mere
picture show could hope to match: society on display, showcased by Tiffany's
tasteful decor.

How could the Ben Ali follow up this auspicious premiere? Assuming that
society could not be expected to arrive decked out in formal attire night after
night, then the 1,500-seat Ben Ali would have to find at least a good number
of its patrons from among Lexington's vaudeville fans and moviegoers. Even
had Berryman wanted to go all "legitimate," the Shubert Agency apparently
did not handle enough combination companies to fill the Ben Ali's schedule
of one- and two-night stands. (In larger cities like Louisville and Cincinnati,
where week-long engagements were common, an exclusively legitimate theater stood a better chance of success.) Thus the Ben Ali from its inception
adopted the type of booking policy that Charles Scott had successfully employed for over twenty years at the Opera House, a policy quite unlike that
of the Ada Meade or the Colonial. The question was, could Lexington—with
a population of about 37,000—support two large, multipurpose venues, especially considering the competition offered by the city's five other downtown theaters?

In the two months following its grand opening, the Ben Ali's schedule included revues, recitals, and band concerts, as well as combination companies
(such as *Bella Donna,* starring Nazimova), and Berryman underscored the
civic role of his new theater by allowing it to be used for a "tuberculosis mass
meeting," a speech by feminist activist Charlotte Perkins Gilman under the
auspices of the Lexington Equal Rights Association, a charity concert staged
by local African Americans, and a Knights of Columbus-sponsored lecture

on the "Menace of Socialism." Berryman also quickly began to book vaudeville and motion pictures. For example, Lexington's first extensive exposure to big-time vaudeville came in November 1913, when an eight-act program of Keith circuit vaudeville began running Thursday through Saturday at the Ben Ali, with performers on the order of Will Rogers and the Three Keatons, featuring Buster.[23] Rounding out the Ben Ali's schedule were such feature-length motion pictures as *The Undying Story of Captain Scott and Animal Life in the Antarctic*—a "living record in motion pictures," complete with lecture—and the "sensational white slave movie," *Traffic in Souls.*[24]

By the early 1910s, the number of special motion picture attractions (e.g., Sarah Bernhardt in *Camille* and Paul Rainey's African travelogues) had also risen at the Opera House, since Scott rarely booked rep troupes and scheduled somewhat fewer minstrel shows and combination companies than he had ten years earlier. He scored a particularly successful coup when Edison's Talking Pictures played to "well-filled" and "highly pleased" crowds at the Opera House in July 1913 and returned the following month during Blue Grass Fair week and again in October.[25] Then *Quo Vadis* had a week's run in November, followed by two bookings of the nine-reel *Les Misérables*, which the *Herald*'s reviewer praised as being "so eminent in its finish, so worthy in its theme that every collegian and school child old enough to understand should see it."[26] These feature-length, "classically" based motion pictures were something of an ideal attraction for venues like the Opera House: cloaked in culture, pedagogically sound, yet more extraordinary, spectacular, and scene-filled than a popular-price melodrama.[27] And for all the benefits it promised to provide students and responsible parents, *Les Misérables*, for example, cost just fifteen cents for matinees and twenty-five cents for evening shows during its return engagement at the Opera House.

The head-to-head competition between the Ben Ali and the Opera House lasted only seven months, for on 6 April 1914 the merger of the two theaters was announced by Berryman, who would serve as general manager while Scott supervised the booking and daily operations of both theaters. Henceforth all "important attractions," such as touring plays and most of the Keith vaudeville dates, would be presented at the Ben Ali, while the Opera House would have "minor attractions," including some vaudeville, amateur theatricals, and sporting events. As it soon turned out, the Opera House was rarely used, except for benefit shows like the First [Colored] Baptist Church's production of *Tallaboo*, "a play portraying the better life of the colored people."[28]

After being leased to a black entrepreneur for vaudeville and motion picture
shows during the 1914 summer season, the Opera House was for all purposes
closed by the Berryman Realty Company for the rest of the year.

Interestingly, the public announcement of the Opera House and Ben Ali
merger did not explain how the touring motion picture programs that had
become increasingly prominent at both theaters figured in the newly defined
split between "minor" and "important" entertainment attractions. Films did,
however, unquestionably remain a significant part of the Ben Ali's schedule.
The 1913–14 season, for example, concluded with a special two-day engagement of *Mexican War Pictures*, and the Ben Ali reopened in August with Annette Kellerman's *Neptune's Daughter* for a week, followed by the "startling
and sensational exposition of crime and vice," *Protect Us*. By the logic of the
merger announcement, these and other films like *America* and *The Last Days
of Pompeii* were *de facto*—and in fact—"important attractions." No minstrel
show or combination company booked into the Ben Ali during this period
received more glowing reviews in the local press than did the spectacular
Italian film, *Cabiria*. On 1 May 1915 Scott and Berryman announced that
henceforth the Ben Ali would drop attractions like the San Carlo Grand Opera Company and John Vogel's Minstrels in favor of an all-motion picture
format. Coming less than twenty months after this "Theatre Beautiful" had
first opened its doors, this change in policy was neither a risky nor a particularly unexpected move, though it did leave Lexington, for the first time in the
twentieth century, without a "legitimate" theater.[29]

A major "rehabilitation" of the Ben Ali signified this change. A gold fiber
screen was installed, as well as a new facade, "emblazoned with myriads of
lights, making the place one of the brightest spots in Lexington at night."[30]
This kind of eye-catching, electrified display apparently was the requisite
indication that the Ben Ali had truly become a moving picture show ready to
compete on a daily basis with the smaller venues just a brief walk away on
Main Street. To corner its proportionate (and therefore large) share of the
market, the Berryman Realty Company offered first-run programs that
screened continuously from 1:00 to 10:30 P.M. and changed almost daily,
thereby vastly increasing the number of potential customers. It did not have
access to the Chaplin shorts that were so successful at the Colonial and the
Orpheum, but the much more spacious Ben Ali could offer major releases
from Paramount, Fox, Mutual, and Famous Players, with stars like Mary
Pickford, William Farnham, and Theda Bara. Tickets were priced at five
cents for children and gallery patrons and ten cents for all other seats. Thus

Interior of the Ben Ali after its transformation into a movie theater. Photo courtesy University of Kentucky Photo Archives.

the Ben Ali's former multileveled stratification, based on the location of seats (box, main floor, front balcony, balcony, gallery) and the time of the performance (matinee versus evening), gave way to certain simple oppositions: children versus adults, gallery dwellers (including all the African Americans who attended this theater) versus everybody else.

Judging from the Ben Ali's promotional material, equally important as the new film schedule and low ticket prices was the newly acquired Hope Jones Unit Orchestra, said to be capable of replacing an entire orchestra, mechanically reproducing real sounds, and "registering in tone every phase of expression in harmony with the expression registered in the pictures."[31] This state-of-the-art Wurlitzer instrument was, in effect, another "marvelous" invention like the motion picture apparatus itself. Furthermore, the attention accorded the Ben Ali's acquisition of a Hope Jones Unit Orchestra strikingly testifies to the prominent role played by music/sound/aural accompaniment in the promotion as well as the exhibition of motion pictures in Lexington.[32]

In August 1915, as the Berryman Realty Company began to profit from the Ben Ali's position as the closest thing in Lexington to a picture palace of truly metropolitan scale, Berryman and Scott let out contracts for the remodeling of the Opera House. They announced that since "the Ben Ali has been a great success as a feature photoplay house and will be so retained now the year round," the Opera House was needed for "legitimate attractions."[33] This decision occasioned much local attention. It was not, however, the promise of Lexington being exposed to the latest Broadway revue or a star-studded revival of Shakespeare that spurred the *Herald*'s reviewer to wax poetic over the resurrection of the Opera House. With the reopening of this theater, "it will be like getting back home to the dear old house," the reviewer confessed, "where mother and the girls wept their gentle eyes red at *Way Down East*, and father and the boys sat in peanut heaven and 'cussed out' Simon Legree."[34] Here, in words as sentimental as the plays it evokes, is a description of the popular entertainment experience that resonates with ideological implications: the theater/house has become the home, a much-beloved site where reenactments of spectacular melodramas ritualistically (and cathartically?) move the entire, unpretentious, unsophisticated family to emotional heights, and in the process reaffirm both on and off stage the most conventional of gender roles. Even the shifting—cinematic?—point-of-view here is revealing, if only to remind us how little we can know in close-up, as it were, about the people who filled the gallery and the various other "subject positions" in a theater like the Opera House.[35]

It is tempting to ridicule this remembrance or submit it to some empirical acid test. As I have noted, the Opera House's schedule always included much more than hoary popular-price melodramas, and the *Herald*'s gushing tribute to a theatrical primal scene tells us nothing about the experiences of actual families at this house/home away from home. But this tableau does takes it place among several "descriptions," evocations, or hailings of the commercial entertainment audience mentioned thus far in this book: the mixed, democratic multitudes gathered for Circus Day or the Elks Fair; the "brilliant" and elegant society types on display during a pricey night at the Theater; the non-rowdy, non-"colored" visitors to well-run Blue Grass Park; the girls enjoying a vaudeville show in utter safety, under the watchful eye of L. H. Ramsey; the habitual movie fans so much desired by nickelodeon operators, and so on. In Chapter 6 we will see how certain of these images—contradictory fragments of what we might call the history of representations of reception—figured in local debates over censorship ordinances and Sunday film screenings.

Way Down East and *Uncle Tom's Cabin* were not among the plays scheduled for the refurbished Opera House as it began its renewed "legitimate" mission in November 1915 with a musical comedy, entitled *The Girl from Utah*. Before the Berryman Realty Company's joint operation of its two Lexington theaters could get fully under way, a large fire probably caused by faulty wiring destroyed the stage and the Hope Jones Unit Orchestra at the Ben Ali in the early morning hours of 11 January 1916. Damage was set at $80,000, and though no one was injured, the aftereffects—as described in the *Herald*—seemed suitably melodramatic: "the Main Street entrance was dark, grim and forbidding," while inside, the stage was "a mass of twisted girders, criss-crossed like straws in the wind, and a black waste of charred timbers and smoking wood."[36] Scott and Berryman immediately shifted the Ben Ali's film schedule to the Opera House, which by default became the site for the Lexington premiere of *The Birth of a Nation* (which will be examined at length in the following chapter). So, perhaps fittingly, the pathetic victims and reprobate villains of spectacular melodrama did return—albeit on screen rather than in the flesh—to the Opera House, home to *The Clansman* and so many revivals of *Uncle Tom's Cabin*.

The Ben Ali reopened on 10 April 1916 with a special three-day engagement of *Battle Cry of Peace*, which proved so popular it returned in May. As nearly as possible, the Ben Ali was restored to its condition before the fire, except that a ten-piece orchestra led by Turner Gregg had replaced the much-acclaimed Wurlitzer and a Saturday morning children's matinee that had been instituted at the Opera House was continued at the Ben Ali. According to an ad published in a special Chamber of Commerce newspaper supplement, the Ben Ali's mission was to provide "beautiful, wonderful and artistic productions of picture drama presented for your entertainment by the dearest idols of the screen with Gregg's Imperial Orchestra to charm the music lovers." We can term this the promise of a "legitimate" photoplay program on a par with any combination company—befitting the status of the Ben Ali, self-proclaimed "most beautiful picture show theatre in the South."[37]

With the Ben Ali back in business, the Opera House was left to draw from an increasingly limited number of touring attractions, ranging from Al G. Fields Minstrels and yet another revival of *Ben Hur* to the Russian Symphony Orchestra and Sarah Bernhardt's latest tour. As it had since its reopening in 1915, the Opera House also offered select motion pictures for multi-day engagements: for example, Metro's *Romeo and Juliet* and Thomas Ince's *Civilization,* the Annette Kellerman vehicle, *A Daughter of the Gods,* which toured with its own twelve-piece orchestra, and D. W. Griffith's *Intolerance,* which came with a quartet of singers as well as an orchestra. The Berryman Realty Company maintained this policy even after Scott left Lexington in May 1917 to aid the war effort by managing theaters at military bases in Iowa and Texas, eventually ending as a sort of trouble-shooter for Klaw & Erlanger.

Strand

The last important addition during the 1910s to Lexington's array of cheap amusement venues was the Phoenix Amusement Company's 1,600-seat Strand Theater. Though it was equipped with dressing rooms and a stage large enough for vaudeville acts, the Strand, unlike the Ben Ali or the Ada Meade, was built expressly as a movie theater. Located at 151 East Main, half a block east of the Ben Ali, across the street from the Phoenix Hotel and Union Station, it occupied a site where a livery stable had long stood.[38] As part of his agreement to lease the property to the Phoenix Amusement Company, Garret D. Wilson became a major stockholder in the new corporation, as did the *Herald*'s owner, Desha Breckinridge (also an investor in the Berryman Realty Company). Although the Phoenix Amusement Company took its name from Lexington's Phoenix Hotel and involved local investors, its first board of directors was from outside Lexington, including a real estate broker and an attorney from Louisville; secretary-treasurer Louis Zahler, from Chicago, who was hired to manage the Strand; and president Michael Switow, who also headed the Switow Amusement Company in Louisville. Thus, unlike the other theaters in the city opened during the 1910s, the Strand was not initially a locally controlled business venture.

The guiding force behind the construction of the Strand was unquestionably Switow, who more clearly fit the standard profile of a metropolitan-based commercial entertainment mogul than did John Elliott of the Colonial or Charles Berryman of the Ben Ali. According to his own promotional information, the self-made Switow began as a "penniless immigrant" with little formal education. Knowing a trend when he saw one, in 1906 he set up a moving picture show inside a restaurant he owned in Jeffersonville, Indiana. Two years later he built Switow's Dream Theater, the first of many venues he erected, operated, bought, and sold in Louisville and southern Indiana.[39] In fact, during the early 1910s, virtually all of the columns datelined "Louisville" in *Moving Picture World* contain a reference to the activities of Switow or another member of his family. He was, in the words of this trade magazine, a veritable "photoplay magnate," whose Switow Amusement Company and Broadway Amusement Company by 1915 controlled a good percentage of the film exhibition business in the Louisville area.[40] The Strand was his first foray into central Kentucky, and though Switow soon sold his share in the Phoenix Amusement Company, he returned to build two more theaters in Lexington in the 1920s.

Designed by the Louisville architectural firm of Joseph & Joseph, the $65,000 Strand sat a thousand people in the main auditorium, two hundred in thirty-two mezzanine boxes, and four hundred in the balcony. While the theater was under construction, the *Herald* reported that a "tier of seats in the upper balcony" would be reserved for black moviegoers, but two days later the Phoenix Amusement Company announced that the Strand would be "exclusively for white patrons," with no "colored" seating at all.[41] Switow and company doubtless reasoned that whatever black customers it lost would be more than made up for by white customers who preferred absolutely segregated commercial entertainment venues. By Lexington standards, the Strand's policy was more racist than the Jim Crow seating of the Ben Ali and the Ada Meade, with their "colored" second balconies: the Strand was, after all, not some storefront nickelodeon or small vaudeville house, but a venue that billed itself as one of the best in the state, a theater that had a balcony with a separate street entrance and yet still had no place for Lexington's African-American residents.

What white patrons would find at the Strand was one more variation on the theme of "beauty, comfort, and restfulness, things to be desired above all others in a picture house." The tiled, mirrored, and mahogany-trimmed front lobby opened onto a small foyer, which led to the main auditorium—all decorated in what promotional notices called an "Italian Renaissance style." Gilded plaster in a "lattice effect" graced the auditorium, which was shaded from dark to light olive green. Two ledges, one eight feet and the other twenty-two feet off the floor extended around the walls and were "used to display many handsome boxes of flowers." This same decorative style was apparent in the design of the Strand's front, with its white enamel brick, trimmed in stone. Rising twenty-five feet above this "Renaissance" facade was a green and white electric sign that flashed and "intermittently spelled out" the name

of the theater.[42] The design of this theater hardly approximates the fantasti-
cal, exotic decor of a 1920s metropolitan picture palace, but the Strand's
"Renaissance" trimmings (and particularly the two flower box-holding
ledges) were at least a modest nod in that direction.

At the same time, as might be expected given the other theaters I have
described, the Phoenix Amusement Company left no doubt as to its commitment to the quite pragmatic virtues of safety, efficiency, and comfort. The
Strand would be not only the "largest and most modern" but also the "most
fire-proof and sanitary theatre in the state of Kentucky." Steam radiators in
the auditorium provided heat, and ceiling fans, large ventilation ducts, and
rows of windows carried away any "fetid air." The 10 × 18 foot operator's
booth was guaranteed to be fireproof, and there were enough exits that the
entire theater could be evacuated in a matter of minutes.[43]

The opening of the Strand on 12 October 1915 was not quite as grand an
event as the premiere of the Ben Ali (or even the Ada Meade), though Lexington's mayor was among the honored guests taking part in the festivities. From
the first, the Strand adopted an all-feature (or "photoplay") policy: each film
played from 1:00 to 10:30 P.M. for one or two days, with music provided by a
"real $10,000 pipe organ."[44] Among the Phoenix Amusement Company's
special promotions were a Saturday morning children's matinee (in imitation
of the Ben Ali), special screenings for the DAR and a local automobile firm,
and even the production of a film that was shot in Lexington.[45]

In July 1916 Switow announced that the Strand was in satisfactory financial shape, though the directors of the Phoenix Amusement Company decided to assess stockholders $10,000, "to be applied in removing all
indebtedness against the company," after which "the stock will then be upon
a dividend paying basis."[46] Rumors circulated about a takeover by the Berryman Realty Company, a move that would have eliminated the "expensive
competition in pictures."[47] But instead it was the Colonial Amusement Company (operators of the Colonial and a string of area theaters) that in November
1916 acquired Switow's stock in the Strand. As a result, John Elliott was
named general manager of the Phoenix Amusement Company, whose new
board of directors included several Lexington residents, notably Democratic
political "boss" Billy Klair.[48] When the board met a month later, Switow resigned as president and Elliott was unanimously elected. The Strand, like
the rest of Lexington's motion picture theaters, was now locally owned and
operated.

Elliott immediately announced plans to improve the projection equipment and reduce the first-floor seating from one thousand to nine hundred, probably to accommodate better a new eight-piece orchestra. He began opening the theater at 10:00 A.M. rather than 1:00 P.M. daily, cut organ performances to only fifteen minutes per hour, and promised "stars of the first magnitude." According to the *Leader*, the Strand's profits in December 1916 had risen 60 percent since Elliott's takeover.[49] A month later the Colonial Amusement Company closed the Colonial Theater for good, and Elliott's motion picture operations in central Kentucky were thenceforth conducted under the banner of the Phoenix Amusement Company, with the Strand as its flagship theater.

Film Exhibition, Commercial Entertainment, and the Status of the Movies in 1917

Surveying theatrical entertainment in Lexington as part of a special "House Warming" issue, the *Herald* in April 1917 declared that with the Ben Ali, Orpheum, and the Strand in operation, "the movies have the day" in Lexington. This article, however, was also quick to point out that the current situation did not reflect any "deterioration" in "the taste for spoken drama among Blue Grass audiences." As in 1897 or 1907, in 1917 this still strong "taste" was assumed to signify an estimable level of refinement several rungs above the habit of moviegoing. Furthermore, the *Herald* reasoned that the higher tastes of Lexington's "cultured and enthusiastic audiences" could not be satisfied because the major theatrical booking agencies were victims of the tasteless "country at large," which had abjured the spoken drama.[50] Yet there still was legitimate theater to be found in Lexington during the 1910s at the Opera House and, for a time, at the Ben Ali. And even though big-time Keith vaudeville never proved economically feasible for any extended period, the inexpensive five- or six-act vaudeville shows at the Hipp/Ada Meade were a mainstay on Main Street. The stage had not disappeared, but as I have noted, motion pictures were essential to the economic survival of even the Opera House (with its booking of touring photoplays) and the Ada Meade (with its regular Sunday screenings).

That the movies were triumphant in the race or battle for Lexington's leisure-time market did not mean that other competitors were in a flash rendered obsolete by the emergent twentieth-century mass media or by an abstraction called "modernity." The cultural history of commercial entertainment—not to mention the workings of local politics, economics, and "taste"—is far more complex than that. Most of the principal forms of commercial entertainment from the pre- and early nickelodeon period continued into the 1910s.

For instance, in 1912, several years after the roller skating fad had peaked, the 4th Street rink briefly reopened, to be joined in 1913 by another short-lived rink located south of downtown in a tobacco warehouse. In November 1916, the 4th Street venue—now called the New Mammoth Skating Rink—was again in business, operated by a pair of Lexington men, and offering two daily sessions with music provided by an "electric orchestrian [sic]" and special events sponsored by local retailers. After the New Mammoth had been "turned over to Negroes" in March 1917, the city commissioners voted not to renew its license, citing protests by white property owners who claimed that the rink was a "fire trap" and a "menace" to the "peace and good order" of their middle-class residential neighborhood.[51]

Protest and official intervention also affected street fairs and carnivals, which continued to be staged by traveling companies under the auspices of local groups, often organizations with strong working-class ties, such as the Street Car Men's Union. By the mid-teens, such shows no longer included moving picture attractions, though otherwise they were little changed from the carnivals of a decade earlier, with a similar blend of wild animal acts, minstrel performers, "mechanical" exhibits, ferris wheels, and the like. Professions of cleanliness, legality, and uprightness were still *de rigueur:* the Blue Grass Federation of Labor, for example, assured the public that its 1916 carnival would contain "no immoral shows and no gambling."[52] But three days after this week-long carnival closed, the city commissioners passed an ordinance banning all street fairs and carnivals from setting up within Lexington's city limits, on the grounds that such attractions bring "disorderly and undesirable people to the city."[53] (Circuses and dog-and-pony shows were specifically excluded from this ban.) In effect, the new ordinance pushed such cheap amusements several miles from the central business district, with its electric marquees and up-to-date theaters that signified Lexington's urbanity.

Unlike street fairs, touring tent shows met with no interference from the city government during the 1910s. Such attractions had, however, become relatively few and far between. Not even the arrival of the Ringling Bros. circus in October 1916 could generate the level of interest common for major touring shows ten or twenty years earlier. Nor, for that matter, could the yearly Blue Grass Fair. The 1912 Blue Grass Fair was apparently the final one to include a motion picture show, and the *Herald* pointed out that this attraction was "patronized by many out-of-town visitors"—no doubt meaning country folk, if not actually bumpkins and rubes.[54] In later years, the fair's midway featured both old standbys (Wild West shows, minstrels, high-wire acts) and novel, "modern" attractions like tango dancers or tabloid shows. But the last glowing editorial I could find in local newspapers celebrating the opening day of the Blue Grass Fair as the "gladdest day of the year" appeared in 1913.[55] At the same time that the movies and other commercial entertainment were thriving in Lexington, the Blue Grass Fair seems to have lost much of its symbolic resonance.

Other summertime venues that I described earlier were also altered or redefined during this period. Woodland Park, for example, no longer had anything to do with the business of entertainment, which was conducted downtown, seven days a week, ten or twelve hours a day. Even a venue like the Lexington Railway Company's Blue Grass Park came to rely less and less on shows and commercial attractions as the decade progressed. In 1914 ads for this amusement park boasted of its dance pavilion, penny arcade, chute-the-chute, Sunday semi-pro baseball games, shooting gallery, and 300-seat airdome theater. Within two years, its prime drawing card was its new swimming facility, and Blue Grass Park had become primarily a site for daytime recreation, catering especially to children, picnicking families, and groups on prearranged outings. With the development of downtown theaters, the Lexington Railway Company (later the Kentucky Traction and Terminal Company) did not in the 1910s exert anywhere near the influence over leisure-time activity as it had when it developed Woodland Park and Blue Grass Park between 1900 and 1910. Yet the Railway Company's legacy was significant, both in terms of its promotion of the idea that leisure was time to be filled away from one's home and immediate neighborhood and in terms of its unequivocal endorsement of racial segregation.

Even this abridged survey of skating rinks, traveling shows, and parks suggests that during the 1910s the movies faced more competition in Lexington than just the spoken drama and inexpensive vaudeville. Yet it is difficult to think of Lexington's movie theaters as actually *competing* for customers with Blue Grass Park or the Federation of Labor's street carnival. Would movie attendance have increased substantially if these other leisure-time sites had not existed? Did movie theaters adjust their exhibition practices because of this "competition?" I think not. To say that the movies did indeed "have the day" in Lexington, as least by the time that the Ben Ali adopted an all-motion picture format in May 1915 means, for one thing, that they defined—for better or worse—what constituted "entertainment." So what was the status of the movies and of film exhibition in Lexington on the eve of the United States' entry into World War I, at roughly the point when, according to Kristin Thompson, the system of classical Hollywood cinema was "complete in its basic narrative and stylistic premises?"[56]

In 1917 Lexington had a population of about 38,000. Even with the closing during 1916–17 of smaller theaters like the Star and the Colonial, the city's movie houses had 3,312 seats, or about one seat for every eleven residents. (If the Ada Meade and the Opera House—which both regularly featured motion pictures—are also included, there were 5,446 seats, or one for every seven residents.) By way of contrast, in 1911, before the opening of the Colonial, Lexington's five nickelodeons had about 1,260 total seats, or one for every twenty-nine residents. Two other factors need to be taken into account in any such tabulations, however: the use of Lexington theaters by people who lived in rural Fayette County (about which no figures are available), and the effect of Jim Crow policies at local theaters. While African Americans in 1917 comprised some 30 percent of Lexington's population, only 12 percent of the seats in local movie houses were in designated "colored" sections. In effect, then, there was in 1917 one movie theater seat for every twenty-nine black residents, and one movie theater seat for every nine white residents.

Not just the number of seats, but the ownership of theaters is also significant. After the Colonial Amusement Company took over the Strand in November 1916, all of Lexington's theaters were locally owned and operated. John Elliott and the Orpheum's owner, John Stamper, had each been in the business for almost a decade; Charles Berryman was one of the better known businessmen in central Kentucky. Both the Berryman Realty Company and the Phoenix Amusement Company counted among their stockholders a good number of men who were very active in the civic and commercial life of the city. Lexington theaters were also local businesses in that their employees— ushers, ticket-takers, operators, and musicians—were virtually all city residents, as were those people who managed the theaters on a day-to-day basis: Stamper lived within a few blocks of the Orpheum; Nelson Gurnee moved his amusement company to Lexington after he leased the Ada Meade; Charles Scott had been associated with the Opera House since 1887; Slaughter Sparks rose from being an usher and then a doorman at the Princess, to become head usher at the Colonial and ultimately manager of the Strand. Being

locally owned and staffed, Lexington's theaters resembled other prosperous
and reputable downtown businesses.

I have no doubt that the experience of moviegoing was affected by the type
of musical/sound accompaniment provided and by the physical environment
of the individual theater: projection equipment, size, decor, luxuriousness,
and so on. I wonder if the knowledge that Lexington's theaters were local
enterprises also influenced the way moviegoers received the fare these theaters offered. In this regard, was attending the Ben Ali or the Colonial more
like shopping in a department store or a chain store or an owner-operated
specialty shop? Did it matter who owned or worked at the theater so long as
new product dependably filled the slots of a familiar format?

One thing that obviously did matter was the fact that programming was by
1917 quite systematic and regularized, no matter how much individual films
might vary from day to day. Within the stable, efficient business of film exhibition in Lexington there was little, if any, place for the occasional oddball
booking of the sort that had appeared at the city's moving picture shows even
five years earlier. No place, that is to say, for attractions like the Japanese
ex-soldier criss-crossing the country with films of the Russo-Japanese War
who was booked into the Princess Theater for a one-day engagement in
1912.[57]

By 1917 the format at the Ben Ali and the Strand was virtually identical:
tickets cost ten cents for adults and five cents for children; music was provided by an eight-piece orchestra (though only the Strand also had a full-
time organist); and the motion picture bill, usually changed daily, consisted
of a first-run multiple-reel film plus one or two short comedies, newsreels, or
serial episodes. Sometimes both theaters offered "double bills" of two- or
three-reel films. In contrast to the Ben Ali and the Strand, the Orpheum
charged five cents for all seats and almost never booked feature films. Stamper's five- or six-reel program, accompanied by a pianist, included four or more
different motion pictures, with at least one comedy on the bill, often paired
with a two-reel western, a serial episode, and/or a cartoon. In effect, film
exhibition in Lexington was now clearly divided into two tiers. The Orpheum
was not so much a second-run as a second-rank theater, featuring a shorter,
more modular program that had no "photoplay" pretensions, and the Sunday
show at the Ada Meade followed this same policy.

It is impossible to tell just how much the Orpheum's regular audience
differed from the Strand's or the Ben Ali's in terms of age, social class, and
gender, but the Orpheum's older-style, continuous exhibition format was

The pleasures and amenities of "high class" moviegoing. Lexington *Herald,* 15 April 1917.

seemingly better suited to lunchtime customers, kids after school, shoppers with only a half-hour or so to spare, and at least some of the Sunday family trade. In February 1918 the municipal government formally codified the distinction between the Orpheum and the city's larger theaters by substituting a graduated license fee scale for the previous flat $200 annual fee. Henceforth, theaters with under four hundred seats (i.e., the Orpheum) would pay $100, while those that sat over eight hundred (i.e., the Ben Ali and Strand) would pay $200. (The Ada Meade and Opera House, presumably because they offered live shows with more costly tickets than the movie theaters, were assessed $250 annually or $25 per month.) By cutting Stamper's license fee in half, the city commissioners affirmed, even if only indirectly, that the small, second-rank theater ought to have a place in Lexington.[58]

The place of motion pictures in general was a basic issue in the ongoing local debate over censorship and Sunday screenings, a controversy I will discuss at length in the next chapter. It was also directly taken up in four different accounts of the city's theatrical activities published in local newspapers. According to a *Herald* feature article, the movies, once merely a "midway attraction" for "younger folks," were by the beginning of 1914 an "enormous business" in Lexington, attracting 25,000 customers weekly.[59] From this view, increasing profits, popularity, and product sophistication all went neatly hand-in-hand, and film exhibition stood as a model of the well-operated, prosperous business. With similar optimism, a *Herald* survey of the city's theaters in 1916 set out to prove that "Lexington can justly claim to be an amusement town," with the Strand and Ben Ali, in particular, as its crowning glory.[60] Here the quality and quantity of commercial amusement are what marked Lexington as an expanding, economically vital urban center, firmly committed to the twentieth century.

In contrast, a *Leader* editorial published in May 1915, the same month that the Ben Ali changed to an all-film format, viewed the progress of motion pictures with some trepidation. For what, the *Leader* wondered, would replace the now outmoded nickelodeon, where "cheap motion pictures" served the "worthy purpose" of entertaining and informing the poor and uneducated and all those in "need of predigested mental food?"[61] This patronizing attitude toward mass culture and its audience informs another *Leader* editorial, this one from 1912, that bemoaned the use of the "alleged 'music'" (or "drivel") called "ragtime" in picture shows, but nonetheless praised the moving picture as "one of the greatest educational forces in our modern amusement life." Why? Because movies so effectively speak to the "thousands who have no opportunity to attend the regular theater."[62] If moving pictures are understood as a pedagogic rather than a business opportunity, then any attempt to elevate moviegoing above the reach of the lowest common denominator must be seen as a betrayal of the medium's important social mission.

Whatever their differences, none of these commentaries doubted the legitimacy of moving pictures, though both local newspapers could strongly oppose particular films. By the mid–1910s, those who entered into the public discussion of the movies in Lexington with few exceptions assumed (1) that film exhibition was a legitimate local business venture, a good investment, and a fit occupation; (2) that the production and distribution of motion pictures was a powerful, important national industry; and (3) that the broad appeal of the movies made them part of the fabric of daily life in America. It was quite a step further to assert that the motion picture, or at least the photoplay, qualified as an art, worthy of comparison with the spoken drama and potentially beneficial in its capacity for being informative and uplifting. Such an affirmation was explicitly made in January 1918, when the Lexington high school debating and literary society took as its topic, "Resolved that the motion picture is a benefit to the United States."[63] That this resolution would be selected as a topic worth debating is perhaps to be expected, given the local sabbatarian controversy; that the resolution passed is a pretty fair indication of the status of motion pictures in Lexington by the late 1910s.

Particularly germane in this context are the handful of reviews of individual films written by local critics for Lexington newspapers. Beginning with *Les Misérables* and *Cabiria* and then on through *The Birth of a Nation* and *Intolerance,* it was almost always the touring motion picture productions screened at the Opera House that the *Herald* and the *Leader* took the trouble to review.[64] Such films would be in town for from three days to a week, so a review of the opening night screening would be topical and even useful for the newspaper's readers. Furthermore, there is the clear sense that, as photoplays, these films merited reviewing by critics who usually covered spoken drama, recitals, concerts, and (less frequently) vaudeville.

Here, then, are contemporary, local reactions to specific motion pictures, something very difficult to come by. Yet as with all reviews that are marshaled as evidence in historical studies of reception, certain questions must be kept in mind: did these reviewers speak to and for the cultured minority? How constrained were they by the conditions under which they wrote? Did the attitudes of local reviewers vary substantially from place to place, or did certain well-entrenched (and ideologically charged) notions of beauty, coherence, refinement, and integrity inform this entire level of discourse about motion pictures in the 1910s? To put the matter concretely, would many other reviewers—or viewers—have agreed with dramatic critic James Ross of the Lexington *Leader,* who concluded that *Daughter of the Gods,* Fox's tropical fantasy starring the "daring, versatile and adorable" Annette Kellerman, was "by far the greatest film ever shown here," "as spectacular as *The Birth of a Nation* without any of the unpleasant features of that picture?"[65] On the one hand, we may justifiably ask which audience Ross represents: which viewers could possibly have seen either Griffith's racism or the crimes committed by his black characters as merely "unpleasant features" of *The Birth of a Nation*? On the other hand, the fact that Ross would have resorted to this euphemism, held Griffith accountable for unpleasantness, and praised *Daughter of the Gods* because it was not unpleasant does say much about the aesthetic and social value of good taste, propriety, and silence in a strictly segregated society. Thus we surely must add Ross's voice to the rest of the evidence we can muster about how a city like Lexington took in and took to the movies, so long as we do not treat it simply as some exemplary instance of reception.[66] And Ross's opinions, like all the information I have offered here about the status of the movies in Lexington, must be seen in the context not only of the greatly expanded local film exhibition business, but also the heightened controversy that accompanied this expansion.

SIX

Reform and Regulation

The opening of the Colonial, Orpheum, and Strand—along with the Ben Ali's adoption of an all-picture format—both affirmed and furthered the popularity of moviegoing in Lexington during the 1910s. That moving pictures came, for better or worse, to be an integral aspect of the city's leisure life is also demonstrated by the ongoing public debate between 1910 and 1916 over film exhibition practices, a debate that involved elected officials, theater operators, clergymen, newspaper editors, and other concerned citizens, both African-American and white. Precisely who promoted government regulation, prohibitive measures, and reform initiatives in Lexington, where such efforts were not primarily directed against "working class institutions and behaviors," as was the case, Roy Rosenzweig argues, in Worcester, Massachusetts?[1] The overarching aim in Lexington during the decade was to assert local control over commercial entertainment. At issue here is whether the campaigns for theater safety codes, local film censorship, strict enforcement of Sunday closing laws, and the banning of *The Birth of a Nation* differed to any substantial degree in their constituencies, rhetorical strategies, and practical methods. What values and assumptions informed this entire discourse about moviegoing and film exhibition, a discourse that directly and

122

indirectly raised questions about political power, social class, race, and ideological priorities in Lexington?[2] By 1917 the movies may have "won the day,"
but not without first giving certain citizens a reason or at least an occasion
for assessing what they expected of small-city life as Lexington moved further
into the twentieth century.

Regulating Theater Safety

One indication that Lexington's moving picture shows had become much
more than a passing novelty is that in 1910 certain municipal officials began
to propose building codes intended to ensure the safety of moviegoers, particularly from the danger of fire. The ensuing three-year effort to enact and im-
plement a theater safety ordinance begins to suggest how the relationship
among local politics, civic demands, and the business of commercial entertainment was negotiated in Lexington. Further, the conflict concerning the
regulation of motion picture theaters can be seen as something of a prelude
to the much more heated controversy later in the decade over censorship and
Sunday film screenings, when a different and more ideologically charged sort
of "safety" was at issue.

In May 1910, I. J. Miller, a successful merchant who was then chairing
the Joint Improvement Committee of the Board of Public Works, attempted
to pass an ordinance to "provide safety to the public against possible disas-
ter" by requiring theaters that show motion pictures to, among other things,
have three easily accessed exits, sufficient lighting at all times, a fireproof
booth for projection equipment, thirty-six-inch aisles, and seats "firmly secured to the floor."[3] Miller's concern was well founded, for catastrophic theater fires were often front page news. If passed and enforced, his ordinance
would, for all intents and purposes, have spelled the end of low-overhead,
under-financed nickelodeons and would have affected the city's larger theaters as well. Opposition to Miller was headed by L. H. Ramsey, who argued
that compliance with the ordinance would place undue financial strain on
theater owners; for instance, it would, he told city officials, "necessitate the
taking out of one entire row of seats . . . and so cut down the capacity of the
house."[4] Even though Miller had the support of the fire chief, Ramsey won
the first round of this "hot battle" when the board of aldermen tabled the
measure.

The following year Miller reintroduced his ordinance, now expanded to include all "places of assemblage, amusement or instruction," though his target was clearly the city's theaters, including the Opera House. The revised ordinance (no. 2693) added new requirements for a fireproof curtain, more stipulations regarding balcony areas, and a number of provisions concerning windows, lighting, and plumbing.[5] A building permit for the Colonial Amusement Company's new movie theater was held up, pending action on the ordinance. Though Ramsey and Charles Scott appeared before the Joint Improvement Committee to challenge the ordinance, the measure passed with only slight modifications on 8 June 1911. On August 29 Miller—motivated in part by a widely reported fire in a Canonsburg, Pennsylvania, movie theater that killed twenty-six people—complained to the mayor that the ordinance was not being enforced and that the Opera House, in particular, was not in compliance. Yet it was not until December of that year, soon after a small fire in the projection room of the Hipp Annex, that city officials issued a resolution prohibiting any further film screenings at the Hipp and the Opera House until changes were made in the fire escapes, exits, and stairways of these theaters.

Notwithstanding this resolution, both theaters continued to conduct business as usual. Ramsey even added a marble and polished glass soda fountain in the lobby shared by the Hipp and the Hipp Annex. After grand jury deliberations in May 1912, Scott received a summons, and Ramsey was indicted for violating ordinance no. 2693, as was John Stamper, whose Orpheum had just opened. In all three cases, however, what the *Herald* called a "satisfactory arrangement" was reached: Ramsey was to fasten the tables and chairs near his soda fountain to the floor; Stamper was to remove bars from the doors of the Orpheum to facilitate exiting; and Scott was to add a new emergency exit.[6] Demands for more costly alterations, including the removal of seats, were dropped after Ramsey met with the Board of Councilmen and Stamper filed for a restraining order from Fayette Circuit Court. Frustrated with the failure of city officials to press the issue, Miller resigned from the Board of Public Works, and the controversy faded away.

Lexington's theater owners had managed to circumvent Miller's civic-minded initiative. In fact, they had used this opportunity to proclaim publicly the absolute safety of their theaters. At no point did local newspapers or reform groups take up Miller's cause, and city officials were in 1910–12 simply not willing, it seems, to enforce regulatory measures that might severely hamper the growing business of film exhibition in Lexington. When it came to legally closing a skating rink in 1906 and again in 1917, the city did not hesitate, and under strong pressure from temperance supporters, local authorities often relied on the yearly ordinance procedure to at least give the semblance of controlling saloons. But if motion picture theaters were to be challenged, it would not be on the basis of their physical design and safety features. Luckily, there were no serious theater fires in Lexington until January 1916, when the Ben Ali suffered substantial damage from an early morning blaze. By a twist of managerial logic, this fire itself became something of a verification of the theater's safety provisions, as the Berryman Realty Company announced: "we are perfectly satisfied with the fire protection in the theater. The fireproof construction and the equipment restricted the blaze to a single location."[7]

While Ramsey and Stamper were taking on Miller and the Board of Public Works, they were also responsible for staging the inaugural convention of the Kentucky Motion Picture Exhibitors League, held in Lexington in April 1912. Presided over by Ramsey, this two-day meeting attracted some fifty "motion picture men" from around the state, as well as representatives of film companies such as Reliance and Gaumont.[8] Stamper was elected president and Ramsey secretary of the new organization, and the convention garnered front page coverage in both local papers.[9] Eileen Bowser notes that by the time exhibitors formed their first national organization—the Moving Picture League of America—in August 1911, it was too late for them to reclaim control of the motion picture industry from the manufacturers.[10] But on a state or local level, formally organized exhibitor groups could still serve important functions. Whatever practical benefits might have been gained by the formation of the Kentucky Motion Picture Exhibitors League—for example, in securing better product or in lobbying against state legislation—the symbolic import in 1912 of the league and its Lexington convention was apparent: film exhibition had nothing to do with itinerant showmanship or shoestring operations, for it was unquestionably a legitimate enterprise, conducted along familiar businesslike lines. The very existence of a League with officers and a convention was itself a testimony to the "safety" of the film exhibition business.

The Problem of Amusement

While the physical well-being of moviegoers was not adopted as a major cause by reformers and concerned citizens in Lexington, the protection of spectators' hearts and minds (and souls) surely was, as evidenced most dramatically by the highly vocal and visible campaign to enforce the Sunday closing law (the so-called "blue law"; see Appendix 2 for a transcript of this statute) and to institute local censorship of moving pictures. Of course, during the progressive era, film exhibition was neither the first nor the sole target for censure and regulation. In Lexington, the proponents of prohibitive social reform cast a wide net, eyeing easily influenced children and corrupt adults, saloons and brothels, dancing and moviegoing. I do not propose here to offer a complete account of this effort, but it would be misleading to suggest that local attempts to regulate the movies were unprecedented and unique.[11]

Thus, to cite an obvious example, sermons on the danger of the theater and amusement in general predate attacks specifically directed against the movies.[12] According to the pastor of the First Presbyterian Tabernacle in 1907, "the word 'amusement' means the absence of thought. In the light of the multiplicity of amusements of the present day, I am constrained to call this a thoughtless age. The world is mad on the subject of amusements."[13] The most dangerous forms of amusement, the Reverend Mark Collis of the Broadway Christian Church told young people and college students in 1909, were "card playing, theater going and the dance."[14] A more complete catalogue from a 1912 sermon lists "dancing, card playing, theater going, picture shows, baseball, excursions, horse racing and so on."[15] New styles of dancing repeatedly drew fire. When the *Leader* surveyed the ministers of prominent white churches in July 1913, they were virtually unanimous in condemning the turkey trot, tango, bunny hop, and other "suggestive" modern dances, which "are doing for our womanhood what the saloons are doing for our manhood." The faculty of Kentucky State University that same year banned such "unconventional dances" at all university-sponsored events.[16]

There was, however, no attempt to legislate control over dancing, aside from certain 1907 city ordinances aimed at so-called "Toledo joints," saloons with dancing that catered to an African-American clientele. When the *Herald* and several outraged citizens protested in 1913 against the "Negro dances" being held downtown at the National Guard Armory, their focus was not on the dancing itself but on the "public nuisance" created for nearby residents and on the harm that late-night cavorting did to young black women, who were thereby rendered "utterly unfit" for their day jobs.[17] Obviously, the problem of dancing—or amusement in general—could be posed in quite different ways, depending on who did the posing and whether the amusement was seen as sinful diversion (according to the church), as nuisance (for us, for our political economy), as threat (to our children, to young women), or as sign (of the present day's "madness," of creeping unconventionality).

Unlike the anxiety about suggestive modern dancing and Toledo joints or the Civic League's protest against street fairs with their "games of chance and other amusements,"[18] the drive for Sunday closing of motion picture theaters coalesced into a movement, with committees, public rallying of support, and political lobbying. Lexington's "crusade" for the enforcement of blue laws first took shape in February 1908, when several Protestant ministers and the secretary of the YMCA organized to take action "toward closing the moving picture shows, skating rinks and even the grocery stores that are keeping open on Sundays."[19] As early as 1896, "red-hot sermons" had denounced Sunday baseball games, though most attention was focused on saloons. In 1906 a successful campaign finally led to new city ordinances compelling saloons to close between midnight Saturday and 4:00 A.M. Monday morning. By 1908 nickelodeons had become a likely target, all the more visible because very little else besides churches, groceries, and barber shops was open downtown on Sundays.

However, for the next several years, other social and moral ills seemed more pressing. When, for example, the Moral Improvement League was formed in October 1911, prompted by the actions of the Ministers Union and headed by representatives of thirty-four city organizations (including the State University and the Central Labor Council, as well as the YMCA and the city's churches), its general aim was the "moral uplift of the city's youth" and its target was vice, in the form of drinking, gambling, and prostitution.[20] The Colored Ministers Alliance followed suit, setting up a series of public meetings to promote the "moral uplift of the colored race," much as the Good Citizens League of Colored Citizens had been organized in 1905 as a complement to the (white) Law and Order League.[21] (These ministerial and reform groups always remained racially segregated, even in the face of a common enemy.) The Moral Improvement League led efforts to strengthen restrictive ordinances dealing with saloons and to force the mayor to take action against "bawdy houses," which he did by ordering the police to close all "dance halls" in the red light district. Given the high profile of the Moral Improvement League in Lexington, it is all the more noteworthy that when prohibition came to a vote in the city in 1914, the "wets" won by a margin of 5,204 to 2,258, with "drys" in the majority in only four upper-middle-class white precincts.[22]

Sabbatarian Campaigns

Having set the Moral Improvement League in motion in 1911, the Ministers Union in January 1912 began circulating petitions calling for the closing of "all forms of amusement and practically all classes of business" on the Sabbath.[23] From the first, film exhibition was singled out, since the moving picture theater open on Sunday "tends to destroy the sacredness of the day and is not in the interest of morality and good order."[24] With the support of their congregations, seven ministers presented a formal resolution to the mayor, who took no action on the matter. A week later the Colored Ministers Alliance entered into the fray by announcing that it would hold weekly "evangelical" meetings on Sunday afternoons in order to "turn our people away from Sunday theaters and other places of questionable amusement."[25]

No doubt this church-sponsored initiative was a response to the growth of the motion picture business in Lexington: the Colonial and the Hipp Annex had opened in 1911 and construction plans had been announced for the Orpheum. The action of the Ministers Union might also have been prompted by the specific kinds of films shown on Sundays. In September 1911 Ramsey began to run a Sunday schedule at the Hipp that included a three- or four-reel film like *The Fall of Troy* or *Jesse James*. Within weeks, the *Herald* reported that Mayor John Skain had received "a number of complaints filed by numerous citizens concerning the character of the moving picture shows presented here on Sunday." Skain told the theater proprietors that "a class of subjects in keeping with the day [Sunday] might be substituted for some of the 'blood and thunder' themes such as hold-ups and robberies. The ladies and children of Lexington patronize these theaters in larger numbers on Sundays than possibly any other day, and it is deemed best to have more refined pictures on the Sabbath than have been exhibited at a number of times previously."[26] Skain's recommendation was similar to that offered by W. Stephen Bush in a December 1911 *Moving Picture World* editorial, "A Practical Solution of the Sunday Problem." Bush advised exhibitors to screen only "educational or religious" motion pictures on Sundays, for "nothing would add more dignity to the moving pictures, nothing would secure more respect for it from among the best classes than a good, clean educational entertainment on Sundays."[27] Such a policy would allow all to bask in the benefits of uplift: the audience, the medium, the industry, and the specific exhibitor.

By identifying the audience as "women and children who usually throng the theater on Sunday," Skain zeroed in on what was at stake in the sabbat-

arian controversy. Women and children had from the first been a much sought
after clientele for Lexington's moving picture shows, yet these same spectators were the people most in need of protection, lest their "sensitive natures"
be subject to "unwholesome effects."[28] (Recall Ramsey's claim that at the
Hipp he presented "clean shows, amusing without vulgarity, thus catering to
women and children.") Inseparable, therefore, from the question of Sunday
closings was the fundamental early twentieth-century problem of how to manage leisure time in a society enamored with or perhaps invaded by mass commercial entertainment. Both sides in the controversy had much to lose, either
in terms of impressionable women and children or in terms of a quite sizeable
chunk of weekly box office revenues.

As might be expected, the problem was not resolved by Skain's mild-
mannered proposal that exhibitors book a better "class of subjects," and it
was not settled via a compromise "arrangement," like the theater safety issue.
The mayor's handling of the situation was, however, typical of the way Lexington's elected officials attempted to placate citizens' complaints without
encroaching on local business practices. In the following years, when pressed
into taking sides, these officials would consistently look more favorably on
censorship demands than on requests that blue laws be rigorously enforced.
No doubt economics entered into the equation: since large Sunday crowds
accounted for well over 14 percent of the weekly box office take, Sunday
closing would cost theater owners much more than would local censorship.

In 1913 the same clergymen again pressed their demands in the name of
a "cleaner and more attractive city," arguing that Sunday movies "lower the
moral tone of a community" and "cultivate in the younger generation a spirit
of profanation . . . which bodes ill for the future of American citizenship."[29]
The Ministers Union fared no better this time around, although their insistence at least forced the terms of disagreement to become publicly clarified.
The city commissioners went on record in favor of allowing Sunday shows to
continue, as did County Judge J. Percy Scott, who offered his opinion in an
interview published in both local newspapers.[30] Challenging the status quo,
a committee of black Baptist ministers presented a resolution to the mayor
and the city commissioners, requesting enforcement of the Sabbath laws and
censorship of "shows that are not conducive to the best morals of the race."
According to this particular resolution, Sunday moving picture shows and
saloons illegally open on the Sabbath were part of the same problem.[31]

The most detailed sabbatarian argument was offered by the Reverend
O. J. Chandler of the First Methodist Episcopal Church, whose lengthy letter

to the editor appeared in both the *Herald* and the *Leader.* Attempting to prove that "Sunday picture shows are both unamerican and unchristian [sic]," this pastor questioned the validity of allowing such issues to be decided by elections or tallies of "public sentiment": who constitutes or speaks for the "public"? Chandler cogently asked. At the same time, Chandler rejected any claim that Sunday movies were harmless diversions or a sort of lesser evil. He condemned the invidious, seductive power of motion pictures, with their "suggestions of infidelity in the marriage relations, and disappointed love and wild west ideals," all of which whet the young spectator's "already sharp appetite for evil." Moreover, the "Sunday picture show is the common meeting place for both boys and girls who are bent on 'seeing life'," and so are led down the most "ruinous course."[32] One could hardly ask for a more striking image of the moviegoer-as-adolescent or more unequivocal (albeit unsympathetic) testimony to the allure of film narratives and to the medium's capacity to fuel *wanderlust* and scopophilic desires.

Critics of sabbatarianism, such as the anonymous "churchman" who wrote a letter to the *Herald,* might share Chandler's assumption that "the trend of the lives of the young is largely determined by what they do in their leisure hours," but they reasoned that concerned citizens should put pressure on the city government to increase playground appropriations rather than attempt to ban Sunday movies, "a form of entertainment and relaxation which to say the least is not opposed by many conscientious citizens."[33] In good progressivist fashion, this argument proposed that there is a reasonable, secular, public solution (playgrounds) to the problem (or, better put, the opportunity) of leisure. This line of reasoning is indicative of those forces within Lexington's reform movement that were committed to amelioration.

Such arguments could do nothing to sway the opinions of the Ministerial Association, and in May 1913 Chandler led another delegation to confront city officials, compelling newly elected mayor J. Ernest Cassidy to justify his defense of Sunday movies. There were three rationales for Sunday shows, according to Cassidy: motion pictures "afforded legitimate amusement, entertainment and instruction to the general public," thus preventing people from being "tempted into other paths much more demoralizing"; theaters did not open until 1:00 P.M. on Sundays, after morning church services; and probably most important, if Lexington offered no Sunday picture shows, then residents would be "forced to leave the city on excursions to secure relaxation and entertainment, spending their money in other cities and towns."[34] In other words, in matters of commercial entertainment, the needs of the "general public" and the health of the local economy took top priority. With the mayor securely in their camp, the proprietors of motion picture theaters did not need to actively promote their own interests, as they had done when faced with the theater safety ordinance.[35]

What the defenders of the Sabbath required was something to forge Lexington's churchgoers into, as one pastor put it, a "spiritual, well disciplined army, able to dominate public thought and control public action."[36] This they got in February 1914, when Charles Berryman announced plans to book Keith vaudeville on Sundays at the Ben Ali.[37] By a three-to-two margin, the city commissioners and the mayor voted to allow Sunday vaudeville on a probationary basis, and the initial performance played to good crowds on February 15. Within days, the sabbatarians had marshaled their forces in a show of strength comparable to the efforts of the Law and Order League in 1904 and the Moral Improvement League in 1911. Bowing to the pressure, Berryman on February 17 canceled plans for additional Sunday vaudeville shows at the Ben Ali, but this did not put an end to the controversy.

Many of the same Baptist and Christian Church clergymen who had been active in years past delivered sermons on the issue and helped to orchestrate public protest. But when the advocates of blue laws gathered at the Opera House (then still in competition with the Ben Ali) on February 22, the principal speakers were all laymen: a bank cashier, a grocer, and the owner of a laundry, as well as the dean of the state university law school and the head of the board of education. The "laymen's committee of fifteen" formed at this meeting was chaired by the president of the Fayette National Bank. These speakers did not so much attack motion pictures and vaudeville as exalt the role of the church in Lexington, defend the "civilizing" effect of Sabbath observance, and call for the closing of all businesses on Sunday, including barber shops and groceries.[38] In so doing, they attempted to transform the sabbatarian debate into something of a referendum on Lexington's very status as a law-abiding, moral community.

The *Leader*, Lexington's Republican newspaper, for the first time overtly took a position in the controversy, running an editorial on February 14 denouncing Sunday vaudeville as an affront to Lexington's "standing as an educational and commercial center."[39] (Berryman, as noted earlier, was a prominent leader in the local Republican party.) Two days later, a more circumspect *Leader* editorial called for a ban on Sunday vaudeville, as well as the censorship of Sunday moving pictures because "Lexington is not a cosmopolitan city. It is a peculiar town. To an unusual degree it preserves the traditions of pioneer days, when the church was the center of the social life of the people. There are few foreign-born residents of Lexington. There is no large factory class here which must of necessity have all forms of amusement open to its members on Sunday."[40] The 1910 census bears out the *Leader*'s description, for less than 3 percent of the population in 1910 were identified as "foreign-born" whites (and a good portion of these were long-time residents born in Ireland or Germany). Even though the city grew by almost 9,000 people between 1900 and 1910, the total number of foreign-born residents had increased by only twenty during this decade.[41]

The *Leader*'s editorial assumed that local conditions should determine how the business of commercial entertainment is conducted. Lexington's "peculiarity"—and implicitly, perhaps, its asset—is here identified as its virtual lack of immigrants and a "factory class"; by remaining true to itself, it could retain the "traditions of pioneer [read: American? ante-bellum?] days." Thus again at issue was the definition, and hence the direction and destiny, of the city itself.

Although the *Leader* estimated that 90 percent of Lexington's residents, "without regard to race or creed, are opposed to introducing the continental or wide-open Sunday into the life of the community,"[42] the public outcry in 1914 succeeded only in preventing further Sunday vaudeville performances at the Ben Ali. When a committee appointed at the Opera House mass meeting presented its proposals to city officials, the mayor based his objection on the citizens' right to "personal freedom": "if this Sunday observance is carried so far as to close the picture shows, barber shops and the ball parks on Sunday, then the thing will become so obnoxious that the citizens will rise in their might and in their demand for personal freedom, everybody will become a law-breaker."[43] Even the *Idea*, the student newspaper at the State University which rarely commented on local (or controversial) issues, ran an editorial that declared: "If closing the grocery stores and pictures shows will also shut the hollow heads that continue to howl about a holy Sabbath, the *Idea* will stand for closing and will almost agree to shut down the preachers in order to give quietude a handicap over quibbilitude, and Holiness an advantage over hollowness."[44]

The rhetoric of the 1914 campaign suggests that the entire sabbatarian movement in Lexington during the 1910s can be understood, in part, as an example of the "status politics" that Joseph R. Gusfield defines in his study of the American temperance movement. "Status issues," Gusfield writes, involve the sense of "opposed systems of moralities, cultures, and styles of life," and campaigns for the closing of saloons (or of theaters) are, in effect, "symbolic crusades" for status, respect, and prestige fought in "public arenas." "What is at stake," he concludes, "is not so much the action of men, whether or not they drink [or go to the movies on Sunday], but their ideals, the moralities to which they owe their public allegiance."[45] The more the defenders of the Sabbath attempted to flush out of hiding the other side (whoever they were), the more the sabbatarians resembled what Gusman calls the "coercive reformer" who "has begun to feel that his norms may not be as respected as he has thought. He is less at home and somewhat more alien to his own society."[46]

By this line of reasoning, the vehemence, visibility, and persistence of the sabbatarian movement in Lexington are indicative of just how anxious traditional-minded, white, middle-class Protestants (and some more Evangelical congregations and black churchgoers) had become about the public status of their values in the second decade of the twentieth century. As a "symbolic crusade," sabbatarianism seems to be of a piece with the temperance movement, and the Sunday moving picture show—set against the Sunday church service—becomes a fit symbol of an opposing "group mentality and life style," one that is secular, consumerist, national, and profit-oriented.

Lexington's sabbatarian movement did unquestionably seek prestige and allegiance; it was not, however, solely a "symbolic" initiative, for it had a precise, tangible agenda and it asserted what power it could to reshape the leisure life of the city. Perhaps Mayor Cassidy was being somewhat disingenuous or simply naive in elevating the question into a matter of "personal freedom," but he did realize that the demands of sabbatarianism, if enacted, would have directly affected the lives of working people and the health of the city at large.

The other point to be raised about Lexington's "symbolic" sabbatarian crusade is that it was fought in the local trenches; it was, in other words, undertaken and negotiated in a quite specific social and historical context. During the mid–1910s the same kind of arguments and the same status seeking would likely have been found in most places where the availability of Sunday movie shows was a heated issue. Still, consider how varied the outcome of such crusades could be, even in as homogeneous a place as Kentucky. In the small western Kentucky town of Cadiz, for example, the owner of the Lyric Theater agreed to close on Wednesday as well as Sunday evenings, since at these times "residents of Cadiz are expected to attend church."[47] However, in Henderson, across the river from Evansville, Ohio, the city council rejected in 1913 and again in 1914 sabbatarian proposals presented by two churches.[48] And in Owensboro (which then had a population of over 10,000), the city council in 1916 passed a resolution allowing Sunday movies, but only for "colored" moving picture shows, since the city's "negroes would be better off at the picture house than in frequenting dives."[49]

The Owensboro plan, no less than the solution in Cadiz, was not a possibility in Lexington, where the proponents of Sunday closing received support in February 1915 from the grand jury, which was acting on instructions from Circuit Court Judge Charles Kerr. Kerr advised the jurists that regardless of the "wisdom of the law," they had "no option but to indict" the operators of moving picture theaters who opened for business on Sundays. As a result, indictments were handed down against the owners of the Colonial, Orpheum, and Gem.[50] The county attorney proposed a compromise solution: if the owners would agree to close their theaters from 6:00 to 7:30 on Sunday evenings—that is, during evening church services—the indictments would be "annulled." The owners rejected this offer because they felt they were already deferring enough to the churches by not opening until 1:00 P.M. on Sundays; any other concessions would be too costly and would imply that the movies were not a form of "innocent amusement."[51] When local theaters continued with business as usual, a second round of indictments was issued, and the Kentucky Motion Picture Exhibitors League resolved to support its Lexington members.

Buoyed by the action of the grand jury and hoping to influence the verdicts when the indictments came to court, the self-styled "Sabbath observance" forces began their 1915 campaign, now led almost exclusively by clergymen and aimed specifically at Sunday moving picture shows. On March 13, local ministers enlisted the aid of Dr. Wilbur F. Crafts, founder of the American Sabbath Union and one of the country's most prominent supporters of federal censorship of motion pictures.[52] Crafts was brought to Lexington for a series of Sunday rallies, including an afternoon address to blacks at the African Methodist Episcopal (AME) Church and a public mass meeting that evening at Woodland Park auditorium, where he spoke to a capacity crowd on "The Uses and Abuses of Motion Pictures and Their Relation to Sunday and Law Enforcement." Crafts attacked the National Board of Censorship and charged that the operation of "commercialized amusements" on Sunday was an affront to the principles of "good citizenship." "There are no 'blue laws'—they are all red, white and blue laws," Crafts declared, and if these laws go unenforced, churches will not be able to fill their all-important civic task of "the making of the youth into good citizens."[53] For Crafts, the heart of the matter was less sinful pleasure and the fate of individual souls than the very existence of a legally constituted commonwealth that depended on "good," law-abiding citizens. "It isn't religious narrowness that prompts the movement" for strict Sabbath observance, the pastor of the Second Presbyterian Church told his parishioners, "it is good citizenship. It is sound statesmanship. It is sound social psychology. It is sound civic idealism."[54]

The mayor and the commissioners were clearly not having any of it. When approached by a delegation of ministers in March 1915, "the City Fathers reiterated more emphatically than ever their approval of the Sunday movies, base ball, and other 'harmless pastimes.'"[55] A *Herald* editorial was not quite so "emphatic," though it did suggest that "the theaters provide for the poorer classes what automobiles and clubs provide for the richer class," and it advised that the matter of Sabbath observance be left for the courts to decide, in accord with the will of the majority.[56] By all appearances, the public was largely satisfied with current arrangements. Seven local theaters were screening films on Sundays, and a Lexington attorney had even begun to circulate petitions opposing Sunday closings—hence the theater owners unwillingness to strike a compromise with the county attorney.

When the grand jury indictments were finally brought to trial in January 1916, each proprietor pleaded guilty and received a very modest ten-dollar fine. The *Herald* reported that "it is not believed that the technical violations of the law will be enforced again."[57] The theater operators decided to pay the fines and not seek a state court ruling on the applicability of blue laws to Sunday operation of moving picture theaters. Economic priorities, "innocent amusements," and "personal freedom" had won the day.

Well, almost won the day. The sabbatarian movement returned with a vengeance in 1918 and again in 1920. Even during 1912–16, efforts at instituting local censorship of the movies succeeded where the campaign for Sunday closings had failed. Wilbur Crafts and several other defenders of the Sabbath had linked censorship and Sunday closings, but there were notable differences between the predominantly Protestant church-led attempts to restrict the operation of moving picture theaters and the push for greater community control over what these theaters showed.

The Fear of Offense

The specific films that sparked controversy in the 1910s, like the stage productions of *Uncle Tom's Cabin* and *The Clansman* some years earlier, are unquestionably significant in any account of how Lexington responded to
commercial entertainment. For the reception of these "dangerous" texts reflects the anxieties felt by various residents of the city, insofar, of course, as
these residents had a voice deemed worthy of being acknowledged by the
local press. The way such texts entered into public discourse and were dealt
with by city officials again brings to the fore the workings of local politics
and the ideological tensions in the community. Yet these particular instances
of censorship in practice are best seen not as ruptures in an otherwise harmonious calm but rather as manifestations of an ongoing concern with the suit-
ability, power, and consequences of popular amusements.[58]

During Lexington's pre-nickelodeon period, this concern showed itself in
a variety of ways: for example, in sermons that condemned the modern stage
as an altar to the "god of pleasure," catering to the "lust of the eye, lust
of the ear";[59] in the mayor's demand in 1903 that an itinerant exhibition of
"anatomical specimens and wax figure novelties" be closed until "certain
objectionable features were removed";[60] and, perhaps most revealingly, in
the way the promoters of commercial entertainment attempted to forestall
reprobation and censorious action even as they hawked their products in the
marketplace. Virtually all entertainment enterprises undertaken in Lexington felt at least some pressure to legitimate the pleasure they promised to
provide, particularly if they sought to attract women and children. Who
knows just how deeply husbands and fathers and the "respectable" class at
large feared the power of amusements to offend and corrupt? But this fear
was regularly—obsessively—addressed in the advertising for popular-price
stage productions, fairs, and all manner of shows. Even a rather innocuous
1899 dog-and-pony show assured would-be patrons that its performances
"may be witnessed by the most refined amusement lovers without fear of offense."[61]

This "fear of offense"—an anxiety concerning impressionability and the
perils of watching—found its corollary in the fear of the audience as a com-
mingled, dangerous crowd. As noted in Chapter 2, a prime selling point of
the vitascope exhibition at Melodeon Hall was that "any lady may visit one
of these performances without an escort with perfect impunity."[62] Customers
were promised an experience untainted by what the proprietors of the 1903

Maccabee Carnival and Jubilee referred to as "a certain worthless and undesirable element."[63] (How *was* this "element" defined? Primarily in terms of
race, class, age, gender, or in terms of employment history, educational level,
rural upbringing, disorderly behavior, bad manners? Were all people deemed
to be "worthless" necessarily "undesirable" and vice versa?) In this manner,
commercial entertainment around the turn of the century was marketed in
Lexington as safe and inoffensive, at times even as uplifting and educational.
However "cheap" it might be, it attempted to situate itself closer to the first-
class offerings at the Opera House and the Chautauqua Assembly than to
the saloon.[64]

The vaudeville theaters and nickelodeons that opened in 1906–8 were
often promoted in a quite similar fashion. The short-lived Lyric Theater, for
instance, promised that a "competent member" of the police force would be
present at every performance; L. H. Ramsey introduced a "censor rehearsal"
on Monday afternoons at the Hipp so "anything which could be objectionable
to ladies and children can be cut out."[65] The first nickelodeons also took the
moral and social high ground in soliciting patrons and attaining some measure of respectability. One of the few large newspaper ads for the Alvin Theater averred that "perfect order will be maintained. Ladies and children
without male escorts will be carefully looked after."[66] Similarly, the Gem
Family Theater advertised "clean, moral, up-to-date entertainment at popular prices"; while the Star Theater offered "polite, fashionable moving pictures."[67] Suitably vague claims of this sort were hardly unique to Lexington.
But it is worth noting how these last two ads find no contradiction in selling
moving pictures as *both* "polite" *and* "fashionable," "moral" *and* "up-to-
date."

Such claims came to be less important (or at least less often explicitly
proclaimed) as moving picture shows became an accepted fact of life in the
city. Daily ads and promotional copy in local newspapers increasingly
focused on the product itself. Yet there was also an undercurrent of what we
might call "defensive" self-promotion, addressed at any abiding misgivings
concerned citizens might have about the legitimacy of the movies. Thus Stanley Platt, the manager of the Princess, reassured potential patrons in October
1908 that "great care is used in selecting the pictures for this popular theater.
All pictures of a sensationalistic nature are rejected and only those that teach
a good moral lesson are accepted."[68] (Promises, needless to say, can be broken: the Princess' schedule at this time was as likely to include *Fun at the
Bridal Party* and the boxing film, *A Battle Royale,* as the *Life of Moses* and

the *Life of Abraham Lincoln*.) What Platt promised was a carefully monitored exhibition policy, overseen by the wise and rigorous guidance of the industry-supported National Board of Censorship of Motion Pictures: "the Princess is licensed by the Motion Picture Patents Company," one promotion notice declared, "and that is assurance that every subject is examined by the 'Board of Censors', who refuse every subject unless it is an attraction of refinement and clarity."[69] Appeals of this sort to the paternalistic authority of the Board of Censors would remain an important recourse for Lexington film exhibitors during the years when advocates of Sunday closing and strict censorship mounted their campaigns.[70] For example, John Elliott of the Colonial defended his Sunday screenings by citing the Board of Censorship, and when Wilbur Crafts attacked the board in the Lexington speeches referred to earlier, Nelson Gurnee of the Ada Meade took out a half-page ad listing the "absolutely unimpeachable" members of the board and defending its integrity and social usefulness.[71]

Local Censorship in Action

Gurnee's testimonial to the National Board of Censorship was published in April 1915, several months before city officials enacted a local censorship ordinance. Up to this date, the few films deemed objectionable were dealt with individually. For example, when the wife of a prominent retailer arrived at a May 1912 session of the Juvenile Court to complain that the motion picture shows in local theaters were not "proper for a young person to witness," the presiding judge told her that no legal recourse was possible, "as long as the shows were decent."[72] But in the case of the motion pictures of black heavyweight Jack Johnson's defeat of the "white hope," Jim Jeffries, in July 1910, action was quick and categorical, as might be expected. Like officials in countless other cities and towns, Lexington mayor John Skain, acting in consort with the police court judge, barred the Johnson-Jeffries fight film, since it would likely "demoralize and appeal to race prejudice" and so disrupt the "friendly relations" that exist between "our people" and the "colored race."[73] The judge cited a law giving him jurisdiction over "all cases of riots, routs or unlawful assemblies within the city"; the mayor said he would invoke the state statute that banned *Uncle Tom's Cabin* and other racially inflammatory performances.[74] The *Herald* and the Women's Clubs of Central Kentucky immediately endorsed this prohibition, and there was apparently no protest by either local theater owners or Lexington's black residents. Unlike the unsuccessful attempt to ban fight films in 1897, the local censure of the Johnson-Jeffries fight film was not a response to prizefighting per se, but rather to racial and racist fears.[75] In fact, the Opera House had in April 1910 shown films of the Wohlgast-Nelson fight, and in August 1911 films of a light-weight championship fight were booked into one of Lexington's nickel-odeons.[76]

Skain's successor as mayor, J. Ernest Cassidy, also had little problem when he sought, for the first time in Lexington, to halt the exhibition of a motion picture being shown by a local theater. After a number of women in September 1912 complained about *Driven by Death*, then booked at the Star, Cassidy dispatched the chief of police to watch this film and stop the show if he deemed it "immoral." And so the chief did, after viewing a reel and a half. The Colonial Amusement Company complied with this ruling, and Elliott turned the situation to his advantage by declaring that his company "desired to show pictures of the best kind and any found to be objectionable would be immediately discontinued."[77]

The limits of the mayor's prerogative in censorship matters and of Elliott's willingness to comply with official edicts were tested less than a week later when *Resurrection*, starring Blanche Walsh, was booked for two days at the Colonial. *Moving Picture World* found this four-reel adaptation of Tolstoy's novel to be "so finished that it may be said to herald the Future Photo-drama."[78] Certain people in Lexington obviously thought otherwise, and Mayor Cassidy, again acting on complaints from local citizens, requested that the Colonial Amusement Company set up a preview screening of the film. To pass judgment on *Resurrection*, the mayor appointed Lexington's first Board of Censors, composed of County Judge A. Percy Scott, the dean of Christ Church Cathedral, and the pastor of St. Paul's Catholic Church. Both clergy-men, however, were dropped in favor of members of the city council, who were more in a position to take action if the situation warranted it.[79]

The newly constituted board, representatives of the press, the chief Juvenile Court officer, and other "invited guests" attended the special screening of *Resurrection*. While several officials found the second and third reels of the film to be "strongly suggestive," only Judge Scott felt that this section justified suppression of the entire film as "immoral." Elliott was not nearly as compliant as he had been regarding *Driven by Death* (no doubt he stood to lose much more money if *Resurrection* were banned since his company had purchased the Kentucky state's rights for the film). He cited the fact that

Blanche Walsh's stage production of *Resurrection* had played the Opera
House in 1910 without any protest whatsoever; he also obtained a telegram
from the National Board of Censorship indicating its approval of the film.
Judge Scott reversed his decision and agreed to allow *Resurrection* to be
shown, provided that children were barred and "young girls under eighteen
be not admitted to the production, unless accompanied by an adult."[80] The
wording of the Colonial's ad was not quite so gender-specific: "No One Admitted under Eighteen Years of Age Unless Accompanied by Parents."

Local censorship, exemplified by the three examples just discussed, could
be a matter of banning a film from being exhibited in the city (the Johnson-
Jeffries fight film), suppressing a film already being shown (*Driven by Death*),
or restricting the audience for a particular film (*Resurrection*). However, with
the number of motion pictures that passed through Lexington during this period of daily changing bills, a truly effective system of local censorship would
have been virtually impossible.[81] Perhaps the best that could have been
hoped for was that exhibitors would find it in their own interest to be (or at
least seem to be) ever vigilant. For almost two years this system—or lack of
a system—worked. The state WCTU in October 1913 emphasized the need
for "supervision over moving picture shows,"[82] and the local chapter of this
organization voiced their concerns to the mayor two months later. But no specific films in 1913–14 were hauled before Lexington's ad hoc Board of Censors, not even sensationalistic "white slave" melodramas like *Protect Us* or
Traffic in Souls, which had much-publicized runs at the Ben Ali at around
the same time that Lexington's Vice Commission was conducting its investigation of "commercialized vice" in the city.[83]

The demand for censorship again became a pressing issue in 1915,
prompted once more by a film booked by the Colonial Amusement Company.
On 30 August 1915, the Board of City Commissioners, based on reports it
had sought from municipal officials in Cincinnati and St. Louis, voted unanimously to forbid the exhibition of the Universal photoplay *Hippocrites* (also
known as *Hypocrites!*), a "film allegory" directed by Lois Weber that featured
"the figure of an undraped woman."[84] Cassidy, according to *Moving Picture
World*, "stated that he did not believe that the Lexington Vice Commission
could gaze upon the picture unmoved."[85] Nonetheless, Elliott went ahead
with the planned screening. In fact, his advertising exploited the sensation
caused by *Hippocrites*, advising patrons to see the first of the thirteen hour-
long performances of this "film classic," lest subsequent screenings be prohibited by city authorities.[86] At a city council meeting one of the commission-

COMING TO THE COLONIAL Fri., Sept. 3

Bosworth's Sensational Four-Act Drama

HYPOCRITES

Written and Produced by Lois Weber.

Courtney Foote as Gabriel, the Ascetic, and as the Minister, one of the most extraordinary pictures ever placed before the public.

By means of an absorbing story and superb allegory, it flays mercilessly those people who, faulty and evil themselves, yet dare to condemn the seeker after Truth. The play is a daring one in its frankness, but has been handled by Miss Weber with the most exquisite delicacy, so that it is entirely without offense to the most critical.

One of her inspirations for the story was the painting by A. Faugerson, now in the Paris Salon, called "The Truth," a painting which has caused more discussion than any painting of late years. Margaret Edwards plays the delicate and unusual role of "Truth." Rôles of great appeal and strong contrast are played by Miss Myrtle Sledman and Miss Dixie Pau.

We are showing this picture in spite of the refusal of the Lexington Board of Commissioners to allow us to do so; because after hearing the views of the cities where it has been shown we honestly think the picture, though involving the use of the figure of an undraped woman, is so artistically done and carries such a strong moral lesson, that after the commissioners see it, instead of condemning it, they will place their stamp of approval on it. However in order to be sure and see this picture you had better come to the first show at 10 A. M., Friday.

In addition to the Hypocrites—the last Chapter of the serial Beautiful—"The Goddess" will be shown. We tried to have The Goddess transferred to some other day but could not do it.

Admission For This Day Only 10c

No Children Under 16 Years of Age Admitted Unless Accompanied by Parent or Guardian.

Show starts 10 a. m., 11 a. m., 12 m., 1 p. m., 2 p. m., 3 p. m., 4 p. m., 5 p. m., 6 p. m., 7 p. m., 8 p. m., 9 p. m., 10 p. m.

Come early if you want to see this film classic and avoid the rush.

Hypocrites screened in defiance of city officials. Within two weeks of this showing, Lexington had a local censorship ordinance. Lexington *Herald*, 3 September 1915.

ers proposed that the chief of police be ordered to "at once stop the exhibition of this picture," but his motion did not receive a second.[87]

Cassidy charged that the Colonial Amusement Company had "insulted" the "dignity of the city government,"[88] and the Women's Clubs lodged a protest against *Hippocrites* and called for the formation of a board of censors. After the city solicitor informed the mayor and the commissioners that current ordinances gave them no legal power to "control the picture business" by barring films *before* they actually were projected in local theaters, the "incensed" commissioners voted unanimously on September 13 to enact a new ordinance that prohibited the exhibition of "lewd, obscene or immoral pictures." Further, the ordinance authorized the Commissioner of Public Safety to demand screenings "in advance of public exhibition" and to bar films deemed unacceptable. Transgressing theater operators could not only be fined from five to fifty dollars for each offense, but could also have their licenses revoked.[89]

The city officials who passed this censorship ordinance clearly did not intend to force local theaters out of business or institute a costly and time-consuming procedure for screening most films slated to appear in Lexington. This ordinance was more in the nature of a symbolic affirmation of government authority and a procedural guide if and when citizens complained about specific films.[90] After being passed in September 1915, the ordinance was not invoked or even referred to again in the press until the following February, when movie censorship for a time replaced Sunday closing and the regulation of saloons as the city's most pressing issue relating to leisure-time activity. "Wanted—A Local Moving Picture Censorship," the *Leader* editorial of 27 February 1916 that initiated Lexington's most heated debate over movie censorship in the 1910s, is worth quoting at length:

> The *Leader*, for many reasons, would very much dislike to begin a fight on the local moving picture houses. . . . However, if the motion picture business in Lexington is to continue to be profitable more care will have to be extended in selecting films.
>
> Within the last two weeks there have been at least three pictures, probably more, exhibited in Lexington which should not have been countenanced and they belong to a class of attractions which, if not abandoned in respectable communities, will do serious damage to the moving picture houses and deprive the public of a source of pleasure and instruction which should be enjoyed to the greatest possible extent.
>
> When a young man takes a young woman to see a motion picture

which he cannot afterward discuss with her fully and frankly—if she is
the right sort of a young woman—it is about time he was changing his
place of entertainment, and certainly a picture of this character is not a
fit object to be displayed to hundreds of morbidly curious boys and girls.

Any picture in which the anti-climax is either a seduction or a criminal assault, clumsily and vulgarly featured, should be barred from respectable picture houses. The writer has seen four such pictures in Lexington
within the space of a few days. . . . There are too many clean plays, too
many engaging and at the same time innocent romances, to say nothing of
patriotic dramas which just at this time would appeal to the public mind,
for theatres to resort to attractions which their audiences suffer rather
than enjoy.

Let us try another course and see if it will be profitable.[91]

Spelling out a clear-cut distinction between "clean" pictures and repre-
hensible films that exploit sex and violence, and setting forth the goal of protecting young couples on dates and "morbidly curious boys and girls," this
editorial generated several supportive letters to the editor. "It is love's labor
lost," wrote a local doctor, "to close up the red light district, and maintain
one of its chief sources of supply," the motion picture theater's "putrid performances."[92] One letter even went so far as to propose that theater managers
actually screen interpretive titles before and during photoplays, pointing out
"the right from the wrong, etc."[93]

The board of education also voiced its concern over motion pictures, citing
in particular one "typical" film, *The Serpent*, which, they declared, climaxed
with a quasi-incestuous "sexual act" and a suicide. Like virtually all advocates of censorship in this period, the board posited the most straightforward
model of causal effect, ignoring completely the fact of representation: "what
difference," they rhetorically asked, "is there between watching the pictures
of an act and watching the act itself?" Both experiences are equally "immoral, degrading and injurious in the extreme to the welfare of our people
and especially the young." Since the board was entrusted with the education,
broadly understood, of the city's children, it felt compelled to pass a public
resolution calling for the city commissioners to take immediate action concerning motion pictures.[94]

Apparently these concerned citizens were not aware of the censorship or-
dinance passed the previous September.[95] The Commissioner of Public
Safety pledged to enforce this ordinance to the letter, and requested the
Leader to reprint it in full, which the paper did on March 1. Meanwhile, the

local press sought out the opinion of theater owners and managers, who were compelled to take a more explicit public stance than they had during the sabbatarian controversy. Though the exhibitors had been accused of endangering local youth and polluting the city's moral atmosphere, they were generally—and understandably—circumspect in their response. While agreeing that "lustily appealing" films had no place on Lexington screens, the exhibitors stood squarely behind the National Board of Censorship and noted, further, that their films had also been approved by the notoriously vigilant Ohio Board of Censorship.[96] (In addition, the *Herald* twice published a glowing full-page account of the National Board of Censorship's indefatigable efforts to "keep the wrong things out of the movies."[97])

Lexington's theater operators were, however, less than enthusiastic about the need for a local censorship body. The most rambunctious of the lot, John Stamper of the Orpheum, declared: "my family witnesses all the films shown by me and what is good enough for them is good enough for anyone else and is also enough censorship for me."[98] As this comment suggests, the exhibitors offered no *mea culpa*. In fact, Louis Zahler, manager of the Strand, accused the board of education of misinterpreting *The Serpent*, which he said he had personally edited before it was screened at his theater.[99] Zahler then submitted a letter to both newspapers pointing out the dangers of censorship. Probably not coincidentally, two weeks later Zahler "resigned" his position at the Strand and returned to Chicago.

Since the exhibitors, even including Zahler, were committed to "clean" films and the city already had a censorship ordinance on the books, one would assume that the matter would have been dropped until another *Serpent* or *Hippocrites* arrived in town. But the *Leader*'s editorial and the board of education's resolution had obviously given voice to a more pervasive anxiety. Ministers, such as the Reverend E. T. Edmonds of the Woodland Christian Church, preached sermons that warned (yet again) of the "special danger" to children who habitually view the movies' constant "story of sorrow and shame."[100] But the censorship campaign presented itself as a predominantly secular, progressive, reform initiative. In addition to letters of support from individual citizens, the board of education's efforts were lauded by the faculty of Transylvania University, which issued a formal resolution that called the "regulation of commercialized amusement" a "community duty of high importance."[101] Then, on March 21, the board of education joined forces with the Women's Club and the Committee on Social Hygiene (successor to the

Lexington Vice Commission) to take up the motion picture "problem," as well as the marked increase in cigarette smoking by young boys.

As critical as the board of education was toward specific exhibition policies, it did not, as did certain evangelical pastors, offer a wholesale condemnation of moving pictures. By 1916 the educational possibilities of the new medium had long been acknowledged and demonstrated in Lexington.[102] Feature articles in local papers, for example, had praised the use of motion pictures for demonstrating "up-to-date" agricultural methods and promoting better personal hygiene.[103] In 1914–15 the Kentucky Tuberculosis Commission extensively used traveling motion picture exhibitions to take its message statewide. Even the purchase of a motion picture "outfit" for the Lincoln School, located in the Irishtown tenement district, had merited front page coverage in November 1913, while screenings of "educational" films for schoolchildren at Woodland Park Auditorium had become relatively commonplace. The rationale for this type of noncommercial film exhibition was clearly stated in a *Leader* editorial published in April 1914 entitled "Motion Picture Education." For all its deep misgivings about the specific practices of local movie theaters, the *Leader* had the highest hopes for the motion picture's potential as a means of adapting famous novels and plays, staging the "great stories of history," and, above all, instructing students and "untrained men." In fact, the *Leader* concluded, "the increasing use of motion pictures by non-commercial agencies, such as schools, churches and recreation centers, is one of the significant signs of the times."[104]

The danger, of course, was that this powerful pedagogic tool would be (or had been) utterly prostituted in the name of profit and cheap amusement. One alternative, posed by school superintendent M. A. Cassidy at precisely the time when the 1916 local censorship controversy was at its most heated, was to equip all public schools with motion picture projectors. In this way, the school system could fulfill an essential twentieth-century task: "training" the "tastes of the child for moving pictures"—as if by such instruction children would learn to forego standard movie fare in favor of "pictures which portray scientific, geological and subjects of a like nature."[105] The members of the board of education and the Civic League were, with good reason, enthusiastic about Cassidy's proposal, for it promised to curb the power of commercial entertainment and return the shaping of "taste" to where they felt it rightly belonged.

A year later, in April 1917, the problem of "taste" had, according to Cassidy, become too acute and dangerous to be solved by providing a projector for every school or even every classroom. Cassidy called principals, teachers, and parents to arms against "the trashy, vulgar improbable motion picture," a form of entertainment so "fascinating" that "no greater menace to childhood and impressionable youth is extant." The only prevention against this plague was for responsible adults to "cultivate" students' "taste for pure, pleasing and instructive motion pictures," not just in the classroom but in the local picture house as well. Abstinence is never mentioned as a viable recourse. Cassidy was duly impassioned about this mission, but he also saw firsthand the prominence of the movies in Lexington and believed that "one immoral and suggestive picture may destroy the long and devoted training of both parents and teachers."[106] In the face of this insidious blight, what beneficial fruits would even the most diligent cultivation bring forth?

A strong censorship board armed with the power to assess fines and revoke business licenses might stand a chance of protecting children from "trashy, vulgar, improbable motion pictures." When the board of education, in league with the Women's Club and the Committee on Social Hygiene, proposed their version of such a plan in 1916, city officials concluded that the existing ordinance was sufficient, meaning that any complaints had to be directed to the Commissioner of Public Safety who, together with the Chief of Police, would conduct an investigation. While the current commissioner did not "claim to be an expert censor," he did claim to be "able to judge whether or not a picture is immoral or will tend to have a bad influence on the children who attend the shows."[107] In this confrontation, which pitted politicians against civic-minded professionals and progressive reformers, the politicians came out on top, probably to the relief of theater owners, since the board of education and the Committee on Social Hygiene not only wanted a more rigorous preview policy, but also stricter control over what they termed "undesirable publicity."[108]

In a certain respect the decision concerning precisely who would act as the community's moral watchdog was something of a moot point, since no more *Serpents* lurked in the garden of Lexington's movie theaters for at least the next several years. Six weeks after the *Leader* had "started the agitation for cleaner films," it ran a self-congratulatory editorial that announced: "there has been a marked improvement in the character of the motion pictures which have been exhibited in Lexington."[109] I doubt whether this change in programming practices (if in fact there was any effort to book "cleaner" films) or the public airing of grievances solved the "problem" of motion pictures or soothed anxieties concerning the pernicious influence of commercial amusements. After all, according to the Committee on Social Hygiene, Lexington was still besieged by "evil influences that stalk the city at noon day, such as liquor, commercialized vice, indecent picture postals, indecent songs and demoralizing shows of all kinds."[110] But possibly the protest against immoral movies was itself sufficient to assure Lexington's concerned citizens that they were, indeed, responsible, morally alert, and progressive. Perhaps what they gained had less to do with the images on downtown movie screens than with the images they held of themselves and their community.

Naming, Counting, Describing the Audience

The other type of "image" central in both the debate over local censorship and the sabbatarian crusade was the image of the audience. On occasion, sermons, letters to the editor, proclamations, and editorials referred to the movie audience as the "poorer class of people" or simply as "the people,"[111] but most often moviegoers were pictured as children irresistibly drawn outside the home to cheap amusements and so in dire need of adult protection. Perhaps children really were flocking to picture shows and beginning to suffer certain ill-effects of this habitual behavior, and prohibitive reform may have been easiest to promote when it was conducted in the name of children. But this way of picturing the audience may have been more of a figurative move that turned all moviegoers into immature, pleasure-seeking children who did not know what was good for them.[112] In any event, minors were obviously the moviegoers who mattered most.[113]

In large measure, children were also the impetus and the focus of the social-scientific recreation surveys that began to appear across the country in this period, conducted under the auspices of the Playground and Recreation Association of America and the Russell Sage Foundation. These reports, replete with graphs and much-emphasized numerical data, were intended to justify the progressive, professional management of local leisure-time activity.[114] Nonetheless, they are useful in giving some empirical support to two rather obvious points: children and young people were a prominent part of the moving picture audience, and the demographics of movie attendance could vary somewhat from city to city.[115]

During the 1910s the closest thing to a formal recreation survey undertaken in Lexington was a master's thesis written by Dudley H. Starns for the University of Kentucky Department of Education in 1917, entitled "A Study of the Relation of the Motion-Picture to the Work and Deportment of Pupils in the School." For his test group Starns used the seventh and eighth graders at two schools and all the students at the city's high school. A total of 620 Lexington students were given questionnaires to chart their movie attendance during a twelve-week period. Starns then compared frequency of attendance with the grades received in various subjects. "Beyond doubt," he concluded, "there is a close correlation between regular [movie] attendance and the work of the pupil in school": for the seventh and eighth graders as well as the high school students, a substantially higher percentage of "C" and "D" pupils were "excessive" moviegoers than were the "A" and "B" students. More significant than Starns' tentative conclusions is the very fact that he took up this topic in the first place. The movies, he reasoned, were worth scholarly attention because "this form of public entertainment is neither a fleeting fad nor a mental epidemic, but a social force that touches and influences all life and one that must be reckoned with." Moreover, he (and the Department of Education) obviously believed that this "social force" could be investigated by quantitative methods, which would yield accurate data of benefit to "parents, school boards, superintendents, principals and teachers."[116] What these figures of authority could actually *do* about students' movie attendance was never explained by Starns.

For my purposes, the most useful part of this thesis is the basic information Starns gathered about the moviegoing habits of Lexington's white adolescents. Less than 3 percent of the students questioned did not attend the movies during this twelve-week period. On average, the rest of the students attended three times weekly. Unfortunately, Starns did not indicate which particular shows and theaters these students attended. He did, however, tabulate the difference between "moderate" attendance (three or fewer times per week) and "excessive" attendance (more than three times per week). According to this criterion, 29 percent of the seventh and eighth graders and 38 percent of the high school students qualified as "excessive" moviegoers—figures that help to explain the concern publicly voiced by the superintendent of schools and the board of education about the need for local censorship and pedagogic initiatives to counteract the effect of moviegoing.

Besides Starns' study, little empirical data exists about Lexington movie-goers. There is, however, a small but quite suggestive body of anecdotal evidence that somehow made its way into local newspapers and public discourse about the movies. These anecdotes are best taken as indications of the kinds of stories then considered worth telling about moviegoing and moviegoers in Lexington.

During the nickelodeon era such accounts from larger cities could resemble naturalistic melodramas, with children—easy prey to enticement—"pilfering or begging to obtain the price of admission."[117] In Lexington, vignettes of this sort were likely to appear, if at all, only in the most virulently anti-amusement diatribes. A quite different type of story was told in a *Herald* article in December 1912 about seven grade-school boys who were brought before the juvenile court because they had staged "miniature moving picture scenes." Specifically, they were charged with capturing an unwilling schoolmate, tying him up, and "putting him through certain bandit performances, particularly applicable to western cowboy life as depicted in moving picture shows." Some of the boys even donned their sisters' dresses to fill the requisite female parts in the (re)production.[118] Like many of the sermons cited earlier, this article highlights the consequences of frequent moviegoing on impressionable youngsters, though the *Herald*'s tone ("boys will be boys") surely works to undercut the magnitude of this "problem." Imitative behavior could, however, be taken more seriously, as when the *Leader* reported that the "desperate acts" of a black teenager arrested for burglary were said to have been "prompted by some of the daring things he had seen delineated in the silent drama," which he attended daily.[119]

As for the actual experience within the moving picture theater, Lexington newspapers contain no references to the sort of "urban" crimes that were reported, for example, in Louisville: "mashers" who "annoyed" unaccompanied female spectators; and "gangs of young toughs" who accosted theater employees and tried to force their way in without paying.[120] For dramatic spectacle, nothing occurred in Lexington movie theaters that rivaled the scene in eastern Kentucky's Prestonsburg in February 1913, when a drunk staggered into a moving picture show, insulted everyone in sight, drew a knife on the constable who tried to arrest him, and was shot dead as the spectators watched.[121] In fact, Lexington papers were more likely to recount comic stories about moviegoing. For example, in August 1917 a brief front page item in the *Leader* reported that three ten-year-old girls, presumed to be lost (or worse), were perfectly safe after all, since they had merely stayed to see the show again at one of the local moving picture theaters.[122] What is the moral of this light-hearted anecdote; that it was foolish of the parents not to think of so obvious an explanation; that children are found, not lost at the movies; that whatever dangers might tempt or prey on unchaperoned girls in Lexington, moviegoing was not one of them?

The sole extended article on Lexington moviegoers, published in the *Herald* in 1916, adopted an even more obviously satirical tone, as it etched in comic-strip fashion the types to be encountered on an average visit to the movies: the usher who "toils and spins" but is ignored by all patrons; the "educated person" who insists on reading aloud all titles; the "young clerk" who explains the subtleties on screen to his date; the "middle-aged man" who "phlegmatically picks the whole picture to pieces"; the girl mooning over Francis X. Bushman; the man who whistles along with the piano player, and so on.[123] This movie audience is somewhat mixed in terms of age, gender, and class and much more free to express itself in this public arena than it would be in a legitimate theater. These harmlessly eccentric spectators are clearly not part of some mass audience entirely given over to "passive" recreation. To be sure, this account proves nothing concrete about daily moviegoing habits. But its tone of gentle mockery suggests how deeply familiar and even mundane the movies had become by the mid–1910s; the article reads like the monologue of a congenial comedian who turns our attention to the routines of life, all that is right before our eyes.[124]

This vision of the audience presents an interesting contrast to certain of Lawrence W. Levine's speculations in *Highbrow/Lowbrow: The Emergence of Cultural Hierarchy in America.* Levine convincingly argues that with the "sacralization of culture" in late nineteenth- and early twentieth-century America came an attempt to "discipline" and "train" theater and concert audiences, so as to make them "less interactive, less of a public and more of a group of mute receptors." This process, he proposes, also affected the patrons of nickelodeons, who "were far from the raucous, independent audiences of the nineteenth century."[125] Set against this backdrop, the *Herald*'s description of comic (almost Bergsonian) types at the picture show becomes all the more notable for its insistence on independent, active viewers, quite at ease (at home, in fact) in a public space. From the *Herald*'s perspective, these far-from-mute receptors either did not need any "training" or would persist in their eccentricities, notwithstanding all admonitions that they adhere to rules of "passive politeness."

The Birth of a Nation

Perhaps it is to be expected that there are no newspaper accounts of what an ordinary Lexington moviegoing experience was like in 1908 or 1915, at the Colonial or the Ben Ali, at a midweek evening show or a Sunday matinee. (As even these options suggest, there was no single "moviegoing experience.") Unfortunately, the same is true for probably the most significant film screening in Lexington during the 1910s, D. W. Griffith's *The Birth of a Nation*. There is, however, a sizable amount of information about the controversy that preceded this film's local engagement.

The Birth of a Nation did not open in Lexington until the week of 20 March 1916, more than a year after its New York City premiere and five weeks after it began a highly successful Louisville run. (Griffith was born and raised in the Louisville area.) It was arguably the most technically sophisticated American narrative film to date, and also the most widely publicized, in part because of the NAACP-led protest mounted against Griffith's film in Los Angeles, New York City, and Boston.[126] The selling of this epic in Lexington relied on basically the same advertising tactics used elsewhere across the nation. Yet the way the exhibiting of *The Birth of a Nation* was negotiated (and perhaps also the way the film was received by audiences) was a reflection of quite specific local conditions, particularly of racial relations in Lexington.[127]

Apprehension about the booking of *The Birth of a Nation* was first voiced by Mayor James C. Rogers, who had taken office on 4 January 1916 and soon thereafter weathered the storm about *The Serpent* and other "immoral" pictures. Directly after *The Birth of a Nation* appeared in a list of the Opera House's coming attractions, Rogers proposed that the city commissioners consider if the film should be banned, citing the Kentucky *Uncle Tom's Cabin* law. The commissioners heartily agreed with Rogers' description of the situation: "In Lexington the most pleasant relations exist between the white and colored races, and we do not want these good relations disrupted."[128] This warning should sound familiar, for it is virtually identical to the rationale offered for banning the Johnson-Jeffries fight film in 1910. Rogers' misgivings about *The Birth of a Nation* quite transparently express a commitment to the status quo, the racial equanimity (not to be confused in any way with racial equality) that made the city so livable for residents well situated enough to reap the benefits of continued "pleasantness."

Yet lying dormant, waiting to be revivified by some outside stimuli, was the specter of unnamed disturbance, which would entail what—passion, violence, dissension not manageable by political arrangements or ordinances or mayoral prerogative? If the true danger went unspecified in Rogers' warning, so did any explanation of how the cause (the screening of *The Birth of a Nation*) would lead to the effect (disturbance). Would the film incite whites not of the "better classes" to abuse "coloreds" in the name of the Lost Cause? Would it energize dissolute blacks to give vent to suppressed bestiality and dreams of license and power? What Mayor Rogers, unlike the NAACP and certain African Americans in Lexington, did not consider was the possibility that Griffith's film might be most damaging and dangerous as a (melo)dramatization of racist ideology and "false" history.[129]

Whatever his fears, Rogers took no precipitous action. With the blessing of the city commissioners, he set up a meeting with Charles Berryman, whose realty company had recently acquired and refurbished the Opera House. Berryman offered to pay for Lexington's Board of Censors to travel to Louisville to see *The Birth of a Nation*. If the board found the film "objectionable," Berryman promised to cancel the booking.[130] For some reason, instead of the chief of police and the commissioner of public safety, two other commissioners—Harry Schoonmaker, a contractor and former city jailer, and Frank G. Ott, a furniture store salesman—made the trip to Louisville on February 26. Schoonmaker was particularly impressed with the "grandeur and sublimity and the great moral truth" taught by Griffith's film, and this special committee advised that the picture be allowed to play the Opera House as scheduled.[131]

Yet when the commissioners met on March 7, the mayor disregarded this recommendation and introduced a motion to ban *The Birth of a Nation* from Lexington, which passed by a three-to-one vote, with Ott maintaining his defense of the film, while Schoonmaker sided with the majority.[132] Berryman continued to run extensive newspaper advertising for *The Birth of a Nation* and considered taking the matter to court. In the end he simply disregarded the commission's motion and screened *The Birth of a Nation* as planned. The city took no legal action, for Corporation Counsel John G. Denny advised the mayor that the *Uncle Tom's Cabin* statute "cannot properly be construed as applying to motion picture productions," because "motion pictures were in a nebulous and undeveloped state when these laws were enacted."[133] So Berryman was able to profit from sell-out crowds at the Opera House, while Mayor Rogers was able to profit with certain constituencies for the stand he had taken against the film.

In the headline for its front page coverage of the March 7 vote, the *Leader*

put the matter succinctly: "Commissioners Decide To Heed Numerous Protests." During the days following the initial council meeting on February 26,
public interest in the controversy rose, and municipal officials came under
pressure from a number of sources, both black and white. The mayor's appre-
hensions about *The Birth of a Nation*'s capacity for disturbing the city's racial
arrangement were echoed by, among others, the Women's Clubs of Central
Kentucky and the Lexington chapter of the WCTU, whose public resolution
called for the "suppression" of *The Birth of a Nation* because the "sad" past
it dwells on has no relevance now that "the races of Central Kentucky are
happy together and are making for the uplift of each other."[134] The *Leader*, in
fact, was so confident about the "harmonious relations as citizens between
the two races in Lexington" that it believed that no "mere picture"—even
one as accomplished as Griffith's—could break up the bonds between "old
friends."[135] The Colored Ministers Alliance and the Colored Boosters Club,
who lodged the first official protests by Lexington blacks against *The Birth of
a Nation*, were less sanguine about the unlikelihood of disturbance, but they,
too, proclaimed their belief in and commitment to "the pleasant relations that
now exist between the races" in the city.[136]

The birth Thomas Cripps in *Slow Fade to Black* examines in detail how the protest
against *The Birth of a Nation* in New York City and Boston underscored the
conflicts among black organizations, particularly the NAACP and the eastern
contingent of Tuskegee supporters.[137] This rift was not noticeable in Lexington, though local black protest was hardly uniform, either in its tone or in its
target. In fact, the *Herald* reported on February 26 that "the sentiment among
negroes in this city as to whether or not the picture [*The Birth of a Nation*]
should be shown seems to be divided."[138]

The largest public display of opposition to *The Birth of a Nation* occurred
on February 27, when Roscoe Conkling Simmons, a nephew and protégé of
Booker T. Washington, came from Louisville to address a gathering at the
AME church.[139] Several prominent white civic leaders, including the editors
of both papers and two city commissioners, were invited guests, seated on
the rostrum. Speaking for what he called "the best of the blacks to the best
of the whites," Simmons used the occasion to present "an eloquent defense"
of African-American accomplishments, emblemized by the rise of Booker
T. Washington. *The Birth of a Nation* deserved condemnation, according to
Simmons, for its grossly inaccurate and prejudicial images of blacks, not for
any potentially disturbing immediate problems it might cause.[140] The whites
in attendance, wrote the *Herald*, were "visibly impressed" with Simmons'

oration, and both papers praised the speech in their editorials the following day. This response by the "best of the whites" is understandable; after all, the meeting showed blacks at their "best" (in one of the largest colored churches), and Simmons' vision of African-American progress was a vindication of how things had got to be the way they were. He accused *The Birth of a Nation* but not society at large of racism.

Two subsequent letters to the editor by local black residents addressed the controversy and the white audience in quite different terms. Unlike Simmons, D. I. Reid (a teacher at one of the colored schools) insisted that *The Birth of a Nation* was of a piece with the "racial restrictions, proscriptions and dire hate and prejudice" facing blacks in the United States. Specifically, Griffith (or actually Thomas Dixon, for Reid was basing his observations on *The Clansman*) was guilty of negating the fact that "the American Negro is the grandest specimen of the achievement of Christian missions. He is solely the production of the white man's consecration to the high Christian ideals that have made his race the favorite of heaven." Reid felt that *The Birth of a Nation*'s "most deadly thrust" was matched by the gross impiety of overly ambitious "Negro politicians," who were leading the race down a false, secular path. For the "swift and certain relief" necessary for his race, so beleaguered "both within and without," Reid could only appeal to (white) "Christian missions everywhere" for protection and preservation.[141]

Ed Willis, editor of the black Lexington *Weekly News* (of which there are no extant copies), put the matter in almost opposite terms. Willis was resolutely secular in his letter to the *Leader*, pointing out, as Simmons had done, the inaccuracies of Griffith's purportedly "historical" view of reconstruction. Willis, however, did not compliment the "best" white people or seek their wise guidance in the local struggle to maintain the peace; and he most definitely did not ask to be protected by benevolent Christian missionaries. Instead, Willis challenged Lexington's whites, since they alone had the power to take action in this situation, to bar *The Birth of a Nation* if they truly wanted to uphold the racial status quo. After all, he concluded, black leaders had done their part six years earlier by complying with the "white men's" decision to ban the Johnson-Jeffries fight film and, further, by not booking Jack Johnson as an attraction at the Colored A & M Fair, although the heavyweight champion was willing to appear and his presence would have "increased the gate receipts considerably." Now, Willis affirmed, it was the duty of white people to act in an equally principled manner, putting their racial and financial interests aside in favor of civic responsibility.[142]

These arguments are worth summarizing in some detail because the protest against *The Birth of a Nation* was one of the few instances in which Lexington newspapers recorded African-Americans' discussion of motion pictures. Moreover, the diversity of even this meager sampling—a speech, two resolutions, two letters to the editor—which, of course, does not take into account opinions expressed in homes, schools, churches, workplaces, and saloons, makes generalizations about *the* black community patently reductive. For, as we will see more fully in the next chapter, even in Lexington, which was hardly a bastion of anti-Tuskegee black activism, there were different stories African Americans told about themselves, different rhetorical strategies and oratorical stances, different reasons for condemning *The Birth of a Nation.*

The *Leader* lauded Roscoe Simmons' speech, as did the *Herald,* whose positive response is particularly noteworthy, given that it was a Democratic paper (with no "Colored Notes" column until 1919) in a city with deep ties to the South. The legacy of the Civil War personally touched Desha Breckinridge, the influential editor of the *Herald,* since his grandfather, John Breckinridge, had formed the Kentucky Brigade and served as secretary of war for the Confederate States of America. Desha Breckinridge was no unregenerate rebel, however; and his paper consistently promoted the efforts of his wife, Madeline McDowell Breckinridge, who was in the forefront of local movements for the development of playgrounds, child labor laws, and educational reforms.[143]

The *Herald*'s racial stance—at once progressive and paternalistic, concerned and condescending—is well exemplified by a 1912 editorial that bemoaned Lexington's lack of suitable "places of amusements," meaning "respectable" sites like city parks and the YMCA. This problem was especially acute, Breckinridge observed, for local blacks, who "need amusement, recreation under proper conditions, with respectable surroundings, more than do the white people, because of the circumstances of their lives, the limitations of their interests and their pleasure-loving natures." He knew this firsthand, having seen his own "colored" servants at a loss for innocent amusement on their days off. Breckinridge therefore implored the white people of Lexington to live up to their "obligation" to dependent blacks, for the "investment" would yield both material and immaterial benefits to the donor as well as the recipient.[144] Breckinridge's polite and humanitarian racism, which seems so blatantly apparent and so potentially insidious to us now, was in early twentieth-century Lexington (and likely in America at large) deemed not to be prejudicial but enlightened.[145] And so, invited by a black "friend" who worked at the exclusive Lexington Club, the editor of the *Herald* took his place at the AME meeting as a representative of the "best white people."

Breckinridge had not planned to speak out on *The Birth of a Nation*, feeling that the spirit of "mutual trust and helpfulness" between the races in Lexington would triumph over any divisiveness the film might promote. Yet after hearing Simmons, Breckinridge felt compelled to offer his editorial opinion, though he never went so far as to call for the banning of the film. Writing very much as a son of the Confederacy who still felt the anguish of "Sherman's raid," Breckinridge nonetheless criticized *The Birth of a Nation*'s "stirring of dead passions" and, especially, its "false history," which unjustly glorified the Ku Klux Klan, vilified southern blacks, and discounted the role of "true" southern gentlemen, like his grandfather, who had honorably guided the reconstruction of the region. Breckinridge hoped that Griffith's lies would not incite "the lower classes of whites or of blacks" to commit acts that might disrupt the "mutual confidence and respect between the better class of whites and the better class of negroes," a "relation upon which in so large a measure depends the prosperity of the community."[146]

The *Herald*'s overall treatment of *The Birth of a Nation* was, however, more ambivalent than just this single editorial would suggest. On the one hand, the paper gave a glowing account of Simmons' speech and also published an editorial deploring the lynching of a black in Georgia, a statement from a Mississippi-born widow of a Confederate soldier staunchly defending the fidelity of Civil War-era blacks to their southern masters, and a letter of protest against the falsehoods of *The Birth of a Nation* from a retired Union officer living in Berea, Kentucky. Yet, on the other hand, Breckinridge's paper continued to accept advertising for the film and indirectly to propose an alternate reading of *The Birth of a Nation*, very much in keeping with Griffith's own defense of his film. For example, the *Herald* reprinted a letter that veterans in the Kentucky Confederate Home had written to the Louisville *Courier-Journal*, testifying to the absolute accuracy of the film. And in the *Herald*'s society column, amid wedding announcements and accounts of fraternity dances and elegant luncheons, there appeared a glowing Birmingham *News*' description of *The Birth of a Nation*, which "Lexington audiences will have the pleasure of seeing this week."[147] (Another such piece appeared in the society column a week later.) Rather than taking the *Herald*'s treatment of the film as a sign of hypocrisy or as a commitment to journalistic fair play, the ambivalence of this paper is better interpreted as indicative of the multiple audiences in even a city the size of Lexington, where *The Birth of a Nation* was pre-viewed in a variety of ways: as a diatribe, a society event, a mere picture, an incitement to disturbance, and/or a page from history.

The promotional campaign for *The Birth of a Nation*, as would be expected, sought to shape this pre-viewing. For ten days before the March 20 opening, both newspapers carried the same large ad, which featured information about the cost and magnitude of the production itself, the film's success in New York City, Boston, and Chicago, its major historical scenes, and its "dramatic narrative" highlights. Two hundred- to three hundred-word promotional notices with publicity stills also appeared daily in both papers, underscoring the time, effort, and money expended on this monumental and meticulous undertaking and praising Griffith's spectacular action sequences and the performances of Mae Marsh and Lillian Gish. *The Birth of a Nation*'s newspaper advertising, in Lexington at least, did not explicitly refer to reconstruction or to blacks, and it did not allude to or exploit the local or national controversy over the film. In effect, Griffith's production was promoted as being above the controversy and any merely local bickering, for it was simultaneously a phenomenal technical achievement (in size, cost, verisimilitude) and a compelling, spectacular, realistic, accessible masterpiece in the grand nineteenth-century tradition.[148]

Fittingly, *The Birth of a Nation* was booked into the Lexington Opera House, which had presented the theatrical version of *The Clansman* a decade before. With the Ben Ali closed after being severely damaged by a fire in January 1916, the Berryman Realty Company had to utilize the Opera House for both touring companies and motion pictures, as well as for local events like the Shrine Minstrels. As a result, March 1916 was a busy month. Along with *The Birth of a Nation*, nineteen different feature films (from Paramount, Metro, and Equitable) were each booked at the Opera House for one day. As for live theater, Johnston Forbes-Robertson's farewell tour played a two-day engagement, and George Arliss arrived for matinee and evening performances of *Paganini*. With tickets set at from twenty-five cents (for gallery seats) to $2.00 (for lower floor boxes) for evenings and from twenty-five cents to $1.00 for matinees, the price of admission for *The Birth of a Nation* far exceeded the standard prices for movie fare and rivaled ticket costs for Forbes-Robertson's productions of *Hamlet* and *The Light That Failed* and even the special appearance of the Minneapolis Symphony Orchestra in January 1916.

Being booked into the recently renovated Opera House meant that *The Birth of a Nation* profited from and enhanced the prestige of a theater that still evoked strong sentimental associations as a Lexington institution for going on thirty years. *The Birth of a Nation*'s six-day engagement was virtually unprecedented in Lexington. Would some 2,500 persons pay top dollar to see the film each day?[149] In spite of or perhaps because of the local protest and the attempt by municipal authorities to prohibit exhibition of the film, *The Birth of a Nation* was an overwhelming box office success. Scott described it as "by far the most largely attended of any production ever billed at a Lexington theatre," with an average of 1,400 patrons at each performance. Based on these figures, the *Leader* called Griffith's epic easily "the most profitable attraction ever offered at a Lexington playhouse."[150] The *Herald*'s society column gauged the film's success in somewhat different terms, noting the fashionable "theater parties" and many out-of-town visitors at the Opera House.[151]

The only clue as to how Lexington audiences reacted to *The Birth of a Nation* is a brief, cryptic paragraph that appeared on the front page of the March 22 *Leader:* "Because of the demonstrations made at the exhibition of *The Birth of a Nation* the first two days the picture has been shown here, the management of the Lexington Opera House . . . has asked Commissioner of Public Safety Land for extra police. Accordingly six extra policemen were scattered throughout the house last night, and while the exhibition provoked several enthusiastic outbursts from the crowd there was no trouble."[152] Neither local paper published a follow-up to this story. I am sure that had the people responsible for the outbursts been black, or had the "trouble" involved physical violence, or had the "demonstrations" actually been a form of protest, press coverage would have been extensive. So I assume that the disturbers of the peace were whites (of the "lower classes," Breckinridge no doubt would have added) overly expressive in their enthusiasm. Still, the notion that policemen would be "scattered throughout the house," instead of being stationed in the lobby or at the entrance shooing away loafers, seems quite remarkable and unprecedented. Were they there to protect the less enthusiastic spectators, to guard the house itself, or to prevent the demonstrations from spilling out into the streets?

These demonstrations were not mentioned by local reviewers, who paid no attention to the audience, one way or the other. In the *Herald,* Enoch Grehan dismissed as "insane twaddle" the very idea that *The Birth of a Nation* could have "unwholesome influences" on either whites or blacks, and he praised the film for exceeding its own reputation as a "stupendous spectacle," even though it did include "necessarily disagreeable scenes of negro attempts at defilement of white women."[153] James Ross in the *Leader* granted that the first half of the film "from an artistic view point was wonderfully done," but he took Griffith to task for seeking to "stir racial feeling."[154] Lexington's newspapers, needless to say, had no African-American critics on staff, but the *Leader*'s Colored Notes did praise Ross for his critique of *The Birth of a Nation.*

The final white word in the local press was accorded to three ministers who took the film as the subject for their Sunday sermons on March 26. At Central Christian Church, the pastor commended *The Birth of a Nation* as a truthful effort "that depicts nothing save better, higher and nobler things," while the Reverend G. R. Combs of the Park Avenue Methodist Episcopal Church declared that the film taught fundamental lessons on the dangers of "abused" power and the "horrors of war." The dissenting view was offered by the pastor of Centenary Methodist Church, who, speaking as a self-styled "cosmopolitan" and lifelong southerner (an interesting combination), scored Griffith on the grounds that the "black man and the white man may have enough of present imperfections to overcome without having their past weaknesses paraded before the public."[155]

Notwithstanding the rare criticism of Griffith for stirring "racial feelings" or parading the "past weaknesses" of blacks and whites, the bottom line was that *The Birth of a Nation* was screened to overflow crowds in Lexington. It returned for a three-day engagement at the Opera House in September 1916, attracting large audiences whose "enthusiasm [was] as great as on its former appearance here."[156] And it would play Lexington, at the Ben Ali, again in 1919, 1924, and 1927. (As far as I have been able to determine, no other feature film was recirculated locally to this extent.) Though black leaders failed to prevent Berryman from showing *The Birth of a Nation,* their campaign was without doubt one of the most well organized public protests mounted by Lexington's African-American community during this period. Yet to take the campaign against *The Birth of a Nation* as the sole or even the primary indication of the reception of motion pictures by local blacks would, I think, be a vast oversimplification. Segregation in the 1910s may have "needed" the melodramatized racism of *The Birth of a Nation,* but Griffith himself did not invent the Jim Crow system, which Lexington's reformers and Christian moralists took completely for granted as the natural, socially efficient course of things. In the next chapter, we will view again the nickelodeon and post-nickelodeon periods, from the perspective of black moviegoing and black-operated theaters, which existed in a segregated world of extraordinarily limited possibilities.

SEVEN

**Another Audience:
Black Moviegoing
from 1907 to 1916**

"Strange thing that moving pictures do not appeal to the masses of negroes," declared an unnamed showman quoted in *Moving Picture World* for 8 June 1907. Admitting that "of course, a moving picture show exclusively for negroes has not yet been tried," this showman then went on to note that "in large towns, where such shows for white people pay handsomely, negro attractions of this character have been started and gone under." Why? According to this observer, blacks shunned motion pictures because, first, "the average negro wants to see a show with an abundance of noise, something like a plantation minstrel, with lots of singing and dancing and horseplay. He doesn't seem to grasp the idea of moving pictures"; and second, "the persons in the pictures are white," and "when a negro goes to a show it pleases him most to see black faces in the performance. But no pictures are made with Senegambian faces."[1]

Even if we assume that these remarks were not uttered with a sigh of relief, several questions remain. Did this showman intend to warn off producers and exhibitors or to urge them on? Could "noise"-loving blacks ever transcend their plantation roots and grasp the "idea of moving pictures," an "idea" that apparently caused no problem for whites (aside from Uncle Josh-styled country bumpkins)? Could this "strange" lack of interest in moving pictures be interpreted as in some manner an oppositional gesture rather than a mark of childish, undeveloped taste? Or if the problem was simply suiting the product to the prospective consumer, within what ideologically acceptable frame could "black faces" be cast upon the screen so as to draw black patrons into nickelodeons?

Perhaps the Selig Company set out to rectify the situation as defined in *Moving Picture World* by releasing in November 1907 a "genuine Ethiopian comedy" entitled *The Wooing and Wedding of a Coon*.[2] One might take up the matter of "noise" and minstrelsy and "black faces" by surveying this and other "coon" comedies like Edison's *The Pickaninnies* (1908), for instance, or Lubin's *Rastus in Zululand* (1910).[3] Or one might examine films produced by as well as featuring blacks, beginning, it would seem, with the Foster Film Company's *The Railroad Porter* in 1913.[4] My concern in this chapter, however, is less with "black faces in the performance" than with black patrons in the audience and black-run movie theaters between 1907 and 1916 in a small city with a substantial African-American community and a tradition of "colored" entertainment enterprises.

As the first producers of "all-colored" motion pictures (like William Foster, Al Bartlett, and Hunter Haynes) realized, the black audience for cheap commercial entertainment during this period was large—and also captive, given the effects of increasing segregation. Judging from advertisements and show business columns in the Indianapolis *Freeman* (a black weekly newspaper that regularly covered theatrical activity in much detail) and brief promotional notices in *Moving Picture World*, providing entertainment for black audiences at least looked to be a profitable enterprise early in the nickelodeon period. For example, in 1908, the Princess Theater, "run exclusively for colored people," opened in Salisbury, North Carolina, as did the Odd Fellows Theater, a six hundred-seat moving picture show, in Louisville;[5] then in 1909 came the Dixie Theater in Lake Charles, Louisiana, the Palace Picture Theater in Wilmington, Delaware, and the Pekin Theater in Cincinnati.[6]

All told, according to show business columnist "Juli Jones" (pseudonym for pioneer black film producer William Foster), there were 112 "colored" theaters in the United States in 1909, with those outside major cities being mostly "five and ten cent theaters, vaudeville and moving pictures."[7] No doubt a good number of the venues Jones referred to were owned by white investors, since the *Freeman* in 1910 put the total number of theaters "owned and operated by Negroes" at fifty-three.[8] Even guessing at the number of black movie theaters is virtually impossible since (as the quotation from Jones suggests) there was little attempt to differentiate nickelodeons from vaudeville houses.[9] Probably the most common exhibition format was a combination of vaudeville and motion pictures, such as played the New Grand Theatre in Chicago, billed in 1911 as the "finest theater in America built for colored people."[10]

Jim Crow and the Frolic Theater

This national trend is an important context for the venues attended, managed, and owned by African Americans in Lexington during this period, including the Frolic Theater, which opened on 28 September 1907, predating all of the examples listed above. My primary intention, however, is to examine the Frolic and the city's other "colored" theaters in relation to the specific conditions of African-American life in Lexington.

While the city's black population increased slightly from 1900 to 1920, the total percentage of blacks in Lexington dropped from 38 percent in 1900 to 31 percent in 1910 and 30 percent in 1920. Even with this decline, Lexington, once a center for slave trading, still had a higher ratio of black residents than any other Kentucky city or town.[11] Most continued to work as laborers, servants, or laundresses, and fully one-third of the blacks over ten years old remained illiterate. The colored public schools, however, were an increasingly prominent part of the community, and by 1910, 81 percent of the city's black youths between six and fourteen years old were attending school.[12] According to the 1910 census, Lexington's racial demographics and also its low number of foreign-born residents closely matched the figures for Atlanta, Nashville, and Little Rock, as well as for those regions of the country designated as the East South Central (Kentucky, Tennessee, Mississippi, and Alabama) and the South Atlantic (the coastal states from Delaware to Georgia).[13]

Lexington's long-standing black community could not help but define itself and live its daily life in relation (though not always in acquiescence) to formal and informal Jim Crow practices. Obviously, the same was true for black-run theaters. Faced with this situation, did these small-scale entrepreneurial enterprises aspire to imitate white-run theaters, or did they seek to make a virtue of their separateness and "colored" status? What was their position in the city's much-contested, ongoing discourse on leisure-time activity and race relations? For even in segregated, "southern" Lexington, such relations were not irrevocably settled, particularly where leisure hours and cheap amusements were concerned. As historian George C. Wright notes, Lexington—more than the rest of Kentucky except for Louisville—exhibited "fluid racial patterns" that left certain boundaries negotiable, subject to rede-scription, and in need of monitoring.[14]

For example, a year before the Frolic opened, Payne's Big Free Shows, a touring medicine show in the middle of a multi-week run in Lexington, felt compelled to announce publicly that "tonight and hereafter the races will be divided at Payne's show grounds . . . without a disagreeable intermingling as heretofore."[15] In this instance, seating blacks on the left side of the tent and whites on the right side was apparently an acceptable solution according to Lexington standards; intermingling, even in a temporary, "popular" venue, was not. Who exactly intermingled and who found it so offensive are never made clear. The point is that it did occur and that it required correction.

What leading spokespersons for the local black community on occasion attempted to monitor was not the seating arrangement of the audience but the show itself, at least when a touring production of Thomas Dixon's *The Clans-man* was scheduled for the Opera House in January 1906.[16] In a long letter to the *Leader,* the presiding elder of the AME Church rhetorically asked: "will the progressive, cultured, and aristocratic city of Lexington encourage such stuff" as Dixon's "race hatred," which will "inflame the ignorant and disso-lute blacks and whites" and undercut the efforts of "the colored professional people of intelligence, ministers, teachers, doctors, and lawyers" who "are daily blanketing race hatred."[17] *The Clansman* went on as planned, appar-ently without any disrupting protest within the Opera House (as had occurred in Atlanta).[18] For "colored professional people" lacked the political power of, for example, the Daughters of the Confederacy, who that same year managed to convince the Kentucky state legislature to pass the *Uncle Tom's Cabin* bill.

Any society or group is revealed in the face of its preferred monsters, and the singling out of monstrous plays or films is no exception. However, what is especially remarkable about this protest against *The Clansman*—and is quite relevant to the historicizing of Lexington's first black nickelodeon—is that the AME Church elder so explicitly posited an absolute social class distinction *within* Lexington's black community: on the one side, the "blan-keters," those "colored professional people of intelligence" who, like the city at its best, were assumed to be "progressive, cultured, and aristocratic"; on the other side, those "ignorant and dissolute blacks," whose passions would likely be inflamed by *The Clansman*.[19]

In Lexington, from the turn of the century on, this image of a bifurcated black community figured prominently in public concern over how to fill and manage leisure time and whether to tolerate or even condone cheap amusements. "Ignorant and dissolute blacks" were, for example, the obvious target of certain 1907 city ordinances that banned combined saloon/dance halls and prohibited women from "entering or loitering around saloons." Since 1905, in fact, these "low dives, where nightly orgies of the more depraved character take place," had been under attack from the Good Citizens League of Colored Citizens.[20] It was also this class of dissolute blacks that Booker T. Washington railed against in a 1908 Lexington speech. Before an audience of twenty-five thousand people at the Colored A & M Fair, Washington demanded that "we must get to the place, as speedily as possible, where the loafers will disappear from our street corners, from around bar-rooms."[21] Taking Washington's cue and operating on the assumption that today's undirected children are tomorrow's dissolute adults, Lexington's preeminent black ministers petitioned city officials in 1909 to hire a full-time truant officer to deal with the problem of "colored children wandering aimlessly about without any fixed purpose in view."[22]

For Booker T. Washington and local ministers, the answer to aimlessness and loafing was work, church-related activity, and enforced school attendance.[23] But a surplus of leisure time was bound to remain, waiting to be filled by easily accessible, inexpensive nickelodeons, skating rinks, and vaudeville theaters. Motion pictures per se, however, posed no problem, for they had become familiar to Lexington residents and had acquired legitimacy during the pre-nickelodeon period by being exhibited at fairs, churches, Chautauqua Assemblies, and, quite often, at the Opera House. Thus local blacks could have watched motion pictures at, for example, the Colored A & M Fair, or, occasionally, at a number of different churches, or from the "colored" seats at the Opera House.

These sites, all free from the taint of criminality or dissipation, were otherwise quite distinct. First held in 1869, the Colored A & M Fair prospered well into the 1920s, guided by successful black doctors, pharmacists, and businessmen. This fair, according to William Henry Fouse, "came to be one of the outstanding Negro institutions of the United States."[24] It was, declared a booster in 1898, a truly "fashionable place where you take your family and spend a delightful day," secure in the knowledge that "this organization has the united support of all the better elements."[25] The A & M Fair's horse races and stock shows attracted white spectators and garnered the most attention in Lexington newspapers, but the four-to-five-day event was similar to the Elks Fair in that it prominently featured a floral house and also a midway, usually under the direction of a traveling carnival company.

Such companies were quite different from the small-scale exhibitors that visited Lexington's black churches. For example, Professor J. V. Snow, the black showman mentioned in Chapter 3, presented his motion picture program in 1903 at both the AME Church and First Baptist, two of Lexington's premiere "colored" churches. Judging solely from newspaper accounts (which very likely did not mention all such traveling exhibitors), this kind of show continued well into the nickelodeon period and was much more commonly offered in black than in white churches.[26] For example, in April 1909 the Wilson Brothers brought their blend of religious films, comedies, and trick films to local black churches. Clearly, motion pictures could be programmed in such a way as to be welcomed into the very churches that were then leading the fight in the black community against vice, drinking, and violation of Sunday closing laws. By scheduling such entertainments, these churches reinforced their central, multifaceted role in the black community.

With a more explicitly commercial intent, Charles Scott opened the Opera House to black theatergoers, who were allowed to occupy balcony as well as gallery seats for professional shows featuring black talent. For "colored" commencement exercises, amateur productions, and benefit shows, Scott made all seats available to African Americans. Thus, at the turn of the century, the Opera House's seating arrangements were more flexible—though no less racist—than, say, schools and streetcars. In 1904 an irate white customer rebuked Scott for this flexibility after "well-dressed, respectable looking negroes" were permitted to sit in the back row of the first floor for a performance of *In Old Kentucky*.[27] A year later Scott added a separate entrance to the gallery of the Opera House, thereby affirming a more rigid and more visible enforcement of Jim Crow demands.

It is difficult to determine the extent to which African Americans formed part of the potential or actual audience for Lexington's first nickelodeons, which did not have balconies. A promotional announcement for the black-run Frolic stated that "the other picture shows have either excluded the colored people or put them in a cramped cage."[28] Presumably, in the "cramped cage" category was the two hundred-seat Blue Grass Theater, for the *Herald* reported in 1907 that a black teenager who had stolen a roll of tickets from this theater was "arrested while looking at the moving pictures, and was so intensely interested in them that he pleaded with the police not to take him out until the show was over."[29]

The seating policies of the competing vaudeville theaters that opened in 1907, the Hipp and the Majestic, are easier to ascertain, since they regularly advertised in both of the city's newspapers. For example, a promotional notice for the Majestic in December 1907 praised the week's "strictly high class" acts and the "fashionable and high-class" audiences that had been frequenting the theater, and then emphasized that "no colored people are admitted."[30] Here the *absence* of blacks is implicitly another signifier of "high class." (Appropriately enough, the motion picture segment of the Majestic's bill that week included a film of the Debeers diamond mine in South Africa.) The day after this Majestic promo appeared, L. H. Ramsey announced: "the Hippodrome admits colored people, it has a balcony for them and a separate entrance, with elegant brass railing to show them where to go."[31] This arrangement assuaged any white fears of intermingling, while promising blacks at least the touch of class/brass. Six months later, citing low "colored patronage," the Hipp adopted a whites-only policy that lasted until the theater became the Ada Meade in 1913. These overtly racist practices were not, of course, unusual at this time, though it is significant that both the Hipp and the Majestic felt it was necessary (and made good business sense) to state their seating policies, publicly implying that other alternatives were at least conceivable.[32]

One obvious alternative was to cater exclusively to a black audience. This was the case with several new ventures after the turn of the century: a plan in 1903 to develop Belt Line Park as a recreational site, centering around Lexington's black baseball team, the Heavy Hitters; the organization of the Lexington Colored Midsummer Fair & Carnival in 1904; the Grand Colored Skating Rink discussed in Chapter 4; and a self-styled "playhouse" opened in Ladies Hall on Church Street at the edge of the central business district. Ladies Hall housed Lexington's first school for blacks, and as the city's "colored" hall, it was used for a range of events, including cakewalk contests and boxing matches. The "enterprising colored citizens" who in 1903 took over the financing and management of "this place of amusement for their own people" had something different in mind. Their playhouse premiered with a "highly artistic program" by a black violinist.[33] It then became a site for dances, civic meetings, and benefit performances—the sort of "amusements" likely to attract and involve the highest strata of the local black community, the same citizens who ran the Colored A & M Fair, participated in literary and debating societies, served on the board of directors of the Colored Orphan Industrial Home, and joined the reform-minded Good Citizens League.[34] Much less respectable than Ladies Hall were such venues as Foster's Pleasure Theater and the Fontenac Roof Garden, which also offered live entertainment. Managed by a black professional actor and songwriter from Lexington, Charles Parker, Foster's Pleasure Theater was housed during 1906–07 in a saloon owned by a white man, while the seven hundred-seat Fontenac Roof Garden was located atop one of Lexington's few black-owned saloons.[35]

Although the Frolic and Foster's Pleasure Theater both sought a black clientele, the new picture show self-consciously posed itself as an alternative to saloon-theaters. The promoters of this nickelodeon were not community leaders and "professional people," but rather a Lexington paperhanger, Webster Thompson, and his partner from Louisville, Pete Walker.[36] They had initially planned to open the Frolic on the very site that had been used for the Fontenac Roof Garden, above one of the several saloons on Water Street, Lexington's so-called "Colored Main Street." Instead, Walker and Thompson opted for a small building at 430 West Main Street that had housed a black-owned restaurant. The 400 block of West Main, on the edge of the downtown commercial district, contained the office of Lexington's black weekly newspaper (the *Standard*), a distillery, a commercial laundry, a large furniture store, and several retail shops. Sharing the west end of the block with the Frolic were two "colored" boarding houses, a junk dealer, a restaurant, a grocery store, and a saloon. Located in an area predominantly patronized by blacks, the Frolic could be described as something of a neighborhood theater. Walker and Thompson's choice of the West Main (as opposed to the Water Street) location is telling, since Water Street was associated by the white press (and, at times, by black clergymen) with crime and dissolute amusements of the worst sort. A 1909 account, for example, describes this area— with its gaudy posted bills, trash barrels, empty beer bottles, and "dirty" lunch stands—as a blight on the city.[37] Thus the Frolic gained some measure of legitimacy simply by being situated in the safer and more stable West Main area.

That Walker and Thompson actively sought such legitimacy is apparent from the way they promoted the Frolic, which defined and hailed its target audience as explicitly as did the Hipp and the Majestic. The sole ad for the

> # COLORED PEOPLE
>
> ## Take Notice
>
> ---
>
> Come where you are welcome and meet your friends.
> The Frolic Theater offers splendid pictures, excellent
> singing and fine music. The leaders of the colored pop-
> ulation endorse it. Open nightly at 7 o'clock. Saturdays
> and Sundays from 2 o'clock until 10:30. Pictures chang-
> ed Sunday, Wednesday and Friday. Come tonight and
> enjoy a good laugh.

The only advertisement run in Lexington's daily papers for the Frolic, the city's first black-operated nickelodeon. Lexington *Leader*, 30 November 1907.

Frolic that ran in the *Leader* announced: "Colored People Take Notice. Come where you are welcome and meet your friends"; and an announcement of the theater's opening beckoned the "colored public" to patronize the Frolic, where "they are welcome and can mingle with their fellows unhampered."[38] Except for the fact that it did not open on weekdays until 7:00 P.M., the Frolic offered basically the same exhibition format as Lexington's other nickelode-ons: five-cent admission, pictures changed three times a week, Sunday show-ings from 2:00 to 11:00 P.M., illustrated songs, and simple musical accompaniment to the films. Would Lexington's black citizens have taken it as an achievement if a "race" theater like the Frolic could match venues catering solely to whites? Walker and Thompson, however, went further: they

promoted the Frolic as being not only equal to but separate from the city's
other theaters, as a site where the vexing problem of "disagreeable mingling"
and the demeaning experience of segregated balconies and "cramped cages"
could be avoided.

What Walker and Thompson attempted to sell was not so much movies
and illustrated songs, or even the act of moviegoing, as the place itself. To
this end, their description of the Frolic emphasized that their storefront theater would be a congenial meeting place, quite lavishly decorated: "the
building has been entirely renovated and papered, and handsome pictures
by Remington in gilt frames adorn the walls. A new front has been built,
which is beautifully panelled with dark red and green ingrain paper set off
with gold molding."[39] Such surroundings (different from the lobbies of the
soon-to-be-built Colonial and Orpheum only in degree, not in kind) were designed to provide a fit environment for "respectable" blacks, including
women and children.[40] The Frolic's interior decoration in some measure con-
notes those socially prized "progressive, cultured and aristocratic" values
referred to by the church elder quoted earlier. Here, then, was an amusement
venue that was "cheap" only in the price of admission, and that, accordingly,
would not be stigmatized by the powers-that-be.

To reinforce this impression and perhaps to suggest just *who* Walker and
Thompson meant when they addressed their advertising copy to Lexington's
"colored people," these two entrepreneurs included in their ad the assurance
that "the leaders of the colored people endorse" the Frolic. A promotional
column quoted one such endorsement from the well-respected secretary of
the Colored A & M Fair Association: "I think the Frolic Theater is a splendid
thing for the colored people. The pictures are excellent and do not hurt the
eyes. It [the Frolic] is elegantly fixed up and I heartily endorse and will patronize it."[41] What the renovation and promotion of the Frolic suggest is that
Walker and Thompson wanted their moving picture show to be perceived
not as an alternative to the saloon but as a complement to Lexington's black
churches, schools, and social clubs.

Gem Theater

Given the paucity of information, it is impossible to tell just who patronized
the Frolic, whether the "elegance" that Walker and Thompson offered trans-
lated into box office receipts, or exactly when this theater closed. The four

subsequent black-operated theaters in Lexington were all located in the same West Main Street area, but none were promoted in a manner that approximated Walker and Thompson's attempt to imbue the Frolic with an air of refinement and respectability.[42] Perhaps such legitimation was deemed superfluous or irrelevant as vaudeville and moving picture shows became commonplace; perhaps the somewhat elitist view of the "colored public" in the Frolic's advertising was not conducive to filling seats on a daily basis.

In September 1909 Robert Geary and C. B. Combs (identified in the 1909 city directory as, respectively, a machinist and a laborer) opened the Pekin Theater in a building at 415 West Main that formerly had been leased to a wholesale liquor distributor. Designed "for the express use of colored people," the Pekin was described in the *Leader* as a 250-seat "moving picture theatre" equipped with a soda fountain, though it also featured vaudeville performers.[43] It was managed by Charles J. Parker, who had served in a similar capacity for Foster's Pleasure Theater. In May 1910 the *Freeman* included the Pekin on its list of theaters "owned and controlled by the Negro."[44] By November 1910, however, the Pekin had closed.

Far more successful than the Frolic or the Pekin was the Gem Theater. The Gem opened in November 1910, taking over a site at 440 West Main that had formerly housed the Blue Grass Theater, one of the city's first nickelodeons. The Blue Grass had changed hands at least four times over the previous three years and had for at least part of its existence admitted blacks, which might account for its booking of black vaudeville acts and its screening of Essanay's *The Making of a Champion,* a six-scene biography that took Jack Johnson from being "a baby in his mammy's arms to the full-fledged gladiator of the fistic arena."[45] After the Blue Grass had been damaged by fire, two "colored businessmen" from Cincinnati refurbished this 250–300-seat theater and opened it as the Gem.

The Gem's first shows placed roughly equal emphasis on motion pictures, local musical talent, and vaudeville acts said to have been booked through Doyle and Company of Chicago, "which handles only the best class of artists, some of whom are white." A laudatory review of the Gem's opening night made no mention of the movies, but particularly praised the "catchy ragtime songs" of a "soubrette."[46] According to the brief promotional notices that ran in the Colored Notes column of the *Leader* during 1911–12, the Gem's programming featured: Sunday shows from 1:00 to 10:30 P.M. devoted exclusively to motion pictures, oftentimes westerns, with musical accompaniment that might include a saxophone trio; daily evening shows combining motion pictures and live acts, usually song-and-dance teams or small groups like Smith's Pickaninnies, though "novelty" acts were also booked, ranging from a female impersonator to a white performer who specialized in "eccentric" dancing and a parodic treatment of *Casey Jones*.[47]

During 1911–12 the Gem first became part of the Central Vaudeville Circuit (serving black theaters in Chicago, Indianapolis, Louisville, Dayton, St. Louis, and Springfield, Ohio), then it was briefly associated with the Dudley Circuit (with fourteen theaters in Washington, D.C., Virginia, North Carolina, Tennessee, Indiana, Ohio, and Kentucky).[48] Thus this small Lexington venue, though it was not one of the premiere black theaters in the country, was able quite regularly to offer acts that also played the Crown Garden Theater in Indianapolis and the Monogram in Chicago. Like the Opera House during its heyday as a one-night theatrical stand, the Gem at times served as a way station for performers en route to larger venues in midwestern or southern cities.[49]

The Gem's promotional notices do not indicate how this theater's exhibition strategy affected the way Lexington's blacks viewed a 101 Ranch western or a one-reel melodrama like *The Gambler's Influence*, or, more generally, how its audience responded to the combination of live black performers and "white" motion pictures. Did moviegoers at the Gem suffer from what the *Freeman*'s editor called the "lack of general education" that "a good many colored people" demonstrate when they laugh "in the serious places of great tragedies" on the screen?[50] Could this so-called "lack" be seen as analogous in any way to what Roy Rosenzweig describes as urban working-class "movie theater conduct," which grew "out of traditions of working-class public recreational behavior based on sociability, conviviality, communality, and informality?"[51] Such unanswerable questions are, of course, endemic to reception studies—probably even more so in the case of marginalized, devalued audiences such as the black residents of a small biracial city.

Compared to "colored" theaters in Indianapolis and Chicago, the Gem was a modest operation, but it was a reasonably successful and therefore exceptional black business venture, afloat for almost six years.[52] Initially, its main competition for the black amusement dollar in Lexington came from the Lincoln Theater, which opened in late 1910 across the street from the Gem at 415 West Main (previously home to the Pekin). In May 1911 the Lincoln was acquired by the Collins brothers of Piqua, Ohio, who briefly booked a stock company that performed productions like *A Walk through Coontown*. However, during the rest of the year that the Lincoln remained open, it stuck to a blend of moving pictures and vaudeville acts, with an occasional special Sunday matinee that featured moving pictures, illustrated songs, and "fifty slides of descriptive pictures of the Holy Land."[53]

In December 1911, after the Lincoln had closed, the theater was "purchased outright" at a sheriff's sale by "Senator" R. F. Bell, a well-known, forty-nine-year-old Lexington native. One of the more entrepreneurial-minded black residents of the city, Bell had been managing the Gem since at least May 1911 and would later became a real estate dealer and co-owner of a grocery and would eventually be given a political patronage job at Lexington's first black park.[54] Bell vowed that the refurbished Lincoln would be "one of the best equipped theaters in the South, controlled entirely by Negroes."[55] This claim is typical of an era when black businesses sought to answer Jim Crow practices by appealing to and capitalizing on race pride. In the same spirit, but with more wit than Bell, a movie theater proprietor in Savannah, Georgia, for example, announced that "the pictures are hand-colored, the performers, the patrons and the proprietor are so by nature. Glad of it, aren't you?"[56]

By early 1912 Bell had acquired the lease on the Gem as well as the Lincoln, thereby cornering most of the local market on black commercial entertainment.[57] Initially he planned to operate both theaters full time, but the Lincoln soon closed except for Sunday screenings (another testament to the drawing power of the motion pictures on the Sabbath). Bell also announced plans for the Gem Theater Company to open a "vaudeville and moving picture house" in nearby Winchester, "the first of a chain of colored houses to be established in towns adjacent to Lexington."[58] In early 1913 Bell moved his entire Lexington operation from the Gem Theater building across the street to the site occupied by the Lincoln. 440 West Main, which had been home to the Blue Grass and the Gem theaters, became a saloon and then the four-lane Elite Bowling Alley.

The Gem's bookings during November 1913 are typical of Bell's exhibition strategy while he ran the theater: Sundays were devoted to four or five reels of motion pictures, with films like Broncho's *The Indian's Gratitude;* regular shows, combining pictures and two small-scale live acts (for example, a "singing and dancing comedian" and "Professor Baryear, the handcuff king") ran for a week; and the only special attraction was a week-long contest involving Lexington's vocal quartets.[59] This schedule looks modest indeed, particularly in contrast to Lexington's white moving picture shows, whose programs changed daily and had begun to include longer films. But the Gem was not in competition with the Orpheum, Colonial, and Star, none of which admitted blacks.[60]

According to the *Freeman*'s Lexington correspondent, Bell survived an attempt by white businessmen to force his "clean, orderly Negro theater" to move to another location in February 1913.[61] He continued to manage the Gem until April 1914, when it was acquired by Willis E. Burden. (Since Burden is not included in any city directories before this date, I assume he came from out of town.) Bell provided competition to the Gem when he leased the Opera House and presented motion picture-and-vaudeville shows for black audiences, but this arrangement lasted only through the summer of 1914.

Under Burden's management, the Gem experimented with a resident stock company and again was briefly allied with the Dudley theater circuit, but for the most part it operated exclusively as a site for "High Class Motion Pictures," with bills changing daily and musical accompaniment provided by a small band featuring a trap drummer and, at times, a trombone soloist.[62] One strategy for staying in business under the dictates of Jim Crow was to provide black consumers with a product comparable to that available in white-only venues. Once Burden stopped showcasing touring vaudeville performers and local acts, the Gem's exhibition format became basically the same as the other movie theaters in town, except that its films were often in at least their second Lexington run. (Thus *Fantomas* was screened at the Gem some four months after it had premiered at the Star.) During November 1915, for example, the Gem offered five or six reels for its daily shows and seven or eight reels on Sundays. The more than one hundred films screened that month included a few five-reel photoplays and a special program of nonfiction war films, though the typical fare was one- or two-reel productions from studios such as Reliance, Broncho, Joker, and Keystone, with serials a staple on Tuesdays (*The Perils of Pauline*), Thursdays (*The Broken Coin*), and Sundays (*The Phantom Extra*).

Unlike the Gem's previous proprietors and like the managers of Lexington's white-owned theaters, Burden advertised his theater's daily schedule, selling and sorting out the mass of product, film by film. The following promotional notice from 29 March 1915 is typical:

> Sunday's program at the Gem Theatre will as usual be one of class. "The Jewel of Allah," an interesting drama of the Orient, featuring Edna Payne and Stanley Wolpole, will be offered, and for real excellence along all

lines ranks with the best films now before the public. "The Kaffir's Skull," a tale of South Africa, which furnishes a thrill a minute, will also be shown. The setting and photography of this offering is unsurpassed and the cast is composed of many of the leading lights of filmdom. "The Call of the Waves," showing life at a famous watering place, with all its attendant attractions, will be seen. This drama is filled with human interest and is always a winner, wherever shown. The famous stars of the "Lucille Love" serial, Grace Cunard and Francis Ford, play the leads in this production.[63]

Included in the "Colored" section of the *Leader*, this promotional notice was placed amid announcements for church-sponsored activities, school achievements, and meetings of fraternal organizations and social clubs like the Maple Leaf Embroidery Club, the WCTU, and the Knights of Pythias. The Gem's "class" program complements the image of an industrious, religious, self-sustaining black community that the *Leader*'s Colored Notes daily celebrated. The movies are in fact the sole "outside" presence in this column/social world. We can only wonder whether the Gem fit as readily into the daily lives of Lexington's African Americans as it did into the Colored Notes of this newspaper.

Burden's decision to drop black vaudeville acts at the Gem in favor of more moving pictures provided his patrons with an increasingly homogeneous entertainment experience, no matter how different individual films might be. *The Call of the Waves* is "always a winner, wherever shown," the Gem's promo claimed, implying that the black spectator, as well as the next (white) person, can see this film and vicariously experience "class." In retrospect, the dilemma of the Gem seems unresolvable: to compete for black patrons, Burden sought to provide an equal, if separate, moviegoing experience, yet the pictures he offered upheld and endorsed, directly or indirectly, the unequal and unjust conditions in segregated America. For example, what are we to make ideologically and culturally of the particular program listed above, which combines Oriental exoticism, South African adventure, and the "human interest" drama of well-to-do white folks at a famous resort? Here was the "world" become story, the Other (as place, race, religion, ethnicity, class) materialized and arbitrarily linked together into a single program— and the process continued, day after day.

The Kaffir's Skull no doubt included "Africans," and therefore provided Lexington's African Americans with screen images, albeit probably perverse and stereotypical, of blacks.[64] Burden did not settle for such images, however, for soon after he took over the Gem he began quite systematically to book films by and about American blacks.[65] A Gem promo on 4 August 1914 lauded the efforts of the Afro-American Film Company, which planned to produce films involving black performers and to record the activities of "notable Negroes" like Booker T. Washington. Later that month and into the fall of 1914, Burden's advertisements prominently mention a series of "race" films: *The Streets of Harlem;* the Afro-American Film Company's comedies, *Jim Dandy's Dream* and *One Large Evening* (featuring Charles Gilpin); the Haynes Photoplay Company's *Uncle Remus' Visit to New York* and its three-reel film of the Odd Fellows Convention in Boston, which included footage of "notable Negro enterprises of the East and many of the most noted Negroes in the United States"; and newsreels focusing on Booker T. Washington and the National Baptist Jubilee in Nashville.[66] Typically these black films played for three days at the Gem, paired in each case with a more conventional offering. *Uncle Remus' Visit to New York,* for example, was co-billed with *The Lady in the Lake* (Vitagraph's 1912 adaptation of Sir Walter Scott's poem). During the three months when he booked these films, Burden's schedule also included other "special" attractions like *Fantomas* and Warner's three-reel *The Daughter of the Confederacy.*

The handful of "race" films screened at the Gem are more than a historical curiosity; indeed, the production of "all-colored" motion pictures before 1916 merits more attention than it has been accorded by film historians.[67] We can assume that these motion pictures were successful in Lexington (as they were in Chicago and New York City), since Burden held them over for three days and continued to book and publicize them.[68] Another cycle of black films at the Gem began in January 1916 with newsreels of Booker T. Washington's funeral. Then on each Sunday in March 1916—the same month that *The Birth of a Nation* drew sell-out crowds at the Opera House—the Gem included a different black film on its bill: the Afro-American Film Company's one-reel comedy, *By the Help of Uncle Eben;* the Historical Feature Film Company's *Money Talks in Darktown* and *The Shooting Star; Mr. Fixit's Birthday;* and *For the Honor of the Eighth,* a newsreel on a crack "colored" National Guard regiment, produced by the Jones Photoplay Company.[69] Regardless of whether or not *Money Talks in Darktown,* for example, reworked "coontown" clichés or the newsreels reified Booker T. Washington's notion of "notable Negroes," the very existence of such films is significant. During those stretches in 1914 and 1916 when Burden scheduled "Negro films," the designation of the Gem as a "colored" theater did not simply mean that it was a second-rate imitation of Lexington's white theaters, but rather that it was a business that promoted the race and helped to link Lexington's black moviegoers with the black community in larger urban areas.

It was in part because the Gem exhibited "colored pictures of a high class nature," that the *Freeman*'s correspondent in Lexington, Hardin Tolbert, enthusiastically championed this theater. For Tolbert the fact that the Gem was a Negro-owned enterprise put Lexington blacks under a moral and racial obligation to support Burden's theater. Why shouldn't they, Tolbert reasoned, since the Gem "was equipped with modern machinery, insuring at all times perfect projection, police [polite?] service and a welcome to all."[70] In Tolbert's eyes, the choice was perfectly clear: attend the Gem or join that

> class of Negroes who will go to the Ada Meade theatre in the Jim Crow department where their legs are cramped up, where there are poor sanitary conditions in the second gallery or rat hold [sic]. There are some of the same people who will go to the Ben Ali theatre where the Negroes are compelled to go in from Short Street [the main, white entrance was on Main Street] to that lofty perch in the roost where, with a little unbalance, they would fall over and break their necks, and there would be nothing done about it. In less time than a year three Negroes have been killed and slayers have been exonerated by the highest authorities, and even some of these Negroes had rather patronize a Jim Crow institution than go to a first class theatre prepared for them to enjoy.[71]

Tolbert's anger and the connection he draws between Jim Crow practices in local theaters and grossly racist miscarriages of justice are quite unlike anything expressed in the city's daily newspapers. With the assistance of the editor of the Lexington *News* (a black weekly), Tolbert announced plans in December 1915 for "mass meetings" to demand equal treatment for blacks at white theaters in the city.[72] His subsequent columns do not refer to this public protest, but through January and February of 1916 Tolbert continued to press his point, by noting, for example, that the Gem employed five blacks, while the white theaters together had only one black employee. He also railed against "the doctor, business man and school teachers who sanction Jim Crow" by patronizing segregated theaters, for these "said-to-be-leaders" are a "menace to society and a disgrace to the Negro race."[73] Tolbert's characterization of Lexington's black elite differs dramatically from the self-image offered by the *Leader*'s Colored Notes, though in both cases the Gem is associated with the "progressive" segment of the African-American community.

Whether or not Tolbert's personal crusade against Jim Crowism, or the screening of black motion pictures, or Burden's reduction of the Gem's admission price from ten to five cents in January 1916 helped fill the theater in the winter and spring of 1916, such measures failed to make the Gem profitable in the long run. It probably closed soon after Burden's last promotional notice ran in the *Leader* in September 1916. I could find no reference in either Lexington newspaper to the precise fate of the Gem, though by late 1918 the building at 415 West Main had become part of a furniture store. It was not until 1921 that another black-run movie theater opened in Lexington.

What factors contributed to the closing of the Gem, by far the city's most successful black-operated theater until the 1940s? It seems clear that official action or organized protest had nothing to do with it, unlike the case of the New Mammoth Skating Rink, which was refused a city license in 1917 after it had been "turned over to Negroes."[74] Though Willis Burden had been indicted in February 1915 for violating Kentucky's Sunday closing law, this ultimately had no effect on Sunday film showings. Nor was the Gem, in contrast to saloons and dance halls, ever targeted by black clergymen and civic-minded reformers.

Lexington at large had surely not forsaken the movies. As noted earlier, the *Herald* declared in May 1916 that some 7,500 people each day attended the city's movie theaters,[75] the largest of which begun booking feature film programs for one- or two-day engagements. Burden, it would seem, could not afford a comparable product, even on a second- or third-run basis, and as Tolbert noted with shame, part of the Gem's potential audience opted for the segregated seating arrangements and ten-cent tickets of the Ben Ali.

Whether or not the Gem—even with its standing as a "colored" enterprise that made some effort to uplift the race—closed because it could not compete in the commercial entertainment marketplace, other factors probably played a role in its demise. For example, in July 1916 Frederick Douglass Park, Lexington's first city-funded black park, finally opened with much fanfare. Sunday afternoon band concerts, recreational and picnic facilities, and supervised playground activities brought large crowds to Douglass Park, which was readily accessible for a good part of Lexington's black population. In addition, like the deep South, Kentucky and other border states were affected by the Great Migration, as blacks left the region and headed to northern cities, particularly during the 1910s. (The black population of Kentucky, for example, dropped by 9.8 percent from 1910 to 1920, more than any other southern state.[76]) One account in a local newspaper stated that blacks were leaving Lexington at the rate of almost one hundred per week in the summer of 1916.[77] This figure is at best a rough estimate (perhaps more a matter of wish fulfillment than hard fact), yet the Great Migration doubtless affected black businesses like the Gem.

Although Hardin Tolbert of the *Freeman* sought to engineer a mass protest against the unjust hiring practices and segregated seating policies of Lexington's white-owned theaters, it took the booking of *The Birth of a Nation* to mobilize at least part of the black community. (The unsuccessful campaign to prevent Griffith's film from being shown in Lexington did not, however, explicitly take up the matter of separate but unequal conditions.) Ironically the Gem probably closed right about the time when Griffith's film returned to Lexington for its sold-out second run. The unprecedented box office success of *The Birth of a Nation* and the enthusiasm with which white spectators greeted Griffith's melodramatic celebration of Jim Crow's founding principles might well be the most telling indication of the movies' place and role in a small biracial city and a racist society. If so, there is all the more reason to pay attention to how black-owned-and-operated theaters like the Frolic and the Gem defined themselves and sought out a clientele in the African-American community; how they negotiated the shifting politics and policies of Jim Crowism; and how they competed with, mirrored, or posed an alternative to white opera houses, nickelodeons, and vaudeville theaters, which often stood as embodiments of white economic, social, and cultural power and prestige in a radically unjust biracial society. The more we learn about early black moviegoing, the less likely we will be to accept and perpetuate well-entrenched and reductive notions of the "mass" audience and of the movies as, in the words of the *American Magazine* in 1913, "art democratic, art for the race."[78]

EIGHT

Movies on the Homefront

Judged solely in terms of theater construction and booking policies, 1917–19 seems to have been a relatively static and uneventful period for Lexington film exhibitors. During the World War I years no black theater sought to replace the Gem, which, along with the Star and the Colonial, had closed, leaving the Orpheum as the only five-and-ten-cent show in town. *The Birth of a Nation* had twice come and gone. Lexington's premiere movie theaters, the Strand and the Ben Ali, having weathered the storm over film censorship in 1916, had both settled into the same predictable format. The Ada Meade did change hands in 1918, yet this was of far less significance than either the transactions conducted by the Berryman Realty Company and the Phoenix Amusement Company earlier in the 1910s or the deals that would be struck after the war.

There is, however, a story well worth telling about 1917–19, for during these years local exhibitors faced a number of problems that together could have been disastrous. Wartime conditions and, in particular, the federal Committee on Public Information (CPI), put special demands on theater owners. City authorities raised license fees and increased safety requirements. From June through August 1918, local sabbatarian forces staged their most con-

180

certed effort to date, focusing all their attention on movie theaters. Two months later, an influenza epidemic struck with deadly force. Under these conditions to conduct business as usual was in itself something of an accomplishment.

Movie Theaters and the War Effort

To an extent, the United States' participation in World War I affected film exhibition in Lexington in much the same way it affected smaller towns and larger cities across the country. For a brief period beginning 22 January 1918, theaters were closed on "heatless" Tuesdays by order of the federal Fuel Administration. Earlier, a 10 percent "war tax" had been assessed on all movie tickets costing more than ten cents.[1] Typically this meant no direct increase in prices for consumers: regular engagements at the Ben Ali, for instance, cost ten and twenty cents, "war tax included."[2] The effect of the war on film programming was more readily apparent. Expanding on a trend begun in 1915–16, all manner of war films were screened at Lexington's commercial venues: official documentaries like *Pershing's Crusaders* (July 1918); melodramatic, patriotic features like *The Kaiser, the Beast of Berlin* (August 1918); and torn-from-the-headlines serials like *The Eagle's Nest* (March 1918).[3] The most acclaimed war film locally was D. W. Griffith's *Hearts of the World*. When Griffith's latest epic played the Opera House for a week in September 1918 at top prices, it "continually" brought Lexington audiences "to their feet and cheering." The *Herald* literally "begged" its readers to see *Hearts of the World*, "one of the greatest films ever made."[4]

Yet despite the wave of highly topical motion picture fare, which peaked in 1918, the war never dominated local screens on a daily basis. For example, during the first week of October 1918, as the armistice neared, the Ben Ali for two days scheduled "Official War Pictures" and then booked a singer who performed "patriotic songs" with "the words flashed on the screen" so that the audience could join in. Some war-related footage was most likely also included in that week's installments of the *Hearst-Pathé News, Current Events*, and the *Universal News Weekly*. But none of the feature films showcased at Lexington cinemas that week were even remotely connected to the war effort. In fact, the only fictional films that might fit into this category were an episode of *The Lion's Claw* serial at the Orpheum and two comic shorts at the Ada Meade.

The war also entered local theaters via speeches delivered by "Four-Minute Men." Historian David M. Kennedy notes that these local volunteers representing the CPI had to be "certified as to speaking prowess and safe political views" and endorsed by "three prominent citizens—bankers, professional or business men."[5] The first group of these speeches was given as part of "Patriotic Wake-Up Week." On 8 October 1917, the Four-Minute Men, including the county attorney and the pastor of the Church of the Good Shepherd, spoke at all the city's theaters between 7:30 and 8:00 P.M. To suit the site and the occasion—and probably in acknowledgment of the moviegoers' amount of patience—speeches were kept briefer than anything else on the bill, about the length of a newspaper editorial. Apparently the "four-minute" appellation was taken quite literally; the *Herald* describes how one speaker "crowded nearly 300 words in four minutes" and "continued speaking as he walked from the stage."[6]

The CPI carried on its campaign in 1918. For example, during the week of 23 July 1918, different speakers were scheduled for Tuesday, Thursday, and Saturday evenings at each of Lexington's theaters, where they addressed moviegoers on "The Meaning of America" and on the differences between democracy and autocracy.[7] After the speeches came such films as *M'liss*, an adaptation of a Bret Harte story, starring Mary Pickford; Sessue Hayakawa in *The White Man's Law;* and a Gloria Swanson vehicle, *You Can't Believe Everything;* as well as assorted short comedies, including a return engagement of Chaplin's *Easy Street.* No doubt few of the speakers or the spectators would have acknowledged that these and the other motion pictures being screened that week and every week were, in effect, part of a deeply influential, ongoing process of defining and redefining the "meaning of America."

What makes the Four-Minute Men campaign particularly significant is that it seems to have been based on the assumption that, in order to influence public opinion, regular moviegoers were a crucial audience to reach. Further, this group was likely to be as (if not more) effectively reached in a theater as by other means, for example, through the press. Perhaps the spectators felt themselves to be more a part of democratic America when they were inside a movie theater (with its inexpensive tickets, open seating, varied programming, and audience mixed in terms of age, class, and gender) than inside a classroom, workplace, or church. Intended to boost patriotism and encourage the purchase of war bonds, the Four-Minute Men speeches also served as one further unqualified acknowledgment of the importance of motion picture theaters within the community. Like the successful, well-respected men who gave these abbreviated pep talks, local film exhibitors were doing their non-partisan civic duty.

Lexington's theaters did their bit for the war effort in other ways as well. In April 1917 Christine Mayo, "the vampire woman of moving pictures," appeared in person at the Strand to promote recruitment and preparedness.[8] Later that year, the Ada Meade, Ben Ali, and Opera House held benefit performances for the Red Cross and the Victory Loan drive. The Strand and the Ben Ali also screened patriotic slides and films of local recruits in training at Kentucky's Fort Benjamin Harrison. Similar events were staged the following year, and in July 1918 the Orpheum and Ben Ali instituted a free admission policy for the four thousand soldiers stationed at Fort Stanley, two miles from Lexington, and the 430 recruits in training at Camp Buell on the University of Kentucky campus.

Whatever income local theaters lost due to admission taxes and benefit performances was probably more than made up for by good public relations and increased patronage for war-related programming. There was no such upside, however, to the influenza epidemic in the fall of 1918 that caused all Lexington theaters to be closed by the state Board of Health from October 8 to December 18.[9] During this ten-week period, there were 1,500 cases of influenza and sixty deaths reported in Lexington. Even after the theaters were allowed to reopen, the mayor insisted that no one under eighteen years old be admitted and no one be allowed to stand in the aisles or crowd theater entrances.[10] In January 1919 the Lexington Board of Health considered reclosing the theaters, but opted instead for authorizing "inspectors stationed in each theater of the city to request all patrons who cough, sneeze or show symptoms of being ill to leave the building."[11]

How did giving up the movies (and vaudeville) for ten weeks stack up against war-related shortages of food and fuel? As would be expected, theater advertisements suggested that Lexington, deprived of the movies, had suffered depression and withdrawal. "Cheer up! The Ada Meade Reopens," declared one ad, while the Strand was billed as being ready to satisfy Lexington's appetite for the movies: "Picture Hungry? Sure You Are. You Didn't Realize How Much You Needed Moving Pictures Until You Were Deprived of Them."[12] This language of need, hunger, and deprivation gains resonance not only in terms of wartime shortages, but also in terms of the increasingly successful temperance movement and the extensive sabbatarian campaign waged in Lexington during the summer of 1918. This new round in the debate over Sunday film screenings centered on the question of whether in wartime America the movies were truly a "necessity" for Lexington residents and for the soldiers stationed in or near the city.

The 1918 Sabbatarian Campaign

Several factors beside the continued popularity of Sunday movies led Lexington's sabbatarian forces in June 1918 to launch another initiative. In April 1918, after a "vigorous protest" by the Ministerial Union, Mayor Rogers banned *Purity*, a film scheduled for the Opera House. Rogers even prohibited this film from being privately shown at the Kentucky Horse Breeders Association auditorium.[13] City officials also gave at least nominal support to a mass anti-vice rally staged by the Ministerial Union and other local organizations in October 1917, as part of a drive to rid Lexington of "disorderly houses" and thus protect Camp Buell recruits. At the same time, the local blue law proponents probably felt themselves at the crest of a national wave, what with the Army's strict policy concerning "sexual vice" and the highly effective activities of the Anti-Saloon League across the country.[14] Closer to home, there was the Kentucky state legislature's overwhelming vote in January 1918 to ratify the proposed eighteenth Amendment.[15]

Sabbatarian hopes were especially encouraged when the Kentucky Court of Appeals in January 1918 upheld a circuit court ruling that "for each employee engaged in operating a picture show on Sunday, moving picture theater proprietors may be fined $50."[16] Then, in March, after a "stormy debate," the Kentucky legislature voted 56–36 to reject a bill that would have legalized Sunday moving picture shows. Opponents "contended that public sentiments in each community can determine the question," thereby to some extent keeping film exhibition and moviegoing under local control.[17] With renewed vigor, sabbatarian forces in Lexington sought to stir up public sentiment and bring exhibitors to task for their violation of the Sabbath.

On the evening of 1 July 1918, (white) Protestant churchmen representing the Laymen's League and delegates from the Ministerial Union met at the YMCA and decided to start a petition drive and to gather evidence of Sunday film screenings so that warrants could be sworn out against theater owners and projectionists.[18] Once this plan had been publicly announced, leaders of the Laymen's League made direct appeals to theater owners and city officials. John Elliott reportedly agreed to close the Strand on Sundays if the other theaters followed suit. But Charles Berryman of the Ben Ali—which was then and would until December 1919 serve as the temporary Sunday morning home of the First Presbyterian Church—absolutely refused to forego Sunday screenings voluntarily, as did John Stamper, who argued that closing on Sundays would assuredly put the Orpheum out of business. (At this time the Ada Meade was closed for renovations and so was not a target of sabbatarian protest.) The city commissioners and Lexington's corporate counsel advised the laymen to take the matter to a grand jury, while Mayor Rogers again came out loudly and clearly in favor of Sunday movies, which he called "a harmless form of amusement, always entertaining and frequently instructive and educational in value."[19]

The sabbatarian strategy was to present the issue as a straightforward legal matter, and prominent laymen—not ministers—initially were the public spokespersons. (Even the first round of sermons on Sunday movies approached the situation from what was dubbed a "statute violation" rather than a "moral" standpoint.)[20] For example, Dr. A. S. Venable, president of Sayre College, then a private girl's school in Lexington, called for a literal interpretation of the blue law, since "it is the duty of every citizen to see that the law is enforced, and when it is enforced impartially, Lexington will be a better city and Lexingtonians better citizens."[21] This appeal to civic responsibility was quite in tune with the diligent earnestness so valued in the homefront war effort. But in this particular case, at least, the rhetoric of good citizenship did not prove to be very persuasive.

The debate that ensued relied on many of the same arguments that had been proffered in Lexington's previous sabbatarian controversies. Berryman, for example, solicited the opinion of ordinary citizens by running a pro/con questionnaire for a week in both papers; this form could be mailed or dropped off in person at the Ben Ali. Similarly, the Orpheum ran slides encouraging its patrons to make their attitudes known. Letters to the editor once more evoked biblical justification for blue laws or condemned its adherents as Philistine meddlers out to restrict individual freedom.[22] In the most extreme antisabbatarian tirades, the supporters of Sunday closing were depicted as repressive autocrats and veritable "Huns of America" offering aid to the "Beast of Berlin."[23] The *Leader* half-seriously proposed in an editorial that the church itself "build an auditorium" and stage a "Sunday afternoon show [with appropriate motion pictures] bigger and better than any other house can put on," one that provides "recreation, entertainment, instruction, amusement and advanced conception of the ideals of citizenship and upright living."[24] The *Herald,* in contrast, called for an increase in "wholesome, healthful rec-

A demand has been made upon the management of the

BEN ALI THEATRE

THAT THEY CLOSE ON SUNDAYS

In order to ascertain the wishes of the citizens of Lexington we ask that you fill in the coupon below stating whether you are in favor of this closing or against it and your reasons therefor.

Kindly sign and mail your reply to Ben Ali Theatre or drop it in the box provided for this purpose at the door of the theatre.

COUPON

Do you think the Ben Ali Theatre should remain open on Sundays?

....

Why? ....

....

....

....

(Signed)

....

Giving the citizens what they desire: the Ben Ali's response to sabbatarianism in 1918. Lexington *Leader*, 10 July 1918.

reation on every day of the week, and particularly on Sunday," for that is what society owes to "those who labor and undergo daily toil and strain."[25] Among these "toilers," as another *Herald* editorial put it, were, most prominently, "the tired housewife" and "our poorest working people, including the colored ones."[26] For the *Herald,* as for outspoken local postmaster Moses Kaufman, the movies were not merely harmless; they were actually instructive and beneficial in their ability to provide restorative diversion.[27]

Thus the two sides in this controversy were no closer to agreement than they had been in 1914 or 1916. What was new in the sabbatarian debate during the summer of 1918 derived to a great extent from the fact of the war and the presence of soldiers in Lexington. Indeed, as soon as the Laymen's League took up the fight against Sunday movies, Lieutenant W. B. Marxsen, adjutant of Camp Buell, came out strongly against the proposed ban. Recruits, he argued, have only Saturday afternoon and Sunday for recreation, and motion pictures provide a much-needed, "harmless means of amusement."[28] A letter to the *Herald* gave even more credit to the role of motion pictures during wartime: after a week of toil, the "heroes of shop, mill and mine" can visit a movie theater on Sunday, see footage of United States and enemy troops, and thereby "gain inspiration for another week's work and further self-denial."[29] Here the theater has essentially taken over a function of the church: inspiring the worker to accept his or her plight and labor for a greater, far-distant good. As these comments suggest, in 1918 Sunday movies were defended as a basic necessity for the boys in uniform and for working people, pictured in these accounts as diligent and easily satisfied, a perfect movie audience (and an image quite suitable for the middle class to contemplate).

With public sentiment in favor of Sunday movies, and theater owners (save Elliott) unwilling to comply with the blue law, the Laymen's League took the matter to court. On Sunday, July 7, league members purchased movie tickets, which constituted evidence sufficient to have warrants issued for the proprietors of the city's three movie theaters. Magistrate Orville Boone scheduled the trial for within the week. (Magistrates at this date were elected officials who needed no special qualifications beyond age and residence.) Members of the Ministerial Union circulated petitions among their congregations, and the Laymen's League hired two lawyers to assist in the county's prosecution of the case. At the same time, city commissioner Wood G. Dunlap, writing as a private citizen, argued against closing Sunday movies in a long letter to the *Herald*,[30] and the Blue Grass Federation of Labor took the same position in a public resolution issued on July 13.

As the trial neared, Corporate Counsel John G. Denny, in response to a request from the city commissioners, weighed the various precedents, pointed out the "elasticity" of blue laws nationwide, and concluded that Kentucky's statute could be interpreted "literally or liberally," depending on how one read the key phrase: "no work or business shall be done on the Sabbath day, except the ordinary household offices, or other work of charity or necessity."[31] Not surprisingly, the attorneys representing the Ben Ali would hinge their case on the proposition that the movies were indeed a "necessity" of life in Lexington in 1918.[32]

After much challenging of potential jurors—most of whom already held strong opinions on Sunday movies—a stockbroker, an insurance agent, and four farmers were seated as the jury, and the trial against the Berryman Realty Company commenced on Saturday, July 13. Preliminary testimony established that the Ben Ali collected $700–$900 per month in war taxes, with considerably more of this total amassed on Sundays than on any other day.[33]

The defense focused on the crucial role of motion pictures during wartime. To this end, Berryman's attorneys called officers from Camp Buell, who testified that the "recreation" provided by motion pictures was "essential to the well-being of the troops." The defense also argued that the Ben Ali aided in military recruitment and provided a forum for the Four-Minute Men, while the motion pictures themselves "keep the minds of the people off the horrors of the present conflict."[34] (Other defenders of Sunday movies made exactly the opposite point, that at local theaters "leading events all over the world are shown true to life," and these news films "bring vividly before Sunday audiences the fact that we are in the midst of the most terrible war history will ever chronicle."[35]) The prosecution sought simply to prove that the Ben Ali had been open for business on the previous Sunday and so had violated state law as recently interpreted by the Kentucky Court of Appeals. Magistrate Boone ruled that "the question of necessity is for the court and not the jury to decide." All that the jury was called upon to determine was whether the Ben Ali showed motion pictures on Sunday and, if so, how much should the Berryman Realty Company be fined—not less than two nor more than fifty dollars. After deliberating for an hour, the jury returned a guilty verdict and recommended a two-dollar fine. Under the conditions Boone had laid down, this was obviously as close as the jurors could come to an outright endorsement of Sunday movie screenings.[36]

Two days later, on July 18, the joint trial of the Orpheum and the Strand began, again with Magistrate Boone presiding. Defense counsel immediately requested a change of venue on the grounds that Boone "entertains bias and prejudice against any work of labor whatsoever on the Sabbath day," and therefore he refused to admit evidence as to the necessity of Sunday motion pictures. Without confessing to any "disqualification," Boone turned the trial over to Magistrate Charles P. Dodd, a wholesale grocer by trade. Once again, jury selection proved to be a problem, as only two of the first twenty-four men called were seated.

Though defense attorney R. C. Stoll was quick to point out that "many things are now necessary which were not necessary before the war," this trial was, in effect, the closest thing Lexington had seen to a public hearing on the movies.[37] For the defense was allowed to present a battery of witnesses, all testifying to the necessity of Sunday motion pictures, particularly given the wartime conditions in Lexington. Stamper, for example, noted that Sunday crowds, mostly composed of the "laboring class," were twice the size of other days and included twice as many soldiers as during the rest of the week. The defense's key testimony came from a quite diverse group of people: Camp Buell officers, the chairwoman of the Kentucky Federation of Women's Clubs, a member of the State Council of National Defense, a locally based navy recruiter, a Lexington policewoman, and a lumber mill foreman and father of seven. All spoke of how necessary the movies were to a broad range of spectators: soldiers, would-be recruits, the "girls of the city," families, and the rural and urban "laboring class."[38] As the front page headline of the *Herald* put it: "Sunday Movies Necessity, Say Many on Stand. Side of Laborer, Soldier, Working Girl and Average Citizen Heard in Picture Trial."[39] The other side seemed to be a beleaguered, short-sighted minority, out of step with the twentieth century, as the prosecution once again called on Protestant ministers and local laymen to decry the desecration of the Sabbath.

Magistrate Dodd instructed the jury to base its verdict on whether or not the movies could be considered a "necessity." After twenty minutes of deliberation, the jurors found the defendants "not guilty under present war conditions."[40] The rationale for this verdict was perhaps best explained in a letter to the *Herald* written by a woman who identified herself as "a church and civic worker and believer in 'law and order'." "There should be," she wrote, "as few restrictions placed upon our movie theaters as possible, because they are democracy's most valuable patriotic asset," given that they cater to "all ages and all classes" and, especially, to "whole families" together. What sabbatarianism threatened was nothing less than what this woman affectionately called the "'dear old movies'," which provide an "inexpensive, all-inclusive, democratic form of amusement, recreation and patriotic instruction."[41] Such arguments were meaningless (or worse) to such die-hard defenders of the Sabbath as the pastor of the Calvary Baptist Church, who had testified at the trial that "he would rather see a son of his lying wounded on a battlefield than in a moving picture show on Sunday."[42]

After losing in Dodd's court, the Laymen's League revised its strategy, returning to sympathetic Magistrate Boone, who issued summonses for the manager of the Ben Ali, as well the machine operator, ticket taker, two cashiers, and five ushers who worked in this theater on Sundays. The Berryman Realty Company was thus charged with ten counts of violating the blue law and could be assessed a maximum fine of $500, if found guilty.[43] The Laymen's League got the endorsement of the Colored Ministers Alliance and further pressed its campaign by taking out a large advertisement on the entertainment page of the *Leader* that enumerated the cities throughout the South in which Sunday movies were prohibited.[44]

Before the third trial could begin, the defense again successfully sought to disqualify Magistrate Boone, and the prosecution, in turn, objected to the four other city magistrates, on the grounds that they favored a "liberal" reading of the blue law as it applied to motion picture theaters. The gavel was eventually passed to one of the county magistrates, G. W. Botkin, owner of a general store in Coletown, a small village some ten miles from Lexington. Botkin regularly conducted his court in his store or, weather permitting, under a large tree in an adjacent field.[45] On the morning of July 30, the concerned parties gathered under "frying pans, tin and galvanized buckets hanging from the ceiling," and heard Botkin's decision to continue the case until mid-August, in part because the farmers who would likely make up part of the jury were then "up to their eyes in work." The sabbatarian campaign of 1918, at least as filtered through the local press, threatened to become a genial farce, a sort of Revenge of Uncle Josh on the Moving Picture Show. The *Herald*, in particular, went to some length to set the scene: prominent Lexington attorneys and dead-serious sabbatarians crowded in Boone's "typical country market place with butter, eggs, cheese and other products sitting on the counters. Boxes, kegs, and rustic benches offer places to sit. On either wall shelfs [sic] are fixed to hold bolts of calico, cotton, bars of soap, cans of corn and tomatoes. Showcases contain combs, pins, razors, candy and other things. On the floor are plough shares, poultry wire and screen wire."[46]

In this quaint rural holdover from the nineteenth century, Sunday movies, and perhaps city life itself, were to be judged. But the trial never did take on quite this weighted symbolic resonance. The court reconvened on August 22, not in the general store but in a small schoolhouse in nearby East Hickman, with the jurors seated in desks designed for grade school children. Defense attorneys objected to the fact that immediately before the trial someone (a minister later confessed) had written on the blackboard: "Remember the Sabbath day and keep it holy." Basically the same witnesses were called as in the second Lexington trial. After a picnic lunch, "followed by cigars, funny stories and jokes," Magistrate Botkin instructed the jurors to base their verdict on whether Sunday moving picture shows were a necessity. After deliberating for half an hour, the jury—composed of three Fayette County farmers, an employee of Eastern Kentucky Hospital, a businessman, and a warehouseman—remained "hopelessly hung," with four of the six in favor of acquittal.[47] A hung jury was tantamount to another not guilty verdict or a two-dollar fine; in the country, as in the city, Sunday movies were vindicated, at least during extenuating wartime circumstances.

The other sort of problems Lexington's theater owners faced during and soon after World War I paled in comparison to the sabbatarian controversy, from which they emerged vindicated, and the influenza epidemic, about which they could do nothing but remain closed for ten weeks. For example, one side effect of prohibition was that Lexington's city officials raised license fees in an attempt to recoup some of the $60,000 formerly paid for saloon licenses. Early in 1919, the commissioners increased fees for movie theaters with under four hundred seats from $100 to $150, and for larger theaters from $200 to $400 annually. Theater proprietors apparently did not protest this substantial increase.[48]

Similarly, no objections were raised when the Board of Public Safety in April 1918 called for an amendment to Lexington's theater safety ordinance that would "prohibit the patrons of shows from standing in the aisles and approaches of the theaters."[49] Movie patrons could use some reassurance about the safety of local theaters after a fire at the Orpheum in January 1918, which caused "smoke with the characteristic odor of burning celluloid" to pour out onto Main Street.[50] Much more significantly, however, at least twelve people, mostly children, had been killed in an accident on 9 March 1918 at the Pastime Theater in nearby Winchester. The building next door to this theater had been gutted by fire, and the only wall that remained standing towered over the roof of the one-floor picture show. Gale-force winds sent the wall crashing down through the roof of the Pastime, burying the first ten rows of spectators in bricks and other debris during a Saturday evening "hair-raising Wild West picture," when the theater was packed with children.[51] With this tragedy striking so close to home, Lexington's theater owners were quick to endorse any action that demonstrated their commitment to the safety of the public. Subsequently, when small fires occurred at the Ada Meade and the Orpheum, the city's precautions against overcrowded theaters apparently paid off, for both theaters were evacuated in an orderly fashion, in one case to the strains of "Dixie."[52]

Heading into the 1920s, local exhibitors had good reason to be confident: their product had been deemed a necessity of life and their standing in the community had probably never been higher. They had withstood a well-orchestrated sabbatarian campaign, absorbed a federal movie tax and an increase in local license fees, and survived an influenza epidemic. What else could stand in the way of steadily profiting from an audience that now included people who had literally been brought up on the movies? Several things, as we will see in the following two chapters: increased competition for the entertainment dollar, another crusade to save the Sabbath, renewed demands for strict, locally based censorship of motion pictures, and the onus of being perceived as guilty-by-association with scandal-ridden Hollywood.

NINE

Movies and Something More:
Film Exhibition from
1919 to 1927

Before moving on to Fatty Arbuckle, Will Hays, and the reform campaigns of the 1920s, I will in this chapter examine the ownership and operation of Lexington's commercial theaters from roughly the end of World War I until mid–1927, when the first local movie theater was wired for sound. "By most criteria," historian George T. Blakely contends, Kentucky at large "did not seem to share in the progress of the 1920s," measured primarily in terms of industrial development, electrification, and highway construction.[1] Being a major tobacco market and regional transportation hub, Lexington, however, remained reasonably prosperous, as evidenced by the continued growth of its commercial entertainment market. While the city's population increased by about 10 percent during the 1920s, from 41,534 to 45,734 residents, two new downtown cinemas were built, along with three short-lived, black-operated neighborhood theaters, an additional amusement park, and several spacious dance halls.

Kristin Thompson proposes that "by the mid-twenties, classical filmmaking had reached a relative stability."[2] The exhibition of this "classical" product in Lexington was also relatively stable, insofar as the Orpheum still occupied the bottom of a two-tier system that had been in place since at least

193

1917. But there was considerable experimentation with different programming formats in local theaters during the 1920s and much variation concerning the type of live performers booked or even co-billed with motion pictures: solo accompanists, house orchestras, traveling "jazz" or novelty bands, tabloid shows, "vodvil," and amateur talent. There is simply no way to explore the reception of Hollywood movies during the late silent period without paying due heed to the way live performance, not simply music, contributed to the moviegoing occasion and experience in sites other than what might have passed for picture palaces.

Beyond the Picture Palace

Statistics can readily be marshaled to offer a national perspective on film exhibition and moviegoing in the 1920s. In January 1923 there were, according to *Film Daily,* some 15,000 motion picture theaters in the United States, with an average size of 507 seats. Weekly attendance totaled 50 million, even taking into account that about 30 percent (4,500) of the theaters were open four–five days per week, and 10 percent were only open one–three days per week. On the basis of such data, Garth Jowett concludes, in *Film: The Democratic Art,* that by 1922 the motion picture was a "normal feature" of twentieth-century life, enjoyed by "every segment of society." And since this period saw "tremendous increases in audiences"—up to an average of 65 million per week in 1928—"it was during the 1920's," Jowett writes, "that the 'movie craze' really became a national phenomenon."[3]

For certain historians the "national phenomenon" that Jowett sketches is aptly and neatly exemplified by the picture palace. But seeing the 1920s through the portals of the picture palace almost invariably privileges the urban—or, more precisely, the downtown, large city—experience and practice of film exhibition.[4] For example, Lary May argues, in *Screening out the Past: The Birth of Mass Culture and the Motion Picture Industry,* that beneath the changes in theater architecture, managerial techniques, and clientele from 1906 to the 1920s "lay one key development: from a pariah nickelodeon, the motion picture had become a major urban institution for the middle class." Metropolitan picture palaces, veritable "cathedrals of the motion picture," play a central role in May's interpretation of this "evolution." The operation and design of these increasingly more exotic picture palaces, he concludes, made manifest the ambivalence of America toward the new, post-Victorian world: on the one hand, this "classless" site "glorified lavish consumption and play" and offered its patrons a "release from restraint"; on the other hand, the picture palace "kept alive very traditional values," including the "symbols of high culture" and the need to pursue success diligently.[5]

Can May's analysis of the cultural function and implicit contradictions of the picture palace be extended to 1920s moviegoing in general, as he seems to suggest? Only if we accept two corollary contentions: that in the 1920s "moviegoing was unquestionably an urban phenomenon" and "a *mass* amusement . . . clearly geared toward middle class aspirations";[6] and, furthermore, that the experience of audiences in a relatively small number of opulent theaters was representative of moviegoing throughout the "urban centers" of the Northeast, which, in turn, was somehow comparable to the experience of going to the movies in the rest of urban (meaning here simply "nonrural") America. As prominent as the picture palace may have been in the motion picture industry's self-promotion during the 1920s, and as evocative as it is now as a nostalgic icon, architectural marvel, or contradictory cultural symbol, there is no reason to conclude that the picture palace represents the typical or the only noteworthy site where Americans took in the movies during the late silent era. David Naylor's *American Picture Palaces: The Architecture of Fantasy* clearly indicates how varied the "palaces" were in terms of design, location, and size. For example, the eleven theaters built in 1925 that Naylor discusses ranged in size from 598 to 4,325 seats and were located in Manhattan, Chicago, Detroit, Brooklyn, San Francisco, Boston, Indianapolis, and Beverly Hills, as well as Shreveport, Louisiana, and Longview, Washington.[7] This sense of variety is even greater in R. W. Sexton's two-volume *American Theatres of Today* (1930), which comes with a foreword by S. L. "Roxy" Rothafel himself, yet is not restricted to palatial metropolitan theaters.

Douglas Gomery's attempt to ground the phenomenon of the picture palace and motion picture exhibition in the 1920s in what he calls a "material" history is particularly germane in this context.[8] For one thing, Gomery provides a more precise and workable definition of the "picture palace": any theater built for the movies that had seating for over 1,500, a fan-shaped auditorium, "much nonfunctional decoration," and, often, a stage show. During the 1920s, there were, he concludes, about one thousand such theaters in downtown urban areas and also in outlying business centers (particularly in Chicago), which together "provided the bulk of the industry's revenue."[9] (Since these first-run theaters charged considerably more for tickets than other houses, this large share of box office revenue would not necessarily mean that a greater number of people saw movies at picture palaces than at other types of theaters.) Gomery is especially interested in how the operators of such theaters, most notably Balaban & Katz, utilized chain-store retailing techniques, air-conditioning, carefully prepared stage shows, and strictly monitored employees to build powerful regional theater circuits. Though his research does not directly take up cities the size of Lexington, Gomery's detailed case studies of specific locales and corporate practices work to snap us out of our lingering fascination with the facades of the great "cathedrals" of the movies and to undercut any simple use of the picture palace phenomenon to explain (away) moviegoing and film exhibition in the 1920s.

From a different angle, Richard Koszarski accomplishes much the same thing in *An Evening's Entertainment: The Age of the Silent Feature Picture, 1915–1928*. This volume in Scribner's impressive *History of the American Cinema* series rightly assumes that any comprehensive examination of moviegoing in this era needs to range far indeed, taking into account, for example, questions concerning audience preferences, promotional activity, the role of music, the various ways of organizing a motion picture "show," and even the quality of projection equipment and film prints. Koszarski does devote considerable attention to the design, management, and exhibition policies of picture palaces in New York, Chicago, and Los Angeles. But these theaters do not serve for him as some all-explanatory metaphor or metonymy. In its glimpses of the "small theaters [that] continued to provide the backbone of national film exhibition" and, more generally, its attentiveness to the workings of American film exhibition outside the grand confines of the picture palace, *An Evening's Entertainment* is at once more national in scope and more open to regional and local variation than previous accounts of this period.[10]

Though none of the six theaters in downtown Lexington would have qualified as a picture palace, by Gomery's criteria, they did evince a good measure of variety in, for instance, the entertainment they offered and the status they held in the community. This is another reason why Lexington seems to be a particularly apt test case.

Orpheum Theater

By the end of the 1910s, John Stamper's Orpheum had settled into place as a second-rank picture show, with a daily changing, continuous program that usually combined a newsreel, a serial episode, a comic short, and a two- or three-reel western—precisely the sort of bill that seems to be tailored especially for schoolchildren. Among Stamper's main drawing cards that year were Chaplin's Mutual films, then in their third Lexington run. The only unusual attraction at the Orpheum during and soon after World War I was *Fit To Win*, a United States Public Health Services "photodrama" made to educate troops about venereal disease,[11] which played for four days, two reserved for men and two for women, with no one under sixteen admitted. Adult ticket prices at the Orpheum rose to sixteen cents in 1920 and then to twenty cents in 1921, with children's tickets increasing to ten cents, but all that changed in the Orpheum exhibition policy was that Stamper came to screen as many as five different serials each week.[12]

Obviously the profit margin at the Orpheum was slight indeed. One way Stamper cut his operating costs was by breaking his contract with Local 346 of the International Alliance of Theatrical Stage Employees. In February 1917 he replaced two union projectionists, who each earned $19 weekly for 6½-hour shifts, with an eighteen-year-old novice who was paid $19 to work the entire 13-hour shift, except for meal breaks when an usher would relieve him. A week later union men abducted the replacement operator late at night and deposited him in Frankfort, Kentucky, with a warning to steer clear of Lexington. Stamper declined to press charges, but from then on, the Orpheum was the city's only non-union theater.[13]

At the same time, Stamper was the Lexington theater operator most active in the Motion Picture Theater Owners (MPTO) of Kentucky, part of a national organization founded in 1920 by independent exhibitors.[14] As the smallest of the independents in central Kentucky, Stamper was drawn to the MPTO, as he had been to the Kentucky Motion Picture Exhibitors League in the early 1910s. When the MPTO state convention was held in Lexington in March 1922, Stamper served as a vice-president and lectured on "The Balanced Program and Cash Booking."[15]

Committed to a "balanced program" of serials, westerns, and comedies, all with minimal musical accompaniment, the Orpheum remained in business through the 1920s. In November 1923 Stamper cut ticket prices to a dime for all seats at all times—by far the cheapest tickets in town, particularly for adults and for moviegoing during prime weekend hours. At the same time, he dropped the daily newspaper advertising that he had run continuously since 1912. Presumably, anybody who wanted to attend the Orpheum either would not care exactly how the slots in the program were filled or would find out what was playing from the publicity material Stamper put up outside his theater. In fact, it was not until October 1927 that Stamper took out another newspaper ad, and that was only because he had managed to book for an exclusive engagement the "official" pictures of the recent Jack Dempsey-Gene Tunney prizefight. Aside from this single ad, the few notable references to the Orpheum in the local press occurred when small fires broke out in the theater's projection booth in 1925 and again in 1926.

Fires notwithstanding, Stamper managed to secure a spot in the marketplace during the 1920s without relying on promotional efforts, all-star feature films, or live musical performers. During this period it seems as if the Orpheum was no longer in competition with Lexington's other theaters, in the sense that a lunch stand would not actually have been in competition with a hotel restaurant, though both served food. While the Orpheum was located in the center of downtown Lexington, its size, exhibition format, and ticket prices reflect what more likely would have been found in an urban neighborhood theater or in the only picture show in a small, rural town. The Orpheum was Lexington's version of what Koszarski calls the "silent majority of picture houses,"[16] except that a small-town theater (for example, say, the Alhambra in Campbellsville, Kentucky) might give more prominence to feature films than did the Orpheum.

The Phoenix Amusement Company: Acquisition and Diversification

Much as the Strand occupied the opposite end of the commercial entertainment spectrum from the Orpheum, Stamper's policy of retrenchment shared little with the aggressive expansionism of John Elliott's Phoenix Amusement Company. By the end of World War I, the Strand was worth approximately $150,000 (or at least this was Elliott's asking price when the Shubert organization expressed an interest in purchasing this theater),[17] and its musical director was advertising in *Billboard* for musicians to join his "high-class

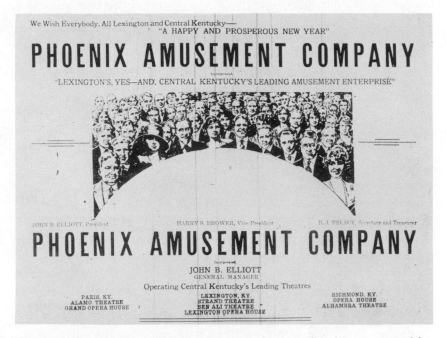

New Year's greetings from the Phoenix Amusement Company, then the most successful commercial entertainment enterprise in the area. Are the smiling faces employees? Investors? Satisfied customers? Lexington *Herald,* 26 December 1920.

picture theatre orchestra of 25 pieces, all concert and no grind."[18] Along with its "continuous musical feast," the Strand typically offered four changes of bill weekly, each comprised of a major studio feature film, a Sennett or Harold Lloyd comedy, and a newsreel (with a serial episode added on Sunday). The only theater in Lexington that could compete with the Strand was the Ben Ali, which featured its own augmented house orchestra and offered special attractions like "Paramount Week," headlined by the latest William S. Hart release.

The competition between the city's two largest motion picture theaters abruptly ended on 2 January 1920, when the Phoenix Amusement Company purchased both the Ben Ali and the Lexington Opera House for $250,000. (As part of this transaction it also agreed to carry $120,000 worth of insurance

on the Ben Ali and $43,000 on the Opera House.) Elliot's company had
filed amended articles of incorporation on 21 December 1919, announcing
its intention to increase its capital stock from $200,000 to $600,000 and
to raise its limit of indebtedness from $100,000 to $1,000,000.[19] With
these additional funds, it planned to add to its central Kentucky circuit,
which then included the Capitol in Frankfort, the Alamo and the Opera
House in Paris, the Colonial and the Liberty in Winchester, the Alhambra
and the Opera House in Richmond, and the Strand in Lexington.[20] With
the acquisition of the Ben Ali and the Opera House, the Phoenix Amusement Company controlled three-fourths of the theater seats in Lexington,
including the city's three most prestigious venues. Now the question was
how best to profit from this domination of the Lexington (and central Kentucky) market.

The Ben Ali, Strand, and Opera House all could have (and had been and
would be) run strictly as motion picture theaters. Elliott, however, chose to
institute a different exhibition strategy for each of his Lexington venues.[21] In
the revised Phoenix Amusement Company scheme of things, the Strand
would serve as the company's premiere picture house, billed as "Lexington's
$150,000 Motion Picture Palace," providing a panoply of goods and services:
"Safe, Sane and Moral Amusement. Entertainment. Education. Recreation.
Comfort. Ventilation. Cleanliness. Courtesy."[22] From 1919 well into 1927,
through two remodelings of the theater's interior, the Strand's film booking
policy remained consistent. Special attractions like *The Sheik* or *Way Down
East* that played for a full week were unquestionably exceptions to the general rule. Ticket prices, too, stayed basically the same, starting the decade at
thirty cents for adults and twenty cents for children, then dropping to ten
cents for children in 1922, with discount ticket books available (five adult
tickets or fifteen children's tickets for a dollar). Bargain matinees were introduced in March 1926, with twenty-cent adult seats between 10:00 a.m and
2:00 P.M.

Comfort, ambience, and the availability of first-run feature films set the
Strand off from the Orpheum and the area's small-town picture shows. And
so, in a quite significant way, did the music at the Strand, which may not
have carried a twenty-five piece orchestra throughout the 1920s but always
featured some type of house band. On 6 February 1921, for example, the
Strand All-American Orchestra (two violins, piano, bass, cornet, trombone,
clarinet, and percussion) performed the following program:

I.   "Strand Theatre March" by A. C. Marshall [the musical director of
     the orchestra].
II. Overture, "Semiramide," by Rossini.
III. Popular Song, "Margie."
IV. Musical Comedy Selection, "Irene."
V.   "Valse Caprice" by Rubinstein.
VI. Popular Songs, "Home Again Blues" and "Avalon."
VII. Grand Opera Selection, "Mignon" by Thomils.
VIII. Popular Songs, "Rosie" and "Cuban Moon."
IX. Caucasian Sketches (Suite in Four Parts).
X.   Second Hungarian "Rhapsody" by Liszt [sic].

As an extra added attraction, one of the orchestra's violinists performed
Mylernski's "Mazurka."[23] This mini-concert, combining different musical
idioms and bridging the "popular" and the "classical," bore no direct connection to the rest of that day's two-hour program: a new Metro feature film
(*Cinderella's Twin*), a Snub Pollard comedy, and an episode of Vitagraph's
serial, *Fighting Fate*.[24] But, then, neither the individual components of the
film program (serial, comedy, feature) nor the eleven selections performed by
the orchestra cohered into a unified whole. An overall sense of continuity,
wholeness, and coherence—those formal and aesthetic qualities integral to
a 1920s high cultural recital, play, or art exhibition—were simply not goals
for this typical evening's entertainment at the Strand. What the Phoenix
Amusement Company's flagship did offer was variety and more-than-your-
money's-worth. Yet no matter how eclectic, the Strand's program remained
within well-understood and rather narrow parameters: "songs" and "selections" drawn from a limited repertoire, and motion pictures produced according to the logic of familiar genres.

What helped to sell the Strand in the 1920s was not only its orchestra
(later dubbed the All-American Jazzo-Concert Orchestra), but also the touring musical groups Elliott booked for one- or two-week engagements, such as
the Tivoli Harmony Maids, the Central American Marimba Band, the Inter-
Fraternity Orchestra, and the eleven-piece Kentucky Kernels, featuring Nan
Blackstone, "Queen of the Blues-Song."[25] Scheduling such acts testified to
the Strand's commitment to providing the last word in contemporary music
as well as in movies. The Inter-Fraternity Orchestra, for example, came to
Lexington "direct" from the Pennsylvania Hotel in Philadelphia and—so the
ad promised—would heat up the Strand with its rendition of "Indian Love

Call" and other current hits.[26] Booking this orchestra or Roland Lewis's Symphonic Syncopating Serenaders was a way to capitalize on "jazz" and perhaps to attract college students, who, as Paula S. Fass documents, "danced whenever the opportunity presented itself," and "the dancers were close, the steps were fast, and the music was jazz."[27] At the same time, the Strand ran little risk of alienating other moviegoers since its musical repertoire was very seldom limited to jazz, and, no matter what the music, the Strand was not a dance hall.

For a year after the Phoenix Amusement Company had acquired the Ben Ali, Elliott employed the same booking policy as at the Strand, including touring musical acts like the Cherokee Indian Maidens, Keith's Famous Chicago Society Jazz Band, and Ruth Denice, noted "rag singer." After a $25,000 facelift in August 1921, the Ben Ali began presenting seasonal Keith circuit "vodvil," with Lexington sharing the same acts as Keith houses in Louisville, Cincinnati, and Dayton. (In the summer, motion pictures remained the Ben Ali's prime fare.) Vodvil bills at the Ben Ali changed twice weekly, with 2:00 and 8:15 P.M. performances daily, except for Saturday, when three shows were scheduled, and Sunday, when only motion pictures and music were featured. Vodvil tickets cost more than the movies, even at the Strand: for matinees, children and gallery seats were twenty-eight cents, and all other seats were thirty-nine cents; for evenings, prices ranged from thirty-three cents (gallery), forty-four cents (balcony), and fifty-five cents (lower floor) to eighty-three cents (box seats).

In 1923 *Equity Magazine* estimated that there were sixty-two "big time" and almost eight hundred "small time" vaudeville theaters in the United States and Canada.[28] I assume that performances at the Ben Ali were fairly representative of "small time" fare: six acts, with no high-priced headliners and no elaborately staged production numbers, plus a "fotofeature." Consider a run-of-the-mill vodvil show at the Ben Ali, for instance, the one that played 17–19 September 1923:

Bowman Brothers: a blackface act, specializing in song and "mimicry"
Frank and Ethel Carmen: novelty hoop rollers and baton experts
Criterion Four: song and comedy
Larry Comer: singer
Armstrong and Gilbert Sisters: "a potpourri of song, talk and steps"
Visser and Company (and their "singing duck"): singing and "feats of
    strength and dexterity"
Fotofeature: *My Friend the Devil* (Fox).[29]

The Phoenix Amusement Company's program for its Lexington theaters. Photo courtesy
University of Kentucky Photo Archives.

Vodvil, a fixture at the Ben Ali for much of the 1920s. Photo courtesy University of Kentucky Photo Archives.

Purely in terms of time, the fotofeature was the major part of the vodvil bill, though Ben Ali ads highlighted the live acts, and the entire show was, after all, called "vodvil." Since there was apparently no attempt to match performers with complementary films, the motion picture spectacle might well have registered all the more strongly when it was juxtaposed with the sort of entertainers listed above. Or perhaps the modular format of vodvil reduced the fotofeature to simply another part of the show. It was within the frame of Ben Ali vodvil that Lexington audiences saw a number of films eventually canonized as silent screen "classics": *I Accuse, Nanook of the North,* and *The Golem* in 1922, and in later years, *Orphans of the Storm, Phantom of the Opera, Moana, The General, Faust,* and *The Merry Widow.* When *The Birth of a Nation* returned yet again to the Ben Ali in 1924 (in a version that ran appreciably under two hours), it screened on a Sunday and then as the vodvil fotofeature for the remainder of the week. *The Covered Wagon* also served as a fotofeature, on its third Lexington run, a little more than a year after it had premiered locally on a pricey road show tour.

By 1925 the Ben Ali's vodvil format was wearing a bit thin, and the Phoenix Amusement Company relied more and more on special promotions, including the exhibition of a life-size oil painting of the birth of Christ and the staging of a "local Charleston contest," which proved popular enough to warrant a "colored Charleston contest," then a children's Charleston contest. During the off-season, Elliott tried out a range of different attractions: a five-day beauty contest, a small stock company, even a combination stage/screen show that paired *Aloma of the South Seas* with a live production called "A Trip to the Hawaiian Islands."[30] On occasion during the summer, the Ben Ali also hosted special week-long motion picture engagements of, for example, *The Ten Commandments, The Big Parade,* and *Ben Hur.* All told, the vodvil format at the Ben Ali lasted until March 1928, meaning that for over six years it had successfully complemented the first-run-motion-picture-and-music format at the Strand. One obvious measure of this success was that when the Phoenix Amusement Company declared a quarterly dividend of 3 percent in July 1927, the *Herald* noted that in years past this Lexington-based corporation had "paid as high as a 17½ percent yearly dividend."[31]

Lexington Opera House

During 1920–21, the Opera House figured in the Phoenix Amusement Company's plans along with the Strand and the Ben Ali. Under Elliott's management, the Opera House gave up its few high cultural bookings and became more exclusively a site for touring shows, particularly revues like *George White's Scandals,* Sunday film programs, and special motion picture attractions like Griffith's *Way Down East* and DeMille's *Male and Female.* But on 4 November 1921 the Phoenix Amusement Company announced that it would soon close the city's oldest theater and dispose of the property because the Security Trust Company, owners of an adjacent building, had served the Opera House with a formal notice to remove fire escapes and to close exits that utilized Security Trust property.[32] Since city fire codes required these safety features, Elliott stated that he had no choice but to close the Opera House, which he did on 24 November 1921, after a week-long engagement of *The Four Horsemen of the Apocalypse.* Six months later, the Phoenix Amusement Company sold the Opera House for $24,000 to R. S. Webb, Jr., a contractor who planned to turn part of the theater into storerooms, then sell or lease the building for a "Negro theater or public hall."[33] Apparently having no luck with this plan, in September 1922 Webb converted the Opera House into a gas station and automobile storage warehouse.

Lary May begins the first chapter of *Screening out the Past* with an image borrowed from *Saturday Review* editor Henry Seidel Canby, who, "looking back on the passing of Victorian America" in 1934, "saw one apt symbol for that change in his home town: the center of local society, the opera house, had been turned into a movie theater."[34] The Lexington Opera House, however, is not nearly so neat and convenient a "symbol" of massive cultural change. For one thing, it had regularly made use of motion pictures from 1896 on. For another, the "symbolic" danger was that this Opera House would be judged unsafe, outmoded, and unprofitable, and then completely closed down and discarded. Or, worse, it might become a "colored" theater. Both outcomes looked like good possibilities in 1914 and again in 1922. Thus there is something a bit anticlimactic (though still "symbolic," I suppose) in the fact that the Opera House became a sort of glorified filling station in 1922. But not for long: one more revivification of this former "center of local society" remained.

Headed by Charles Berryman and Harrison Scott (son of the former long-time operator of the Opera House), this restoration effort presented itself as being more a civic gesture than a solely financial transaction. In February 1923 Berryman announced his intention to purchase and restore the Opera House, if he could obtain funds from two hundred stockholders, half of whom would invest $500 each, the other half $200 each.[35] This public call succeeded, and in May 1923 the Lexington Opera House Company was incorporated, with 115 local stockholders and $50,000 in capital. The company's directors were Berryman, Scott, James A. Todd (president of the Union Building and Loan Association), J. C. Carrick (a physician), and E. L. Hutchinson (an attorney).[36] After major renovations, the Opera House reopened on 18 September 1923, "resplendent in entirely new furnishings and appointments throughout." "The gathering," announced the *Herald*'s reviewer, "partook especially of the nature of a good, old-fashioned homecoming."[37] Appropriately, the "rejuvenated" house premiered not with a risqué Broadway revue but with a touring minstrel show—the traditional season opener for the Opera House in years past and a suitably conventional, nostalgic, regionally flavored accompaniment for an "old-fashioned homecoming."

Berryman and Scott believed that there was a market in Lexington for an Opera House schedule based, as it had been ten years before, on touring attractions and occasional local benefit shows. (But not high cultural recitals, operas, ballets, or concerts, which were then being conducted under the auspices of the Lexington College of Music at Woodland Park Auditorium.) For two seasons the Opera House was relatively well booked, sometimes with performers on the order of Otis Skinner in *Sancho Panza* and Eubie Blake in *The Chocolate Dandies*. But tickets for a Broadway revue like *The Passing Show* were fifty cents to $3.00, much higher than vodvil prices at the Ben Ali; and it cost from fifty cents to $1.50 to see *The Thief of Baghdad* and other touring films at the Opera House, well above the prices at even the Strand.

The 1924–25 season turned out to be the last full theatrical season at the Opera House or any other Lexington venue. Signs of the times were apparent in September 1925, when Scott booked the Gross-Ross Players, a stock company that performed a different (usually well-known) play each week, for much of the fall and again in May 1926. The Opera House's 1926–27 season opened as usual with a minstrel show, but within two weeks Scott announced that the theater would close, blaming its demise on the exorbitant demands of union musicians and stagehands. *Ben Hur* was the last road show motion picture exhibited at the Opera House—almost thirty years to the day after the premiere of the cineomatragraph. On 21 December 1926, Charles Berryman resigned as president of the Lexington Opera House Company, and a week later Harrison Scott resigned as manager, their civic gesture/investment having failed.

During 1927–29 three different stock companies tried to make a go of the Opera House, the most successful of which was the Robertson-Smith Players, who in September 1927 began what was billed as an "indefinite engagement." This company charged from twenty-five cents to $1.00 for Jazz Age plays like *6-Cylinder Love* and *Dancing Mothers* ("If you've seen the picture, be sure and see the play") and time-tested melodramas like *Way Down East*.[38] The Robertson-Smith Players remained at the Opera House for over a year, until late in 1928. Thus even when sound films were a novelty item much in demand, there was still at least some audience for stock company theater at prices roughly comparable to small-time vaudeville.[39] But it was not enough to support the Robertson-Smith troupe or the Alney Alba Players, who lasted from June to December 1929. Four months later the Lexington Opera House Company sold the theater and the property at an auction to Transylvania University for $22,014, the amount owed on the existing mortgage.[40]

Overseen by Charles Scott, the Opera House between 1889 and 1914 had been a profitable, well-run, one-owner commercial entertainment operation. It was Scott's model that the Lexington Opera House Company had in mind

when it attempted in 1923 to maintain the Opera House as a venue for live
theater. Yet in the mid-1920s the Opera House could no longer fall back on
vaudeville (since the Ben Ali had established itself as a vodvil house) or on
traveling repertory companies (which had become relegated to the tent show
circuit). Concerts by touring symphonies and other high-cultural performances were now scheduled elsewhere, more completely segregated from
commercial entertainments. Fewer "serious" dramas, star vehicles, and hal-
lowed revivals were on the road in the 1920s. The prime touring attractions,
with ever-increasing ticket prices, were musical comedy revues, which were
often barely a shell of the original Broadway productions.[41] Other than that,
each season offered a handful of road show motion pictures and minstrel
shows, and virtually none of the popular-price attractions that had been
touring mainstays a generation earlier.[42] In the fate of the Lexington Opera
House we can readily see the effects of the "decline of the road" so often
bemoaned in the 1920s. The motion picture industry, of course, contributed greatly to this decline, as the movies first drew away the gallery patrons,
then even more of the theater audience.[43] Given this situation, it is significant that Lexington investors revived the Opera House in 1923 precisely
because they assumed there was a local market (and a need?) for touring
productions.

It is also easy to picture the string of stock companies that leased the
Opera House between 1926 and 1929 as harbingers of this theater's (and *the*
theater's) decline and fall, a pathetic, backward-looking coda to Lexington's
supposedly glorious years as "America's best one-night stand." Yet, in fact,
the decline of the road gave stock companies a major boost in the 1920s.
Alfred L. Bernheim in *The Business of the Theatre* (1932) held out the hope
that these companies might help assure the future of the American stage by
becoming "distributors of drama throughout the country."[44] At least one of the
stock troupes that played the Opera House found enough support to warrant a
fifteen-month engagement. Theater historian Jack Poggi, however, notes that
the stock company revival "spent its force about the end of the decade,"[45]
and by 1930 it looked as if no professional form of legitimate theater could
remain commercially viable in Lexington.

Lafayette Amusement Company:
Breaking into the Lexington Market

A different sort of theater performance had long been associated with the
Ada Meade, which, under the ownership of William James, was by 1919 offering three acts of Keith vaudeville and a feature film, with three shows daily
and bills changing on Monday and Thursday. Once the Ben Ali began booking six-act vodvil programs in September 1921, James switched to an all-
picture policy, though to some extent this was a holding action, for he had
already entered into negotiations with several Kentucky film exhibitors, including Lee Goldberg, who was then secretary of the First National Exhibitors Picture Association, and Michael Switow, who had built the Strand in
Lexington in 1916. On 31 December 1921, James announced that the Ada
Meade would henceforth be operated by the newly formed Lafayette Amusement Company.

When this company had filed its articles of incorporation on 3 December
1921, it offered no public sale of stock. Among its investors were several
prominent, longtime Lexington residents: Louis des Cognets (president of the
Lexington Coal and Coke Company), David L. Ades (owner of a large dry
goods store), L. B. Shouse (president of the Lafayette Hotel), and George
Graves and Charles N. Manning (chief officers of the Security Trust Company). The showmen who ran the Lafayette Amusement Company were William James (secretary), Michael Switow (vice-president), and Colonel Fred
Levy (president).[46] The forty-four-year-old Levy was a Kentucky native whose
family earned its substantial wealth from a Louisville department store. He
had worked for the Keith circuit in Louisville and was a member of the executive committee of Associated First National Pictures. Levy prided himself on
his ability "to follow the methods of up-to-date merchants" in his "progressive" film exhibition policies.[47] While Levy had the title of "president," it
was actually Switow who turned out to be the key figure in the Lafayette
Amusement Company, although it was not until 1927 that Switow finally
bought out Levy's interest in the company.

The main reason the Lafayette Amusement Company was formed in December 1921 was to build what it would consistently refer to as a new "palatial photoplay house," the Kentucky Theater. Why then did the company
bother to acquire the Ada Meade, which was no match in size or elegance to
the Ben Ali and the Strand? Presumably Switow and Levy felt that they
needed to control more than one theater in downtown Lexington, so as to

Palatial luxury as Lexington's due: the grand opening of the Kentucky. Lexington *Herald*, 1 October 1922.

better challenge the Phoenix Amusement Company and capture different parts (and therefore more) of the local market. In fact, the Ada Meade and the Kentucky turned out to be so distinct in format (and probably in audience) by the mid-1920s that the Lafayette Amusement Company never ran any joint advertisements for these theaters, as the Phoenix Amusement Company was wont to do with the more complementary Strand and Ben Ali.

Soon after the Ben Ali introduced its vodvil policy in September 1921, Switow finalized plans for his return to the film exhibition business in Lexington. The Lafayette Amusement Company signed a lease for a 76 × 220 foot piece of property owned by Graves, Manning, and des Cognets. This lot, previously occupied by an automobile dealer and the McAlister grocery store, was adjacent to the Lafayette Hotel, about a block and a half east of the Strand on Main Street. The three-story building that housed the new theater was designed by the prominent Louisville architectural firm of Joseph & Joseph, which was responsible for the Rialto Theater and a number of institutional buildings, schools, and factories in the Louisville area.[48] The actual construction was carried out by Platoff & Bush of Louisville and overseen by Michael Switow's twenty-four-year-old son, Harry. While construction work continued in the spring of 1922, the Lafayette Amusement Company generated publicity by offering twenty dollars in gold to the person "first suggesting the name that will be used" for the new theater.[49] "Kentucky" was the winning suggestion, a name less generic than "Strand" and less idiosyncratically local than "Ben Ali" or "Ada Meade." "Kentucky" was also the name of another theater Switow had recently opened in Louisville.

Like the Colonial in 1912 and the Strand in 1916, the Kentucky was billed as a veritable "palace of enchantment." Was it truly a "picture palace?" From the point of view of the Lexington market, this question is irrelevant: the Kentucky was the newest, costliest, and most impressive first-run movie theater in Lexington and its environs. It announced its presence on Main Street with a four thousand-bulb marquee, topped by a twenty-five-foot vertical sign. The Lafayette Amusement Company clearly marketed this 1,276-seat, one-floor theater as a classy and costly investment, built expressly for the pleasure and comfort of local moviegoers at a cost of approximately $250,000. Within its immediate frame of reference, then, the Kentucky was palatial.[50]

In terms of its interior decoration, the Kentucky was built too early to have been influenced by either John Eberson's "atmospheric" picture palaces (in which the theater interior was designed to suggest an "open-air illusion") or the "exoticism" of theaters like Grauman's Egyptian.[51] The Lafayette Amusement Company touted its new theater as a masterpiece in the "Italian Renaissance style of architecture," but, according to architectural historian Walter E. Langsam, the Kentucky's style could more accurately be said to combine Beaux Arts and Adamesque.[52] Joseph & Joseph's design was not nearly as devoted to ornate embellishment as, for example, the well-known motion picture theaters created by New York architect Thomas Lamb, whose "preferred trademark" from 1914 on was also "Adamesque design."[53] The Kentucky aspired to a somewhat more conservative standard of taste, one that would

The lobby of the Kentucky. Photo courtesy University of Kentucky Photo Archives.

have valued matched marble walls in the vestibule, "deeply cushioned" carpets, mirrors framed by hand-carved woodwork, variable indirect lighting, and, on the walls of the auditorium, "exquisite examples of tapestry work and hand painted landscape scenes."[54]

Befitting this sort of decor, the Kentucky promised that its staff would be models of courtesy and efficiency. The comfort of its "guests" would also be assured by a ventilation system that was supposed to keep the air absolutely pure and the temperature at a constant 70 degrees. All these attributes of the new theater were played up in the Kentucky's promotional material, particularly in a special six-page "Kentucky Theatre Section" of the Lexington *Herald* issued to commemorate the grand opening on 1 October 1922.

One significant detail concerning the Kentucky was, however, not directly referred to by the local press: even though the site of this new theater could have accommodated two or three tiers of seats, it had no balcony and therefore no "colored" seating section. The Lafayette Amusement Company did

The auditorium of the Kentucky. Photo courtesy University of Kentucky Photo Archives.

not base this decision on abstract philosophical principles, for the Ada Meade (which it also owned) courted the local black audience. Maybe the absence of a balcony—and of all those people, black or white, who would sit above and apart from the more expensive seats below—somehow itself signified that the Kentucky was a "high-class" house. Judging from oral history accounts of the 1920s and 1930s, the Kentucky's position as Lexington's premiere movie theater derived in part at least from a whites-only admission policy that did not end until the early 1960s.

The premiere of the Kentucky was a gala local event, reflective of a time when the construction of a large new movie theater could be taken as what one speaker at the ceremony called "an expression of faith in the future of Lexington."[55] The evening began with an overture performed by H. Haden Read on the Kentucky's highly touted $25,000 Wurlitzer organ. After touring as an organ demonstrator for the Wurlitzer company and serving as organist at the Rialto Theater in Louisville, Read became a major draw at the Kentucky for several years, adding a certain measure of prestige to this theater since, as Koszarski notes, "the 'mighty' Wurlitzer" was "the trademark of the picture palace."[56] Following the organ overture, city commissioner Wood Dunlap led the audience in a rendition of "My Old Kentucky Home," with the lyrics projected on the screen. It was an appropriate choice, given the name of the theater, its commitment to segregation, and the way that the theatrical "house" was at times described with much affection as a "home."

Governor Edwin P. Morrow then formally dedicated the "magnificent building" and "declared that he believes in the motion picture because he believes in art, in education, in recreation, in laughter and in humanity." Colonel Fred Levy, in turn, vowed that "it is our intention not to permit a picture in this house that the good people of Lexington cannot come to freely and permit their wives, children and sweethearts to come without fear."[57] As we will see in Chapter 10, Morrow's encomium to the motion picture and Levy's assurance that the Kentucky would be a morally safe environment take on special significance because 1922 had already seen the Fatty Arbuckle scandal and the Kentucky state legislature's debate over the creation of a state censorship board. In this climate, local film exhibition—and the new, lavish Kentucky Theater in particular—had to sell itself both as an up-to-date supplier of a national commodity (a "necessity," in fact) and as a local enterprise, duly aware of its place within and obligation to the community and its "good people."

It is difficult to see any direct correlation between Levy's statement of principle and actual booking practices at the Kentucky. After the speeches, the opening night crowd saw *The Eternal Flame* (a historical drama starring Norma Talmadge), a two-reel Christie comedy that parodied *The Sheik*, and a First National "Kinogram" newsreel. Initially, much was made of the Kentucky's special arrangement with First National, the company with which Levy was associated. And two weeks after its opening, the Kentucky seemed to score a special coup by presenting what it billed as the "world's premiere showing" of *Oliver Twist*, with each child attending the show promised a special souvenir autographed by Jackie Coogan.

Aside from the emphasis placed on Read and his Wurlitzer, the Kentucky's format and prices were comparable to the Strand's, the city's other first-run movie theater.[58] Open from 11:00 A.M. to 11:00 P.M. daily and from 1:00 to 11:00 P.M. on Sundays, with two changes of bill weekly, the Kentucky charged ten cents for children at all times, twenty-five cents for adults at matinee shows, and thirty cents for adults in the evenings and on Sundays and holidays. Its programming varied little during 1922–24, except for the occasional added attraction: the Kentucky Six (a jazz band featuring several Lexington residents), Victor recording artist Barney Rapp and his orchestra, or a tabloid show with Dorothy Bush and her Cinema Girls Revue. In June 1924 the Kentucky brought in a different sort of added novelty: "Plasti-grams," described as a "third dimension movie."[59]

Like the Strand, the Kentucky increased its special attractions in 1925, which clearly suggests that these two theaters were in direct competition for patrons. In addition to musical acts like the Royal Holland Bell Ringers and the Alabamians (a seven-piece jazz band), a handful of motion picture double bills were also booked at the Kentucky, as was, for the first time, heavily publicized films complete with their own staged "prologues," when *The Thief of Baghdad* played in April 1925 and *The Lost World* in October 1925. Usu-ally, however, the Kentucky's special attractions had no thematic or even complementary relation to the main bill. *Quo Vadis* (starring Emil Jannings), for example, shared its Lexington dates with a pair of dancers who performed the Chicago Charleston, and other feature films were co-billed with the "an-nounced play-by-play through direct wire" of out-of-town University of Ken-tucky basketball games and other sporting events. Even with these added attractions, the core of the Kentucky's exhibition policy continued to be a program composed of a feature film, newsreel, comic short, and organ perfor-mance. In fact, in February 1926 the Kentucky with much fanfare premiered its new custom-made Wurlitzer, said to be capable of producing "every sound needful for the interpretation of a picture . . . from the most difficult classical compositions, to the weird groans, numerous squeaks, and the sudden an-nouncements of the cuckoo clock, always good for a laugh."[60]

With the Kentucky in 1922 established as its first-run movie house in Lexington, the Lafayette Amusement Company seemed to be at something of a loss concerning what to do with the Ada Meade, whose sketchy and diverse schedule then included Sunday movie programs, local benefits, touring stage shows, and even a few boxing matches. In June 1923 James instituted daily changing motion pictures at the Ada Meade, with all tickets priced at ten cents, except for weekends, when adult tickets were twenty cents. This strat-egy positioned the Ada Meade with the Orpheum at the bottom of the Lexing-ton market, rather than at the top with the Kentucky and the Strand.

On 1 January 1925 the Lafayette Amusement Company again revamped the Ada Meade's exhibition format, this time by adding live entertainment,

The outer limits of programming possibilities: *Metropolis* and University of Kentucky basketball co-billed at the Kentucky. Lexington *Herald,* 13 November 1928.

quite unlike anything the Orpheum, or any other theater in town, had to offer. Co-billed with the "usual picture program" was the Mildred Austin Musical Comedy Company, complete with "Beauty Chorus." The movies still changed daily (with Sundays, as before, reserved for "fast action Western features"), but the musical comedy only changed twice a week. Tickets remained close to the cheapest in town, twenty cents for adults and a dime for children.[61] Except for summers, this format lasted until well into 1927. Like revues and tabloids, Austin's 30- to 45-minute shows were "filled with catchy tunes and embellished with pretty girls."[62] Yet on occasion this troupe also performed farcical comedies and even social problem melodramas like *Ten Nights in a Bar Room* and *The Unmarried Mother*. During this period the Ada Meade also regularly staged Friday night amateur hours (which sometimes included boxing matches) and "colored" Charleston and buck-dancing contests, also showcasing local talent. These participatory events were combined with a Mildred Austin performance (maybe a revue, maybe a melodrama), and a feature film, comic short, and serial episode to form an evening's entertainment that would, it was hoped draw customers from the Orpheum and from the cheap vodvil seats at the Ben Ali.

With all phases of the motion picture industry coming under what Koszarski calls "increasing centralization" after World War I,[63] the experience of going to the movies would seem to have been more homogeneous in the 1920s than in the nickelodeon period or the mid-1910s. Jowett, for example, argues that the industry's "wholesaling practices" (like block booking) and its "mass production" system made it unable to cater to "America's regional-cultural variations."[64] Simply put, this means that the same movies, produced and distributed by a relatively small number of companies, were shown throughout the United States. Thus, particularly when it came to feature films, local theater owners could not tailor their offerings along some "regional-cultural" line, even if they had wanted to. Obviously, some variation from theater to theater was inevitable in terms of precisely when a given film was scheduled and how long it ran, and, as Koszarski points out, in terms of the quality of the print and even the speed at which it was projected.[65] Against exhibition practices of the 1990s (saturation bookings, multiplex cinemas), such variations are quite striking, but they do not fundamentally challenge Jowett's claim that there was during the late silent era a "mass," national product called the movies.

Just as film exhibition in the 1920s looks appreciably more varied if we

can see beyond the picture palace, when we take into account, as does Koszarski, not just the motion pictures screened but the whole "show," the
multipart bill, the "balanced program," then moviegoing in this period looks
far less homogeneous. Surveying the theaters on Lexington's Main Street from
the end of World War I to the late 1920s proves that there was considerable
variety in precisely how motion pictures were programmed, even within one
small city that had no bona fide picture palace and no successful theaters
located outside the central business district.

There were, for instance, readily apparent differences between the Kentucky's typical motion picture program and the Orpheum's feature-less bill.
However, variety and heterogeneity were most strikingly and tellingly evident
in the various ways motion pictures and live entertainment were combined
in the city's theaters.[66] As noted earlier, the Kentucky offered "acted prologues" for *The Thief of Baghdad* and *The Lost World* in 1925, yet this type
of "multimedia performance," associated with large city picture palaces, was
rarely seen in Lexington. Local residents were more likely to be entertained
by a bill in which motion pictures were preceded by an organ solo, six acts
of vodvil, an orchestral concert, a stock company revue or melodrama, a touring jazz ensemble, a Charleston contest, or a marimba band.

Koszarski rightly notes that "the one element that linked all silent-movie
exhibitions (and that remains the most difficult to recapture for modern audiences) was the musical setting."[67] If Lexington is any indication, this same
element also served to differentiate programming strategies and moviegoing
experiences in the late silent period. Add to the notion of the multimedia
performance and the "balanced program" the physical differences among local theaters and also the less readily demonstrable ways that audiences
seemed to have differed from theater to theater in terms of age, race, and
social class, and going to the movies in Lexington between 1919 and 1927
seems to have been far indeed from a unilaterally homogeneous experience.[68]

TEN

Movies, Culture, and the
"Jazz Environment"

From the standpoint of film exhibition practice, Lexington's theaters were quite distinct during the 1920s, though all were in the business of importing entertainment and marketing Hollywood. This business put them very near the heart of Lexington's social and cultural life during this period. The local significance of the booking policies, programming decisions, and daily operating procedures of the city's theaters becomes even more apparent if we once again attend to the larger context for and reception of commercial entertainment in Lexington. For example, sabbatarian demands, voiced with even more evangelical fervor, carried over from the 1910s. So did calls for censorship, with attention refocused on the need for action at the state rather than the city level. These campaigns, coupled with the high visibility of Fatty Arbuckle and Will Hays, helped to assure that Hollywood would figure prominently in local discourse as place and symptom, multiform trope and terrifying reality, wellspring of narrative pleasure and formidable American industry.

At the same time, demand seemed to increase for a recognizably twentieth-century version of high culture that was—usually for a steep price, under special conditions—made available to "all." This type of imported culture

219

Downtown Lexington in the 1920s. Photo courtesy University of Kentucky Photo
Archives.

was in part a way of compensating for provincialism and answering the excesses of cheap amusements. Yet commercial entertainment did not wilt under the pressure of criticism or culture: the 1920s saw the opening of a new amusement park and several large dance halls, even as the Lafayette Amusement Company and the Phoenix Amusement Company invested heavily in downtown theaters and jockeyed for position and profit. Beyond providing "colored" balconies in some of their venues, these companies, however, did little to seek out specifically the still substantial African-American audience in Lexington. Primarily from within the black community came a range of initiatives—movie screenings, concerts, community theater, dance halls—that sought to fill this gap in the name of race pride, uplift, or profit.

All these developments underscore the distance the city had traveled since the turn of the century, when major public activities for Lexington's black residents were generally held at the Opera House, as were the occasional high culture event and the most popular-price touring attractions. The Opera House may not have actually promoted a sense of community across racial and class lines, but it was able to serve a range of audiences. By the 1920s no single venue could hope to play this role in Lexington—the population was too large, commercial entertainment too widespread and ever-present, high art and African-American culture too separate by design or by circumstances.

Imported Culture

Lexington's theaters were able to find a place for marimba bands, blackface comedians, and Charleston contests, but they made little use of what passed as high culture in the 1920s. I refer here not to literary clubs or amateur recitals but to those special events that were publicly advertised and open to whoever could afford a ticket: Culture in the marketplace, Culture acknowledged in the entertainment section instead of (or at least as well as) the society pages of Lexington's newspapers.

One example of this phenomenon, held over from the 1910s, was the Redpath Chautauqua, which arrived in June or July for a six-day engagement. This version of "circuit" Chautauqua had changed somewhat since it had first pitched its tents in Lexington in 1916 under the auspices of the Ministerial Union, which felt that the Redpath series could provide an affordable, enlightening alternative to "the cheap entertainments that are generally en-

joyed."[1] While the 1920s version of tent Chautauqua was less directly concerned with political issues, it still featured bowdlerized drama, various types
of musical performance (though no "jazz"), and edifying lectures, including
in 1921 a speech by a former Chicago policeman who advocated the creation
of local motion picture censorship boards because "juvenile crime has increased 56 percent since the advent of the movies."[2]

The Redpath Chautauqua had nowhere near the level of local support,
prestige, and influence that the Lexington Chautauqua Assembly had
wielded. But during a period dominated by national media—such as motion
pictures and, later, radio—the annual Redpath visit did link Lexington to
regional circuits (stretching further south, as well as north into Indiana and
Ohio) and, more generally, to the rural, small town, predominantly middle
western America that made up the prime audience for what one circuit owner
called "culture under canvas."[3] Arriving from outside and providing a week-
long hiatus that was part recreation and part retreat, tent Chautauqua in fact
seemed more suited to the rhythms of an agrarian community.

Viewed in this light, the Redpath Chautauqua was the opposite of the annual Artist Concert Series, first organized in 1917 by Anna Chandler Goff,
Lexington's chief high culture impresario. Each of the five or six concerts in
Goff's series, spread out over several months, was a unique event, a special
night of Culture set apart from the quotidian offerings of Lexington's downtown theaters. Series tickets, ranging from $7.70 to $11.00, could be purchased at Goff's Lexington College of Music or at the Ben Ali, which in this
way helped to shoulder its civic responsibility.

Goff made available to those residents who could afford the rather steep
price of admission an appreciably more elevated level of art than that provided by the Redpath Chautauqua or the minstrel shows and revues booked
into the Opera House. The 1922–23 series, for example, featured Serge
Rachmaninoff and vocalists from the Chicago and the Metropolitan Opera
Companies. Two *Leader* editorials from 1923 testify to the gap between tent
Chautauqua and the Artist Concert Series. The Redpath visit to Lexington
was praised in matter-of-fact words for being "a part of and supplemental
to our system of education."[4] Jan Paderewski's Woodland Park Auditorium
appearance, however, elicited boundless enthusiasm: through the performance of this "great artist," the *Leader* affirmed, ordinary people are "lifted
into a realm of pure idealty, beauty and sublimity," and the United States as
a nation is "aroused to a higher appreciation of art in all its forms."[5] This

SEASON 1922-1923

IGNACE PADEREWSKI

in

Piano Recital

WOODLAND AUDITORIUM

Lexington, Kentucky

Friday, January 26, 8:15 P. M.

Auspices:

The LEXINGTON COLLEGE *of* MUSIC

ANNA CHANDLER GOFF, Director

Member National Concert Managers Association

Direct from the "realm of pure idealty, beauty and sublimity," Paderewski in Lexington.
Photo courtesy University of Kentucky Photo Archives.

encomium is indicative of a much broader trend toward the "sacralization of art."[6] And art, for a small city like Lexington in the 1920s, was free of the regional and the provincial; it was predominantly the product (or gift) of major dance and opera companies, metropolitan symphony orchestras, and internationally renowned masters: Paderewski, Rachmaninoff, Jascha Heifetz, Pablo Casals, and Fritz Kreisler.[7]

Art could also arise from local sources, as the "little" or "community" theater movement in the 1920s proves.[8] Underwritten by some fifty city residents, Lexington's two hundred-seat little theater, the Romany Theater, was housed in a former Negro church then owned by the University of Kentucky (UK). It was under the supervision of the chairman of the UK's Department of Art, and its mission was to use primarily Lexington talent to mount one production a month during the winter and spring. In January 1924 the Romany premiered, appropriately enough, with a play from the Theater Guild in New York City, Franz Molnar's Lilliom, which drew, the Herald noted, "fanciers of the higher form of dramatic art," including "many of the most cultured folk" in the area.[9]

In its choice of plays, its use of local performers and stage personnel, and its commitment to the "higher form of dramatic art"—loosely identified with contemporary stagecraft and plays outside the Broadway mainstream—the Romany marked its distance from mass culture. However, this nonprofit community theater was not interested in promoting regional or local drama. Like the Artist Concert Series, the Romany Theater was an attempt to plug Lexington into a larger, more cosmopolitan cultural circuit. This goal made the city's little theater the antithesis of, for example, blackface benefit shows or amateur night at the Ada Meade, even though these performances also relied on local talent.

University support of the Romany Theater led to the construction of a new on-campus facility in March 1927, which was described as "essentially a university enterprise, although the support of the citizens of Lexington is equally essential." Like its predecessor, the New Romany took as its aim "the elevation of standards of cultural appreciation," a process that had been and would increasingly become part of the university's public mission.[10] Art had found one of its prime twentieth-century havens.

Nontheatrical Exhibition of Motion Pictures

The significance of the University of Kentucky and other area colleges for the local entertainment scene extended well beyond UK's funding of community theater. From the first, college students had been among the most vocal "gallery gods" at the Opera House, and during the 1910s the UK student newspaper ran reviews of and advertisements for vaudeville at the Ada Meade and the Ben Ali. Movie theaters also regularly advertised in the *Kernel* and occasionally hosted pep rallies and fund raisers. Meanwhile, university administrators, city officials, and theater managers attempted to discourage underclassmen who, after home football games, would "form themselves into 'wild groups,' rush downtown and storm the theaters."[11] Rushing the movies, however, remained a fall ritual throughout the 1920s.

Underclass antics aside, college students formed an audience well worth capturing because of their age, leisure time, and disposable income. And, as I have suggested, individual faculty members and administrators often played a role in local debates on the reform and regulation of cheap amusement. The broader institutional effects of the university on the cultural life and leisure-time activity of the community at large are more difficult to gauge, in part because Lexington—which had long prided itself on being the educational center of the state—was not, strictly speaking, a college town. What can be ascertained, and is relevant to the larger concerns of this study, is the public use that UK made of motion pictures.[12]

The key qualification here is the notion of *public* use. Incorporating motion pictures produced by the State Department of Roads into engineering classes or even offering a short-lived course in 1915 on "photoplay writing" is one thing. Arranging screenings open to the public or making motion pictures available for use outside the university is another. These latter activities in effect made the university a nontheatrical, noncommercial film exhibitor and distributor and could only serve to reinforce the notion that the motion picture was potentially a valuable pedagogic tool. How soon did students of all ages come to take for granted that films screened under the auspices of a school were simply not the movies?

UK announced its first public film series in April 1916, the same month that saw the Daughters of the American Revolution try to "inspire patriotism" among children by sponsoring a Saturday morning program of "historical pictures" at the Strand.[13] (This was also the same month that the *Herald* began a five-part series of quasi-educational, syndicated articles on "How To Become a Motion Picture Actress.") UK's series grew directly out of the classroom use of motion pictures, for the university invited the public to attend screenings being held in conjunction with engineering classes. The films scheduled, all produced by private companies, included industrials (*The Making of High Grade Tools*), travelogues (Northern Pacific Railway's *Yellowstone Park*), and special "welfare" subjects (like Carnegie Steel's *Play Ground and Welfare Work*).[14]

Through the next decade there were other public screenings at UK announced in local newspapers, including films about cancer and evolution, a cinematic version of *Julius Caesar*, and even a reel of tennis instruction. The university's Engineering Society sponsored a series of "industrial pictures" like *Coal Is King* in November 1920, and another, more general interest summer series in 1928. Not surprisingly, the films exhibited by UK from the mid-teens through the 1920s were all offered as being the equivalent to public service lectures; the very act of screening them on campus gave them credibility, whether the subject was "the lives and customs" of Mexicans or the production of vaccines.[15]

In its capacity as a film distributor, UK also sought to increase its public visibility and influence statewide. Motion picture documentation of World War I and the use of this footage for propaganda purposes had brought home in an unprecedented way what the *Leader* called the "almost endless" "educational possibilities of motion picture photography."[16] In February 1920, UK opened a "Film Library," housing some 75,000 feet of film, principally travelogues (for example, *A Trip to Los Angeles*) and World War I footage produced by the Committee on Public Information. This library's holdings (as well as portable projection equipment) were provided free to any school in the state through the newly formed Department of University Extension.[17]

I could find no indication that this new university policy was considered at all controversial. Indeed, from one perspective, it was simply a matter of common sense and keeping up with the times. "There is no more delightful way to supplement textbook teaching" of "geography and history" than the motion picture, a *Leader* editorial declared in November 1919.[18] There also seems no doubt that ideological as well as "practical" ends were served by an arrangement whereby government-produced films were distributed through a state university and exhibited in elementary and secondary schools. Classrooms, needless to say, are not movie theaters, but to ignore nontheatrical film exhibition is to underestimate the extent to which the motion picture medium had made its presence felt throughout American society by the 1920s.

Public Entertainment, Commercial and Noncommercial

As the number of high culture performances and nontheatrical motion picture screenings increased in Lexington during the 1920s, so did the venues for and varieties of commercial entertainment and public recreation. One holdover from previous decades were fair weather traveling shows, the one or two large circuses or Wild West shows that played Lexington each year, as well as the smaller troupes and carnival companies that were regarded with more apprehension by, among other groups, the National Child Labor Committee, which concluded that "Kentucky is infested with traveling carnivals" that "represent commercial amusements at their very worst, not merely because of cheapness and vulgarity but because of brazen defiance of civic virtue and moral decency."[19] The only tangible effect of such protest in Lexington was that by the mid–1920s carnivals had been moved to a site just beyond the city line near tobacco warehouses and lower-income neighborhoods.

Locally owned and operated amusement parks met with nowhere near the reprobation heaped on the traveling carnival. As the 1920s began, the Kentucky Terminal and Traction Company's Blue Grass Park still made do with a few mechanical rides, a swimming area, Sunday baseball games, midway-style concessions, and nightly dancing. In 1921 it reinstituted free moving pictures on weekday evenings, but Blue Grass Park was soon to be displaced by a larger, more modern facility—another visible token of the city's "progress" and the quite remarkable commercialization of leisure-time activity in Lexington over a thirty-year period.

In November 1922 John W. and F. Keller Sauer, who had run several concessions at Blue Grass Park, went into partnership with Frank Brandt and leased with an option to buy twenty-five acres of farmland (including a large house) for $25,000. Located some two and a half miles north of Lexington, this property was easily accessible by streetcar, auto, and bus. In January 1923 Brandt and the Sauers formally incorporated their venture, dubbed Joyland Park, for $30,000 in capital stock.[20] Among the initial attractions when this amusement park opened in late May were well-equipped picnic grounds, Sunday baseball games, food stands, and a midway. The park also housed the Joyland Dance Casino, where, for a separate admission charge, patrons could dance nightly under Lexington's first revolving crystal ball.[21] The Sauers would soon add "thrilling amusement rides" and live performers, including the future state governor and baseball commissioner, Happy Chandler, then billed simply as a "popular tenor."[22]

Given its spacious grounds and dance hall, as well as the fact that it was open after dark and on Sundays, Joyland, even at this relatively late date, required some measure of legitimation. To dispel any fear that their amusement park would promote unsupervised, licentious activity, the Sauers emphasized Joyland's commitment to propriety and order. In words that recall the first ads for Blue Grass Park fourteen years earlier, the Sauers promised that "any and all entertainments have our guarantee for cleanliness, and a moral code will be strictly maintained at the highest. We want every one to have a good time. You may be as jovial and jolly as your nature will permit, that is what you come for, but order will be maintained at all times." To guarantee the maintenance of order, they vowed that a "uniformed officer" would be on duty day and night.[23]

The Sauers expanded and improved their enterprise throughout the 1920s, in the process forcing the Kentucky Terminal and Traction Company to close Blue Grass Park when its lease expired in June 1925. One of the few things that Joyland did not add was a moving picture show. The Sauers built a children's zoo and introduced three daily vaudeville performances in 1924; a roller skating rink and pony rides in 1926; and a $75,000 swimming pool in 1928. Meanwhile, their dance casino began to feature nationally known orchestras and became "the most popular dance spot in the Blue Grass."[24]

Joyland's success during the 1920s was matched by Lexington's municipal playgrounds, whose total attendance almost doubled from 1923 to 1927, when the nine and a half-week summer session drew close to two hundred thousand people.[25] A highly organized schedule of special events arranged by the Civic League was designed to involve children in a steady round of activities. One typical week in July 1923 featured boxing, archery, and tennis tournaments, storytelling contests, lantern carnivals, "pioneer parties," and nature activities.[26] Later years saw the introduction of beauty contests, amateur vaudeville shows, musical concerts, and pet shows, all usually scheduled for Friday and Saturday evenings so as to attract parents as well as children. For instance, in July 1927 some four thousand people attended a

water pageant at Woodland Park with floats built by children at neighborhood playgrounds.[27]

No doubt a strong pedagogic and social rationale lay behind the various
contests, tournaments, pageants, and performances arranged by the Civic
League at city playgrounds during the 1920s.[28] As in the past, the local press
continued to provide strong support. Editorials regularly sang the praises of
the "gospel of play,"[29] though at times the "playground" these journalists
evoked was a recreational site that had little room for pageantry and spectacle. Describing the "value of playgrounds" in 1928, for instance, the *Leader*
concluded that "there should be available to every section open spaces beau-
tified by trees, grass and flowers, where adults and entire families can pass
the early evening hours pleasantly and where social contacts can be made
and the neighborhood spirit cultivated."[30] Such visions of an edenic refuge
within the city die hard, even when they are not nurtured by a playground
system committed to time-filling and event-staging.

In fact, scheduling policies at Lexington's playgrounds shared much with
certain strategies of film exhibitors and the Sauer brothers, who also sought
an audience of repeat customers. Playgrounds were not merely well-tended
grounds on which to play, but sites for a virtually nonstop series of special
events that often culminated in some sort of public display or spectacle. Perhaps this type of "play" could best compete with the ever-changing fare at
downtown movie houses and with the increasing range of attractions at Joyland Park. *More* was the operative principle: live entertainment in addition
to movies (and serials and comedies in addition to features); a children's zoo
and a swimming pool in addition to midway attractions; water pageants and
beauty contests in addition to sporting events and arts-and-crafts projects.

Dance Halls and Blue Laws

What most set Joyland apart from city-operated recreational facilities was its
dance casino, which was closer to a night club than to the sort of open-air
pavilion found at Blue Grass Park. It was billed as "the place of refinement
where social life centers," yet it rarely charged more than ten cents for admission and five cents a dance.[31] By 1925 the Sauers had contracted with the
National Attraction ballroom circuit, which routed New York-based orchestras through various cities for week-long engagements. Musicians like "the
Columbia Record Artists," Earl Gresh and His Orchestra, became major

drawing cards.[32] In effect, Joyland was operating by the same logic that led the Strand and the Kentucky in the 1920s to book touring "jazz" orchestras and stage Charleston contests.

As would be expected, success bred imitation. The first large dance hall downtown, the Rosalind Dance Casino, opened in November 1924 on the third floor of the Lafayette Hotel garage, a few doors down from the Kentucky. This site could accommodate several hundred couples on its dance floor and initially was open from November through April, those months when Joyland was closed. In 1925 white investors financed a large "colored" dance hall on West Main Street, which will be discussed later in this chapter. Downtown nightlife became even fuller when the Olympia Dance Club premiered in November 1926 on the same block as the Strand and the Ben Ali.

This highly visible commercial exploitation of "modern" dancing and music loosely labeled as "jazz" occurred in an environment in which the Elkhorn Baptist Association, comprised of thirty-three congregations from Lexington and surrounding areas, could declare at its 1921 convention that "dancing is one of the most dangerous of worldly amusements, and is making one of the greatest inroads on the churches. The dance is indecent, immoral, and immodest."[33] Such fears led the Lexington Ministerial Union to object to the opening of the Rosalind Dance Casino and to oppose the granting of "public dance hall licenses to any person or concern in this city."[34] In this way the ministers hoped to secure Lexington proper against infection (Joyland being technically outside the city limits) and to forestall any chance that dance halls might fill the void left by the closing of saloons. After the city commissioners set a precedent by granting the Rosalind a license to operate downtown, the Elkhorn Baptist Association reminded easily swayed local residents that "60 percent of the fallen women attribute their downfall to the dance, mostly the public dance hall."[35]

According to area Baptist churches, the movie theater was cut from the same cloth as the dance hall, the only difference being that local theaters were permitted to violate the Sabbath. The new sabbatarian campaign these churches mounted in 1920–21 was more explicitly evangelical than the failed legal maneuverings of 1918. Informing this struggle was the firm belief that, in the words of a formal resolution passed by the Blue Grass Baptist Young People's Union, moving pictures are "the outstanding evil of the day, injurious and very degrading to all that is moral, high and holy. They encourage and magnify all the things that are immoral; they emphasize shooting, killing, gambling, divorce, elopements, unfaithfulness in the home life, free love, appealing to the sex [sic] and such like."[36]

The leaders of this resurgent sabbatarianism were the Reverend Arthur Fox, whose church was in nearby Paris, and the Reverend J. W. Porter of Lexington's First Baptist Church. Both men were uncompromising in their criticism of "Sunday pleasure seeking," which Porter deemed a "deliberate disobedience to law" that contains the "germ of anarchy" and is "usually the first sin in the long catalogue of crime."[37] Fox was, if anything, more explicit: "pictures shows are nightly crowded," he declared, "and whole families are becoming picture show fiends. The moving picture show is the devil's work shop."[38] Fox, in particular, was able to publicize his views in letters to the *Herald* and the *Leader*, which also reprinted several of his sermons and issued editorial responses.[39] Inspired by Fox, the Elkhorn Baptist Association voted unanimously in September 1921 to begin a "united campaign against moving pictures, dancing, immodest 'undress,' mixed bathing, divorce, Sunday baseball, card playing, horse racing, gambling and violation of prohibition laws."[40]

The larger backdrop for these actions by Lexington-area Baptist churches was a national campaign in favor of blue laws, which had enlisted William Jennings Bryan as its major representative. Opponents were organized under the banner of the Anti-Blue Law League, and included such diverse supporters as Luther Burbank, Douglas Fairbanks, and Joseph Lee, the president of the Playground and Recreation Association of America.[41] Locally, the *Leader* decried the materialism of theater proprietors and called for a "sane" Sunday but never actually endorsed the Elkhorn campaign.[42] The *Herald*, in contrast, reprinted articles critical of the national blue law movement and rejected Fox's initiative as a vain attempt to turn back the clock.

Exhibitors did not feel compelled to answer sabbatarian charges, city officials steered well clear of the controversy, and no formal indictments were issued, as had been the case during the 1910s. One incident epitomizes the futility of sabbatarianism in Lexington during the early 1920s: in July 1920 two churches complained about Sunday evening band concerts at a city park. When the fifteen hundred people attending one of these concerts were asked to vote on whether this form of entertainment should be continued, they unanimously voiced their approval and the band played on.[43] Obviously the question was loaded, the electorate was not representative of the city at large, and the audience's choices were limited. But they did vote to maintain what had been a long-standing practice. Compare the scene some thirty miles away, in the town of Danville, Kentucky, where the voice of the people had something quite different to say when an exhibitor trying to screen movies on Sunday was stopped cold by city police who were "followed by a large group of towns-people."[44]

Censorship in the 1920s

Unlike sabbatarianism, which came to be associated with certain specific churches that were bucking the tide of modernity, censorship remained an issue of more general concern in Lexington. However, unlike the 1910s, the 1920s saw much less active involvement in censorship campaigns by civic groups and public school officials. The Central Kentucky Women's Clubs did form a committee in 1921 to promote "cleaner and better amusement for the children and young people," and the "motion picture department" of the WCTU worked to the same end.[45] But in Lexington, at least, there was no strong sense in the 1920s that *local* control over commercial entertainment was a possible or even a desirable goal. This could well have been an acknowledgment of the magnitude of the amusement "problem" or a realistic assessment of how little city government was willing and able to accomplish, given the distribution of power in a mass society.

Municipal officials, for their part, took very few prohibitive actions concerning public amusements. For example, the city board of health in October 1925, and again in August 1927, barred children from attending motion picture theaters for a week after a case of infantile paralysis was discovered in Lexington.[46] In 1929 the police closed down several games of chance at a traveling carnival, and that same year the board of commissioners, after receiving a number of complaints, passed an ordinance banning any shows from starting after 10:30 P.M. at Lexington theaters.[47] Mayor Thomas C. Bradley ordered that posters of "dancing girls in abbreviated skirts" for the *Marcus Show of 1920* (a revue booked for the Opera House) be removed,[48] but as far as I have been able to determine, Lexington's censorship ordinance was never enforced.

The abandonment of local censorship as a goal did not mean the end of all efforts to assert government control over commercial entertainment. Early in the 1920s, censorship at the state level became a distinct possibility in Kentucky, as elsewhere.[49] In response to "popular demand throughout the

state," State Senator Hiram Brock, representing the town of Harlan, introduced a bill in January 1922 providing for a state board of censorship. "It is
the duty of the state," Brock announced, "to look out for the welfare of its
children . . . this measure is for the boys and girls of Kentucky."[50] This proposed board would be comprised of three people selected by the governor:
one chosen at large, one from three candidates proposed by the state Federation of Women's Clubs, and one from three candidates proposed by the Kentucky Education Association (KEA). Each would be paid an annual salary of
$3,000 (with funds coming from a $2.00-per-thousand-foot fee assessed to
motion picture companies) and empowered to demand cuts or to reject any
film that was not "moral and educational or amusing and harmless."[51] Thus
once again the same basic dichotomies—moral/amusing and educational/
harmless—served as the means for categorizing and eventually managing
commercial entertainment.

Brock's proposal was considered in the same legislative session that saw
heated debate over an anti-evolution bill that ultimately was defeated by a
42–41 vote. This call for state censorship generated rather intense lobbying
efforts. The Motion Picture Theater Owners of Kentucky, for example, reiterated their stand against both censorship and "salaciousness in film," and
tried to deflect attacks by pointing to carnivals as the real "menace to a high
standard of community morals."[52] Advocates of censorship successfully enlisted the support of the WCTU and service organizations like the Lions Club.

The censorship bill also became a topic for newspaper editorials statewide, whose views were typified by the positions taken by Lexington's two
daily papers. The *Herald* (like the Frankfort *State Journal* and Louisville's
major newspapers) came out adamantly against the bill, linking it with "puri-
tanical" attempts to censor the press and enforce blue laws.[53] The *Herald*
strongly questioned giving such sweeping authority to any three individuals
and argued that the vague, prescriptive criteria laid out in Brock's proposal
raised the possibility that motion pictures based on the plays of Shakespeare,
Molière, and even John Galsworthy would be prohibited. Similar arguments
were offered in a letter to the *Herald* from Kentucky native D. W. Griffith,
who had recently been invited by the governor to the Louisville premiere of
Orphans of the Storm and who had addressed the state legislature in person
on February 20. Griffith reminded Kentuckians that if state censorship had
been in force, "*The Birth of a Nation* would never have shown in any Northern
State [sic] under the rule of censorship, and the cause of the South would
never have been told."[54] (The irony here is that the *Herald* in 1916 had

strongly attacked *The Birth of a Nation,* but when Griffith returned to Kentucky in 1922 he was greeted only with accolades for being a "moral force in moviedom.")[55]

The *Leader* (and small-town newspapers like the Stanford *Interior Journal*) argued for censorship, as it had done in 1916 and would continue to do for most of the 1920s. The *Leader* reasoned that, first, this extreme measure was warranted because "something is radically wrong with the film world," as proven by its frequent portrayal of violence, crime, "adultery and fornication," and the "coarse and the vulgar"; and, second, because it is the responsibility of society to protect itself (and particularly its children) against "those amusements which constitute a menace to the general welfare and tend to deprave the morals of the community."[56]

Even with considerable statewide support and a favorable senate vote of 24–5, Brock's bill was killed by the Rules Committee before it ever reached a general vote in the house. (It fared no better when it was reintroduced in the next two legislative sessions, 1924 and 1926.) The hiring of the Harding administration's postmaster general, Will Hays, in January 1922 to head the newly formed Motion Picture Producers and Distributors of America (MPPDA) probably managed to deflect interest from state censorship campaigns.[57] From January through March 1922, Hays received extensive coverage in the Lexington press, particularly in the Republican *Leader.* This strongly pro-censorship newspaper would have been precisely the sort of opponent the motion picture industry had in mind when it enlisted Hays.

The *Leader* had begun the 1920s by calling for federal censorship of motion pictures as a means of "suppressing" all that was "salacious, vulgar and immoral" and encouraging the movies' "vast possibilities of good."[58] It endorsed Brock's efforts to create a Kentucky board of censorship and enthusiastically applauded the appointment of Will Hays, whose organizational skills and "reputation for probity and moral idealism" were exactly what the *Leader* felt was needed to "control the [motion picture] business and to clean it out and tone it up."[59] In 1925 it congratulated Hays for leading the industry to adopt a self-censorship plan based on the ideal of "common decency."[60] But this newspaper never lost its deep misgivings about commercial amusement and what it referred to in 1923 as the shallow and dangerous "jazz environment."[61] Four years (and another Republican administration) later, when local theaters and dance halls were regularly booking "jazz" orchestras, the *Leader* sounded the same note, ruefully acknowledging that "jazz reflects modern American life . . . our life nowadays is flippant, hurried and superficial and so is our music."[62] No wonder the *Leader* pined for the bucolic "playground" mentioned earlier.

This newspaper also remained steadfastly ready to condemn transgressive texts: for example, "gutter plays" of the stage as well as the screen that "pander to what is lowest and basest in human nature"; "pictures which glorify vice and licentiousness" and "ostentatious wealth"; and specific films like First National's *Chickie*, which the *Leader* deemed "unfit for consumption" since it could not be "discussed frankly and without reserve by a respectable young man and a modest young woman in the presence of the parents of the young woman."[63] (Even respectability and modesty must still be held accountable to the parental presence.) Such motion pictures "give to the immature and the unsophisticated boy and girl false conceptions of the standards of the average American family and doubtless in many instances thruout [sic] the nation lead them into bypaths which bring shame, misery and ruin."[64] From the *Leader*'s perspective, while Hays' right-minded cleansing of the film industry was all well and good, even one *Chickie* was too dangerous to tolerate.[65]

In effect, the *Leader* offered itself as Lexington's vigilant watchdog for decency, on the lookout for violations of "common" moral standards. But like Hays, the *Leader* could only accomplish its noble goals if the "fundamental decency" of America rose up against "commercialized obscenity."[66] It is difficult, however, to tell just how widespread such opinions were, even among the *Leader*'s readership. After the 1922 state censorship bill was defeated, there were no letters to the editor on the merits of censorship and apparently no major lobbying efforts on this front by area women's clubs or local educators. The rhetoric of the *Leader*'s editorials suggests a possible explanation for this lack of local involvement. Increasingly, the *Leader* came to pose the problem of movies and commercial entertainment as a *national* problem, not something particular to Lexington and not something that Lexington's theatergoers or theater owners could really do anything about, except to reject specific films and movie stars that promoted "loose morals" and "free living" and trust leaders like Will Hays to do their duty.[67]

The *Herald*, in contrast, placed considerably less emphasis on Hays and argued that "better movies" would come only as a result of consumer demand, enacted in the equitable and democratic domain of the marketplace: "the best way to eliminate bad pictures is by creating an overwhelming desire for clean, constructive plays both in the legitimate theater and in moving pictures."[68] The *Herald* believed that this process would succeed because the "great film production companies" are run by responsible men, who are well aware that the "motion picture industry, that is a combination of art and business, has taken rank with the great industries of the country."[69] Having faith that the good sense of the American public and of industry leaders would bring about the progressive improvement of the movies, the *Herald* rejected government censorship, which would, it concluded, inevitably be bound up with party politics, intolerance, and bigotry.[70] Rabbi Theodore Lifset of Lexington's Temple Adaith Israel (one of two small Jewish congregations in the city) strongly agreed, declaring in an April 1927 sermon that it was the task of the clergy to educate the masses, who then would freely reject the obscene and the indecent.[71] Lifset and the *Herald* differed from the Elkhorn Baptist Association and the *Leader* in terms of precisely how they defined "obscenity" and assessed the audience's capacity for determining its own leisure-time (and moral) destiny. But all these discussions of censorship during the 1920s began with the assumption that the movies and the motion picture industry constituted an extraordinarily pervasive and significant presence in American life. The Hollywood scandals early in the decade had made this situation painfully clear.

Fatty Arbuckle and the Discourse of Hollywood

The most prominent among these scandals involved popular screen comedian, Fatty Arbuckle, who was charged with manslaughter after the death of Virginia Rappe at a party in September 1921. From this date until early 1923, through the comedian's three trials and Hays' deliberations concerning Arbuckle's future in the industry, this situation remained prime copy for newspapers in Lexington and across the country. Virtually every day between September 11 and 29, 1921—during the height of the Elkhorn Baptist Association's "united campaign" against immoral amusements—the case was front page news. The same was true during Arbuckle's first trial for manslaughter (November 14–December 6, 1921), which ended in a hung jury, and his two subsequent trials, which took place between January and April 1922. The sheer quantity of front page coverage, often including photographs of Arbuckle, Rappe, the witnesses, and their high-flying life-style, attests to the drawing power, if not the symbolic import, of this story of decline and fall.[72]

Spurred by press coverage, the local response to the Arbuckle "tragedy" or "scandal" was immediate. The Phoenix Amusement Company publicly announced its ban on all Arbuckle films at the Strand and Ben Ali. The *Leader* voiced its support of the ban, and—even as it prominently featured this story—called for a "withdrawal of publicity" of "all of the details of this tragedy."[73] The *Herald* interpreted the American public's response to this "scandal" as indicating that the "California moving picture colony" must learn to respect the "public moral sense."[74] And for Reverend Arthur Fox, the "Arbuckle tragedy" was proof positive of civilization's "shame" under the sway of the movies, whose "whole tendencies" and whose "leaders are evil."[75]

There had been no such local outcry after potentially scandalous events involving picture personalities in 1920: Charles Chaplin's divorce from Mildred Harris; the suicide of Jack Pickford's wife, Olive Thomas; or Mary Pickford's divorce and quick marriage to Douglas Fairbanks. In fact, during the month that the Arbuckle story first broke, the *Leader* was running a ten-part syndicated autobiography of Mary Pickford, "our Mary, the movie queen." Once his first trial ended in a hung jury, it became even more apparent that Arbuckle was, in Richard deCordova's words, "a site of struggle between reformers and the industry, the subject of social controversy."[76] And also, we should add, a subject of pressing interest to the reading public. The *Herald* ruefully announced that "the result of the Arbuckle case has caused more telephone calls to newspaper offices than all the propositions for naval reduction and all the plans of the representatives of the great nations of the world for bringing about an era of international tranquility."[77] The American people had good reason to be preoccupied with the unrepentant, unremorseful Arbuckle and "his companions in debauch," since—the *Leader* reasoned—"the motion picture public, too, is on trial."[78] So would be Will Hays, soon after he took office with the MPPDA in January 1922.

During Arbuckle's retrial, another scandal broke, the mysterious murder of film director William Desmond Taylor, which also received front page coverage for more than two weeks, often sharing the limelight with news concerning Hays' appointment and legislative efforts to create a state censorship board. Even though Arbuckle was acquitted and the Kentucky censorship bill defeated, the *Leader* found some consolation in Hays' decision in April 1922 to cancel all contracts for the exhibition of Arbuckle's films. Six months later, the *Leader* could look upon the whole sordid Arbuckle affair as an uplifting melodrama, with Hays and the American people winning a clear "moral victory" over that part of the "film world" that trafficked in "the erotic, the false [and] the vulgar."[79]

Little wonder, then, that the *Leader* and others of a like mind were so distressed by Hays' decision in December 1922 to allow Arbuckle to return to work in the motion picture industry. The Kentucky Federation of Women's Clubs immediately protested the action, and one city commissioner presented a motion "requesting" local theaters not to show Arbuckle's films. Mayor Bradley cast the deciding vote to defeat this measure, declaring that Fatty deserved another chance.[80] As would be expected, the city's religious community felt otherwise. The Lexington Ministerial Union and the Blue Grass Baptist Ministerial Association adopted resolutions calling for the city commissioners to prohibit the exhibition of Arbuckle's films. The WCTU followed suit, and on 10 January 1923 Lexington's theater owners collectively agreed not to book them.[81] Hays responded to comparable pressure nationwide and reinstituted his ban. For the *Leader,* this epilogue to the Arbuckle affair only made the moral victory that much more worth savoring. In fact, the *Leader* affirmed, "there has never been a more striking demonstration of the power of public sentiment in America": the banishment of Arbuckle demonstrated and vindicated the nation's "high moral purpose" and the efficacy of its democratic processes.[82]

At the local level, the victory over Arbuckle did not turn out to be the first skirmish in a broad-based campaign to reclaim territory lost to the encroaching Jazz Age. Given the rest of the decade, Arbuckle looks more like a convenient scapegoat, and his affair an isolated occasion for oratory and intervention. None of the Hollywood scandals of the early and mid–1920s seems to have led directly to an increase in local sabbatarian efforts, for example, or to campaigns for greater regulation of motion picture exhibition in Lexington. The effects were more diffuse and dispersed, perhaps most evident when exhibitors engaged in public relations activities that also qualified as gestures toward (re)legitimation.

For instance, the Phoenix Amusement Company in November 1923 allowed the congregation of the fire-damaged Centenarian Methodist Church to hold Sunday services at the Strand, and several years later special interdenominational services were held at the Kentucky on Thanksgiving and during Easter week. Exhibitors also supported secular organizations and progressive social welfare initiatives by running special shows for children under the auspices of the League of Women's Voters in 1921–22 and the University of

Kentucky Women's Club in 1928; screening the Automobile Club's safety slides and the Kentucky Hygiene Association's instructional films; and staging benefit shows for the Daughters of the American Revolution, the American Legion, the Society for Crippled Children, and the Red Cross relief effort for Kentucky flood victims. Such actions no doubt reinforced the sense that the Strand, Ben Ali, and Kentucky were valuable, upstanding members of the business community. These theaters brought Hollywood to Lexington but somehow were not themselves tainted in the process.

Of course, "Hollywood," broadly understood as site and subject of discourse during the 1920s, included much more than Will Hays and Fatty Arbuckle. "Hollywood" was constructed on a national scale, through shorts and features and newsreels, and all manner of publicity and promotional material. As commentators have long noted, fanzines, trade journals, and general interest magazines all played crucial roles in this discourse.[83] So, I would propose, did local newspapers, with their publication of advertising, editorials, and syndicated or wire service material.[84] In this regard, several things struck me in surveying Lexington's two daily newspapers throughout the 1920s: the sheer number of pertinent editorials; the extensive coverage of the Arbuckle scandal and then, later in the decade, the death of Rudolph Valentino and the divorce of Charles Chaplin and Lita Gray; the presence of serialized feature articles, including Thomas Ince's autobiography (1924), weekly pieces on "star beauty secrets" (1925) and on movie men's notion of the "ideal girl" (1926), even a serialized novel, *It Can't Be Done* (1928), "a story of love, adventure and the movies," set in Hollywood; the regular publication of front page filler items, usually accompanied by photos, that introduced new starlets, detailed terms of contracts, and provided gossip about the "private" lives of screen celebrities; the use of Hollywood stars and directors in advertising campaigns for Lucky Strikes and Old Gold cigarettes and Lux soap;[85] and, perhaps most interesting (because least analyzed), the representation of moviemaking and Hollywood in syndicated comic strips like *Boobs McNutt, Bringing Up Father,* and particularly *Freckles* (March–April 1923) and *Etta Kett* (November 1928), whose principal characters made extended journeys to Hollywood.

I will not here attempt to synthesize a multisided picture of "Hollywood" from this newspaper material, none of which, except for the editorials, was unique to Lexington. Yet it all was disseminated (and contextualized) in local papers, as opposed to national mass-market magazines. The *Leader*'s editorial staff might find movie stars to be "enormously overpaid and vastly overrated,"[86] but other sections of the paper told a different story altogether. These syndicated articles and wire service releases collectively attest to a broad-based fascination with Hollywood; they prove that Fatty Arbuckle and Will Hays, however prominent, shared column inches with other symbols of and spokespersons for the movie colony; and they stand as alternatives, correctives, supplements, or reaffirmations of the more patly "local" perspective offered by the editorials in the *Herald* and the *Leader*.

Entertainment and Culture in the Black Community

Thomas Cripps' excellent survey of the representation of African Americans in Hollywood films of the 1920s gives some indication of how black spokespersons and key African-American newspapers responded to the motion picture industry during this decade.[87] Much less accessible is any sense of what Hollywood or commercial entertainment, broadly understood, might have meant to the African-American residents of a city like Lexington. The best that I can provide in this regard is another look at the topics covered in this chapter, this time from the perspective of Lexington's black community.[88]

At the beginning of the 1920s, "colored" balconies accounted for one hundred fifty seats at the Ada Meade and about four hundred at the Ben Ali. The Strand refused to admit African Americans until 1922, when, faced with increased local competition, the Phoenix Amusement Company turned the Strand's three hundred-seat second balcony into a "colored" section, with ten-cent general admission tickets and thirty-cent loge box seats. It was these loge seats, in particular, that led the author of *Negro Problems in Cities* to affirm that the Strand offered "easily one of the best appointed galleries open to them [Negroes] in the South."[89] In 1928, however, the Phoenix Amusement Company reverted to its all-white policy, reminding Lexington blacks that even segregated seating arrangements continued to be an arbitrarily determined, revocable privilege accorded by whites.[90]

During the 1920s, as in the nickelodeon era, small "colored" theaters offered an alternative to the Jim Crow practices at Main Street venues. None of the three black moving picture shows that opened in Lexington in the 1920s fared as well as the Gem had between 1910 and 1916 or as Louisville's New Lincoln Theater and Grand Theater in the mid–1920s.[91] Yet their very existence was noteworthy, for this was the decade of the "New Negro," when, in George C. Wright's words, "all over Kentucky the opening of a movie house, clothing store, or any business was proclaimed as a step forward for the race."[92]

In January 1921, almost five years after the Gem closed, the Star Theater began operation at the corner of Wilson and East Short streets in a predominantly black residential area located several blocks northeast of the Strand and the Ben Ali. Managed by former laborer J. H. Bibbs, this was a neighborhood theater that opened at 3:00 P.M. daily, with Sunday shows from 2:00 to 10:00 P.M. The few ads Bibbs ran in the "colored notes" of the *Herald* promised a program consisting of live vaudeville acts, a pianist, and five or six reels of motion pictures. For its premiere the Star scheduled a bill roughly comparable to the sort of fare regularly offered at the Orpheum: an episode of the *Masked Rider* serial, a Fatty Arbuckle comedy, and a W. S. Hart western. An ad from April 1921, however, described an evening's entertainment more directly tailored to the Star's audience: a ten-piece "jazz" orchestra and *The Depths of Our Hearts,* a feature film with an "all-colored cast."[93] Given the paucity of "race" movies in this period, Bibbs did not have the option of scheduling films like *The Depths of Our Hearts* night after night, and in any case, the Star seems not to have stayed open much beyond April 1921. Indeed, the early 1920s were particularly difficult years for all black-run businesses in Lexington. According to city directories, between 1921 and 1923 the number of "colored" groceries, for example, dropped from nine to three, the restaurants from fourteen to ten, and the former saloons become "soft-drink" parlors from nine to four. By the mid-1920s the prospects for black-operated businesses seem to have improved, in part because "race" enterprises had begun to congregate in one area, around Deweese Street, close to where the Star had been located.

When the Lincoln Theater—"exclusively for colored people"—opened in May 1926 at the corner of Spruce and 2nd streets, near Deweese, it shared a block with a grocery store, a restaurant, and several private residences. Within the next few years, this area would become the major center of African-American life in Lexington, home to barbers, physicians, taxicab companies, and life insurance agencies, as well as various sites for leisure-time activity. Like the Star, the Lincoln was managed by a former laborer and was operated along the same lines as black-run theaters of the 1910s, with continuous programming between 1:30 and 10:00 P.M. and admission set at a dime. An early ad for the Lincoln promised "the latest Western photoplays" changed daily, highlighted by a special first-run screening of Tom Mix's *The Wagon Trail.*[94] Westerns dominated the Lincoln's schedule, as they did the

DIXIE THEATRE

(SECOND STREET NEAR DEWEESE)

Exclusively for High Class Colored People

Will Open Saturday, September 3

WITH

LON CHANEY'S MASTER PLAY

TELL IT TO THE MARINES

and a

HAL ROACH COMEDY

ADMISSION

Sundays and Saturdays—Adults 20¢ — Children 10¢

Matinees and Other Days—From 2 to 5 P. M. 10¢

A short-lived black neighborhood theater. Lexington *Leader*, 2 September 1927.

Sunday programming at the Ada Meade.[95] Booking this "low" genre may have had less to do with "colored" tastes than with rental rates and print availability and with an attempt to attract customers of a certain age or a certain social class. The preference for westerns suggests that the Lincoln was a scaled-down version of the Orpheum or the Ada Meade, until we also note that co-billed with *The Wagon Trail* was Jackie, "the Charleston kid, Queen of the Blues Singers"; similarly, *Sons of the West* shared the Lincoln's stage with a spiritualist act and with the music of the Dare Devil Jazz Foot Warmers.[96] Bills like this would seem to have held out the option for what Miriam Hansen calls a "locally specific, potentially interactive and aleatory" moviegoing experience.[97]

Westerns, often co-billed with jazz or blues performers, remained the standard fare when the Lincoln reopened as the Dixie Theater in September 1927. The Dixie—"exclusively for high class colored people"—did, however, have a slightly more flexible exhibition schedule than the Lincoln: occasionally it ran all-motion picture programs (centered on a feature-length western) or a revue like Clarence E. Muse and his twenty-five-piece Charleston Dandies; more often, it offered a small-scale vaudeville act plus daily changing motion pictures. The Dixie apparently stayed in business well into 1928, as the larger theaters downtown converted to sound. The *Herald* reported in June 1929 that the projector had been stolen from the Dixie, which "had not been used for some time."[98] This news item also noted that the owners of the property itself were from Lawrenceville, Kentucky and were represented locally by a white real estate agent, suggesting that neither the Lincoln nor the Dixie had been a black-owned operation.

Watching vodvil or the movies from a balcony seat at the Ben Ali, Ada Meade, or the Strand was inevitably a reminder and a reaffirmation of Jim Crow policies. Thus the very existence of "exclusively colored" theaters signified the possibility of an alternative way of taking one's place in a biracial society. Just how much this "exclusively colored" experience sought to be or succeeded in being separate is impossible to tell. (Were westerns, in some way, always westerns?) What is clear is that none of these theaters was commercially successful. Maybe the necessary capital investment simply was not available; maybe there were not enough African-American moviegoers who would choose the Dixie over the Ben Ali. For whatever reason, the Dixie, Star, and Lincoln did not become a source of "race" pride, a symbol of the community's "better" aspirations, or, for that matter, a dangerous target of fear and loathing.

Set against the relative insignificance of black theaters in Lexington during the 1920s is the prominent role of African-American public schools and churches as sites for motion picture exhibition.[99] As a community service activity and a way to fill and monitor leisure time, virtually all local African-American churches, Baptists included, offered motion picture programs during the 1920s, continuing a tradition that went back to the pre-nickelodeon period.[100] Quite often churches stuck to "sacred moving pictures": religious parables, dramatizations of scripture, or, more rarely, documentary accounts of missionary work. As late as 1930, for example, a traveling exhibitor toured area Baptist churches with "the Hell-bound excursion train in moving pictures, including 78 scenes, 50 characters and 6 reels."[101] Purely secular moving pictures were common only at Methodist and Episcopal churches, with one important exception: nonfiction compilation films like *Colored Fighters of the World's War* played locally during 1920–21 at all of the largest African-American churches in Lexington.

Quite understandably, these documentaries were also presented at the city's "colored" schools, whose purchase of a motion picture projector early in 1921 was taken as proof that they ranked among "the most progressive schools of the country."[102] In fact, the regularly scheduled screenings at Booker T. Washington, Russell, and Constitution grade schools during 1921–22 stand as the most extensive and probably the most significant nontheatrical exhibition of motion pictures in Lexington during the silent era.[103] Certain of these programs had clear-cut pedagogic and racial goals: for example, *Negro Soldiers Breaking the German Lines* and *A Day in the Magic City,* which was billed as a "new type of production featuring the progress and pride of colored people" in Birmingham, Alabama.[104] These schools also arranged for weekly programs principally designed for children, with ten- and fifteen-cent admission prices. One such show at Constitution school featured a Bray cartoon and three recycled short films: Griffith's *The Last Drop of Water,* Mary Pickford's *The Lucky Toothache,* and W. S. Hart's *Prowlers of the Plain.*[105] Such exhibitions, set for Monday or Wednesday evenings, continued through the summer of 1921 and at least into early 1922, when notices stopped appearing in local newspapers.

For African-American educators, the advantages of these programs were obvious: regular screenings under school auspices could generate income, underscore the school's role in the community, allow for some control over motion picture fare, and provide black children and their parents with an alternative to segregated balcony seating. However, the arranging of motion picture programs for children was apparently not perceived as a potentially valuable "race" initiative on the order of staging historical pageants and bringing nationally known African-American performers like Roland Hayes to Lexington.

These performers fell into three distinct categories. Parallel to the high-cultural luminaries of the Artist Concert Series were the renowned African-American singers, Roland Hayes and Marian Anderson, who performed at Woodland Park Auditorium, with part of the lower-floor seating reserved for whites. (Hayes visited Lexington in 1924, 1926, and 1928; Anderson in 1930.) From 1922 on, each year also saw at least one major choral concert, featuring groups like the Tuskegee Singers, Williams World Famous Colored Singers, and the Fisk Jubilee Singers. Such events were sponsored by religious and educational organizations and were strongly supported by African-American social clubs like the Acme Art & Culture Club.

A quite different side (or level) of contemporary black culture was represented by recording artists who were among the major figures responsible for the popularization of blues and jazz. For example, booked into the Woodland Park Auditorium or the Opera House during the 1920s were Mamie Smith and her Jazz Hounds, W. C. Handy, Ida Cox, Ma Rainey and her Southern Troopers, the Fletcher Henderson Orchestra, and, in July 1930, Duke Ellington. Such performances, as well as the availability of "race" records at the black-operated Parker's Melody Shop and other local music stores, helped to bring the new music of the 1920s into the commercial mainstream. Though jazz and blues artists did not come stamped with the institutional imprimatur that underscored the high cultural status of Roland Hayes or the traditional (and overtly regional) value of the Fisk Jubilee Singers, there is no evidence that the audiences for Hayes, choral concerts, and jazz musicians did not overlap.[106]

Much more distinct in their aims and probably in their audiences were pageants and dance halls, two other significant aspects of local African-American public life during the 1920s. A pair of grand-scale "community dramas," *Milestones of a Race* (performed in 1924) and *Loyalty's Gift* (performed in 1925)—as well as various church-sponsored plays and the operetta, *Arrival of the Negro*—drew almost unprecedented support from Lexington's newspapers and from the leaders of the black community. *Milestones of a Race,* for instance, utilized a local cast of nearly five hundred to present its ten episodes, which moved from ancient Egypt through Africa, antebellum life, and reconstruction to end with a celebration of the contemporary achievements of the race. Looking backward, it is easy to be cynical about the myth of progress that informed such grand historical spectacles, but the popularity of motion pictures about the exploits of black soldiers during World War I indicates just how vital race pride was as the inequities of Jim Crow dragged on and the Ku Klux Klan became active in central Kentucky.

Milestones of a Race was directed by a representative of the National Recreation Association and sponsored locally by the newly formed Community Service League, whose executive committee included Lexington's wealthiest and most civic-minded African Americans. This pageant played to overflow crowds at the Opera House in February, then again in March 1924, and it exemplified the Community Service League's commitment to "wholesome recreational, educational opportunities for young and old, through music, drama and play."[107] Thereafter the League's major efforts were directed toward the operation of playgrounds for black children, though it also sponsored various community dramas and the 1930 appearance of Marian Anderson.

Short-lived movie theaters like the Lincoln and the Dixie were never successful enough to pose a threat to the Community Service League's nonprofit, civic-minded agenda. Commercial dance halls were another matter entirely. For one thing, dance halls were able to find a steady, large audience where black-run movie theaters were not. Dreamland, a dance hall located on the north side of Lexington near Frederick Douglass Park, was opened in 1923 by two former black saloon keepers. Taken over in 1925 by the black janitor of the white Central Christian Church and renamed the Palm Garden Dance Hall, it remained in business for the rest of the decade, occasionally booking special acts like the Bandanna Girls, billed as the "world's greatest colored girls' band."[108] On the south side of town a "colored" skating rink and dance hall was housed in a building that served for part of the year as a tobacco warehouse. Dances also continued to be held near downtown at Jackson Hall, leading to protests by area residents that "dancing, accompanied by jazz music, laughter and conviviality, is frequently protracted long after midnight."[109]

Given the larger framework I have been considering—the Jim Crow policies of downtown theaters, the small-scale efforts at promoting black-operated neighborhood movie houses, and the concern of churches, school officials, and the Community Service League with the filling of leisure-time activity—the opening of a "$10,000 Colored Dance Casino" capable of holding more than one thousand people was a particularly significant event. The Land O' Dreams dance hall, occupying the second floor of a large garage located on the same West Main Street block that had housed the Gem Theater a decade earlier, was financed by two white men, a lawyer and the city license inspector. This was by far the biggest investment of white capital for a "colored" venue in Lexington, and given the political influence of the investors, it faced no problem in getting or keeping a license.

The Land O' Dreams' opening festivities in October 1925 were conducted under the glow of "hundreds of multi-colored lights with a gorgeous crystal ball suspended from the center of the ceiling."[110] An investigator for the New York-based Institute of Social and Religious Research found quite a different scene when he visited the Land O' Dreams as part of the research for a national study entitled *Negro Problems in Cities*. This dance hall was indeed "beautifully decorated and very spacious," but it was, he concluded, a "most unsuitable place for the many young boys and girls" in attendance: "working girls, high-school girls, demi-mondes and young men of all strata were there," drinking corn liquor and engaging in "dancing [that] became more orgiastic as the evening progressed." What made this dance hall such a menace to the community at large was that it allowed the youth of "different classes [to] mix," putting a generation in danger of being lost, making it harder for "strata" (and hence progress) to be maintained.[111] If concerned citizens breathed a sigh of relief when the Land O'Dreams was destroyed by fire in March 1926, they soon realized that the flames had not eradicated the problem. Six months later, the Land O'Dreams—renamed the Pontiac Dance Hall—was again in business and would remain so, impervious to criticism from within the black community and undisturbed by white city officials. Through the 1930s no new black-operated neighborhood movie theaters opened in Lexington, but dance halls continued to flourish. In 1931, for example, commercial sites in Lexington hosted, among others, Louis Armstrong, Noble Sissle, Erskine Tate, and Cab Calloway—quite an extraordinary lineup of nationally known talent.[112]

Once African-American initiatives, the Artist Concert Series, and the University of Kentucky's cultural activities are taken into account along with the downtown commercial theaters, the growth of the local market in the 1920s can be better appreciated. And so can the way that Lexington experienced the "nervousness" that Roderick Nash finds to be definitive of the era—at least in the form of nervous anxiety typified by the *Leader*'s editorial stance toward the movies and the entire "jazz environment."[113] The old-style legitimate theater may have lost much of its local prominence during the 1920s, but there were efforts on all sides to take up the slack and offer Lexington audiences art, progressive social values, or the latest styles, imported from far beyond the limits of the provincial. The sites and occasions for this experience, however, remained resolutely local.

ELEVEN

The Coming of Sound
and the Restructuring
of Local Film Exhibition

On 20 February 1927, six months after the Warner Bros. public premiere of Vitaphone sound films, the Lafayette Amusement Company announced that it would install Vitaphone equipment at the Kentucky Theater, one of the first fifty theaters in the country, the company claimed, to be so singled out. For the next two months readers of Lexington's newspapers were treated to virtually daily advertisements and promotional notices touting Vitaphone, the "eighth wonder of the world."[1] The installation began on April 10 and the system premiered on April 24, with six daily screenings of a program comprised of a Felix the Cat cartoon, a newsreel, MGM's feature-length World War I comedy, *Tin Hats,* and four Vitaphone shorts: Will Hays' spoken introduction, Roy Smeck's novelty instrumental performance, selections by a Metropolitan Opera Company tenor, and Mary Lewis' rendition of traditional songs from the South.[2] As Douglas Gomery notes, during the early sound period "the centerpiece of the Warner Bros.' strategy was the regular production and release of vaudeville shorts," but the premiere Vitaphone show at the Kentucky presents a more varied—and more interesting—mix, combining a high art selection, a decidedly regional offering, a vaudeville number, and an appearance by Will Hays himself.

Through the rest of 1927, sound shorts were similarly inserted into an otherwise quite familiar programming format. The Lafayette Amusement Company's advertisements continued to highlight Vitaphone acts and, particularly, the week-long engagement of *Don Juan* in May 1927. But other promotions continued as well: for example, an elaborate "Fall Style Show," cosponsored by several retail stores, and a publicity stunt in which tickets for Harold Lloyd's *The Big Brother* were dropped from an airplane. In other words, during 1927 the Kentucky presented itself not so much as Lexington's Vitaphone theater than as a venue that had added Vitaphone technology (and its roster of bravura performers) to an already rich array of products and services.

Over the next three years the introduction of sound film technology would substantially alter film exhibition in Lexington. One more immediate consequence, however, was that the American Federation of Musicians (AFM) local demanded in July 1927 that the Lafayette Amusement Company hire a five-piece orchestra for the Kentucky and a four-piece orchestra for the Ada Meade, both of which had long made due with only organists. When the company refused to comply, the AFM called for the organists to walk out, with the six union projectionists at the Kentucky and the Ada Meade to follow suit, in a "sympathy strike." The Lafayette Amusement Company took its case to the public in a large newspaper advertisement, then sought recourse in Fayette Circuit Court. Both sides agreed to a temporary restraining order pending a hearing.

The hearing did not directly take up the ramifications of sound film technology for those unionized musicians who, as we have seen, had become a vital part of the entertainment package at local motion picture theaters. The real issue locally was whether the president of the AFM local (who was an employee at the Ben Ali) had been pressured into calling a strike against the Lafayette Amusement Company by John Elliott of the Phoenix Amusement Company, which after three years of holding out had agreed in March 1926 to hire union musicians, stagehands, and projectionists at the Strand and Ben Ali. It was not until July 1928 that the judge finally decided that, while the organists could walk out at the Kentucky and Ada Meade, the projectionists had no legal ground for a sympathy strike. The AFM did not, however, press its demands on the Lafayette Amusement Company, and soon the very best that it could hope for in Lexington, as elsewhere, was simply to maintain a pre-Vitaphone level of employment.[3]

Unveiling the "New Strand." The façade is basically the same as it was when the theater opened in 1916. Lexington *Herald*, 2 September 1928.

Investment and Expansion

During the time it took to settle this labor dispute, the sound film proved that it had come to stay in Lexington. The year 1928 was the crucial one in this regard. Fox Movietone News premiered at the Kentucky on 5 January 1928, then came a series of highly publicized (more-or-less) sound feature films: *The Jazz Singer;* the "first 100 percent talking picture," *Lights of New York;* and *The Singing Fool,* for which the Lafayette Amusement Company instituted a new policy of Saturday midnight premiere screenings. The Kentucky also used its sound equipment to offer direct wire, play-by-play of UK football and basketball games "announced through the Vitaphone."[4] It was not, however, until December 1929 that the Lafayette Amusement Company chose to spend the money necessary to convert the Ada Meade to sound.

In the summer of 1928, the Phoenix Amusement Company responded to its local competition by undertaking a major renovation of the Strand, said to cost $100,000. (The Strand's competition probably also included the dance halls that continued to do good business downtown.) This investment covered much more than the installation of sound equipment. For example, the Strand was outfitted with a twenty-seven-stop Wurlitzer organ ("second largest and finest organ in the South") housed in a special area built over the stage, and the Phoenix Amusement Company hired organist Heyde Conrad away from Louisville's Rialto Theater.[5] It added new Simplex projectors and an Arctic Nu-Air cooling and ventilation system, and—first and foremost—it redecorated the entire theater, from the new solid brass entry doors to the specially designed red velour and gold curtain and the floral arrangements on stage. Refined luxury remained the ideal, with no traces of avant-garde design or flamboyant excess at the "New Strand." After this renovation, African Americans were again excluded from this theater, as they had been before 1922; the absence of a "colored" section most likely also served as an indication of "high-class" status and of the restored Strand's desire to compete with the Kentucky as Lexington's premiere showplace. Accordingly, ticket prices rose by at least 20 percent, from forty to fifty cents for regular adult admissions and from ten to twenty cents for children.

Thus the Phoenix Amusement Company's installation of sound equipment was but one part of a larger investment in the technological updating and interior renovation of the Strand. In fact, during the fall of 1928, the new Wurlitzer was more prominently featured in ads for this theater than was the Vitaphone, Movietone, and Photophone equipment, which went into full operation in December 1928 without a great deal of fanfare. During this transitional period, the Strand's booking policy changed only to the extent that sound films and daily organ performances took the place of touring orchestras.

In the summer of 1928, the Phoenix Amusement Company also spent $35,000 to renovate the Ben Ali, with most of the costs going to replace the 1,500 seats, lay new carpeting and terra-cotta tile, and add drapery, chandeliers, and furniture in the foyer, men's smoking room, and women's rest room. Late in 1928, sound equipment was installed, though the Ben Ali retained its house orchestra and continued to offer both live entertainment and motion pictures. Usually this meant a full-length film coupled with a musical comedy company, whose revues changed weekly. Live performers, not sound films, got top billing in advertisements for the Ben Ali.

Clearly, neither the Lafayette Amusement Company nor the Phoenix Amusement Company, even after the stock market crash, was about to retrench in the face of costly renovations or the success of radio in the late 1920s. Lexington retailers estimated in January 1928 that there were five thousand radios in Fayette County, making for a substantial listening audi-

The Strand's new organ, not its sound equipment, received top billing in the fall of 1928. Lexington *Herald*, 18 November 1928.

ence. To court and help create this audience, the *Herald* and the *Leader* published daily broadcast schedules, news items, and feature articles on all aspects of radio.[6] The broadcasting of the Tunney-Dempsey fight in September 1927, for example, was accorded the status of a major event, pitched via full-page advertisements underwritten by local businesses, including the Kentucky, which promised "fight returns received by radio and amplified by Vitaphone," and the Ben Ali and Strand, which for this special occasion would be equipped with radios on loan from a local store.[7]

The competition between the two regional exhibitors who dominated the Lexington market continued in 1929, as it became clear that the sound film was not merely a novelty or an attraction destined only for picture palaces.[8]

The Phoenix Amusement Company's investment in renovating the Ben Ali and Strand was matched by the Lafayette Amusement Company's opening of its third Lexington theater, the State, in April 1929. Virtually next door to the Kentucky—a passageway connected the projection booths of the two theaters—the State had no facilities for live entertainment and a quite narrow auditorium. It had 888 seats, 98 of which were upstairs in a "colored" balcony that had its own separate entrance on Main Street. Designed by the Lexington firm of Frankel and Curtis, the State was said to have cost $200,000 and was complete with Western Electric sound equipment and a Buffalo Duplex cooling system that would quietly circulate "cool, fresh and pleasant" air without any noticeable currents or drafts. The chief selling point, however, was the State's "Spanish-influenced" decor, with the entire interior designed to resemble "an exterior scene of an ancient Spanish castle." Appropriate decorative motifs linked the floor tile, carpeting, hardware, and lobby furniture with the auditorium, which represented the "patio" of an elegant estate, and the proscenium arch, which represented the castle's front wall. The walls were textured and painted so as to "appear stained and tarnished with age" and covered by flowers and vines. The blue, domed ceiling, on which were projected clouds and stars, resembled a soothing night sky, and all the lighting bore "a close resemblance to moonlight." This "bit of Old Spain in the Bluegrass" was the closest Lexington came to an "atmospheric" theater, albeit on a quite modest scale in what was, from the first, a distinctly popular-priced venue, with three changes of bill weekly, and tickets cheaper than next door at the Kentucky.[9]

A "bit of Old Spain in the Bluegrass": the new State Theater seen from the "colored" balcony. Photo courtesy University of Kentucky Photo Archives.

Exit the Orpheum, Enter Publix

Under the pressure of what Alexander Walker calls "the irreversible establishment of talkies,"[10] Lexington saw a major overhaul of the local film exhibition business during the late 1920s. Corporate investment, technological updating, and extensive redecoration, however, were only one side of the equation. The market for commercial entertainment in Lexington also changed considerably during this period. For example, one obvious sign of the times was the shift of the Lexington Opera House to a stock company format (1927–29) before the then-vacant theater was purchased by Transylvania University in April 1930. Except for political rallies during the 1930 campaign, the Opera House gathered dust until it was leased in April 1931 to the Great Lakes Company of Ashtabula, Ohio, which operated three theaters in Ohio, one in Erie, Pennsylvania, and another in Louisville. Great Lakes reopened the Opera House as a cut-rate venue with all seats at ten cents and a daily changing bill of mostly second- or third-run films.[11]

Two other highly visible events marked the early sound period as a key transitional moment in local film exhibition. The Orpheum, in continuous operation in the middle of downtown since 1912, finally closed, but not until April 1930. John Stamper had long since foregone newspaper advertising, so it is difficult to determine the precise booking policy he pursued as Lexington's larger theaters converted to sound. Yet two brief news items published in the *Leader* in 1930 hint that little had changed at the Orpheum since the early 1920s: in January an eighteen-year-old boy from rural Fayette County accidentally shot himself with a cheap pistol while he sat in the Orpheum "enthralled by a western thriller."[12] And in March, when yet another fire started in the Orpheum's projection booth, several "western thrillers" were destroyed, though none of the seventy patrons was injured.[13] Quite unlike the once elegant and civic-minded Opera House, the poorly attended, unsafe Orpheum was a kind of comic curio that evoked no nostalgic reminiscences. With its juvenile (and predominantly rural?) clientele and clichéd genre films, Stamper's theater had become simply an anomaly in the central business district. Nothing, it seemed, could be further from the moviegoing experience that the Lafayette Amusement Company and the Phoenix Amusement Company tried to promote for their top-rank Lexington venues. Yet as the Kentucky and the Strand competed for prestige releases and the Depression deepened, "western thrillers," serials, and cheap seats—the basis of Stamper's exhibition policy in the 1920s—would become the chief selling points of the Ada Meade and the Opera House in the mid–1930s.

So it is with signs of transition rather than absolute ruptures and clear boundary points that we are finally left: the success of sound films, the corporate investment in new technology and redecoration, the end of legitimate drama at the Opera House, the opening of the State, the closing of the Orpheum. To these interrelated events we must add what may arguably have been the most important alteration in the business of film exhibition, and therefore the conditions of moviegoing, in Lexington in the late 1920s. On 29 October 1929, six months after it opened the State, the Lafayette Amusement Company leased both the State and the Kentucky to the Publix Theaters Corporation, a subsidiary of Paramount Studios.[14] Paramount was well on its way to controlling the largest theater chain in the world, and the State and the Kentucky were among five hundred theaters the company acquired between September 1929 and May 1930.[15] They were also the first theaters in the state of Kentucky to become Publix houses, as Paramount sought to expand its domination of film exhibition in the South.

Negotiations with the Lafayette Amusement Company had begun in August 1929, and the final agreement called for a twenty-year lease, with Publix paying $35,000 annually for the Kentucky and $15,000 for the State. The Lafayette Amusement Company also received $25,000 for the lease of the equipment in the State and $50,000 for the equipment in the Kentucky.[16] This transaction, Michael Switow declared, "is a marvelous thing for the city of Lexington as it assures the very highest class of entertainment under the Publix theatres direction."[17] No "immediate changes in the personnel of either house" were announced, though the two theaters would henceforth be "under the direction" of Publix's "central division" director of theater management.[18]

The real question is precisely how much Publix's commitment to "efficient modern retailing" procedures, so ably documented by Douglas Gomery, affected the way movies were packaged, marketed, and exhibited at the Kentucky and the State. Is it still valid or worthwhile to speak of "local" (and therefore, in some important way, idiosyncratic) exhibition practices in an age of theater chains and, moreover, in an age when the soundtrack had replaced live musical accompaniment, rendering screenings much more standardized and less beholden—for better or worse—to local talent? Tracing the way the Kentucky and State operated as Publix theaters is beyond the scope of this book, though we can note that 1930 saw, for example, the replacement of the longtime manager of the Kentucky by a Publix employee from New York City; the hiring of a new "art director" responsible for promotions and advertising at the Kentucky and the State; and greater insistence on elaborate ballyhoo and on the Publix corporate identity (through, for instance, a "Miss Publix" contest). At the same time, however, these theaters continued to underscore their obligation and ties to the local community, with special theater parties for the employees of "Lexington stores and business concerns";[19] "Merchant's gift night" and other promotional tie-ins with downtown retailers; benefits for the Family Relief Society; and special Easter week noontime church services. Even if these activities were dictated by Publix's national policy, they still bring us back to one of the messy "problems" with which this book began: the role of regional and local variation in the promotion, exhibition, and reception of commercial entertainment during the first three decades when Americans took in and took to the movies.

Of course, neither the movies nor the process of taking them in stopped in 1930. The end of the silent film era provides a fit, if not an absolute, conclusion for *Main Street Amusements.* With time and energy and pages to spare

THE COMING OF SOUND

I would continue the story at least up to the local emergence of commercial television, testing how the methods of chain-store management worked in Lexington theaters, how public leisure-time pursuits were affected by the Depression, and how African-American residents continued to foster civic initiatives and to support commercial entertainment. I would also move laterally, as it were, to explore the local history of smaller towns and rural communities in Kentucky, as well as further afield for a broader sampling of regional practices.[20] Sabbatarianism as a national phenomenon surely deserves a book-length study, as does the local amusement park (beyond Coney Island and Chicago's Riverview Park), the multipurpose opera house, the role and operation of "colored" theaters, the nontheatrical exhibition of motion pictures in the silent era, the discourse of Hollywood in local newspapers, and the presentation of movies and moviegoers in editorial cartoons and comic strips from the turn of the century on.

As well as pointing out these and other lines of inquiry, I hope to have demonstrated the usefulness of, first, approaching the social history of a city like Lexington in terms of how commercial entertainment was promoted, consumed, and reacted to locally; and, second, seeing the larger cultural history of film in the United States in terms of a small city, far from the sites of motion picture production and far from the teeming metropolis. Like certain work that has been published since I began my project, most notably the first three volumes of Scribner's *History of the American Cinema* and Douglas Gomery's *Shared Pleasures: A History of Movie Presentation in the United States,* I have brought matters of exhibition, marketing, and programming to the fore. Specifically, *Main Street Amusements* serves as a counter-example to those influential studies of the nickelodeon era that focus exclusively on the urban centers of the industrialized Northeast, and it challenges histories of the 1920s that fail to look very far beyond the picture palace.

I have elected to look beyond even the movie theater—a route also taken in different ways by recreation surveys of the 1910s, *Middletown,* and more recent working-class history like Roy Rosenzweig's *Eight Hours for What We Will,* which all situate film exhibition and moviegoing in what Bruce A. Austin calls the larger "framework of related commercial and spectator leisure activities."[21] My framework has stretched from store window displays to dance halls, from the Colored A & M Fair to the University of Kentucky-sponsored Romany Theater. And I have looked beyond screened images to consider the design, ownership, daily operation, and marketing of theaters. Entrepreneurial schemes, the legitimation of exhibition, labor relations, corporate expansion, managerial prerogative—these are all aspects of social as well as business history. By keeping my focus on Lexington, I have been able to ascertain what Miriam Hansen calls "the initiative of the individual exhibitor" and to chart over an extended period of time the course of quite distinct individual theaters (the Opera House, the Orpheum, the Hipp/Ada Meade), decision makers (Charles Scott, John Elliott, Charles Berryman), reformist concerns (playgrounds, Sunday screenings, censorship), and booking policies (the illustrated song-and-motion picture format, the popular-price theatrical attraction).[22]

Taking up the first three decades of the twentieth century in a small Kentucky city makes matters of race and region inescapable, as well they should be. To attend solely to Hollywood's images of blacks or even to "all-colored" motion pictures misses much of the significance of race in the cultural history of American film, as Mary Carbine so aptly demonstrates in her analysis of racial identity and black moviegoing in Chicago between 1905 and 1928.[23] My research suggests that the ongoing negotiation of Jim Crow policies in Lexington—the effects of and the response to everyday racism—can be vividly seen in the way the city's African Americans took their seats at the Opera House and other white-owned theaters, started their own entrepreneurial ventures, protested against Sabbath screenings and *The Birth of a Nation*, and attempted to promote the race culturally through church, school, and community activities.

From the perspective of commercial entertainment, regionalism seems to me a much less tangible factor than race, though the situation in Lexington strongly suggests that regional ties mattered. These were most evident in certain bookings at the Opera House (popular-price mainstays like *In Old Kentucky*, minstrel shows), for example, and in the way Lexington was linked via the itineraries of traveling shows with Appalachia and points south. (Yet Lexington's preference before 1906 for "Tom" troupes and its support of inexpensive vaudeville after 1907 distinguish it from much of the South.) I have documented the importance of the local throughout this book, as manifested in specific programming decisions, the hiring of home talent, the regulatory uses of city ordinances, and so on. There are commentators who put unqualified faith in the local or the regional as Lexington's true identity, the last bulwark against the rising tide of modernity. But a more global view of the city between 1896 and 1930 reveals a complicated problematic, for the regional could also be the much-dreaded "provincial" and the local under some conditions could not hold a candle to the "latest" metropolitan product. Part of the historical significance of the growth of commercial entertainment in the early twentieth century was that it deepened and made prominent this problematic. The role of theater chains—and of forging such chains or even dreaming of chain-making—is a revealing case in point.

Like race, region and locality ought to figure more prominently than heretofore in the historical study of reception. Though I have no desire to give up Hollywood texts, my research seconds Janet Staiger's contention that "looking just at celluloid texts will no longer do in writing film history," for "a study of the textual features of early cinema without regard to historical context and the spectator of those films is theoretically and critically fallacious." Staiger, however, approaches reception in terms of "dominant and marginalized historical interpretive strategies as mediated by language and context," and this leaves her basically dependent on what has been written about particular films, in other words, on movie reviews and film criticism.[24] Such material definitely has historical interest, as I have suggested in my comments on local newspaper reviews in the 1910s, but it seems to me that a richer vein of information concerns what Hansen calls the "public dimension of cinematic reception."[25]

Like Kathy Peiss, among others, Hansen bases her argument on the urban situation of "immigrant working-class audiences" and "women across class and generational boundaries."[26] The public I have studied is quite different (though it did, of course, include women and the working class). And I have taken "the public dimension" to include not only what went on in theaters but also the way audiences were represented, the attempts to assert local government control over cheap amusements, the various religious and secular reform campaigns, and the influential role of the local press in promoting, reporting on, and editorializing about the movies. This body of material provides a handle on what happened when imported amusement hit the provinces, when the latest national product was marketed and consumed locally, when commercial entertainment became a fact of daily life in cities large and small across the United States.

APPENDIX 1

**Local Films
and
Local Filming**

Listed here are all projects mentioned in Lexington newspapers between 1896 and 1930: local productions, films shot on location in Lexington, planned film projects, noncommercial motion pictures, and newsreel footage. All available information is cited, including producer and Lexington screening (if any). As far as I have been able to determine, none of these films has survived.

Multiscope Company (10–14 Sept. 1897): W. N. Selig of the Multiscope & Film Company of Chicago films in central Kentucky for three days. On September 10, filming of: on-board caboose view of a Cincinnati Southern train crossing High Bridge; hemp farm with Negro workers; railroad men, Charles Scott, newspaperman, and Colonel James E. Pepper (of Old Pepper distillery) relaxing at the hemp farm; mares and foals at a horse farm; the Queen and Crescent's southbound Florida Limited train (apparently the fastest train in the area) whizzing by at sixty-five miles an hour near Danville; view from off the tracks of northbound Florida Limited crossing High Bridge. On September 14, filming of C & O train speeding past the camera. Then train backed up a mile, and a large piece of cloth bearing the advertisement for Jas. E.

Pepper Co. (painted by Ramsey's sign company) was spread across the track; Selig filmed the train bursting through the canvas sign, "like a bareback rider through a paper hoop" (LH 15 Sept. 1897, p. 3).

German & Swanson (22–/23 Jan. 1903): Gorman and Swanson film all the vehicles of the Lexington Fire Department racing past camera downhill on North Broadway in a prearranged scene and also various department officials and citizens walking and "disporting themselves before the camera." Plan to film a panoramic view from rear of streetcar moving through downtown Lexington. When this footage was shown at a Fireman's Benefit show at Lexington Opera House on 2–3 February 1903, it was advertised as also including motion pictures of "the actual life of firemen, the alarm, the hitch, the run to the fire, the burning building, the leap for life, the fire boats throwing water, the return to the engine house" (LL 2 Feb. 1903, p. 2).

Queen & Crescent Railroad (23 May 1906): A special train on the Queen & Crescent line equipped with a motion picture camera films along the Queen & Crescent route, including the Lexington train station and the Yerkes horse farm.

Gaumont (26 April 1912): As part of the first meeting of the Kentucky branch of the Motion Picture Exhibitors League of America, a Gaumont representative films scenes around Lexington for use in *Gaumont's Weekly.*

Imp Film Company (6–7 June 1912): Part of the two-reel *Winning the Latonia Derby* (directed by Otis Turner, starring King Baggot) filmed by Imp crew at John E. Madden's Hamburg Place stock farm near Lexington. While in town Baggot and the rest of the cast make an appearance at the Hipp Annex. *Winning the Latonia Derby* plays at the Hipp Annex on 18 July 1912.

Cinematograph Company (19–20 Oct. 1912): L. H. Ramsey of the Hipp hires C. A. Taylor of the Cinematograph Company of New York to make a two-thousand-foot motion picture of Lexington. Filming of city schools, fire department, Woodland Park, and the Hipp, with local people prominently featured. Also a scene filmed from a car as it circled the Kentucky Trotting Horse Breeders Association racetrack. Shown at the Hipp on Sunday, 3 November 1912, then again on November 5, and at the Hipp Annex in addition to the regular bill on November 11.

Chicago Feature Film Company (24 March, 1 April 1914): J. Law Siple of the Chicago Feature Film Company staged fire fighting and rescue scenes at the Cliver-Donovan Shirt Company, using the Lexington Fire Department; then scenes at James Ben Ali Haggin's Elmendorf Farms The sights of Lexington are "deftly woven into a pretty little running story" (LH S May 1914, p. 7). Shown at the Ben Ali on May 5, 1914, then the second "series" of this company's local films shown at the Ben Ali on May 25–26.

S. J. Needham (2 Sept. 1914): S. J. Needham of Cincinnati films one reel of motion pictures of the Odd Fellows Home; includes twenty-three scenes, mostly of the children at the home.

Frohman's Famous Players (13 Sept. 1914): Crew in Lexington to film scenes at the fall races for use in *His Last Dollar.*

Karnix Movie Company (1–8 Nov. 1914): Miller H. Karnix of Chicago writes and directs a two-reel comedy, *When the Tango Craze Hit Lexington,* in which an amateur chemist invents a powder that causes anyone inhaling it to immediately begin to tango. He tries it on "mammy," the family maid. His young daughter and two nephews then use the powder on relatives, a society party, and the State University football team and drill squad. This film uses all local performers and is filmed entirely in Lexington: in the downtown business district, at the home of Louis des Cognets, at the State University, at a football game, and on sets constructed at the lumber yard of Hendricks, Moore, Young & Company. The total cost is $500, and the film is screened for two days at the Ben Ali, with proceeds above the cost of production donated to the Baby Milk Supply Fund. Plans announced to exhibit this comedy at various small towns in Central Kentucky. Karnix declares that he will open a "branch office" in Lexington and film "My Old Kentucky Home."

International Film Company (17 Nov. 1914): Lou Green and A. L. Wiswell of the Cincinnati-based International Film Company in Lexington to film parks, businesses, and historical sites for use as part of a larger promotional film about Kentucky, to be shown at the 1915 San Francisco Panama-Pacific Exposition.

———— (15 Jan. 1915): One-reel motion picture of Pythian Home in Lexington. Scheduled to be shown at the Colonial on 1 February, then at other theaters throughout the state.

———— (22 Oct. 1915): Two reels of motion pictures taken during the recent appearance of the Barnum & Bailey Circus in Lexington as well as other unspecific local scenes. Shown at the Colonial, then at the Gem.

———— (29 Oct. 1916): Motion pictures of annual tug of war between freshmen and sophomores at State University. Shown at the Ben Ali in addition to regular show.

H. H. Freeman (29 Sept. 1916): John Stamper of the Orpheum hires H. H. Freeman of Los Angeles to produce a film in Lexington called "The Belle of the Blue Grass." The local girl who receives the most votes in a month will get the leading role.

McHenry Film Corporation (25–27 May 1916): Director William Conklin of the McHenry Film Corporation of Akron and Cleveland films *The Manhaters* in Lexington. Casting of the leading role (Lucy Chenault) and fifteen other parts determined by vote sponsored by the Strand, which promises that "everything in the picture will be absolutely local" (LL 17 May 1916, p. 7). Several scenes of women being rescued by firemen from a burning building were staged at the Phoenix Hotel. *The Manhaters* shown at the Strand for a week beginning June 1916 along with the regular bill.

———— (17 May 1916): Motion pictures taken of May Day celebration at Woodland Park. Shown at the Strand on 1 June 1916.

Hearst (14 December 1916): Hearst newsreel cameraman in Lexington to film thoroughbreds and horse farms.

———— (6 June 1917): Motion pictures of Lexington recruits training at Fort Benjamin Harrison. Shown at the Ben Ali and the Strand as part of government war loan campaign.

———— (15 Aug. 1917): Plan to film local women "doing their bit" for the war effort; this footage will be used as part of a motion picture produced by the National League for Women Service.

———— (18 Feb. 1919): Lexington Board of Commerce contracts with un-named industrial film company to produce film about Kentucky oil fields to be shown at future meeting of Kentucky Oil Men's Association.

———— (3 April 1919): Motion pictures taken of the Lexington school-children's victory parade to begin their "school garden campaign." This film funded by United States School Garden Commission and shown at the Strand.

First National (20 June 1919): Alfred Green of Anita Stewart Productions in Lexington scouting locations for *In Old Kentucky,* a First National film directed by Marshall Neilan and starring Anita Stewart. Plans announced to film at two horse farms—Hamburg Place and Walnut Hill—and at High Bridge and Shakertown. *In Old Kentucky* premieres locally at the Ada Meade on 8 Feb. 1920.

Herald Screen Review (28 Jan. 1920): Lexington *Herald* hires Jack E. Dadswell, cameraman for *Pathé News* responsible for Kentucky, Indiana, Ohio, and West Virginia, to film "the big events in Lexington and the Blue Grass as they occur" (LH 28 Jan. 1920, p. 1). The weekly program will be shown at the Strand and various cities serviced by the *Pathé News Service* and *Pathé Educational Review.* Dadswell declares that the most exciting time he spent as a cameraman was filming in Mexico as a war correspondent fol-lowing Pershing in the employ of Chicago *Tribune* (LH 8 Feb. 1920, p. 1). The *Herald Screen Review* shows on Sunday-Monday-Tuesday, and the rest of the week this slot on the bill is filled by *Pathé Educational Review* and Prizma Natural Color Pictures. After Review no. 7, there are no more references in the *Herald* and no more mention in Strand ads; the Strand then begins to use a Snub Pollard or other one-reel comedy to fill the slot.

Herald Screen Review no. 1 (29–31 Jan. 1920): First edition of this news-reel includes views of the Strand and its manager; officials of the *Herald;* damage done downtown by ice storm; the "pretty girls" in the chorus of *Fri-volities of 1920,* then playing at the Opera House; John Elliott, head of the Phoenix Amusement Company; Mayor Thomas C. Bradley in his office; the cameraman himself as he films; buildings and horses at Kingston Stud Farm; property sold on corner of Main and Limestone; and prize winners at the Farm and Home Convention held at the University of Kentucky. Shown 1–3 February 1920 at the Strand.

Herald Screen Review no. 2 (4 Feb. 1920): Coverage of Will Lockett, black man arrested for murder of ten-year-old school girl; he is caught and immediately rushed from Lexington in fear of mob violence. Report that the Movie Man took films of Madden's Hamburg Farm during a sale (for use by Pathé). Plans also to film legislators who will come from Frankfort to visit the University of Kentucky, as well as university coeds. On 6 February 1920, the cameraman returning from Frankfort sees a car careen off the road in front of him and turn over four times. He films the "after effects"; also films the field where the schoolgirl was killed, her broken umbrella, the corn stalks under which she was hidden, her five brothers, and the murderer's trail as he left the spot. Dadswell will head to Hyden, Kentucky, to try to film the reputedly oldest man in America, Uncle Johnny Shell. This week's edition will also include footage of an "old Kentucky home" that was recently auctioned and close ups of university president Frank McVey. Screened at the Strand 8–10 February 1920.

Herald Screen Review no. 3 (7 Feb. 1920): Plans announced to film anyone who is in front of the Strand at 3:00 P.M. on Tuesday. Attempt to lynch Will Lockett; national guard fires into the crowd, six dead and twenty-two shot and wounded in the melee. The trial itself lasts thirty-five minutes, and Lockett is sentenced to death. The Screen Review has footage of the riot, but the Strand decides not to show it, figuring that authorities would demand a private screening and ban it anyway. No local showings after Dadswell screens riot footage at UK for military officers and local sheriff. These officials decide that "deletion of several scenes and other factors had made it valueless as legal evidence"; Mayor Bradley still bans any public screening.

Herald Screen Review no. 4 (20 Feb. 1920): This installment introduces Miss Gladys Moore, "Queen of the Lexington Turf" and "girl reporter" of the *Screen Review*. Moore checks out the Kentucky Derby prospects with Dadswell. Other subjects include a "party of Mexican" farm workers on their way to a farm near Paris, Kentucky, the annual meeting of the American Berkshire Congress (swine breeders), with close-ups of the prize winners, and a new carburetor invented by a UK engineering professor. One segment shows Moore in jockey attire giving the horse Cottonblossom a "breezing." Shown at Strand 22–24 February 1920.

Herald Screen Review no. 5 (28 Feb. 1920): Details the visit of A. Mitchell Palmer, United States Attorney General (in midst of red scare) to Frankfort; views of lobbyists, politicians, the capitol building, and the governor's mansion; "preparations for summer traffic on the Kentucky River"; the "wreck scene" of Louisville & Nashville freight train in rural Fayette County; the awarding to Major Albert Tucker of an official record of his citations by the commandant of cadets at UK; the Wilbur Smith residence, which was purchased by Charles Baker as site for funeral home. Shown at Strand on February 29, March 1–2 1920.

Herald Screen Review no. 6 (7 March 1920): Section on tobacco industry to be used by *Pathé News* as representative scenes of "the tobacco growing capital of the United States": tobacco-laden wagons and trucks; carts on streets in the "weed district"; public loose-leaf sale; processing of tobacco; Dorothy Harriss, daughter of a Woodford county planter. Also scenes of city "traffic squad" pushing away automobiles parked for more than one hour, part of the "war on traffic stalling"; police officer John Clancy, who lost an arm in the courthouse riot, shown with his daughter; First Division artilleryman exhibiting a 155 mm howitzer in Georgetown and showing the locals "how we did it in France"; the *Herald* movie girl visits Walnut Hill Farm and exercises sheep, horses, and poultry. This edition to be shown at Strand and then at other Central Kentucky theaters.

Herald Screen Review no. 7 (12 March 1920): Footage of Jurd Horn of Wilmore who climbs 312 feet up the girders of High Bridge—these scenes "furnish an interesting dougfairbanks [sic] sort of chapter" for the *Review;* also Jerry Walker, Lexington's child musical wonder.

Kentucky News Pictorial Company (23 May 1920): Ed McClure, Elmer Bryant, Carl F. Neal, Fred J. Erd, and W. P. Roberts, all of Lexington, file articles of incorporation for this company on 22 May 1920, with thirty-five shares of capital stock, totaling $3,000. McClure will serve as chief cameraman, having gotten much experience as a cinematographer with the U.S. Signal Corps in France. The company plans to release a weekly newsreel of Kentucky events.

Kentucky Pictorial News no. 1 (20 Oct. 1920): Planned topics for the first edition of this newsreel include: aerial shots of Lexington; the University of Kentucky and other colleges and public schools in the city; hotels, newspaper offices, and other "principal buildings"; city and county officials, and members of the Board of Commerce and the Ministerial Union.

Kentucky News Pictorial Company (5 Feb. 1921): Motion pictures and colored slides taken of the owner, stock, and operation of Coldstream Farm. Shown at the Ada Meade.

———— (17 Feb. 1921): Plans to film local public schools and the Kentucky Educational Associational meeting; to be used for purposes of fund raising.

Kentucky News Pictorial Company (23 April 1921): Board of Commerce hires this company to film the board's "Lexington booster" trip through eastern Kentucky. The fifteen-hundred-foot motion picture, filmed by R. J. Long, is shown at Board of Commerce meeting, then begins a tour of eastern Kentucky cities. On 5 July 1921, the Kentucky News Pictorial Company shows the film on Main Street on an "open air screen" (LH 5 July 1921, p. 15).

Harrill Production Company (5 Feb. 1922): Lexington women, Mrs. Addie Harrill and Mrs. W. S. Hamilton, together with motion picture producers from Tennessee, form the Harrill Production Company. They plan to feature child actress Hanna Lee in "fairy stories" and "southern" stories with central Kentucky background.

Universal Studios (4–8 May 1922): Crew for *The Kentucky Derby,* written by and starring King Baggot and co-starring Reginald Denny, plan to film for two days in Lexington area at famous horse farms and the Kentucky Jockey Club. While in town Reginald Denny makes a personal appearance at the Strand.

Associated First National Pictures (28 June–3 July 1922): Lexington *Herald* and Ada Meade are local sponsors for *The Crossroads of Lexington,* a one-reel comedy using local amateur performers and directed by A. W. Sobler of Associated First National, with R. J. Long serving as cameraman. This project is part of promotional effort for Mack Sennett's *The Crossroads of New York,* and the Lexington film is presented as a sort of talent search by Sennett for new comedic talent. After an open call for participants, Dick Garland and Violet Young are selected for the major roles, but anyone who attends the filming will be included in crowd scenes. The story is patterned on *The Crossroads of New York:* opening with a traffic cop having problems with lawbreaking motorists at the busy intersection of Limestone and Main, then finally driving off with a pretty young woman. In the second episode, the cop stumbles into a student rush at the University of Kentucky campus, flirts with some coeds, and is chased off. In the last episode (filmed at a ball field in Cynthiana and at Lexington's Devereaux Park), the cop poses as a baseball player who pinch hits for the home team in the ninth inning, strikes out, and flees from the fans. *The Crossroads of Lexington* played for a week at the Ada Meade, beginning 12 July 1920, along with Sennett's *The Crossroads of New York.*

——— (2 Nov. 1922): Motion pictures of Lions Club members taken after a luncheon meeting; to be shown at a local theater.

Pathé (28 May 1923): Pathé correspondent to film events at the University of Kentucky, including ROTC march and women's baseball game.

——— (7 July 1923): Motion pictures taken at Lexington's Eastern State Hospital for the Insane show the improvements and the "life and customs at the institution," particularly the work done with occupational therapy (LH 7 July 1923, p. 1). This film shown to the patients at the hospital, then for a week at the Kentucky in August 1923.

Garsson Enterprises (13–14 July 1923): Murray Garsson and crew from General Film Manufacturing Company, making a feature film entitled *The Toll* for the National Farmers Union, come to Lexington to film the McKee brothers hog farm, the Farmers Union picnic in nearby Clark County, area farms, and the State Farmers Union meeting in Maysville. This film will show "the development of American farmers through cooperative efforts" (LL 12 July 1923, p. 7).

Pathé (23 Oct. 1923): Pathé correspondent films horses and horse farms in Lexington area.

———— (9 Nov. 1923): Motion picture company from Miami, Florida, hired by businesses, tobacco growers, and American Legion branch in Georgetown, Kentucky, to film the story of Georgetown's "history and development." This three-thousand-foot film shown for a week at Georgetown cooperative tobacco warehouse under auspices of American Legion on 15 Nov. 1923.

Fox Film Corporation (July 1924): Cameraman Edward Reek and actress Elizabeth Pickett (who has relatives in Lexington area) from Fox Film Corporation film footage for one-reel Fox Special, *Kings of the Turf.*

Feature Film Corporation (3 July 1924): Feature Film Corporation in Lexington to film for approximately ten days at Idle Hour Farm for a serial entitled *Purebreds* to be released by Pathé.

Reel Town Company (6 July 1924): Plans announced by Lester Park of New York-based Reel Town Company for a multi-reel program entitled *The Kentucky Reel* to be produced in Lexington. This will include a two-reel comedy, a "tabloid fairy tale classic" starring Hanna Lee, a screen magazine, and a feature film, "A Kentuckian There Was," based on the eighteenth-century adventures of Kentucky pioneers.

———— (26 July 1924): Motion pictures taken of a pageant staged by the Fayette County Burley Tobacco Cooperative Association. This film, *Court of Agriculture,* shown to the association on 17 August 1924.

Fox Film Corporation (1–10 Oct. 1924): Fox production crew headed by director John Ford (and also including Elizabeth Pickett), in Lexington to film various scenes for as yet untitled horse race feature film, including a fox hunt in nearby Woodford County, famous horses and grounds at area horse farms. This footage was most likely used in Ford's *Kentucky Pride,* released by Fox in August 1925.

———— (27–29 October 1924): Filming under auspices of Daughters of the American Revolution as a fund-raising activity and a way to "preserve in film form a permanent record of historical facts and traditions for which Lexington and Fayette County are noted" (LL 27 Oct. 1924, p. 7). A "Movie Carnival" with working "movie studio" set up at Woodland Park Auditorium to film local residents; also footage of Transylvania University buildings and library holdings, local historic homes, portraits of famous residents, the city police force passing in review, the fire department on a run, the University of Kentucky playing Centre State in football, and a class in "physical culture" at Lexington's settlement school. Shown at the Kentucky, 19–21 February 1925.

Kentucky Newsreels (6 June 1925): Kentucky begins to promote its own newsreels: one features footage of local sesquicentennial parade (shown on 6 June 1925); another features University of Louisville versus Transylvania University in football game (31 October 1925).

———— (12 April 1926): Lexington Board of Commerce plans to film Lexington Easter parade to be shown at the Kentucky.

———— (17 Aug. 1926): Civic League plans to take motion pictures of pet show winners at Woodland Park playground.

Fox Newsreel (21 Jan. 1928): Roy Anderson of St. Louis films Idle Hour farm and thoroughbreds for Fox newsreel service.

Paramount News Service (25 Jan. 1928): J. H. Hamilton, Paramount News Service cameraman from Cincinnati, will film Farm and Home Convention in Lexington, as well as thoroughbred farms.

———— (3 June 1928): Kentucky advertises exclusive motion pictures of Lexington public schools' May Day parade.

Gullette Film Company (13 June 1928): Sponsored by the Lexington *Herald* and the Kentucky, "Our American Girl" (Agnes Condon) visits Lexington and is filmed upon her arrival by airplane and then touring the city's "many points of natural beauty and historic interest" with Miss Lexington (Lettie Lee). Intended to "stimulate civic pride and unfold pictorially the many advantages Lexington has to offer" (LH 19 June 1928, p. 1). Shown at the Kentucky on 8–11 July 1928.

——— (4 July 1928): Kentucky Progress Commission sponsors filming in Lexington, directed by H. N. Brice of Covington, Kentucky, designed to promote state history and to attract the "motoring public" to the state. An aerial view of Fayette County and footage of local historic sites, Transylvania University, the racetrack, airport, Calumet and Idle Hour farms, downtown Lexington, and area highways to be incorporated into a larger film promoting the state. This film, *Kentucky,* premieres at the Kentucky Theater on 22 February 1929.

Paramount News Service (25 Sept. 1928): Filming of the Lexington Trots, a fall horse racing meet, for newsreel use.

——— (29 Dec. 1928): Strand screens a short, *Blue Grass and Blue Blood,* billed as having been shot in Fayette County.

——— (19 May 1929): Ben Ali will show for a week motion pictures of the consecration of the new bishop of Lexington.

Fox Motion Picture Company (22 May 1929): Director Lou Seiler heads Fox crew in Lexington to film several scenes at area horse farms (particularly the Faraway farm) and the Iroquois Hunt Club for use in sound film that will also include scenes from Churchill Downs in Louisville.

Fox Movietone News (24 May 1929): Filming of horse farms for use in newsreel.

——— (25 May 1929): Lexington Chamber of Commerce and Automobile Club sponsor a travelogue designed to attract motorists to the area.

Billy Curry (19 July 1929): Local resident shows his own films of his trip to Yellowstone Park, the 1928 Woodland Park Doll Show, and the 1928 flood in Lexington at city parks.

APPENDIX 2

City Ordinances
and
State Legislation

These ordinances and statutes were all printed in full in Lexington newspapers.

Kentucky's Blue Law

No work or business shall be done on the Sabbath Day, except the ordinary household officers or other work of necessity or charity, or work required in the operation of a ferry, skiff or steamboat or stream or street railroads. If any person on the Sabbath Day shall be found at his own, or any other trade or calling, or shall employ his apprentices, or other persons in labor or other business, whether the same be for profit or amusement, unless such as is permitted above, he shall be fined not less than two or more than fifty dollars for each offense. Every person or apprentice employed shall be deemed a separate offense.

Lexington "exhibition" ordinance (January 1896)

Any person desiring to give any sort of exhibition, or open any museum or other show in the city, unless the same be a circus menagerie, or a performance at some licensed theater or opera house, shall make an application in writing to the City Clerk, stating the character of the entertainment he desires to give, and the prices of admission to the same. If the Clerk believes that the said exhibition is not immoral or hurtful, he shall upon the payment of $5.00 for each day or $25.00 for each week said exhibition shall continue, grant a license for the same, unless said exhibition shall be for the benefit of some charitable object, in which event no license fee shall be required. But the Mayor shall have the power to revoke said license whenever he shall deem said entertainment or exhibition to have become a nuisance, or in any way hurtful or offensive to public morals.

Kentucky "Uncle Tom's Cabin" statute (1906)

Section 1. That it shall be unlawful for any person to present, or to participate in the presentation of, or to permit to be presented in any opera house, theater, hall or any other building under his control, any play that is based upon antagonism alleged formerly to exist, between master and slave, or that excites race prejudice.

Section 2. Any person violating the provisions of this act shall be subject to a fine of not less than $100 nor more than $500 or to imprisonment in the county jail for not less than one nor more than three months, or both such fine and imprisonment.

Lexington theater safety ordinance (1911)

Section 1. In all theaters, public halls, churches, and other buildings used or intended to be used for purposes of public assembly, amusement or instruction, the doors, stairways, seats, passageways and aisles shall be arranged to facilitate egress in cases or fire or accident, and to afford the requisite and proper accommodations for the public protection in such cases.

Section 2. All aisles and passageways in said buildings shall be kept free from camp-stools, chairs, sofas and other obstructions, and no person other than an employee or policeman or fireman shall be allowed to stand in or occupy any of said aisles or passageways during any performances, service, exhibition, lecture, concert, ball or any public assemblage.

Section 3. The Board of Public Works may at any time serve a written or printed notice upon the owner, lessee or manager of any said public buildings, directing any act or thing to be done or provided in or about the same buildings and the several appliances therewith connected, such as halls, doors, stairs, windows, seats, aisles, fireballs, fire apparatus and fire escapes as they may deem necessary for the safety of the occupants or the public.

Section 4. Every building mentioned in Section 1 shall have at least one front on a street which shall be not less than thirty feet in width, and in such front there shall be suitable means of entrance and exits for the audience. The stage shall be at the end of the building opposite to the main entrance.

Section 5. The width of the main entrance or corridor leading from the street to the main auditorium shall be not less at any point than fifteen feet. The width of the main entrance or corridor shall be estimated on a basis of not less than twenty inches for each 100 persons for whom seats are provided, and who may gain access to the corridor as a means of entrance or exit.

The main corridor may serve as a common place of entrance and exit for the main floor of the auditorium and the balcony or first gallery, provided its capacity be equal to the aggregate capacity of the outlets from said main floor and balcony or gallery as provided for above in this section.

The width of all entrances and exits for each distinct and separate division of the auditorium shall be based upon the same estimate of not less than twenty inches for each 100 persons served by such entrances or exits.

In case the balcony or first gallery, in addition to the stairway or stairways connecting it to the main auditorium floor or main corridor, has an inside stairway or stairways leading direct to the street or public way, then the capacity of this stairway may be taken into consideration in determining the width of the main corridor above the minimum width of fifteen feet herein provided for.

Section 6. From the auditorium opening into a side street or public way, there shall be not less than two exits in each tier from and including the ground floor and each and every gallery. Each exit shall be at least four feet wide in the clear and provided with fire doors. All of said doors shall open outwardly and shall be arranged to open by a slight pressure from the inside without the unfastening of bolts or latches. No circular or winding stairs for the use of the public shall be permitted, either inside or outside of the building.

Section 7. No theater shall have more than three floor tiers above the main floor of the auditorium. Distinct and separate places of entrance and exit shall be provided for each gallery above the balcony or first gallery, by means of inside stairways leading to the street or other public way and not through the main auditorium balcony.

No passage leading to any stairway communicating with an exit (not including fire exits) shall be less than four feet in width. The width of all stairs shall be measured in the clear between hand rails. All stairs within the building hereafter erected shall be constructed of fire proof material throughout Stairs from balcony or galleries shall not communicate with the basement or cellar. No stairs from galleries shall be less than four feet in width. When the seating capacity of the galleries is for more than 100 people there shall be at least two stairs extending to the ground arranged on opposite sides of the galleries.

Section 8. All doors shall open outwardly as herein before provided in the case of emergency exits. No door shall open immediately upon a flight of stairs, but in all cases, a landing at least the width of the door shall be provided. All stairs shall have treads of uniform width and risers of uniform height throughout in each flight. All enclosed staircases shall have on both sides, strong hand-rails firmly secured to the wall about three inches distant therefrom and about three feet above the stairs.

Section 9. In buildings hereafter erected a fire wall built of bricks, or its equivalent not less than thirteen inches to any potion of same shall separate the auditorium from the stage, and the same shall extend at least four feet above the stage roof, or the auditorium roof, if the latter be the higher, and shall be coped. Above the proscenium opening there shall be an iron girder of sufficient strength to safely support the load above and the same shall be covered with fireproof material not less than four inches in thickness.

Section 10. The proscenium opening shall be provided with a fireproof metal curtain or a Obtain of asbestos or other fireproof material approved by the Board of Public Works, overlapping the brick proscenium wall at each side within iron grooves or channels to a depth of not less than twelve inches. Said curtains to be hung or suspended by steel cables passing over wrought iron or steel sheaves supported by wrought-iron brackets of sufficient strength and well-braced. Said fireproof curtain shall be raised at the commencement of each performance, lowered between each act and lowered at the close of said performance, and be operated by the approved machinery for that purpose. The curtain shall be placed at the nearest point at least two feet distant from the footlights.

No doorway or opening through the proscenium wall, from the auditorium, shall be allowed above the level of the first floor, and such first floor openings shall have self-closing standard fire doors at each side of the wall and openings, if any, below the stage shall each have a self-closing fire door, and all of said doors shall be hung so as to be opened from either side of the wall at all times.

Section 11. None of the windows in outside walls shall have fixed sashes, fixed for grills or bars; these may be arranged to hinge and lock, but must be left unlocked during performances.

Section 12. All seats in the auditorium, excepting those contained in boxes, shall not be less than thing inches from back to back, measured in a horizontal direction and firmly secured to the floor. No seat in the auditorium shall have more than six seats intervening between it and aisle on either side. No stool or seat shall be placed in any aisle. All aisles on the respective floors in the auditorium having seats on one or both sides of same, shall be not less than two and a half feet wide, where they begin and shall be increased in width toward the exits in the ration of one and a half inches to five running feet.

Section 13. Standpipes of not less than four inches in diameter shall be provided, same to be supplied by a main not less than four inches in diameter to be connected to the street main, not less than six inches and extended to the inside of the proscenium wall under the stage, where suitable fittings must be installed to allow a four inch lead to either side of the building for standpipe service. All standpipes to be free from obstruction; said standpipes to be supplied with hose connections as follows: one on each side of the auditorium on each tier.

The supply of water to be received from the city mains. Pipes shall be constantly filled with water under pressure and be ready for immediate use at all times. A sufficient quantity of approved hose not less than two and a half inches in diameter, in not less than fifty foot lengths, shall be fitted with washers and supplied with couplings and nozzles, the thread of which shall be uniform with that in use by the local fire department.

Section 14. Every portion of the building devoted to the uses of accommodation of the public, also all outlets leading into the streets, and including the corridors, shall be well and properly lighted during every performance, and same shall remain lighted until the entire audience has left the premises. There shall be one light within a red globe or lantern placed over each exit opening on the auditorium side of the wall. Every exit shall have over the same on the inside the word "EXIT" in legible letters not less than six inches high.

Any person or persons, firm or corporation violating any of the terms or provisions of this ordinance, and any such person, firm or corporation failing to conform to any of the provisions of this ordinance, or failing to obey any order of the Superintendent of Public Works, issued in pursuance of this ordinance, shall be deemed guilty of misdemeanor and upon conviction thereof shall be fined not less than ten and not more than 100 dollars; and where such violation is of a continuing nature each day such person, firm or corporation violates any such provision, or fails to conform to any such provision of this ordinance, or any such order of the Superintendent of Public Works, shall be deemed a separate offense.

Lexington censorship ordinance (1915)

Section 1. It shall be unlawful for any persons to exhibit or place on exhibition before the public lewd, obscene or immoral pictures of the kind known as moving pictures. Any person violating this section shall be punished by a fine of not less than five nor more than fifty dollars, and, in addition thereto, the license of such person to operate a picture show shall be subject to revocation or suspension by the Board of Commissioners as provided in Section 3 of this ordinance.

Section 2. Whenever the Commissioner of Public Safety shall deem it necessary or proper he may require that a motion or moving picture, intended to be exhibited before the public, be first placed on exhibition for inspection by himself or the chief of police and other city officials whom he may designate to observe and inspect the picture, and if he shall determine that such picture is lewd, obscene or immoral he shall have the right to forbid and prohibit its exhibition before the public by his written order delivered to the person intending to exhibit such picture. Any person who shall refuse to exhibit any such picture for inspection as herein provided or who shall exhibit any such picture to the public after it has been prohibited and forbidden by the Commissioner of Public Safety, as herein provided, shall, upon conviction, be fined not less than five nor more than fifty dollars for each offense, and, in addition thereto, the license of such person to conduct a picture show shall be subject to revocation or suspension by the Board of Commissioners as provided in the next section of this ordinance.

Section 3. If any person having a license to conduct a picture show shall be convicted in a court of competent jurisdiction of violating either of the two preceding sections of this ordinance, and a copy of the judgement of conviction be certified to the Board of Commissioners, the said board shall have the right and power, by order entered in its journal, to revoke and forfeit the license of such person or suspend such license and the right to do business thereunder for such length of time as the Board may deem proper and no appeal from such judgement of conviction shall operate to suspend the power of the Board of Commissioners to revoke or suspend a license as provided in this section. If the Board of Commissioners shall be informed or have reason to believe that any provision of this ordinance has been violated or is being violated by any such person, his agents or employees, whether such person has been convicted of such violation or not, the said Board shall have the right and power to hear evidence of such violation and if the Board be satisfied upon such evidence that such person, his agent or employee has violated any provision of this ordinance, the Board may, by order entered upon the journal of its proceedings, revoke and forfeit the license of such person or suspend his license and the right to do business thereunder for such time as the Board may deem proper. If any such person shall continue to operate or conduct his picture show after his license has been revoked, or during the time for which it may be suspended as herein provided, he shall be subject to the same punishment as provided by ordinances of this city for carrying on such business without a license.

NOTES

Abbreviations used in the notes:

IF   Indianapolis *Freeman*
LH   Lexington *Herald*
LL   Lexington *Leader*
MPW *Moving Picture World*

Preface

1. In *Film History: Theory and Practice* (New York: Knopf, 1985), pp. 193–212, Robert C. Allen and Douglas Gomery call for work in the "as yet virgin territory of local film history," then offer three sample projects.

2. Robert S. Lynd and Helen Merrell Lynd, *Middletown: A Study in Contemporary American Culture* (New York: Harcourt, Brace, 1929), pp. 225–312.

3. Lynds, *Middletown*, p. 265.

4. Roy Rosenzweig, *Eight Hours for What We Will: Workers and Leisure in an Industrial City, 1870–1920* (Cambridge: Cambridge University Press, 1983), p. 2.

5. Bruce A. Austin, *Immediate Seating: A Look at Movie Audiences* (Belmont, Calif.: Wadsworth, 1989), p. 28.

6. George T. Blakely, *Hard Times and New Deal in Kentucky, 1929–1939* (Lexington: University Press of Kentucky, 1986), p. 4.

7. Miriam Hansen, *Babel and Babylon: Spectatorship in American Silent Film* (Cambridge, Mass.: Harvard University Press, 1991), pp. 94–95.

8. Rosenzweig, *Eight Hours,* p. 172.

9. Lawrence W. Levine, *Highbrow/Lowbrow: The Emergence of Cultural Hierarchy in America* (Cambridge, Mass.: Harvard University Press, 1988), pp. 240–41.

Chapter 1: Lexington at the Turn of the Century

1. LH 9 Aug. 1896, p. 6; LL 9 Aug. 1896, p. 4.

2. LL 30 April 1893, p. 3.

3. Lexington Opera House file, Lexington Historical Commission. For information on early theatrical activities in Lexington, see West T. Hill, Jr., *The Theatre in Early Kentucky: 1790–1820* (Lexington: University Press of Kentucky, 1971).

4. LH 17 April 1900, p. 4.

5. LH 6 Jan. 1924, p. 4.

6. Robert C. Allen, "The Movies in Vaudeville: Historical Context of the Movies as Popular Entertainment," in *The American Film Industry,* rev. ed., ed. Tino Balio (Madison: University of Wisconsin Press, 1985), p. 65.

7. LH 3 Jan. 1896, p. 5. See Charles Musser in collaboration with Carol Nelson, *High-Class Moving Pictures: Lyman H. Howe and the Forgotten Era of Traveling Exhibition, 1880–1920* (Princeton: Princeton University Press, 1991), pp. 31–35, on the type of entertainment that "constituted a major cultural activity for middle-class groups" during the late nineteenth century.

8. LL 9 March 1896, p. 7; LH 11 March 1896, p. 6.

9. LH 12 Jan. 1896, p. 6.

10. LL 10 Dec. 1896, p. 3.

11. Musser, *High-Class Moving Pictures,* pp. 12–46, provides extensive background on the more legitimate forms of traveling exhibitions during this period.

12. LH 8 Jan. 1896, p. 2.

13. LH 2 Jan. 1896, p. 5. "Lessons" of this sort soon became standard motion picture fare, long before *Nanook of the North,* and this well-attended exhibition reflects on a small scale the ideological imperatives of ethnographic attractions at large fairs like the Chicago World's Columbian Exposition in 1893, which, according to Robert W. Rydell, "provided visitors with ethnological, scientific sanction for the American view of the nonwhite world as barbaric and childlike and gave a scientific basis to the racial blueprint for building a utopia" (*All the World's a Fair: Visions of Empire at American International Exhibitions, 1876–1916* [Chicago: University of Chicago Press, 1984], p. 40).

14. LH 29 Oct. 1896, p. 5.

15. LL 1 Nov. 1896, p. 5.

16. LL 3 March 1896, p. 3; LH 4 March 1896, p. 4.

17. Musser, *High-Class Moving Pictures,* p. 12.

18. LL 29 March 1896, p. 6; LL 4 Oct. 1896, p. 6.

19. LL 20 Dec. 1896, p. 11.

20. LH 26 March 1896, p. 6.

21. John Higham, *Writing American History: Essays on Modern Scholarship* (Bloomington: Indiana University Press, 1970), pp. 77–88. The formation of the Lexington Golf Club in November 1896 is also relevant in this regard.

22. LH 30 June 1896, p. 6.

23. LH 19 April 1896, p. 11.

24. LH 29 Feb. 1896, p. 5; LH 12 Sept. 1896, p. 2.

25. LH 8 Sept. 1896, p. 1.

26. LL 30 April 1896, p. 3.

27. LH 4 April 1896, p. 5.

28. LH 3 June 1896, p. 2.

29. *Population, Twelfth Census of the United States, 1900* (Washington, D.C.: U.S. Census Office, 1902), vol. 1, table 22, p. lxx.

30. According to the *Leader*, Lexington's "suburban population" numbered "two or three thousand" (LL 11 Sept. 1900, p. 1).

31. *Population, Twelfth Census*, vol. 1, table 4, p. 21; table 8, pp. 452–54.

32. LH 3 Oct. 1900, p. 6.

33. LH 22 Feb. 1903, sec. 2, p. 6.

34. *Population, Twelfth Census*, vol. 1, table 86, p. 958.

35. *Population, Twelfth Census*, vol. 1, table 35, pp. 796–99. The city's annual police report statistics for the "nativity" of people arrested in 1898 generally correspond with the federal government's tabulation of foreign-born residents (LH 5 March 1899, p. 1).

36. *Population, Twelfth Census*, vol. 1, table 59, pp. 874–75; table 61, pp. 882–83.

37. In addition, the local German Aid Society was founded in 1882 and maintained an office downtown. The most overt—and anomalous—acknowledgment of the local German residents was the *Herald*'s publication in October 1900 of a page printed in German (LH 21 Oct. 1900, p. 3). The Irish presence in Lexington was most noticeable in the police and fire departments and the city government.

38. *Population, Twelfth Census*, vol. 1, table 57, p. cxix; table 30, pp. 708–9.

39. *Population, Twelfth Census*, vol. 1, table 57, pp. cxix–cxxi.

40. LH 21 Jan. 1896, p. 6.

41. *Population, Twelfth Census*, vol. 1, table 78, p. clxvii.

42. *Population, Twelfth Census*, vol. 1, table 57, p. cxix.

43. John Kellogg, ("The Formation of Black Residential Areas in Lexington, Kentucky, 1865–1887," *Journal of Southern History* 48, no. 1 [Feb. 1982]: 25) notes that "Lexington itself, as well as the surrounding Bluegrass region, was distinctly southern in terms of racial composition, antebellum extent of slaveholding, and attitude of the white population toward Negroes and their place in society."

44. LH 21 March 1896, p. 6.

45. LL 20 Oct. 1901, p. 10.

46. Lawrence H. Larsen, *The Rise of the Urban South* (Lexington: University Press of Kentucky, 1985), p. 45. See also Blaine A. Brownell and David R. Goldfield, eds., *The City in Southern History: The Growth of Urban Civilization in the South* (Port Washington, N.Y.: Kennikat Press, 1977); and David R. Goldfield, *Cotton Fields and Skyscrapers: Southern City and Region, 1607–1980* (Baton Rouge: Louisiana University Press, 1982).

47. LH 16 Nov. 1896, p. 1; LL 20 Dec. 1896, p. 11.

48. LH 2 March 1896, p. 4.

49. *Manufactures, Twelfth Census*, vol. 7, table 5, p. 281. In terms of wages paid, by far the largest local enterprise was lumber mill work, which had a payroll of $64,000, at least twice as large as the combined total of the next largest industries: carpentry, printing and publishing, and the production of men and women's clothing. However, judged in terms of the number of employees, the largest industry was dressmaking (134 women), followed by lumber mill work (122 men and 3 children), and upholstery work (119 men) (*Manufactures, Twelfth Census*, vol. 7, table 8, p. 290).

50. LH 21 Sept. 1903, p. 4. See also a front-page article, "Boom Is On" (LH 24 Oct. 1901, p. 1), which particularly played up the economic significance of the new interurban rail lines.

51. This list comes from a long feature article, "Big Industries Which Are Booming in Lexington" (LH 16 Dec. 1900, pp. 17–18).

52. LL 29 March 1903, p. 4.

53. See Howard N. Rabinowitz, "Continuity and Change: Southern Urban Development, 1860–1900," in *The City in Southern History*, pp. 107–10, on the role of industry and the make-up of the work force in southern cities during the late nineteenth century.

54. *Population, Twelfth Census*, vol. 2, table 94, pp. 571–73.

55. Goldfield, *Cotton Fields*, p. 110.

56. *Population, Twelfth Census*, vol. 2, table 94, pp. 571–73. Surprisingly, there was 256 people in Lexington categorized as "actors, professional showmen, etc."—more than Kansas City or Los Angeles, for example. Among this group were Billy Young and several other well-known black minstrel performers.

57. LH 5 March 1899, p. 1.

58. Kellogg, "Formation of Black Residential Areas," pp. 39, 41.

59. See James Duane Bolin, "From Mules to Motors: The Street Railway System in Lexington, Kentucky, 1882–1938," *Register of the Kentucky Historical Society* 87, no. 2 (1989): 118–43.

60. LH 29 Jan. 1896, p. 3.

61. LH 29 Jan. 1896, p. 4.

Chapter 2: Introducing the "Marvelous Invention"

1. LH 15 Dec. 1896, p. 2.

2. Terry Ramsaye, *A Million and One Nights* (1926; rpt. New York: Simon and Schuster, 1986), pp. 308–9.

3. Charles Musser, *The Emergence of Cinema: The American Screen to 1907* (New York: Scribner's, 1990), p. 170. Musser's voluminous work on early film production, exhibition, and reception, much of which appeared in print well after I had begun this project, has proven to be invaluable. One of the most detailed case studies of local exhibition is George C. Pratt's "'No Magic, No Mystery, No Sleight of Hand': The First Ten Years of Motion Pictures in Rochester," in *'Image' on the Art and Evolution of Film*, ed. Marshall Deutelbaum (New York: Dover, 1979), pp. 39–46.

4. Gene G. Kelkres, "A Forgotten First: The Armat-Jenkins Partnership and the Atlanta Projection," *Quarterly Review of Film Studies* 9 (Winter 1984): 45.

5. Kelkres, "Forgotten First," pp. 46–58; Musser, *Emergence of Cinema*, pp. 100–105, 159–61.

6. Ramsaye, *Million and One Nights*, pp. 272–73.

7. LL 6 Dec. 1896, p. 6.

8. On this particular tour, Holmes & Wolford arrived in Lexington from Winchester, Kentucky, then went on to Danville, Kentucky, and to Knoxville and Chattanooga, Tennessee (*New York Dramatic Mirror*, 12 Dec. 1896, p. 10).

9. LH 16 Dec. 1896, p. 2.

10. In fact, Melodeon Hall was used for commercial entertainment as early as 1850, when General Tom Thumb appeared for a three-day engagement; see John D. Wright, Jr., *Lexington: Heart of the Bluegrass* (Lexington: Lexington-Fayette County Historic Commission, 1982), pp. 82–83.

11. LH 5 Oct. 1896, p. 8.

12. See Musser's survey of local debuts of the vitascope (*Emergence of Cinema*, pp. 122–28); and Douglas Gomery, *Shared Pleasures: A History of Movie Presentation in the United States* (Madison: University of Wisconsin Press, 1992), pp. 7–8. For some sense of just how varied the "initial diffusion" of motion pictures was, see Charles Musser in collaboration with Carol Nelson, *High-Class*

Moving Pictures: Lyman H. Howe and the Forgotten Era of Traveling Exhibition, 1880–1920 (Princeton: Princeton University Press, 1991), pp. 59–63.

13. LH 23 Dec. 1896, p. 10; LL 23 Dec. 1896, p. 6.

14. LH 22 Dec. 1896, p. 7.

15. LL 21 Dec. 1896, p. 2. In advertising his motion picture theater, Thompson was following the lead of Raff & Gammon, who initially promoted the vitascope "as the latest of the marvels produced by the wizardly Edison" (Ramsaye, *Million and One Nights*, p. 226). For a critical assessment of the "wizard's" actual role, see Gordon Hendricks, *The Edison Motion Picture Myth* (Berkeley: University of California Press, 1961).

16. Musser, *Emergence of Cinema*, pp. 113–15.

17. Robert C. Allen, "Vitascope/Cinematographe: Initial Patterns of American Film Industrial Practice," in *The American Movie Industry: The Business of Motion Pictures*, ed. Gorham Kindem (Carbondale: Southern Illinois University Press, 1982), pp. 5–6.

18. LH 22 Dec. 1896, p. 7.

19. LH 20 Dec. 1896, p. 3.

20. LL 20 Dec. 1896, p. 6.

21. LL 24 Dec. 1896, p. 4.

22. LL 22 Dec. 1896, p. 6.

23. Musser, *Emergence of Cinema*, p. 117.

24. LH 22 Dec. 1896, p. 7. Thompson's theater was somewhat different from the "Vitascope parlors or Vitascope halls" in other cities such as New Orleans, Los Angeles, and Buffalo, where the vitascope was booked along with a range of other "Edison products": the Kinetoscope, phonograph, and even an X-ray machine (Charlotte Herzog, "The Archaeology of Cinema Architecture: The Origins of the Movie Theater," *Quarterly Review of Film Studies* 9 [Winter 1984]: 25).

25. LL 24 Dec. 1896, p. 4.

26. LH 27 Dec. 1896, p. 3.

27. Allen, "Vitascope/Cinematographe," p. 9. See Musser, *Emergence of Cinema*, pp. 126–28; and Ramsaye, *Million and One Nights*, pp. 349–50.

28. LH 25 Feb. 1897, p. 2.

29. Ramsaye, *Million and One Nights*, pp. 301, 391; Musser, *Emergence of Cinema*, pp. 162–63. The *Leader* of 18 April 1897 included a brief article on the use of a magniscope to film a Chicago & Northwestern train; both Spoor and Amet are mentioned in the article. See Appendix 1 for more information.

30. LH 27 Dec. 1896, p. 3.

31. LH 26 Dec. 1896, p. 5.

32. See Harry Birdoff, *The World's Greatest Hit: 'Uncle Tom's Cabin'* (New York: S. F. Vanni, 1947), pp. 355–56, 436–37.

33. LH 27 Dec. 1896, p. 3.

34. LL 3 Jan. 1897, p. 4. Charles Musser notes that phonograph concerts in the 1890s were often conducted under the auspices of church groups and arranged so as to at least seem to be both "morally uplifting and enjoyable" (*High-Class Moving Pictures*, p. 45). The scanty evidence available about George Walker suggests that he, too, followed this model in his concerts. For example, he operated— in an altogether "polite and painstaking" manner—the "phonograph parlor" at the 1896 Chautauqua Assembly in Lexington, where audiences could hear John Philip Sousa's "King Cotton March" as well as "Gladstone's Speech before the Commons" (LL 4 July 1896, p. 4).

35. LH 25 Feb. 1897, p. 2.

36. The Woodford *Sun*, a weekly newspaper in Versailles, reported on 11 March 1897 that the magniscope attracted "grand-sized audiences" for three days at the courthouse: "all marvelled at the wonderful animated pictures, which were startlingly natural and life-like. A phonograph with funnel

attachment discoursed music by Gilmore's and Sousa's bands, songs, cornet solos, etc., during the evening." Why would the tour head for DeFuniak Springs, a small Florida panhandle town? Perhaps Scott, in his capacity as business manager of the Lexington Chautauqua, had connections with the "Florida Chautauqua" that had been a winter event at DeFuniak Springs since 1885. A mid-March 1897 exhibition of the magniscope would have been during the Chautauqua session. A historian of this particular assembly notes that it brought to its patrons "the new media . . . the project-scopes, motion pictures, gramophones, stereopticons, and slides" (W. Stuart Towns, "The Florida Chautauqua: A Case Study in American Education," *Southern Speech Communication Journal* 42 [Spring 1977]: 244).

37. LL 2 July 1897, p. 4. See Musser, *High-Class Moving Pictures*, pp. 61–63, for information on the "many small enterprises . . . created specifically to show motion pictures" during this period.

38. LL 2 March 1897, p. 4; LH 2 March 1897, p. 2.

39. Musser, *Emergence of Cinema*, p. 183.

40. Miriam Hansen, *Babel and Babylon: Spectatorship in American Silent Film* (Cambridge: Harvard University Press, 1991), p. 94.

Chapter 3: Situating Motion Pictures in the Pre-Nickelodeon Period

1. Charles Musser, "Another Look at the 'Chaser Theory'," *Studies in Visual Communication* 10, no. 4 (Fall 1984): 33. George C. Pratt notes that "for some unstated reasons, between March 1901 and January 1903 motion pictures vanished completely from Rochester theater programs" ("'No Magic, No Mystery, No Sleight of Hand': The First Ten Years of Motion Pictures in Rochester," in *Image on the Art and Evolution of the Film*, ed. Marshall Deutelbaum (New York: Dover, 1979), p. 52. In Lexington, motion pictures were still being screened during this period at the Chautauqua Assembly, the 1901 Elks Fair, street carnivals, and at the Opera House (by certain rep troupes).

2. LL 7 April 1904, p. 5.

3. See, for example, Roy Rosenzweig, *Eight Hours for What We Will: Workers and Leisure in an Industrial City, 1870–1920* (Cambridge: Cambridge University Press, 1983); Cary Goodman, *Choosing Sides: Playground and Street Life on the Lower East Side* (New York: Schocken, 1979); and Kathy Peiss, *Working Women and Leisure in Turn-of-the-Century New York* (Philadelphia: Temple University Press, 1986). George Lipsitz surveys various new historical approaches to media studies in "'This Ain't No Sideshow': Historians and Media Studies," *Critical Studies in Mass Communications* 5 (June 1988): 147–61. See also Robert Sklar, "Oh! Althusser!: Historiography and the Rise of Cinema Studies," *Radical History Review* 41 (Spring 1988): 10–35.

4. On sports in this period, see, for example, John Rickards Betts, *America's Sporting Heritage, 1850–1950* (Reading, Mass.: Addison-Wesley, 1974) and Donald J. Mrozek, *Sport and American Mentality, 1880–1910* (Knoxville: University of Tennessee Press, 1983).

5. See *A Century of Speed: The Red Mile, 1875–1985*, ed. Tom White (Lexington: Thoroughbred Press, 1975), pp. 14–26.

6. LL 27 Dec. 1903, p. 1.

7. See Melba Porter Hay, "The Lexington Civic League: Agent of Reform, 1900–1910," *Filson Club History Quarterly* 62 (July 1988): 336–55.

8. LL 1 Feb. 1903, p. 4.

9. LH 30 Jan. 1903, p. 2.

10. LL 31 May 1901, p. 4.

11. Lawrence W. Levine, *Highbrow/Lowbrow: The Emergence of Cultural Hierarchy in America* (Cambridge: Harvard University Press, 1988), p. 195.

12. LL 17 April 1896, p. 5.

13. LL 13 Feb. 1900, p. 6.

14. The Theatrical Syndicate was formed in 1896 when Marc Klaw and Abraham Erlanger, who owned or leased theaters in several large cities and had exclusive booking rights to some two hundred one-night stands in the Southeast, merged with other interests who had similar rights for large blocks of eastern and western theaters. This merger was the culmination of the increasing centralization of the American commercial theater during the final decades of the nineteenth century. 15. Alfred E. Bernheim, *The Business of the Theatre: An Economic History of the American Theatre, 1750–1932* (1932; rpt. New York: Benjamin Blom, 1964), p. 51.

16. Benjamin McArthur, *Actors and American Culture, 1880–1920* (Philadelphia: Temple University Press, 1984), p. 9.

17. Jack Poggi, *Theater in America: The Impact of Economic Forces, 1870–1967* (Ithaca: Cornell University Press, 1966), p. 14.

18. Contemporary observers, like Norman Hapgood in *The Stage in America: 1897–1900*, bemoaned the constraints the Syndicate imposed on the art of American drama, but Klaw & Erlanger's monopolistic policies could also be said to have promoted the nationwide diffusion of drama or at least of particular types of theatrical entertainment. During this period, McArthur argues, the American theater was a "national institution" and "the stars of the legitimate stage reigned unchallenged in the amusement world" (*Actors and American Culture*, pp. x–xi). One revealing sign of the times locally was that Lexington's newspapers each Sunday ran syndicated columns filled with news and photographs of the latest Broadway productions and the lives of leading actors. Readers of columns such as "Stage Gossip from Gotham" or "Rialto Gossip" likely had or would have the opportunity to see such stars and productions live onstage at the Opera House.

19. Bernheim, *Business of the Theatre*, p. 52.

20. Quoted in Bernheim, *Business of the Theatre*, p. 75.

21. LL 25 Feb. 1900, p. 9. One proof of just how "fortunate" Lexington was in this regard occurred in 1903, when a production of *Romeo and Juliet* sandwiched a performance at the Lexington Opera House between engagements at major theaters in Cincinnati and Louisville, before moving on to the Chicago Opera House (LL 5 April 1903, sec. 2, p. 2).

22. LL 27 Nov. 1898, p. 7.

23. I am not suggesting that the Lexington Opera House was a typical provincial theater. For some sense of the variety among theatrical venues in the provinces, contrast the Opera House with the theaters described in Harlowe R. Hoyt, *Town Hall Tonight* (Englewood Cliffs, N.J.: Prentice-Hall, 1955); and Douglas McDermott and Robert K. Sarlos, "Founding and Touring in America's Provincial Theatre: Woodland, California, 1902–1903," in *Theatrical Touring and Founding in North America* ed. L. W. Conolly (Westport, Conn.: Greenwood Press, 1982), pp. 57–76. Scott's theater was appreciably larger and more elegant than any of the other opera houses in smaller central Kentucky towns, which, according to the 1901–2 edition of *Julius Cahn's Official Theatrical Guide*, ranged in seating capacity from 610 to 1,000.

24. See John Coleman Arnold, "A History of the Lexington Theater from 1887–1900," diss. (University of Kentucky, 1956), which chronologically covers each season at the Opera House in an attempt to determine the extent to which the European "theater of ideas" made it to the American provinces.

25. LL 13 May 1902, p. 2.

26. LL 27 Dec. 1899, p. 4.

27. LL 1 Nov. 1903, p. 5.

28. LH 14 Sept. 1903, p. 5.

29. LH 11 Jan. 1902, p. 1.

30. LL 21 Jan. 1902, p. 1. Four years earlier Scott had told the *Leader* that "we have to have Uncle Tom once a year for the benefit of the rising generation and if we don't we are pretty apt to get complaints. That may seem strange but nevertheless it is true" (LL 4 Dec. 1898, p. 7). We might even say that Scott had already indirectly answered any complaints about *Uncle Tom's Cabin*, since he had regularly booked touring productions such as *In Old Kentucky* and *The South before the War*, which offered an idyllic version of the Old South perfectly suited to any second- or third-generation child of the Confederacy.

31. LH 13 March 1906, p. 5. See Appendix 2 for the full text of this statute.

32. LL 23 Feb. 1901, p. 2.

33. LL 27 April 1900, p. 6.

34. See Robert C. Toll, *Blacking Up: The Minstrel Show in Nineteenth-Century America* (New York: Oxford University Press, 1974).

35. LL 13 Sept. 1900, p. 8; LH 11 May 1902, p. 14.

36. Charles Musser, *The Emergence of Cinema: The American Screen to 1907* (New York: Scribner's, 1990), p. 366. For an exhaustive study of Howe and the phenomena of the traveling motion picture exhibitor, see Charles Musser in collaboration with Carol Nelson, *High-Class Moving Pictures: Lyman H. Howe and the Forgotten Era of Traveling Exhibition, 1880–1920* (Princeton: Princeton University Press, 1991). From the first, local newspapers praised Howe's shows because "the colored light effects and sound imitations added much to increase the reality of each picture" (LL 6 Dec. 1903, sec. 2, p. 1).

37. Professor Swanson was probably William Swanson, who toured with prizefight films and operated a nickelodeon in Chicago before opening the Swanson Film Exchange (Musser, *High-Class Moving Pictures*, pp. 171–72).

38. For some background on the commercial use of local films, see Musser, *Emergence of Cinema*, pp. 266, 334, 405; Musser, *High-Class Moving Pictures*, pp. 109–10, 149–52; Robert C. Allen, "The Movies in Vaudeville: Historical Context of the Movies as Popular Entertainment," in *The American Film Industry*, ed. Tino Balio rev. ed. (Madison: University of Wisconsin Press, 1985), p. 72; and Miriam Hansen, *Babel and Babylon: Spectatorship in American Silent Film* (Cambridge: Harvard University Press, 1991), p. 31. In September 1897, W. N. Selig of Chicago filmed several scenes of railroads and rural sights in the Bluegrass with his multiscope camera (LL 12 Sept. 1897, p. 3). Scott announced plans to exhibit these motion pictures at the Opera House, but no such screening is mentioned in local newspapers.

39. LH 23 Jan. 1903, p. 3; LH 3 Feb. 1903, p. 8.

40. See Dan Streible, "A History of the Boxing Film, 1894–1915: Social Control and Social Reform in the Progressive Era," *Film History* 3 (1989): 235–57.

41. For a discussion of the role of kinetoscope fight films, see Gordon Hendricks, *The Kinetoscope: America's First Commercially Successful Motion Picture Exhibitor* (1966; rpt. New York: Arno Press, 1972). Hendricks concludes that the six-round bout between Corbett and Courtney filmed for the kinetoscope in September 1894 "served to focus, as no other event had yet done, national attention on the kinetoscope and the motion picture" (p. 79). On the controversy surrounding prizefighting and fight films, see Streible, "History of the Boxing Film," pp. 237–40.

42. LH 24 March 1897, p. 1.

43. LH 7 May 1897, p. 1.

44. LH 26 Sept. 1897, p. 6.

45. LL 1 Oct. 1897, p. 2.

46. Terry Ramsaye, *A Million and One Nights* (1926; rpt. New York: Simon and Schuster, 1986), p. 289.

47. LH 26 Sept. 1897, p. 6.
48. LL 20 Sept. 1897, p. 3.
49. LL 30 Sept. 1897, p. 6.
50. LL 1 Oct. 1897, p. 2. See Hansen, *Babel and Babylon*, pp. 1–2.
51. He might well have taken these measures because the film to be exhibited turned out to be a staged reproduction of the fight. See Musser, *Emergence of Cinema*, pp. 202–3.
52. LL 25 Aug. 1899, p. 6.
53. LL 26 Jan. 1900, p. 8.
54. See Musser, *Emergence of Cinema*, pp. 208–21.
55. LH 21 April 1899, p. 6.
56. Musser, *Emergence of Cinema*, p. 219.
57. For commentary on the films themselves, see, for example, the essays in *Film before Griffith*, ed. John Fell (Berkeley: University of California Press, 1983); Tom Gunning, "'Primitive' Cinema— A Frame-up? or The Trick's on Us," *Cinema Journal* 28 (Winter 1989): 3–12; and Noel Burch, *Life to Those Shadows* (Berkeley: University of California Press, 1990). 58. LL 11 June 1900, p. 3.
59. LL 26 Oct. 1900, p. 5.
60. See LH 25 Oct. 1903, p. 9; and James Duane Bolin, "From Mules to Motors: The Street Railway System in Lexington, Kentucky, 1882–1938," *Register of the Kentucky Historical Society* 87 (1989): 118–43.
61. The involvement of the local streetcar company in the business of commercial entertainment was hardly unique to Lexington. In his study of the urban South, Howard N. Rabinowitz notes that even those people "too poor to ride the [street]cars regularly to work could take them to pleasure grounds like Atlanta's Ponce de Leon Springs or Nashville's Glenwood Park that the lines operated to increase their ridership" ("Continuity and Change: Southern Urban Development, 1860–1900," in *The City in Southern History: The Growth of Urban Civilization in the South*, ed. Blaine A. Brownell and David R. Goldfield [Port Washington, N.Y.: Kennikat Press, 1977], p. 114).
62. LL 19 April 1896, p. 3.
63. LL 10 June 1900, p. 3.
64. LL 1 Sept. 1904, p. 4.
65. Theodore Morrison, *Chautauqua: A Center for Education, Religion, and the Arts in America* (Chicago: University of Chicago Press, 1974), pp. 162, 165.
66. Morrison, *Chautauqua*, p. 27.
67. Joseph E. Gould, in *The Chautauqua Movement: An Episode in the Continuing American Revolution* (Albany: State University of New York Press, 1961), p. 10, puts the relationship between the original Chautauqua and the independent assemblies (like the one in Lexington) in these terms: "Assemblies . . . varied widely in size, in program, and in denominational or other sponsorship, but they had certain basic features in common. Automatically, it would seem, the reputation for quality, respectability, and integrity that the original Chautauqua had earned was inherited with the name. Healthy fun, wholesome recreation, religious reverence, good taste, and honest inquiry—these qualities were associated in the public mind with the word 'Chautauqua'." For case studies of other Chautauqua Assemblies, see, for example, Jan T. Younger, "The Maumee Valley Chautauqua, 1902–1912," *Northwest Ohio Quarterly* 49 (Spring 1977): 56–68; Doris Lanier, "Henry W. Grady and the Piedmont Chautauqua," *Southern Studies* 23 (1984): 216–42.
68. LH 10 July 1898, p. 1; LL 23 June 1901, p. 2.
69. Apparently 1,300 people (about the seating capacity of the Opera House) constituted a good-sized Chautauqua crowd, while to break even, the assembly had to sell some 1,000 season tickets, averaging $3.00 each.
70. LL 23 June 1901, p. 2.
71. LL 3 July 1903, p. 2.

72. Like the other entertainments, motion pictures constituted a separate "act" within the tightly organized Chautauqua program. However, by 1901 motion pictures also began to be used as illustrative accompaniment for lectures. For example, a lecture on the Paris Exhibition at the 1901 Assembly was "illustrated by the ever popular and wholly beautiful moving pictures" (LL 26 June 1901, p. 4).

73. LL 7 July 1899, p. 4. On the question of motion pictures as chasers, see Robert C. Allen, "Contra the Chaser Theory," *Wide Angle* 3 (1979): 4–11; and Musser, "Another Look at the 'Chaser Theory,'" 22–44, 51–52.

74. Given the WCTU campaign against fight films, it is noteworthy that the Vitagraph pictures were scheduled on "Temperance Day," following a magician and illustrated songs. Obviously, the cinema was by no means universally perceived as a "low" medium, even by those people who glimpsed the danger it posed when put in the service of an activity like prizefighting.

75. LL 5 July 1899, p. 8. At the Assembly in 1898, however, the situation was quite different. Of that exhibition, the *Leader* wrote: "the moving pictures, accompanied by songs corresponding to the scenes, were principally views of the soldier boys in Cuba, and though excellently presented, were a little too realistic and pathetic, considering the grief and anxiety of the present hour" (LL 3 July 1898, p. 7). American Vitagraph also presented films at Lexington Chautauqua Assemblies in 1900–1903.

76. Allen, "Movies in Vaudeville," p. 74. See also Musser, *Emergence of Cinema*, pp. 240–61. "Prior to the sinking of the *Maine* on February 15, 1898," Musser notes, "moving pictures were shown only at a limited number of vaudeville houses and then for a few weeks in between very long hiatuses. With the Cuban crisis and war, many theatres showed pertinent 'war films' for weeks and then months without interruption," though the motion picture segment of the vaudeville bill combined war films with, for example, panoramas or fantastic pictures ("American Vitagraph," *Cinema Journal* 22 [Spring 1983]: 12, 20).

77. Allen, "Movies in Vaudeville," pp. 73–75.

78. For a time, rep companies that played the Opera House also specifically advertised specialties like "Moving War Pictures" (LL 7 Aug. 1899, p. 5) and "moving pictures of the Galveston Flood" (LH 19 Dec. 1900, p. 3). During this period, among the very few articles in local papers on motion pictures (aside from local screenings) were descriptions of the filming of Queen Victoria's jubilee (LL 28 Nov. 1897, p. 1) and of the pope (LL 15 Jan. 1899, p. 13).

79. Charlotte Herzog, "The Archaeology of Cinema Architecture: The Origins of the Movie Theater," *Quarterly Review of Film Studies* 9 (Winter 1984): 17. On the European tradition of traveling fairground film exhibition, see Mark E. Swartz, "An Overview of Cinema on the Fairgrounds," *Journal of Popular Film and Television* 15 (Fall 1987): 102–8.

80. LL 5 Sept. 1897, p. 7.

81. LH 6 June 1899, p. 3.

82. LH 6 Aug. 1899, p. 9.

83. LH 15 Aug. 1902, p. 1.

84. LL 12 April 1897, p. 8.

85. LH 30 April 1896, p. 6.

86. LL 4 July 1901, p. 1. See Rosenzweig, *Eight Hours for What We Will*, pp. 153–68, for the "struggle" over the Fourth of July in Worcester during this period.

87. LH 9 Sept. 1900, p. 5; LL 21 Sept. 1905, p. 6.

88. LL 16 Aug. 1899, p. 2.

89. LH 12 Aug. 1900, p. 10.

90. LH 6 Aug. 1899, p. 9.

Chapter 4: Moving Pictures, Vaudeville, and Commercial Entertainment in the Nickelodeon Period

1. On the nickelodeon period, see Charles Musser, *The Emergence of Cinema: The American Screen to 1907* (New York: Scribner's 1990), pp. 418–89; Eileen Bowser, *The Transformation of Cinema, 1907–1915* (New York: Scribner's, 1990); and Douglas Gomery, *Shared Pleasures: A History of Movie Presentation in the United States* (Madison: University of Wisconsin Press, 1992), pp. 18–23. Of particular interest are the weekly columns in *Moving Picture World* that report on local exhibition practices around the country and, in particular, MPW 29, no. 3 (15 July 1916), a special issue of this trade journal that included various reminiscences concerning the previous ten years of film exhibition. (This issue contains an article on Louisville, but not one on Lexington or any comparable small city.) The text for Q. David Bowers' *Nickelodeon Theatres and Their Music* (Vestal, N.Y.: Vestal Press, 1986) is primarily composed of material quoted from *Moving Picture World* and other trade magazines and is of far less value than the reproductions of Bowers' extensive collection of photographs of nickelodeons across the country. An attempt to identify the "first motion picture audiences" at large is offered by Garth Jowett, *Film: The Democratic Art* (Boston: Focal Press, 1976), pp. 35–42. Jowett emphasizes that the "most important group" in this regard was drawn from "the large urban working class," particularly immigrants (p. 38). Two first-rate studies that examine the location of and the audience for nickelodeons in large urban areas are Robert C. Allen, "Motion Picture Exhibition in Manhattan, 1906–1912: Beyond the Nickelodeon," in *The American Movie Industry: The Business of Motion Pictures*, ed. Gorham Kindem (Carbondale: Southern Illinois University Press, 1982), pp. 12–24; and Russell Merritt, "Nickelodeon Theaters, 1905–1914: Building an Audience for the Movies," in *The American Film Industry*, rev. ed., ed. Tino Balio (Madison: University of Wisconsin Press, 1985), pp. 83–102.

2. See David Bordwell, Janet Staiger, and Kristin Thompson, *The Classical Hollywood Cinema: Film Style and Mode of Production to 1960* (New York: Columbia University Press, 1985), p. 129; and Robert C. Allen, *Vaudeville and Film 1895–1915: A Study in Media Interaction* (New York: Arno, 1980), pp. 230–88.

3. Kathy Peiss, *Cheap Amusements: Working Women and Leisure in Turn-of-the-Century New York* (Philadelphia: Temple University Press, 1986), p. 149. Particularly revealing as a contrast to the situation in Lexington is Roy Rosenzweig's analysis of the function of nickelodeons as sites for urban, immigrant, working-class recreation in Worcester, Massachusetts, in *Eight Hours for What We Will: Workers and Leisure in an Industrial City, 1870–1920* (Cambridge: Cambridge University Press, 1983), pp. 191–208. See also Miriam Hansen, *Babel and Babylon: Spectatorship in American Silent Film* (Cambridge: Harvard University Press, 1991), pp. 60–68.

4. LL 20 Feb. 1908, p. 7. For comparison's sake, see "The Nickelodeon as a Business Proposition," a detailed article from the Grand Rapids *Press* that was reprinted in the MPW 3, No. 4 (25 July 1908): 61–62. After surveying the moving picture shows in Grand Rapids, the *Press* concluded that daily operating costs were likely to range from $20 to $50, with monthly rent from $100 (for "outlying" theaters) to $400 (for downtown theaters). Initial start-up costs totaled about $3,500. All of these figures seem to be significantly higher than the costs of opening and operating a moving picture show in Lexington. For an estimate of nickelodeon costs in a small town, see "Plain Talks to Theatre Managers and Operators: Selecting a Small Town Location," MPW 5, no. 20 (13 Nov. 1909): 676, which suggests that $100 a week (including operating expenses and rent) can provide a "really acceptable show." David S. Hulfish, in his *Cyclopedia of Motion-Picture Work* (Chicago: American Technical Society, 1911), II, pp. 16–19, estimates the operating cost of a theater in a "non-competitive small town" to be $83 per week, with start-up costs of not more than $600; a "high-class store-

front picture theater" would cost between $2,000 and $6,000 to set up and about $215 a week to operate.

5. LL 25 Oct. 1906, p. 6. For information on Hale's Tours, see "Hale's Tours and Scenes of the World," MPW 29, No. 3 (15 July 1916): 372–73; Raymond Fielding, "Hale's Tours: Ultrarealism in the Pre–1910 Motion Picture," *Cinema Journal* 10, No. 1 (Fall 1970): 34–47; Noel Burch, *Life to Those Shadows* (Berkeley: University of California Press, 1990), pp. 34–39; and Lauren Rabinovitz, "Temptations of Pleasure: Nickelodeons, Amusement Parks, and the Sights of Female Sexuality," *Camera Obscura* 23 (May 1990): 79–82.

6. LH 7 Oct. 1906, sec. 2, p. 6; LH 18 Oct. 1906, p. 5.

7. LH 31 Jan. 1907, p. 8.

8. See, for example, Jowett, *Film: The Democratic Art*, pp. 108–18; and Kathleen D. McCarthy, "Nickel Vice and Virtue: Movie Censorship in Chicago, 1907–1915," *Journal of Popular Film* 5, No. 1 (1976): 37–55. The Lexington *Herald* often reprinted articles from reformist periodicals such as *Charities and the Commons,* including a piece entitled, "Chicago City Club to Investigate Cheap Theatres" (LH 23 June 1907, p. 7), which concluded that "the general influence of the penny arcade and the cheap theater with its games of chance, kidnappings and its murders cannot be for good."

9. The surrounding central Kentucky towns quickly followed suit, with moving picture shows opened in downtown Nicholasville, Versailles, and Paris in July 1907, and four months later in Winchester. Unlike the small opera houses in these communities, which could not match the attractions at the Lexington Opera House, the storefront moving picture shows in Versailles or Winchester could offer basically the same programs as Lexington's nickelodeons. Thus the degree to which Lexington's movie theaters attracted out-of-town patrons becomes even more difficult to gauge. In his first column, *Moving Picture World*'s Louisville correspondent noted that "it seems as if all Louisville now has the moving picture craze. Our country cousins have it, too, for on coming to town they seek the moving picture shows" (MPW 3, no. 22 [28 Nov. 1908]: 427).

10. Merritt, "Nickelodeon Theaters," pp. 86–87, 92–95.

11. T. J. Jackson Lears, *No Place of Grace: Antimodernism and the Transformation of American Culture, 1880–1920* (New York: Pantheon, 1981), pp. 10–11.

12. Bowser, *Transformation of Cinema,* p. 15. See, for example, the "Song Slide Review" in MPW 1, no. 2 (10 March 1907): 3; this column includes two songs, one with twenty-five slides and the other with seventeen. Describing the songs in nickelodeons, Michael M. Davis, Jr. observed, in *The Exploitation of Pleasure: A Study of Commercial Recreations in New York City* (New York: Russell Sage Foundation, 1911), p. 24, that "no warm-blooded person can watch the rapt attention of an audience during the song, and hear the voices swell as children and adults join spontaneously in the chorus, without feeling how deeply human is the appeal of the music, and how clearly it meets a sound popular need."

13. Merritt, "Nickelodeon Theaters," pp. 86–87.

14. Rosenzweig, *Eight Hours for What We Will,* p. 195.

15. Lary May, in contrast, argues that "when film makers tried to reach into middle-class markets, they found themselves thwarted by the continuing strength of Victorian assumptions about amusements" (*Screening Out the Past: The Birth of Mass Culture and the Motion Picture Industry* [New York: Oxford University Press, 1980], p. 28).

16. MPW 3, no. 4 (25 July 1908): 61.

17. MPW 3, No. 18 (31 Oct. 1908): 336; MPW 1, No. 25 (24 Aug. 1907): 391.

18. See, in particular, Hansen's convincing interpretation of the "nickelodeon myth" as "legitimation for capitalist practices and ideology" (*Babel and Babylon,* pp. 63–65).

19. LL 24 May 1907, p. 12.

20. LL 25 Oct. 1906, p. 6; LL 21 Oct. 1906, p. 2. Elaborate sound effects were also cited as a selling point in the promotion of nickelodeons. The new manager of the Kentucky Theater in Padu-

cah, Kentucky, promised patrons that at his theater "if you see a lunatic asylum scene, you can hear the maddened cries of the 'nutty ones,' you can hear the horses run in fire alarms; can in fact get the benefit of every effect possible to make the scene more realistic" (MPW 1, no. 19 [13 July 1907]: 297). The same page of *Moving Picture World* included a short column on how to achieve certain sound effects using whistles, bells, sandpaper blocks, and coconut shells.

21. Charles Musser argues at length that Howe's programs constituted a "cinema of reassurance" (*High-Class Moving Pictures: Lyman H. Howe and the Forgotten Era of Traveling Exhibition, 1880–1920* [Princeton: Princeton University Press, 1991]).

22. LH 7 Oct. 1907, p. 7.

23. LL 27 July 1906, p. 7.

24. The opening of nickelodeons in Lexington and a host of other Kentucky towns and cities did not immediately spell the end of small-time touring moving picture shows (as opposed to major operations like Howe's High-Class Moving Pictures). Reports from Kentucky correspondents for *Moving Picture World* indicate that, in isolated areas of the state, itinerant motion picture exhibitors were still on the road well after the end of the nickelodeon period. *Moving Picture World* noted in December 1913, for example, that two men from Cadiz, Kentucky, had mounted their motion picture outfit on a "two horse wagon" and begun a "trip which covers most of the smaller towns in Kentucky which have no picture show" (MPW 18, no. 13 [27 Dec. 1913]: 1563). In 1915, a traveling exhibitor from Hawesville set up a weekly circuit covering six small towns to which he would transport his tent and gas-powered projector (MPW 24, no. 7 [15 May 1915]: 1119). Another regional touring strategy was to bring enough films to each site for a multi-day engagement and then enlist the support (and the quasi-authorization) of a local church by donating to it a percentage of the profits (MPW 25, no. 3 [17 July 1915]: 521).

25. LH 4 Nov. 1905, p. 8.

26. LH 14 Nov. 1906, p. 4; LH 23 Dec. 1906, p. 8; LH 25 Dec. 1906, p. 5.

27. LL 31 Jan. 1907, p. 9.

28. See, for example, "Georgie Takes Wifey to the Roller Skating Rink" (LH 13 Jan 1907, p. 8). Musser notes that the first film produced by the Essanay Company in July 1907 was a comedy entitled *An Awful Skate or the Hobo on Rollers* (*Emergence of Cinema*, p. 486).

29. LH 28 Feb. 1907, p. 9; LL 28 March 1907, p. 1.

30. LH 17 Oct. 1907, p. 5; LL 20 Oct. 1907, p. 5.

31. LL 19 Dec. 1907, p. 3.

32. LL 2 April 1907, p. 5.

33. *Variety* 10, no. 3 (28 March 1908): 13.

34. In this regard, it is particularly revealing that certain phonograph ads of this period begin to picture the *home* as an alternate site for entertainment. "Enjoy yourself at home these long nights," declared an ad for Edison and Columbia Talking Machines in the *Herald* (5 Dec. 1907, p. 6).

35. LL 8 Dec. 1907, p. 11.

36. Located well outside the city limits, the Lexington Country Club was literally as well as figuratively far removed from Woodland Park and the central business district. Its founding members included no men who were then associated with the amusement business in Lexington.

37. See the speculations of David O. Thomas's about the reasons for the success and failure of specific nickelodeons in Winona, Minnesota ("From Page to Screen in Smalltown America: Early Motion Picture Exhibition in Winona, Minnesota," *Journal of the University Film Association* 33, no. 3 [Summer 1981]: 3–13).

38. LL 30 Jan. 1908, p. 5; MPW 2, no. 6 (8 Feb. 1908): 100.

39. MPW 1, no. 39 (30 Nov. 1907): 631.

40. James Duane Bolin, "Bossism and Reform: Politics in Lexington, Kentucky, 1880–1940," Ph.D. diss. (University of Kentucky, 1988), 48.

41. In cities like Lexington, municipal license fees would also have to be taken into account, though these could vary considerably. For example, in Scranton, Pennsylvania, as late as 1912, the yearly license fee was $25 for theaters with less than three hundred seats and $50 for those with more than three hundred seats (Lavera Berlew, *Recreation Survey of Scranton* [Scranton: Playground Association, 1912], p. 9).

42. LL 20 Feb. 1908, p. 7.

43. LL 6 Feb. 1908, p. 7; LL 8 April 1908, p. 6.

44. LL 11 Sept. 1910, p. 7.

45. LL 11 Sept. 1910, p. 6; LL 28 Sept. 1910, p. 11; LL 18 Dec. 1910, p. 32.

46. LL 30 Oct. 1910, p. 21. The attempts by the proprietors of the Princess to lure the "best class of people" are quite similar to Hulfish's advice in 1911 on how to attract a "*clientele de luxe*" to the nickelodeon (*Cyclopedia of Motion-Picture Work*, vol. 2, pp. 4–5). *Moving Picture World*, as might be expected, clearly saw the benefit of a "better-class" audience. In September 1901 it declared that "it is a very powerful sign of the situation that the better classes are patronizing moving picture theaters in such large numbers" (MPW 5, no. 13 [25 Sept. 1909]: 406). Presumably these "better" patrons would only somehow add to the grand democratic motion picture audience that I described earlier.

47. The 24 March 1912 Princess program is typical: two Essanay split-reel comedies, a Lubin drama entitled *The Handicap*, and the song "I'm Lonesome without You, My Dear."

48. See Bowser, *Transformation of Cinema*, pp. 167–89, on the role of genre films in the industry before the advent of the multi-reel "feature" film.

49. MPW 19, no. 8 (21 Feb. 1914): 982; MPW 17, no. 10 (13 Sept. 1913): 1194.

50. LH 1 May 1914, p. 16; LL 19 May 1914, p. 5; LL 20 May 1914, p. 12.

51. Merritt, "Nickelodeon Theaters," p. 91.

52. Musser, *High-Class Moving Pictures*, pp. 9–11.

53. According to *Billboard*, there were more than four hundred vaudeville theaters operating in the United States in 1906 (quoted in Robert C. Allen, *Vaudeville and Film 1895–1915: A Study in Media Interaction* [New York: Arno Press, 1980], p. 36).

54. Quoted in Allen, *Vaudeville and Film*, p. 203.

55. LH 28 March 1907, p. 7.

56. LH 3 April 1907, p. 4.

57. LL 27 Sept. 1908, p. 26; LH 4 Oct. 1908, p. 8. Swanson was then a prominent Chicago-based motion picture distributor and exhibitor. Most likely he was the same man who came to Lexington in 1903 and produced the local films for the fire department benefit show. In 1908 there were, according to ads in *Moving Picture World*, ten companies of "Swanson's Marvelous Talking Pictures" touring Texas and eight more in the territory around Denver (MPW 3, no. 22 [28 Nov. 1908]: 440). See also Bowser, *Transformation of Cinema*, pp. 19–20; and Musser, *High-Class Moving Pictures*, pp. 184–88.

58. In June 1909 *Moving Picture World* published an article on how to use a "Baby Show Contest" to draw patrons, and the same issue included advertisements for slides specifically relating to such contests (MPW 2, no. 26 [26 June 1909]: 869, 877).

59. In 1896 Ramsey had also served as first president and chief spokesperson for the newly formed Blue Grass professional baseball league (LH 28 July 1896, p. 8).

60. LH 31 Aug. 1909 p. 4; LH 26 Sept. 1909, p. 8.

61. LH 21 Feb. 1909, p. 8; LH 30 Aug. 1912, p. 12.

62. LL 12 June 1909, p. 5.

63. LL 26 Sept. 1909, p. 25.

64. Albert F. McLean, Jr. *American Vaudeville as Ritual* (Lexington: University of Kentucky Press, 1965), p. 70. In 1899 playwright and actor Edwin Milton Royle wrote: "the vaudeville theatres may be said to have established the commercial value of decency. This is their cornerstone" ("The

Vaudeville Theatre," in *American Vaudeville as Seen by Its Contemporaries*, ed. Charles W. Stein [New York: Knopf, 1984], p. 24). Or as B. F. Keith, the "founder" of American vaudeville, put it: "Two things I determined at the outset should prevail in the new scheme. One was that my fixed policy of cleanliness and order should be continued, and the other that the stage show must be free from vulgarisms and coarseness of any kind, so that the house and entertainment would directly appeal to the support of ladies and children" ("The Vogue of Vaudeville," in *American Vaudeville as Seen by Its Contemporaries*, p. 17). McLean discusses this aspect of American vaudeville in the context of changes in Protestantism from the nineteenth to the twentieth century (pp. 66–83).

65. LH 28 Nov. 1909, p. 7.

66. There is also no doubt some truth to McLean's contention that "for the vaudeville audiences themselves, the appeal to purity and uplift was more a snobbish identification with upper-middle class taste than it was a matter of religious conviction" (*American Vaudeville as Ritual*, p. 82). On the female audiences for urban nickelodeons, see Hansen, *Babel and Babylon*, pp. 114–19; and Peiss, *Cheap Amusements*, pp. 139–62.

67. McLean, *American Vaudeville as Ritual*, pp. 94–105.

68. Allen, *Vaudeville and Film*, pp. 46–51.

69. *Variety* 8, no. 1 (14 Sept. 1907): 6; *Variety* 10, no. 9 (8 Aug. 1908): 36; *Variety* 19, no. 9 (6 Aug. 1910): 17. See also the anecdotal account of life on the "small time" vaudeville theater circuits in John E. DiMeglio, *Vaudeville U.S.A.* (Bowling Green, Ohio: Bowling Green University Popular Press, 1973), pp. 171–94. It is difficult to tell whether the ten-cent vaudeville offered at the Hipp and Lexington's other theaters between 1907 and 1911 differed in kind as well as in degree from metropolitan houses booked by the major circuits. McLean, for example, does not discriminate among different types of vaudeville in his analysis of the "ritual" function of this form of popular entertainment. One problem with McLean's provocative argument that vaudeville presented "industrialization and urbanization in symbolic terms" for an audience enamored with the "myth of success" (*American Vaudeville as Ritual*, p. 24) is that he posits a rather homogeneous audience and an equally homogenous vaudeville experience.

70. LH 14 May 1911, p. 3.

71. LH 16 June 1909, p. 5; LL 22 May 1909, p. 4.

72. Bowers includes several photos of motion picture shows at parks and notes that "by 1910, just about every amusement park in America had a moving picture theatre" (*Nickelodeon Theatres*, p. 56).

73. LL 19 June 1910, p. 6. Blue Grass Park, it would seem, was a far cry from urban amusement parks, which, according to Peiss, "beckoned young women who desired spaces for social experimentation, personal freedom, and unsupervised fun" (*Cheap Amusements*, p. 186).

74. *Dante's Inferno* (1911) played for a week's run in November and again in December. Actually, Ramsey arranged these screenings and rented the Opera House for these two weeks. Both this feature film and Howe's exhibitions could be considered, in Musser's words, "an upscale alternative to nickelodeon fare," an alternative often relied on in larger cities to "maintain a respectable image yet still reap financial rewards from showing films" (*High-Class Moving Pictures*, p. 183). W. Stephen Bush repeatedly pitched the value of films like *Dante's Inferno*. "There is," he wrote, "in view of the success of these features, no getting away from the fact that high art, beauty of form, magnificence of theme, epic grandeur, lofty morality and appeal to the finest and deepest emotions have found favor with the American public" (MPW 12, no. 6 [11 May 1912]: 505–6).

75. In 1909 the Shubert theatrical syndicate succeeded in leasing the auditorium over the objections of Charles Scott; this was part of the Shuberts' attempt to "open up the South" (LH 22 Aug. 1909, p. 8). See Jack Poggi, *Theater in America: The Impact of Economic Forces, 1870–1967* (Ithaca: Cornell University Press, 1966), p. 19. The auditorium was remodeled and opened in October 1909 as a direct competitor to the Opera House. Scott took an active role in the National Theater Owners

Association, which was formed in June 1910 to resist any further encroachment by the Shuberts in small cities. In December 1910, after the new auditorium showed only modest success, the lease was canceled.

76. By way of contrast, Wheeling, West Virginia, with a population of 60,000, at this time had fourteen movie theaters. Three of these theaters were owned by one man, who also operated a film exchange in the city (MPW 9, no. 10 [16 Sept. 1911]: 812).

77. LH 18 July 1913, p. 8.

78. MPW 9, no. 4 (12 Aug. 1911): 471. In most of these respects, the Colonial seems to have been typical of the new "movie palaces" that opened, according to Bowser, in 1911–12 (*Transformation of Cinema*, pp. 121–29). See also the quite detailed suggestions for upgrading movie theaters offered by the *Moving Picture World* in articles entitled "Swelling the Box Office Receipts" (MPW 8, no. 19 [13 May 1911]: 1059–60; and MPW 8, no. 20 [20 May 1911]: 1117–18).

79. MPW 5, no. 14 (2 Oct. 1909): 442. See, in this regard, the advertisements for usher uniforms in *Moving Picture World* (MPW 6, no. 11 [19 March 1910]: 423), which declare that "The Uniform means Deference—Courtesy—Attention—Respect to the Public," as well as "Cleanliness—Neatness—Punctuality—Obedience." But the Colonial was no match for Louisville's Novelty Theater, whose attendants were "attractive Bluegrass maidens in Russian soldier garb" (MPW 11, no. 8 [24 Feb. 1912]: 676).

80. LH 30 July 1911, p. 5.

81. Judging from its Vitagraph offerings, at least, the Colonial was a first-run theater. For example, *Vanity Fair* played the Colonial only ten days after what Anthony Slide identifies as its opening release date, and the same was true for Vitagraph one-reelers like the John Bunny comedy, *In the Clutches of a Vapor Bath* (*The Big V: A History of the Vitagraph Company*, rev. ed. [Metuchen, N.J.: Scarecrow Press, 1987], pp. 208–9).

82. Staiger notes that "many trade paper writers advised exhibitors to raise the [admission] price to at least 10 cents (which even the poor could afford) to avoid the appearance of a 'cheap and common' show" (*Classical Hollywood Cinema*, p. 129). In Lexington, at least, this advice was rarely followed, perhaps because exhibitors did not face the same sort of problem with legitimation as in a larger urban setting.

83. LH 9 March 1913, p. 6.

84. LL 24 Aug. 1913, p. 3; LL 3 Aug. 1913, sec. 2, p. 6.

85. LL 14 Jan. 1917, p. 11.

86. LL 21 March 1911, p. 9.

87. Charles Kerr, ed., *History of Kentucky*, vol. 3 (Chicago: American Historical Society, 1922), p. 181.

88. LL 24 March 1913, p. 1.

89. See Richard deCordova, *Picture Personalities: The Emergence of the Star System in America* (Urbana: University of Illinois Press, 1990), pp. 50–97.

90. LL 14 Jan. 1912, p. 1. This would seem to have been part of a trend across the state. The Kentucky Motion Picture Exhibitors League estimated in July 1913 that there were 250 theaters in Kentucky owned by about one hundred different companies (MPW 17, no. 2 [13 July 1913]: 162.

91. Even as the start-up costs increased for more elaborate and permanent moving picture theaters like the Colonial and the Orpheum, a cheaper venue could still be built, depending on the location of the theater. Thus the *Herald* in November 1913 reported that certain men from Lexington invested only a total of $3,000 to prepare and open a four hundred-seat movie theater in Frankfort, Kentucky (LH 12 Nov. 1913, p. 9).

92. LL 21 April 1912, p. 4.

93. Ideals are one thing and practice another. Two months after the Orpheum opened, one of the

modern wall fans safely mounted for ventilation purposes in the auditorium fell and hit a little girl in the head (LH 10 June 1912, p. 4).

94. LL 21 April 1912, p. 4.

95. LH 23 Nov. 1913, p. 5. These union musicians briefly walked out because Stamper repeatedly kept them overtime on Sundays, yet this controversy apparently did not hurt the Orpheum's business. Nor did the fact that Stamper, after divesting himself of his controversial grocery store, was arrested in March 1914 after he struck one of his female ticket-takers.

96. Gomery, *Shared Pleasures*, p. 23.

Chapter 5: The Business of Film Exhibition in the 1910s

1. LH 1 Dec. 1912, sec. 4, p. 8.

2. LH 24 March 1912, p. 4.

3. LH 6 May 1912, p. 4. See Q. David Bowers, "Souvenir Postcards and the Development of the Star System, 1912–1914," *Film History* 3 (1989): 39–45.

4. MPW 14, no. 9 (30 Nov. 1912): 908.

5. LH 29 Jan. 1914, p. 1.

6. LH 21 Oct. 1913, p. 4; LH 19 Oct. 1913, p. 5.

7. LH 21 Oct. 1913, p. 1.

8. Eileen Bowser notes that "Kinemacolor was important to the cause of uplifting the industry and attracting a middle-class audience" (*The Transformation of Cinema, 1907–1915* [New York: Scribner's, 1990], p. 228). Ramsey's advertising for Kinemacolor tended to emphasize the novelty and technological wizardry of this color process. On the very interesting Kinemacolor enterprise, see also Gorham Kindem, "The Demise of Kinemacolor: Technological, Legal, Economic, and Aesthetic Problems in Early Color Cinema History," *Cinema Journal* 20, no. 2 (Spring 1981): 3–14; and Charles Musser in collaboration with Carol Nelson, *High-Class Moving Pictures: Lyman H. Howe and the Forgotten Era of Traveling Exhibition, 1880–1920* (Princeton: Princeton University Press, 1991), pp. 217–19.

9. LH 5 April 1914, p. 6.

10. LL 2 Sept. 1915, p. 2. See, for example, on the "science" of vaudeville: George Gottlieb, "Psychology of the American Vaudeville Show from the Manager's Point of View" (1916) in *American Vaudeville as Seen by Its Contemporaries*, ed. Charles W. Stein (New York: Knopf, 1984), pp. 179–81.

11. Gurnee also announced that he would book the Ada Meade through the United Booking Organization (UBO), which was then struggling for domination of the industry with Loew's. Robert C. Allen notes that Loew's had started to book Gus Sun theaters in late 1913 (*Vaudeville and Film, 1895–1915: A Study in Media Interaction* [New York: Arno, 1980], p. 286). In any case, the shift had little effect on the bookings at the Ada Meade.

12. Abel Green and Joe Laurie, Jr., *Show Biz: From Vaude to Video* (New York: Henry Holt, 1951), p. 72.

13. LL 27 March 1916, p. 12.

14. Charles Kerr, ed., *History of Kentucky*, vol. 4 (Chicago: American Historical Society, 1922), pp. 569–71. Local lore has it that Haggin decided that Lexington needed a new theater when tickets for his wife's favorite box seats at the Opera House were sold to someone else (LL 9 Sept. 1964, p. 12).

15. LL 30 May 1915, p. 4. Kerr, *History of Kentucky*, vol. 4, pp. 175–76.

16. LH 10 Jan. 1912, p. 6; LH 11 Feb. 1912, pp. 1–2. Berryman, Haggin, and Breckinridge were members of the first board of directors of the Berryman Realty Company, along with five other

local men, including the owners of a major hardware store, a commercial laundry, and an insurance agency (LH 11 Feb. 1912, p. 2).

17. The Ben Ali also did not face daily competition from Woodland Park Auditorium, whose attractions were decidedly high cultural, like the appearance of the Ballet Russe and the Boston National Grand Opera Company in 1914. Seats for this particular engagement cost from $1.00 to $5.00, though the audience—according to the *Herald*—was not all "fine feathers," for "in the furthermost seats in the gallery were the truest of true lovers of music—the Italian fruit vendor, the Greek bootblack" (LH 20 Oct. 1916, p. 1).

18. *Ben Ali Theatre Magazine* (Nov. 1913), p. 2.

19. LL 25 June 1912, p. 1. A *Leader* editorial on the "Stage Predicament" in December 1913 explained that the decline in attendance for stage productions was a result of high ticket costs, increased automobile use, and especially the motion picture business, which "during the past few years has been a miracle and a revelation" with such films as *Quo Vadis* and *Les Misérables* (LL 4 Dec. 1913, p. 4).

20. LL 24 Nov. 1912, p. 6.

21. LH 21 Sept. 1913, p. 1.

22. LH 24 Sept. 1913, p. 5.

23. In April 1914 Will Rogers and the Keatons appeared on the same bill with a shadowgraphist, novelty roller skaters, and "Eight Girls of the Golden West" (*Ben Ali Theatre Magazine* [April 1914], pp. 3–4).

24. On the role of full-length documentaries in this period, see Musser, *High-Class Moving Pictures*, pp. 229–36. What should be noted here is that in a city the size of Lexington, documentaries like *The Undying Story of Captain Scott* were exhibited at the same venue that screened a sensationalized, highly topical white-slave melodrama like *Traffic in Souls*. For information on this and other early feature films, see Ben Brewster, "*Traffic in Souls:* An Experiment in Feature-Length Narrative Construction," *Cinema Journal* 31, no. 1 (Fall 1991): 37–56.

25. LH 25 July 1913, p. 8.

26. LH 3 Dec. 1913, p. 5). *Quo Vadis* got similar praise from a *Herald* reviewer who called it "an educational feature neither collegians nor school children of the city can afford to miss" (LH 4 Nov. 1913, p. 3).

27. Janet Staiger notes that "the evidence overwhelmingly supports a connection between the famous play, novel, and story adapted into film and the increasing length of the product. The longer film enabled a more faithful reproduction of these classics well-known to a middle-class audience, a ploy in step with contemporary exhibition practices" (*The Classic Hollywood Cinema: Film Style and Mode of Production to 1960* [New York: Columbia University Press, 1985], p. 131). Such films in Lexington were virtually always shown at the Ben Ali or the Opera House and promoted and scheduled much like the other touring productions staged at these venues.

28. LL 5 April 1914, p. 8.

29. Soon after the Ben Ali's shift to an all-film policy, Local 346 of the International Alliance of Theatrical Stage Employees demanded that an extra stagehand be hired to look after the theater's asbestos curtain and electrical switchboard. Even this problem proved to be slight, for a compromise was reached whereby the wages of existing employees were raised and the union gave up their demand (MPW 25, no. 1 [3 July 1915]: 94).

30. LL 18 April 1915, p. 6.

31. LH 25 April 1915, sec. 2, p. 7. See Q. David Bowers, *Nickelodeon Theatres and Their Music* (Vestal, N.Y.: Vestal Press, 1986), pp. 129–89, for a discussion of organs and a range of other music machines used in motion picture theaters up to 1915. The Ben Ali is not included in Bowers' list of the various Hope Jones Unit Orchestras shipped by the Wurlitzer Company during this period.

32. For example, even as late as June 1913, the Colonial's advertising could include a detailed account, complete with photo, of its new singer, but no mention at all of the moving pictures being offered on the bill (LH 29 June 1913, p. 4).

33. LH 22 Aug. 1915, p. 3.

34. LH 7 Nov. 1915, p. 3.

35. The other principal way of remembering and memorializing the Opera House, particularly in later years, was as a site where international artists and the foremost theatrical stars "graced" the stage. In this view, Lexington stood as the "best one night stand in America" because of the Opera House and the sophisticated tastes of the local audience.

36. LH 12 Jan. 1916, pp. 1, 5.

37. LH 15 April 1917, p. 6.

38. This replacement of a livery stable by a movie theater jumps out as a fit trope for Lexington's movement into the twentieth century. Yet, in fact, the Strand made use of the original brick side walls of the stable, so the rather pat symbolism looks somewhat less tidy: was the past being incorporated, salvaged, or dismantled?

39. LH 1 Oct. 1922, p. 6.

40. MPW 11, no. 8 (24 Feb. 1912): 676; MPW 23, no. 10 (6 March 1915): 1470.

41. LL 31 Aug. 1915, p. 8.

42. LH 13 Oct. 1915, p. 5; MPW 27, no. 4 (22 Jan. 1916): 610–11.

43. LH 30 April 1916, sec. 4, p. 5.

44. LH 10 Oct. 1915, sec. 4, p. 3. Staiger notes that by 1916 the multiple-reel feature film had become standardized as the "dominant exhibition practice" (*Classical Hollywood Cinema*, p. 132).

45. This local film was called *The Manhaters;* see Appendix 1.

46. LL 19 July 1916, p. 8.

47. MPW 29, no. 7 (12 Aug. 1916): 1136.

48. James Duane Bolin, "Bossism and Reform: Politics in Lexington, Kentucky, 1880–1940," diss. (University of Kentucky, 1988), 70.

49. LL 24 Dec. 1916, p. 4.

50. LH 15 April 1917, p. 4.

51. LH 12 Nov. 1916, p. 12; LL 30 March 1917, p. 11.

52. LH 28 May 1916, p. 8.

53. LH 6 June 1916, p. 6.

54. LH 15 Aug. 1912, p. 12.

55. LH 11 Aug. 1913, p. 4.

56. Thompson, *Classical Hollywood Cinema*, p. 157.

57. LH 1 Nov. 1912, p. 5.

58. LH 27 Feb. 1918, p. 12.

59. LH 25 Jan. 1914, sec. 4, p. 4.

60. LH 30 April 1916, sec. 4, p. 5.

61. LL 20 May 1915, p. 4. See Miriam Hansen, *Babel and Babylon: Spectatorship in American Silent Film* (Cambridge, Mass.: Harvard University Press, 1991), pp. 67–69, on the "rhetoric of uplift." By 1915 this rhetoric expressed what was already a sort of missed opportunity according to the *Leader.*

62. LL 18 April 1912, p. 4. Compare W. Stephen Bush's comment in *Moving Picture World* in 1913: "the kinematograph," Bush wrote, "is the people's theater and the poor man's amusement" (MPW 16, no. 2 [12 April 1913]: 140).

63. LH 19 Jan. 1918, p. 8.

64. The films reviewed in local papers up to 1917 were: Edison's Talking Pictures, *Les Misér-*

ables, Neptune's Daughter, Cabiria, The Birth of a Nation, The Little Girl Next Door, Daughter of the Gods, and *Intolerance.* On early film reviewing, see Richard Koszarski, *An Evening's Entertainment: The Age of the Silent Feature Picture, 1915–1928* (New York: Scribner's, 1990), pp. 191–92.

65. LL 30 Jan. 1917, p. 5.

66. We cannot even take any single review as exemplary of local movie reviewing. For example, two reviews of *Intolerance,* one from the *Herald,* the other from the *Leader,* prove that substantial variation was possible even in the highly circumscribed mode of local film reviewing. The *Herald's* reviewer offered tempered praise for the film, but worried about Griffith's treatment of reformers (the *Herald* prided itself on its activist, progressive stance toward local reform) and wondered if in playing to the "excited gallery," Griffith had foregone "the real art of finished and sequent [sic] narrative" (LH 27 Feb. 1917, p. 8). The *Leader's* review voiced only unqualified condemnation of *Intolerance,* not on "narrative" grounds, but because Griffith in his "lame attempt to degrade mankind and blacken the history of the human family" was "animated by a deliberate purpose to distort history and mock Christianity" (LL 27 Feb. 1917, p. 7). Though both reviews take *Intolerance* seriously, they bring appreciably different sets of assumptions to bear on Griffith's film. The *Herald* reviewer held this photoplay up to aesthetic standards of completeness and coherency, regardless of what the easily moved gallery might desire. The *Leader's* reviewer demanded not so much formal "finish" or verisimilitude as truthfulness to an ideological system whose linchpin was a sanctified view of mankind, the family, and Christianity. Such truthfulness would inevitably be uplifting rather than degrading.

Chapter 6: Reform and Regulation

1. Roy Rosenzweig, *Eight Hours for What We Will: Workers and Leisure in an Industrial City, 1870–1920* (Cambridge: Cambridge University Press, 1983), p. 208.

2. See Lary May, *Screening Out the Past: The Birth of Mass Culture and the Motion Picture Industry* (New York: Oxford University Press, 1980), pp. 43–57, on urban reform movements and the movies. I found little evidence in Lexington to support May's contention that "small towns and rural areas" were deeply anxious about and alarmed by the prospect of motion pictures.

3. LL 5 May 1910, p. 7.

4. LH 5 May 1910, p. 7.

5. LL 9 May 1911, p. 9.

6. LH 12 June 1912, p. 12; LH 3 July 1912, sec. 2, p. 1; LH 14 Aug. 1912, p. 2.

7. LH 12 Jan. 1916, p. 5. In certain other areas of the country the situation was quite different. New York City, for example, passed an elaborately detailed ordinance in 1913 governing the construction and operation of airdomes (open-air theaters) and motion picture theaters with fewer than six hundred seats. This ordinance specified, among other requirements, that all such venues must provide toilets "separate for sexes" and, when appropriate, heating to a temperature not less than 62 degrees or more than 70 degrees (MPW 17, no. 5 [4 Aug. 1913]: 526–27). State legislation was another option, and a series of articles in *Moving Picture World* in 1914–15 listed state-by-state all laws that dealt not only with safety but also license fees, qualifications for operators, and censorship practices. The only such law in Kentucky was a county license fee, depending on the size of the city. (This amounted to $20 a year per theater in Lexington.) Otherwise, "the [Kentucky] laws applying to common shows regulate the moving picture houses" (MPW 23, no. 3 [16 Jan. 1915]: 357). In its lack of state laws specifically concerned with moving picture theaters, Kentucky was comparable to a good number of other states, including Alabama, Arkansas, Colorado, Minnesota, New Hampshire, Nevada, and Nebraska. This series starts in MPW 22, no. 8 (21 Nov. 1914): 1061–62 and runs through several later issues: MPW 22, no. 10 (5 Dec. 1914): 1372; MPW 22, no. 12 (19 Dec. 1914): 1667; MPW 24, no. 10 (5 June 1915): 1610; and MPW 25, no. 4 (24 July 1915): 664. Earlier efforts at

imposing government safety standards are surveyed in Charles Musser, *The Emergence of Cinema: The American Screen to 1907* (New York: Scribner's, 1990), pp. 443–44. In 1916 a bill providing for statewide moving picture theater safety codes was introduced in the Kentucky legislature, but it "died with hardly a gasp" (MPW 28, no. 1 [1 April 1916]: 19). The newly appointed state fire marshal then simply announced that he would begin enforcing fire-prevention regulations; according to *Moving Picture World*, these would most affect "small theaters in isolated districts" rather than venues in Lexington or Louisville (MPW 29, no. 6 [5 Aug. 1916]: 903; MPW 29, no. 8 [19 Aug. 1916]: 1275).

8. LH 26 April 1912, p. 1.

9. For information on the 1913 Kentucky Motion Picture Exhibitors League convention, see MPW 16, no. 6 (10 May 1913): 578; and MPW 17, no. 2 (12 July 1913): 162–63. By 1914, when the convention returned to Lexington, the membership had grown to around two hundred (LH 21 April 1914, p. 11). Both Ramsey and Stamper were often delegates to national meetings of this organization as well.

10. Eileen Bowser, *The Transformation of Cinema 1907–1915* (New York: Scribner's, 1990), p. 85.

11. On the anti-saloon campaign in Lexington, see Thomas H. Appleton, Jr., "'Like Banquo's Ghost': The Emergence of the Prohibition Issue in Kentucky Politics," diss. (University of Kentucky, 1981), 63–66, 93–94.

12. This topic was not restricted to the pulpit. When the local Colored Debating Club met for the first time in March 1901, it addressed the question: "Has the stage a moral tendency?" (LL 2 March 1901, p. 3).

13. LH 6 May 1907, p. 8.

14. LH 4 Oct. 1909, p. 10.

15. LL 11 March 1912, p. 4.

16. LL 6 July 1913, sec., p. 1; LL 11 Feb. 1913, p. 3. These opinions apparently had little effect on theater owners. By the end of 1913, one local theater was prominently advertising "Motion Picture Dance Lessons," with "practical instruction in the tango, turkey trot and Viennese hesitation waltz" (LL 18 Dec. 1913, p. 3).

17. LH 4 June 1913, p. 7.

18. LL 5 June 1906, p. 2.

19. LL 12 Feb. 1908, p. 8.

20. LL 12 Oct. 1911, p. 1.

21. LL 1 Feb. 1912, p. 10.

22. LH 29 Sept. 1914, p. 1. James H. Timberlake, *Prohibition and the Progressive Movement, 1900–1920* (New York: Atheneum, 1970), pp. 150–51, notes that the South was the strongest area for temperance reform, so that by 1908 more than half of the counties in Kentucky and other border states had voted to go dry. While Lexington voters defeated prohibitionist initiatives, Birmingham, Alabama, Jackson, Mississippi, and Asheville, Charlotte, and Durham, North Carolina all voted to go saloonless.

23. LH 22 Jan. 1912, p. 1.

24. LH 31 Jan. 1912, p. 5. Along with its usual amusement ads, the *Leader* on Sunday, February 4 1912 reprinted "A Protest against Sunday Closing" from the *Motion Picture Story Magazine*. Obviously this piece was germane to the local debate then shaping up, and it was, the *Leader* noted, "reprinted by request," though the actual requester was not identified.

25. LL 6 Feb. 1912, p. 9.

26. LH 20 Sept. 1911, p. 6.

27. MPW 10, no 12 (23 Dec. 1911): 969. Bowser notes that "Sunday closing laws were a topic of warm interest throughout the period [1907–15] . . . where Sunday movie showings were permitted, exhibitors took pains to show particularly educational films and hired lecturers for their showing even

if they could not afford them the rest of the week" (*Transformation of Cinema*, p. 48). *Moving Picture World* throughout this period often reported and editorialized on sabbatarian campaigns across the country. See, for example, reports as early as 1907 on the controversy over Sunday screenings in Brooklyn (MPW 1, no. 34 [26 Oct. 1907]: 539); Bush's series, "The Campaign for a Modern Sunday" (MPW 11, no. 8 [24 Feb. 1912]: 658–59; MPW 11, no. 9 [2 March 1912]: 759; MPW 11, no. 10 [9 March 1912]: 845); other Bush editorials (e.g., "Sunday Openings—A New Departure" [MPW 24, no. 8 (15 May 1915): 1232]); and an editorial cartoon entitled "The Fight for a Modern Sunday," in which the opponent of Sunday movies is a "Bigot" preventing a kid from watching "pictures of China," while the *World* itself appears in the allegorical guise of a classical figure defending "freedom of the screen" (MPW 27, no. 5 [5 Feb. 1916]: 825).

28. LL 19 Sept. 1911, p. 1.

29. LH 17 Feb. 1913, p. 8; MPW 15, no. 9 (1 March 1913): 903. When the Kentucky Motion Picture Exhibitors League met in Louisville in April 1913, high on its agenda was "combating or quelling the agitation against Sunday performances. This has been marked in Lexington and other Central Kentucky cities recently. Sundays are big days with the exhibitors, and they would suffer a severe blow were they forced to suspend on that day" (MPW 16, no. 1 [5 April 1913]: 66).

30. LL 4 Feb. 1913, p. 7; LH 6 Feb. 1913, p. 1.

31. LL 11 Feb. 1913, p. 10; MPW 15, no. 11 (15 March 1913): 1116.

32. LH 8 Feb. 1913, p. 4; LL 9 Feb. 1913, p. 5.

33. LH 18 Feb. 1913, p. 5.

34. LL 21 May 1913, p. 1.

35. The fight for strict enactment of blue laws also carried over to the Kentucky state legislature, where early in 1914, for example, two bills were introduced to prohibit Sunday picture shows. According to *Moving Picture World*'s Louisville correspondent, "the House Committee on Kentucky statutes decided . . . to report unfavorably on the bills prohibiting moving picture shows, baseball games, and other Sunday amusements" (MPW 19, no. 8 [21 Feb. 1914]: 982). Such actions only boosted sabbatarian campaigns at the local level.

36. LH 9 March 1914, p. 1.

37. Berryman at this date was chairman of the Lexington Business Association, the major "wet" organization in the city, but there seems to be no reason why he would intentionally want to provoke churchgoing sabbatarians (who also were very likely to be prohibitionists). In fact, he would in 1916 serve on the Lexington Vice Commission with several of the same people who protested against the Sunday vaudeville shows he attempted to introduce.

38. LH 23 Feb. 1914, pp. 1, 3.

39. LL 14 Feb. 1914, p. 4.

40. LL 16 Feb. 1914, p. 4.

41. *Abstract, Thirteenth Census of the United States, 1910* (Washington, D.C.: Government Printing Office, 1912), table 2, p. 620. It is also telling that the total number of wage earners employed by and the total amount of capital invested in what the census broadly identified as Lexington's "manufacturing" concerns had by 1909 actually decreased slightly from the already low totals of 1904 (*Manufactures, Thirteenth Census of the United States, 1910* [Washington, D.C.: Government Printing Office, 1912], vol. 9, table 1, p. 409).

42. LL 16 Feb. 1914, p. 4.

43. LL 3 March 1914, p. 1.

44. *Idea*, 12 March 1914, p. 4.

45. Joseph R. Gusfield, *Symbolic Crusade: Status Politics and the American Temperance Movement* (Urbana: University of Illinois Press, 1966), pp. 173, 19, 177.

46. Gusman, *Symbolic Crusade*, p. 87.

47. MPW 15, no. 9 (1 March 1913): 903.

48. MPW 16, no. 6 (10 May 1913): 612; MPW 19, no. 7 (14 Feb. 1914): 827.

49. MPW 27, no. 9 (4 March 1916): 1510.

50. MPW 23, no. 8 (20 Feb. 1915): 1167.

51. LL 6 Feb. 1915, p. 1; MPW 23, no. 9 (27 Feb. 1915): 1320.

52. *Moving Picture World* during this period is filled with references to Crafts' activities on behalf of federal censorship. According to Terry Ramsaye, "the Reverend Mr. Crafts was violently aggressive, always sincere and sometimes misinformed in his extravagant enthusiasms" (*A Million and One Nights* [1926; rpt. New York: Simon and Schuster, 1986], p. 482. Musser notes that Crafts had been involved with the very first protests mounted against fight films in 1897 (*Emergence of Cinema*, p. 195).

53. LH 12 March 1915, p. 1; LL 14 March 1915, p. 1; LH 15 March 1915, p. 1.

54. LH 28 March 1915, sec. 3, p. 4.

55. LH 14 March 1915, p. 4.

56. LH 15 March 1915, p. 1.

57. LH 11 Jan. 1916, p. 5.

58. *Moving Picture World* provides much information about censorship of motion pictures on the local, state, and federal levels between 1907 and the late 1910s. Of course, this exhibitors' trade magazine had a vested interest in this issue, and its adamant anti-censorship position is evident in "news" articles as well as a host of editorials such as "ABC of Censorship" (MPW 15, no. 11 [15 March 1913]: 1081); "Why Is a Censor?" (MPW 16, no. 6 [10 May 1913]: 572); and "Are We Outlaws?" (MPW 23, no. 10 [6 March 1915]: 1582–83). *Moving Picture World* was particularly concerned with mobilizing the industry to combat proposed federal censorship of the movies; to this end it even offered for sale sets of colored "Anti-Censorship Slides," which were designed to be shown in theaters so as to "help create a strong public sentiment against this unnecessary and un-American form of legislation" (MPW 28, no. [1 April 1916]: 177). Bowser, like most historians of this period, devotes some attention to censorship, emphasizing the activities of the National Board of Censorship (*Transformation of Cinema*, pp. 48–52). See also Nancy J. Rosenbloom, "Between Reformers and Regulation: The Struggle over Film Censorship in Progressive America, 1901–1922," *Film History* 1 (1987): 307–25; and Charles Matthew Feldman, *The National Board of Censorship (Review) of Motion Pictures: 1909–1922* (New York: Arno Press, 1977), pp. 58–86, for background information on the "censorship battle on state and local levels" in 1911–15. Kathy Peiss focuses on attempts to "regulate" gender relations in the movies (*Cheap Amusements: Working Women and Leisure in Turn-of-the-Century New York* [Philadelphia: Temple University Press, 1986], pp. 158–62. Garth Jowett in *Film: The Democratic Art* (Boston: Focal Press, 1976), pp. 113–19, offers information on municipal and state censorship.

59. LH 6 April 1903, pp. 1, 6.

60. LL 7 June 1903, p. 5.

61. LH 5 May 1899, p. 7.

62. LL 24 Dec 1896, p. 4.

63. LL 27 May 1903, p. 3.

64. Such claims continued to be a feature of entertainment advertising, particularly for fairs and tent shows. The midway exhibitions at the Colored A & M Fair in 1916, for example, were touted as being "clean, wholesome and up-to-the-minute, nothing of an offensive nature being tolerated" (LL 27 Aug. 1916, sec. 4, p. 4).

65. LL 17 March 1907, p. 8; LH 2 Dec. 1907, p. 5.

66. LL 3 Nov. 1907, p. 19.

67. LL 30 Aug. 1907, p. 10; LH 21 Oct. 1906, sec. 3, p. 6.

68. LL 11 Oct. 1908, p. 26.

69. LH 25 April 1909, p. 8. See also LH 29 Dec. 1909, p. 7. On the formation and policies of

the board, see, for example, Feldman, *National Board of Censorship,* pp. 20–41; an early public policy statement by the board (MPW 5, no. 16 (16 Oct. 1909): 524–25; and an interview with John Collier, general secretary of the board (MPW 16, no. 1 [5 April 1913]: 25–26.

70. Judging from Lexington, the Motion Picture Patents Company (MPPC) was quite successful at generating positive national publicity. Syndicated articles in both local papers heralded the MPPC's endorsement of censorship efforts in March 1909 (LH 20 March 1909, p. 1; LL 20 March 1909, p. 3), and a June 1909 column that dealt with local amusements lauded the stringent policies of the Board of Censorship (LL 20 June 1909, p. 15). Comparable pieces appeared several times during the next few years, including a *Leader* editorial in July 1913 that noted with approval the existence of the board and advised that it be diligent in protecting "the minds of the rising generation" (LH 8 July 1913, p. 4).

71. LH 22 Sept. 1911, p. 6; LH 4 April 1915, sec. 2, p. 4.

72. LL 19 May 1912, p. 6.

73. LL 6 July 1910, p. 1.

74. LH 7 July 1910, p. 1.

75. The only Kentucky cities that did not issue comparable bans were Frankfort and Covington. On the larger response to the Johnson-Jeffries fight film, see Dan Streible, "A History of the Boxing Film, 1894–1915: Social Control and Social Reform in the Progressive Era," *Film History* 3 (1989): 241–47.

76. One of the few times when a Lexington exhibitor publicly announced that he would not book a particularly controversial motion picture also involved Jack Johnson. In December 1912 Ramsey demonstrated his sense of social (and racial) responsibility by announcing that he would not book at his theaters any motion pictures of Johnson's marriage to a white woman (LH 6 Dec. 1912, p. 5).

77. LH 10 Sept. 1912, p. 5.

78. MPW 13, no. 6 (10 Aug. 1912): 522.

79. Jowett concludes that throughout the silent period, "the great majority" of local censorship duties "were left to the police department" (*Film: The Democratic Art,* p. 114).

80. LL 16 Sept. 1912, p. 1.

81. In Portland, Oregon, for example, the "Advisory Committee on Motion Picture Shows" formed in March 1911 included twenty-eight volunteer "viewers" who watched an average of 128 total reels per week at the city's five film exchanges (William Trufant Foster, "Vaudeville and Motion Picture Shows: A Study of Theaters in Portland, Oregon," Reed College *Social Servis [sic] Series* 2 (1914): 29–30).

82. LL 7 Oct. 1913, p. 3.

83. See *Report of the Vice Commission of Lexington, Kentucky* (Lexington: J. L. Richardson & Company, 1915).

84. Before it reached Lexington, *Hippocrites* was an important, controversial text in various censorship debates. It was, for example, banned by the mayor of Minneapolis (MPW 24, no. 5 [1 May 1915]: 761) and declared to be "not immoral" by a jury in San Jose, California, which overruled the judgment of city officials (MPW 24, no. 8 [22 May 1915]: 1293). Exhibitors in Corsicana, Texas, attempted to get around the protests of local ministers by segregating screenings by gender and then by billing *Hippocrites* "like a circus" rather than a motion picture (MPW 24, no. 3 [17 April 1915]: 375). According to *Moving Picture World*'s correspondent, exhibitors in Louisville feared that the booking of *Hippocrites* in the city would lead to the establishment of "the dreaded censorship board arrangement" (MPW 25, no. 6 [7 Aug. 1915]: 1028). The expected furor did not occur, and *Hippocrites* was even scheduled for three additional days in Louisville after the controversy in Lexington over the film had begun (MPW 26, no. 1 [2 Oct. 1915]: 105). George Bleich, who ran the Empress Theater in Owensboro, Kentucky, came up with an alternative solution to the problem of *Hippocrites.* He

previewed it for members of the Women's Club, three pastors, the mayor, and the local press, and promised to follow their recommendations. They found no fault with the film, which then brought in "monster patronage at advanced prices." Even if *Hippocrites* was rejected, Bleich figured he would come out on top, since by closing he would "gain in the estimation of the public" because of his own vigilance. The moral of Bleich's story, according to Epes Winthrop Sargent in *Moving Picture World*, was that "deliberate action" was much more effective than "hasty and ill-considered" confrontations with local censors (MPW 26, no. 5 [30 Oct. 1915]: 806).

85. MPW 25, no. 12 (18 Sept. 1915): 2025.

86. LH 3 Sept. 1915, p. 9.

87. City Council *Minutes,* 3 Sept. 1914 (reel 11, p. 138).

88. MPW 25, no. 13 (25 Sept. 1915): 2213.

89. City Council *Minutes,* 7 Sept. 1915 (reel 11, p. 153); LH 13 Sept. 1915, p. 1; LH 14 Sept. 1915, p. 12; MPW 26, no. 1 (2 Oct. 1915): 105). See Appendix 2 for a full transcript of this ordinance.

90. Local censorship, as might be expected, could vary considerably, even in Kentucky. In Bell County, adjacent to Cincinnati and home to the city of Newport, the censorship board was composed of the probation officer and two county patrolmen (MPW 24, no. 8 [22 May 1915]: 1299). In Louisville a privately organized "Censorship Board of Motion Pictures for Children" began its activities in April 1915 and particularly promoted regular children's shows (MPW 24, no. 1 [3 April 1915]: 93). This group was headed and staffed entirely by women and was linked to the Kentucky Federation of Women's Clubs (MPW 24, no. 10 [5 June 1915]: 1647). City ordinances could also be quite diverse and considerably more precise than Lexington in terms of what constituted taboo subjects. In the eastern Kentucky mountain town of Pineville, for instance, an ordinance declared it "unlawful for any owner, manager, or operator of any theater, carnival, circus or other place of amusement in the city to exhibit any moving pictures wherein is depicted tragic or murderous feud scenes" (MPW 19, no. 8 [21 Feb. 1914]: 982).

91. LL 27 Feb. 1916, p. 4

92. LL 29 Feb. 1916, p. 10.

93. LH 8 March 1916, p. 4.

94. LL 28 Feb. 1916, p. 1; MPW 27, no. 11 (18 March 1916): 1866.

95. Clearly the board of education, like most other advocates of censorship in Lexington, was most concerned with local measures, not with the creation of a state board of censors, such as was proposed in an unsuccessful bill submitted to the legislature by a Louisville representative in mid-February 1916 [MPW 27, no. 9 (4 March 1916): 1510]).

96. LL 29 Feb. 1916, p. 1; LH 29 Feb. 1916, p. 7.

97. LH 14 Feb. 1916, p. 7; LH 2 March 1916, sec. 2, p. 4.

98. LL 29 Feb. 1916, p. 1. Stamper's faith in the moral acuity of his immediate family did not prevent him from making public points for the Orpheum by requesting the Board of Censors to preview a film entitled *Born of the People.* Acting on the board's recommendation, Stamper promised to cut one scene featuring a "nude model" from this three-reel film, thereby forestalling any potential complaints and gaining a front page commendation from the *Leader* (LL 18 March 1916, p. 1).

99. Richard Koszarski notes that exhibitors on occasion cut films "more severely than any censor" (*An Evening's Entertainment: The Age of the Silent Feature Picture, 1915–1928* [New York: Scribner's, 1990], p. 61).

100. LL 6 March 1916, p. 7.

101. LH 10 March 1916, p. 8.

102. The line between educational motion pictures and advertising films was fine indeed. In 1913 the Princess, for instance, screened an "educational" film that detailed how stoves are constructed. This film was produced by the Detroit Stove Works, and the screening coincided with a

special sale on this company's stoves at a local department store (LL 27 Feb. 1913, p. 2). Or, in a less literal sense, consider what ideological values were being "advertised" in certain nonfictional, noncommercial motion pictures specially screened for school children, for example, the Civic League's "city beautiful" films mentioned in Chapter 4 or the "historical pictures" designed to "inspire patriotism in the young" sponsored by the Daughters of the American Revolution at a Saturday morning children's show at the Strand (LL 28 March 1916, p. 8).

103. LL 21 June 1914, sec. 4, p. 1; LH 25 Nov. 1912, p. 6.

104. LL 11 April 1914, p. 4. Other "non-commercial agencies" that used motion pictures in Kentucky included the state penitentiary in Frankfort, where in December 1911 motion pictures began to be shown to inmates in the chapel: "only the well-behaved will be allowed to see the show. Wild West pictures, hold ups, and similar films will, of course, be tabooed" (MPW 10, no. 11 [16 Dec. 1911): 913–14. Moving Picture World also reported in February 1915 that a large state-run "insane asylum" near Louisville had been screening comedy films on a weekly basis for over two years, and these films "have the effect of educating the patients to some extent and get their minds working in normal channels" (MPW 23, no. 9 [27 Feb. 1915]: 1320).

105. LH 1 March 1916, p. 5.

106. LH 27 April 1917, p. 3. Particularly before the debate over federal censorship took center stage, Moving Picture World frequently argued that producers and exhibitors should strive to uplift the public's taste. See, for instance, Louis Reeves Harrison, "Much More Than That" (MPW 17, no. 6 [9 Aug. 1913]: 612), which announced that "the men of this paper have consistently combated what is primitive, putrid or brutal in this splendid new means of communicating thought, have conceived life to be something better than an existence of vengeance and slaughter, have hoped that the beauty, grandeur and charm of our God-given progression might be communicated to those whose dark hours need illumination." Cassidy's views can also be compared to the opinion of Francis R. North, field secretary of the Playground and Recreation Association of America. "There is," North warned, "another real danger because of the mediocrity of many films in respect to good taste and dramatic or other educational value. Such conditions likewise constitute a lost educational opportunity. Taste is lowered and mental alertness deadened by constant attendance at picture shows of this character, even though in the course of an evening's program there may be no features which can positively be termed harmful" (A Recreation Survey of the City of Providence, Rhode Island, [Providence: Providence Playground Association, 1912], p. 59).

107. LH 25 March 1916, p. 6; MPW 28, no. 3 (15 April 1916): 481.

108. MPW 28, no. 4 (22 April 1918): 662. For an example of a model "progressive" motion picture ordinance, see Shelby M. Harrison, Recreation in Springfield, Illinois (Springfield: Russell Sage Foundation, 1914), pp. 124–26, which called for no combination motion picture-and-vaudeville performances; for segregated seating for all unaccompanied children under sixteen years old; and for both city inspectors and also a citizens committee to check for any "offense against morality, decency, or the public welfare."

109. LL 16 April 1916, p. 4.

110. LH 23 Feb. 1916, p. 1.

111. LH 15 March 1915, p. 4; LL 14 March 1915, p. 3.

112. Rosenzweig notes that "for many reformers," particularly those concerned with play and leisure, "the entire working class appeared as a group of children whose behavior needed to be reshaped and controlled" (Eight Hours for What We Will, p. 144).

113. The president of Reed College, investigating vaudeville and moving picture shows in Portland, Oregon, in 1914, put the matter in this way: "nearly all the plays in the legitimate theaters, nearly all the vaudeville acts, nearly all the motion pictures are intended for adults. They are not adapted for children. This is unfortunate because so many children attend, and because the effect of

all these performances on children is of far greater significance to society than the effect on adults" (Foster, *Vaudeville and Motion Picture Shows*, p. 41).

114. See the discussion of the Playground Association of America in Cary Goodman, *Choosing Sides: Street Life on the Lower East Side* (New York: Schocken, 1979), pp. 61–80.

115. Shelby M. Harrison, for instance, found that 85 percent of the high school students in Springfield attended the movies, averaging about 1.75 visits per week (*Recreation in Springfield*, pp. 40–41). In Milwaukee, according to Rowland Haynes' calculations, 40 percent of the motion picture audience on Sundays was under fifteen years old, while young people between fifteen and twenty-five years of age constituted the largest segment of the audience for all motion picture and vaudeville shows ("Recreation Survey," *Bulletin of the Milwaukee Bureau of Economy and Efficiency* 17 [March 1912], pp. 10–11). Similarly, investigators in Portland, Oregon, ascertained that 90 percent of all schoolchildren went to the movies, often at night, and 28 percent of these children attended twice a week or more (Foster, *Vaudeville and Motion Picture Shows*, p. 17). In Waltham, Massachusetts, however, less than 20 percent of the total audience was made up of children under sixteen years old, and these children virtually always attended in the afternoon. The Waltham survey also noted that twice as many females attended as males (Francis R. North, *A Recreation Survey of the City of Waltham, Massachusetts* [Waltham, Massachusetts: E. L. Barry, 1913], pp. 60–61).

116. Dudley H. Starns, "A Study of the Relation of the Motion-Picture to the Work and Deportment of Pupils in the School," master's thesis (University of Kentucky, 1917), pp. 1, 22.

117. Louise de Koven Bowen, "Five and Ten Cent Theatres: Two Investigations by the Juvenile Protective Association of Chicago" (1910–11), pp. 2, 4–5.

118. LH 15 Dec. 1912, p. 7.

119. LL 1 Oct. 1916, p. 1. A different sort of effect was noted by Lexington's head librarian, when she arranged for illustrated readings of fairy tales at the library: "children are so interested in the 'movies' that we have found that a lecture not illustrated will not attract them as readily as one in which pictures are used" (LH 19 Dec. 1914, p. 6).

120. MPW 23, no. 3 (16 Jan. 1915): 401; MPW 24, no. 7 (15 May 1915): 1119.

121. LL 9 Feb. 1913, p. 9.

122. LL 26 Aug. 1917, p. 1.

123. LH 19 Nov. 1916, p. 6.

124. Some of the same types noted in this *Herald* article are also listed in a *Moving Picture World* account of moving picture audiences, except that for the trade magazine the person who reads titles aloud or "barks when he laughs" or brings a crying infant to the show is grouped with the masher and the drunk as a problem that must be solved by the efforts of the theater manager (MPW 23, no. 5 [30 Jan. 1915]: 710).

125. Lawrence W. Levine, *Highbrow/Lowbrow: The Emergence of Cultural Hierarchy in America* (Cambridge: Harvard University Press, 1988), pp. 195–98. Similarly, Hansen argues that the "implementation of the rule of silence in the motion picture shows" during the nickelodeon era "contributed to the cultural homogenization of a mass audience" (*Babel and Babylon*, p. 95).

126. See Thomas Cripps, *Slow Fade to Black: The Negro in American Film, 1900–1942* (New York: Oxford University Press, 1977), pp. 41–69; and Richard Schickel, *D. W. Griffith: An American Life* (New York: Simon & Schuster, 1984), pp. 246–47, 271–93.

127. Of course, it is not surprising that there was much public discussion in Lexington of *The Birth of a Nation*, which bore all the marks of a highly "controversial" text. Maybe the telling point is to note just what passed for noncontroversial, run-of-the-mill films in March 1916: these included, for example, *Blue Blood, but Black Skin* ("a real old time black face comedy"); *Marse Covington* (a drama of the "romantic South"); *The Suppressed Order* (a Civil War drama); and *Fighting Blood* (based on "My Old Kentucky Home"). Janet Staiger, in *Interpreting Films: Studies in the Historical Reception*

of American Cinema (Princeton: Princeton University Press, 1992), pp. 139–46, examines the national reception of Griffith's film.

128. LL 21 Feb. 1916, p. 1. Louisville's mayor, in contrast, simply declared that his administration would not "suppress" Griffith's film (MPW 27, no. 10 [11 March 1916]: 1683). The NAACP also argued that screening *The Birth of a Nation* constituted a "threat to public safety." The Los Angeles chapter of the NAACP first attempted to obtain an injunction against the premiere of the film on the grounds that "the picture might so heighten racial tensions as to lead to riots" (Schickel, *D. W. Griffith*, p. 246).

129. See, among other readings of the film, Michael Rogin, "'The Sword Became a Flashing Vision': D. W. Griffith's *The Birth of a Nation*," *Representations* 9 (Winter 1985): 150–95.

130. City Council *Minutes* 25 Feb. 1916 (reel 11, p. 397).

131. LL 27 Feb. 1916, p. 2.

132. City Council *Minutes* 7 March 1916 (reel 11, p. 415).

133. LL 17 March 1916, p. 1; MPW 28, no. 2 (8 April 1916): 299. In January 1916 Lexington representative W. C. G. Hobbs introduced a revised version of the *Uncle Tom's Cabin* statute in the state legislature; this revision, supported by the Daughters of the Confederacy, would have expanded the law specifically to include motion pictures (LH 19 Jan. 1916, p. 1).

134. LL 7 March 1916, p. 1.

135. LL 28 Feb. 1916, p. 4.

136. LH 27 Feb. 1927, p. 5.

137. Cripps, *Slow Fade to Black*, pp. 56–63.

138. LH 26 Feb. 1916, p. 4.

139. Simmons had appeared in the city on 3 January 1916 to address a rally on Emancipation Day, and the local chapter of the Tuskegee Club was quite active, hosting one of Booker T. Washington's sons earlier in February (LL 16 Feb. 1916, p. 8).

140. LH 28 Feb. 1916, p. 16.

141. LH 15 March 1916, p. 5.

142. LL 13 March 1916, p. 6.

143. See James C. Klotter, *The Breckinridges of Kentucky: 1760–1981* (Lexington: University Press of Kentucky, 1986), pp. 208–43; and Melba Porter Hay, "The Lexington Civic League: Agent of Reform, 1900–1910," *Filson Club History Quarterly* 62, no. 3 (July 1988), 336–55.

144. LH 5 July 1912, p. 4.

145. See Idus A. Newby, *Jim Crow's Defense: Anti-Negro Thought in America, 1900–1930* (Baton Rouge: Louisiana State University Press, 1965).

146. LH 29 Feb. 1916, p. 4.

147. LH 12 March 1916, sec. 2, p. 4.

148. An advance "force of advertising men" arrived in town on March 9, but I could find no evidence of precisely what sort of posters, billboards, or theater displays were used to sell *The Birth of a Nation* in Lexington, though one bookstore ran ads tieing the film to Thomas Dixon's novel (LL 19 March 1916, sec. 4, p. 5). The promoters of the film were no doubt also responsible for placing two rather long articles (not identified as advertisements) in local papers: a biographical profile of Kentucky-born Griffith, the "gentle, unassuming, neighborly" "Genius of the Screen" (LH 17 March 1916, p. 12); and an unqualified endorsement of *The Birth of a Nation* by the Reverend Charles Parkhurst, a prominent New York City Presbyterian minister and anti-vice crusader, whose statement had been used by Griffith and his colleagues in defending the film against NAACP objections (see Schickel, *D. W. Griffith*, pp. 286–87). If Griffith's scrapbooks on *The Birth of a Nation* are any clue, both of these articles were consistently used in promoting the film in the Midwest as well as the South (see D. W. Griffith Papers, series 3, Publicity Scrapbooks, box 24).

149. Obviously, Griffith and his associates did not seek to attract black spectators, though pre-

sumably the Opera House gallery remained open to blacks as it had always been. That it was at least possible for Lexington's blacks to see the film is suggested by the fact that the PTA at a colored elementary school resolved to use its "utmost efforts to have the Negroes of Lexington refrain from attending" *The Birth of a Nation* (LL 12 March 1916, sec. 4, p. 6).

150. LL 26 March 1916, p. 1. *The Birth of a Nation* was also a great success in Louisville, but the protest there continued after the film had begun its two-week engagement at Macaulay's Theater. During this engagement, the manager of the theater was arrested for violating the *Uncle Tom's Cabin* statute. This action was initiated by a local attorney who, according to *Moving Picture World*, was really prompted by "prominent negroes" in the city (MPW 27, no. 10 [11 March 1916]: 1683).

151. LH 21 March 1916, p. 10.

152. LL 22 March 1916, p. 1.

153. LH 21 March 1916, p. 16.

154. LL 21 March 1916, p. 14. These reviews basically parallel the initial reviews of *The Birth of a Nation* that Schickel summarizes (*D. W. Griffith*, pp. 276–80).

155. LH 27 March 1916, p. 16.

156. LH 8 Sept. 1916, p. 5.

Chapter 7: Black Moviegoing, 1907–1916

1. MPW 1, no. 14 (8 June 1907): 216–17. Thanks to Charles Musser for pointing out this reference.

2. MPW 1, no. 38 (23 Nov. 1907): 619.

3. See Charles Musser, *Before the Nickelodeon: Edwin S. Porter and the Edison Manufacturing Company* (Berkeley: University of California Press, 1991), pp. 312–14.

4. According to the Chicago *Defender*, 9 August 1913, p. 6, William Foster was "refused support by monied men of the race. Finally a white gentleman loaned him enough money to get the machine. These pictures [*The Railroad Porter*] are the first to be placed on the market by a member of the race."

5. IF 8 Aug. 1908, p. 5; MPW 3, no. 25 (19 Dec. 1908): 502.

6. IF 11 Sept. 1909, p. 6; IF 23 Oct. 1909, p. 5; IF 8 Aug. 1909, p. 5.

7. IF 13 March 1909, p. 5.

8. IF 7 May 1910, p. 6.

9. Louisville's Odd Fellows Theater, for example, initially featured local amateur performers in addition to motion pictures, then over the next several months it changed names (to the Thirteenth Street Theater, the New Odd Fellows Theater, and the New Pekin) and started to feature "real Negro vaudeville." There is also no way of determining how many tent shows there were that featured moving pictures with or without vaudeville acts, like the one opened in 1908 by the black principal of the Negro school in Pine Bluff, Arkansas, much to the chagrin of the white residents of the town (MPW 2, no. 23 [6 June 1908]: 490).

10. IF 20 May 1911, p. 5. See also, for example, the theater section of the Chicago *Defender*, 17 June 1911, p. 4, which includes ads for the Monogram as well as the New Grand ("Built for the Colored People") and the Phoenix ("First Class Colored Orchestra").

11. *Abstract, Thirteenth Census of the United States 1910* (Washington, D.C.: Government Printing Office, 1912), table 2, p. 620.

12. *Population, Thirteenth Census* (Washington, D.C.: General Printing Office, 1912), vol. 2, table 2, p. 752.

13. *Abstract, Thirteenth Census*, table 14, p. 86. By way of contrast, here are some 1910 census figures for other cities in the 30,000–40,000 population range (table 19, pp. 95–96):

	Foreign-born residents	Black residents
Lexington, Ky.	2.7%	31.4%
San Diego, Calif.	18.6%	1.5%
Joliet, Il.	30.1%	1.4%
Cedar Rapids, Iowa	16.2%	0.6%
Quincy, Mass.	33.3%	0.1%
Galveston, Tex.	16.7%	21.7%
Huntington, W.Va.	1.6%	6.7%
Butte, Mont.	32.9%	0.1%
Niagara Falls, N.Y.	39.6%	0.9%

14. George C. Wright, *A History of Blacks in Kentucky: In Pursuit of Equality, 1890–1980* (Frankfort: Kentucky Historical Society, 1992), p. 61.

15. LH 13 Aug. 1906, p. 6.

16. *The Clansman* subsequently met with black protest in Washington, D.C., New York City, Philadelphia, and Norfolk. See IF 20 Jan. 1906, pp. 1, 6; IF 17 Feb. 1906, p. 2; IF 13 Oct. 1906, p. 5; IF 27 Oct. 1906, p. 6; IF 22 June 1907, p. 4.

17. LL 18 Jan. 1906, p. 4.

18. John Dittmer, *Black Georgia in the Progressive Era: 1900–1920* (Urbana: University of Illinois Press, 1977), pp. 66–67.

19. LL 18 Jan. 1906, p. 4. Lexington's daily (white) newspapers frequently reaffirmed the same sort of distinctions, both in terms of their reporting of black activities (which, broadly speaking, were depicted as exemplary, farcical, or criminal) and in their use of specific phrases like the "colored elite" (LL 10 May 1900, p. 7). For an overview of social class distinctions in various black communities during this period, see: George C. Wright, *Life behind a Veil: Blacks in Louisville, Kentucky 1865–1930* (Baton Rouge: Louisiana State University Press, 1985), pp. 134–39, on the "social elite" in Louisville; David A. Gerber, *Black Ohio and the Color Line 1860–1915* (Urbana: University of Illinois Press, 1976), pp. 325–30, on the black "upper classes" and the phenomenon of "passing" in Ohio; Kenneth L. Kusmer, *A Ghetto Takes Shape: Black Cleveland, 1870–1930* (Urbana: University of Illinois Press, 1976), pp. 91–112, on the "Negro elite" and the middle class in Cleveland; and Dittmer, *Black Georgia,* pp. 59–62, on social clubs and class structure in Georgia.

20. LL 26 Feb. 1907, p. 6; LH 23 Jan. 1905, p. 5; LL 26 Jan. 1905, p. 1.

21. IF 12 Sept. 1908, p. 1; IF 3 Oct. 1908, p. 7; LH 12 Sept. 1908, p. 1.

22. LL 5 June 1909, p. 6. The leisure time of white as well as black children was thought to require socially acceptable filling and regulation, and from 1898 on there was a highly vocal, reformist drive in Lexington for a centralized, citywide park and playground system. But public oratory was one thing and "natural" priorities another. The Lexington Civic League did not begin sponsoring a black playground until July 1912, and the city did not purchase land for a black park until March 1915. The same rule held true for the private sector: the Lexington (white) YMCA facilities—complete with swimming pool and spacious auditorium—were open for several years before even a temporary Colored YMCA began operating in 1905, and it was not until 1907 that permanent space was leased for the Colored YMCA.

23. For a discussion of the National Negro Business League and Washington's notion of "black capitalism," see Gerber, *Black Ohio,* pp. 378–90; and Lester C. Lamon, *Black Tennesseans, 1900–1930* (Knoxville: University of Tennessee Press, 1977), pp. 167–73. James D. Anderson, in *The Education of Blacks in the South, 1860–1935* (Chapel Hill: University of North Carolina Press, 1988),

pp. 79–109, situates the Hampton-Tuskegee doctrine promoted by Washington in the context of the "struggle for ideological hegemony" over the education of blacks in the New South.

24. William Henry Fouse, "Educational History of the Negroes of Lexington," M.A. thesis (University of Cincinnati, 1937), p. 31. See also *Negro Business Directory and Fair Souvenir* (Lexington: Standard Printing Company, 1899).

25. LL 24 Sept. 1898, p. 2.

26. A more elaborate program was offered by the Brooks Brothers, traveling evangelists who during their appearance at Woodland Park Auditorium in May 1909 offered moving pictures, as well as songs and lectures illustrated with slides "from their own photographs" (LL 31 May 1909, p. 10). Tent show evangelists also used moving pictures. When R. W. N. Tracy conducted a "temperance revival" in Lexington in 1907, for example, his sermon about the prodigal son "was illustrated in pantomime by moving pictures" (LH 6 May 1907, p. 1). I assume that Tracy and the Brooks Brothers were white since the newspapers do not suggest otherwise.

27. LH 11 Oct. 1904, p. 8.

28. LL 7 Nov. 1907, p. 9.

29. LH 20 June 1907, p. 2.

30. LH 10 Dec. 1907, p. 2.

31. LH 11 Dec. 1907, p. 11.

32. Jim Crow policies and the degree of segregation could differ from city to city, especially in Ohio. See Kusmer, *Ghetto Takes Shape,* pp. 57–59, 178–80; and Gerber, *Black Ohio,* pp. 257–62. For information on Kentucky, see Wright, *History of Blacks in Kentucky,* pp. 43–79. *Moving Picture World* occasionally provides some indication as to how segregated movie theaters operated. For example, a theater owner from Louisiana wrote to the trade journal inquiring whether it was possible to hang a curtain across the middle of his theater so that the projected images could simultaneously be seen by black and white spectators on opposite sides of the curtain (MPW 6, no. 9 [5 March 1910]: 337). A theater owner in Jeffersontown, Kentucky (a small town outside of Louisville), took a different approach by "inaugurating special hours during which colored patrons in Jeffersontown and vicinity could be accommodated" (MPW 13, no. 1 [6 July 1912]: 56).

33. LH 15 March 1903, p. 3; LL 17 April 1903, p. 3.

34. See, for example, Lauretta F. Byars, "Lexington's Colored Orphan Industrial Home, 1892–1913," *Register of the Kentucky Historical Society,* pp. 147–78. This board often used "entertainments" to raise funds, though they also realized that such benefit shows must be carefully monitored since "in some cases the entertainments have not been in keeping with the dignity and tastes of the institution" (quoted in Byars, p. 150).

35. IF 29 Dec. 1906, p. 6; IF 16 Feb. 1907, p. 5.

36. The Pete Walker who was a co-owner of the Frolic could well have been the Louisville resident and "expert electrician" of the same name mentioned in the *Freeman* (IF 2 Feb. 1907, p. 6; IF 24 Dec. 1910, p. 4).

37. LH 24 Jan. 1909, sec. 3, p. 1.

38. LL 30 Nov. 1907, p. 8; LL 7 Nov. 1907, p. 9.

39. LL 7 Nov. 1907, p. 9.

40. The Frolic, probably like most nickelodeons, was a far cry from what Robert C. Allen and Douglas Gomery call the "dark, smelly, sawdust-covered storefronts [nickelodeon] of traditional film-lore" (*Film History: Theory and Practice* [New York: Knopf, 1985], p. 204).

41. LL 22 Nov. 1907, p. 5.

42. The number of black-operated theaters is noteworthy since the 1909 Lexington city directory lists only eight saloons, six retail grocers, and twelve restaurants owned by blacks. The statewide figures for Kentucky, according to the 1910 Census, were comparable: out of 1,113 saloon keepers,

only 25 were black; out of 20,300 "retail dealers," only 542 were black (*Population, Thirteenth Census,* vol. 4, table 7, p. 464). On the difficulties faced by black businesses in this period and the push for "race" enterprises, see Gerber, *Black Ohio,* pp. 309–19; and Wright, *Life behind a Veil,* pp. 96–99.

43. LL 12 Sept. 1909, p. 12.

44. The only other theater in Kentucky that was mentioned was the Taft Theatre in Louisville (IF 7 May 1910, p. 6).

45. An ad for the Blue Grass Theater appeared in the IF 9 March 1907, p. 5; a description of *The Making of a Champion* appears in MPW 4, no. 8 (20 Feb. 1909): 278.

46. LL 4 Dec. 1910, p. 22; LL 15 Dec. 1910, p. 9.

47. LL 5 April 1911, p. 11.

48. IF 4 Feb. 1911, p. 5; IF 14 Dec. 1912, p. 4.

49. For information on the white-owned Theatre Owners Booking Association and the major black vaudeville circuits in the 1910s and 1920s, see William Barlow, *'Looking up at Down': The Emergence of Blues Culture* (Philadelphia: Temple University Press, 1989), pp. 119–22.

50. IF 9 July 1910, p. 9.

51. Roy Rosenzweig, *Eight Hours for What We Will: Workers and Leisure in an Industrial City, 1870–1920* (Cambridge: Cambridge University Press, 1983), p. 203.

52. According to *Moving Picture World,* "colored" theaters were fairly common during this period, and quite a few such theaters opened in smaller Kentucky cities and towns during the mid–1910s: for example, the Paul Dunbar Theater, which occupied an old church in Earlington (July 1913), as well as short-lived ventures in Russellville (March 1914), Maysville (May 1915), Owensboro (January 1916), and Mt. Sterling (May 1916). From trade magazine accounts, it is difficult to determine precisely how many of these theaters were black-owned and operated. Larger cities in the region, like Nashville and Chattanooga, had what *Moving Picture World* referred to as substantial "colored patronage" for black theaters (MPW 28, no. 13 [24 June 1916]: 2276). Louisville, with more than 40,000 blacks among its 200,000-plus population, supported at least one and sometimes three black theaters throughout this period, including a 350-seat venue located in the Knights of Pythias building (MPW 27, no. 2 [8 Jan. 1916]: 275).

53. LL 5 March 1911, p. 13.

54. See Lawrence Harris, *The Negro Population of Lexington in the Professions, Business, Education and Religion* (Lexington: n.p., 1907), p. 12.

55. LL 22 Dec. 1911, p. 7.

56. Quoted in Dittmer, *Black Georgia,* p. 67.

57. A fourth black theater, the 150-seat Dixie Theater, was announced in August 1912 by Charles Parker, actor and one-time operator of the Pekin Theater. It is especially noteworthy since it was to be located more than a mile south of downtown in a black residential area, thus making the Dixie in all senses of the word a neighborhood theater. The only subsequent reference to this theater I have come across is a two-line notice in the *Leader* when the Dixie opened in October 1912. In September 1913 a black Lexington resident leased a vacant building on Spring Street near West Main, with the intention of transforming it into a hotel for blacks, complete with a moving picture show, but this project was apparently not realized (LL 10 Sept. 1913, p. 8).

58. LL 19 May 1912, p. 4. Plans for a moving picture theater in Winchester "for colored people exclusively" were first announced in MPW 11, no. 3 (20 Jan. 1912): 220. The Winchester *Sun's* Colored Notes for 25 May 1912 mentions that the Lincoln Theater is prospering under new management (presumably Bell's), and a notice for this theater in Winchester appeared later that summer in the *Freeman* (IF 17 Aug. 1912, p. 2).

59. LL 9 Nov. 1913, p. 5.

60. Basically the same situation was in effect in Paducah, Kentucky, where only one of the four theaters allowed blacks to sit in the gallery (IF 4 Jan. 1913, p. 2).

61. IF 15 Feb. 1913, p. 8.

62. LL 29 March 1915, p. 6; LL 22 Nov. 1915, p. 4.

63. LL 29 March 1915, sec 4, p. 6. *The Kaffir's Skull* was a one-reel mystery released by Reliance on 28 November 1914 (MPW 22, no. 10 [5 Dec. 1914]: 1430); *The Jewel of Allah*, "a mystic story of the Hindus," was a one-reel film released by Eclair on 20 December 1914 (MPW 22, no. 12 [19 Dec. 1914]: 1681); and *The Call of the Waves*, a two-reel romance involving a "young man of wealth and excellent parentage" and a fisherman's daughter who is an "athletic, carefree child of Nature," was released by Gold Seal on 22 December 1914 (MPW 22, no. 13 [26 Dec. 1914]: 1892).

64. See Thomas Cripps, *Slow Fade to Black: The Negro in American Film, 1900–1942* (New York: Oxford University Press, 1977), pp. 8–40; and Daniel J. Leab, *From Sambo to Superspade: The Black Experience in Motion Pictures* (Boston: Houghton Mifflin, 1975), pp. 7–22, for a survey of the image of blacks in film before *The Birth of a Nation*. Presumably the fare in Lexington was standard, for instance, the "polyscopic motion picture scenes of darkies picking cotton in the land of the banjo," which were shown as part of an illustrated lecture at the YMCA in 1908 (LL 2 April 1908, p. 2). Recall that the one film that truly "set the house in a roar" at the Opera House during a magniscope exhibition in 1897 was the "very funny" vignette of "an old colored woman washing a baby" (LH 2 March 1897, p. 2).

65. One notable precursor to this trend was *A Day in Tuskegee*, which screened locally at the First Baptist Church in November 1913.

66. IF 8 Aug. 1914, p. 6; IF 10 Oct. 1914, p. 5.

67. See Cripps, *Slow Fade to Black*, pp. 70–79; Leab, *From Sambo to Superspade*, pp. 58–81.

68. IF 12 Sept. 1914, p. 7.

69. IF 15 Aug. 1915, p. 1. For a synopsis of the Historical Feature Film Company's productions, see MPW 23, no. 6 (6 Feb. 1915): 898.

70. IF 1 April 1916, p. 1; IF 22 Jan. 1916, p. 5.

71. IF 3 April 1915, p. 4.

72. As far as I have been able to determine, there was no official protest in Lexington over segregated seating policies, unlike in Louisville, for example, where black lawyer and newspaper editor William Warley in 1914 led a boycott against the gallery seating and "colored" back entrance at the National Theater. Warley "won a partial victory when the management of the National Theater allowed blacks to enter from the main street and to have accommodations in the first balcony" (Wright, *Life behind a Veil*, p. 200).

73. IF 18 Dec. 1915, p. 1; IF 1 Jan. 1916, p. 6; IF 5 Feb. 1915, p. 9.

74. LL 30 March 1917, p. 11.

75. LH 21 May 1916, p. 7.

76. Robert B. Grant, *The Black Man Comes to the City: A Documentary Account from the Great Migration to the Great Depression, 1915 to 1930* (Chicago: Nelson-Hall, 1972), pp. 25–26.

77. LL 18 July 1916, p. 5.

78. "In the Interpreter's House," *American Magazine* 76 (July 1913): 105.

Chapter 8: Movies on the Homefront

1. See William Marston Seabury, *The Public and the Motion Picture Industry* (New York: Macmillan Company, 1926), pp. 325–29, for a summary of the various federal Revenue Acts bearing on motion picture exhibition between 1918 and 1924.

2. LH 6 Oct. 1918, p. 5.

3. On the range of war films produced during this period, see Craig W. Campbell, *Reel America and World War I* (Jefferson, N.C.: McFarland & Company, 1985).

4. LH 1 Sept. 1918, sec. 2, p. 7. See Richard Schickel, *D. W. Griffith: An American Life* (New York: Simon & Schuster, 1984), pp. 358–60, for a survey of other reaction to *Hearts of the World*, which does not seem to have been nearly as enthusiastically received as in Lexington. Campbell does, however, describe a comparable reception of the film in Atlanta, Los Angeles, and across the country (*Reel America*, pp. 97–98).

5. David M. Kennedy, *Over Here: The First World War and American Society* (New York: Oxford University Press, 1980), p. 61.

6. LH 9 Oct 1917, pp. 1–2.

7. LL 23 July 1918, p. 2.

8. LH 30 April 1917, p. 3. See Campbell, *Reel America*, p. 54.

9. Campbell notes that during the height of the epidemic, "representatives of 18 producing and distributing companies gathered to hear Adolph Zukor report that 75 percent of the nation's theaters had closed" (*Reel America*, p. 106).

10. LH 13 Dec. 1918, p. 1.

11. LL 22 Jan. 1919, p. 3.

12. LH 18 Dec. 1918, p. 2.

13. LH 26 April 1917, p. 6.

14. See Kennedy, *Over Here*, pp. 186–86.

15. Kentucky was the third state to ratify this amendment. See Thomas H. Appleton, "'Like Banquo's Ghost': The Emergence of the Prohibition Issue in Kentucky Politics," diss. (University of Kentucky, 1981), pp. 218–22.

16. LH 23 Jan. 1918, p. 5.

17. LL 16 March 1918, p. 1.

18. LH 2 July 1918, p. 1; LL 2 July 1918, p. 1.

19. LL 5 July 1918, pp. 1–2; LH 6 July 1918, p. 8.

20. LL 8 July 1918, p. 1.

21. LL 5 July 1918, p. 2.

22. A writer to the *Herald*, for example, put the matter thus: "what is at the bottom of the effort to close the motion picture shows in Lexington" is "religious interference with the natural rights of the citizens" (LH 14 July 1918, p. 5).

23. LH 1 July 1918, p. 10.

24. LL 2 July 1918, p. 4.

25. LH 7 July 1918, p. 4.

26. LH 14 July 1918, p. 4.

27. LH 7 July 1918, p. 5.

28. LL 2 July 1918, p. 5.

29. LH 1 July 1918, p. 10.

30. LH 12 July 1919, p. 12.

31. City Council *Minutes*, 13 July 1919 (reel 11, p. 279); LL 13 July 1918, pp. 1, 3.

32. For the domestic film industry at large, the key word was not "necessary," but "essential." The industry successfully campaigned to have its skilled employees categorized as "essential" workers who would thus be exempt from the government's "work or fight" mandate (Campbell, *Reel America*, pp. 82–83).

33. LH 14 July 1918, p. 1.

34. LL 16 July 1918, p. 5.

35. LH 12 July 1918, p. 2. On 7 July 1918, the specific date of the alleged blue law violation, the actual movies shown at the Strand and Ben Ali (the Orpheum ran no ad that day) were:

Strand: *Confession* (Fox) starring Jewel Carmen in "an eventful story of a society girl's interrupted honeymoon"; and episode no. 15 of *The House of Hate,* featuring Pearl White and Antonio Moreno;

Ben Ali: *The Maid of Belgium* (Brady-World Feature Film) starring Alice Brady as, according to Craig W. Campbell, "a pregnant Belgian woman, amnesiac after the invasion and her family's murder," who is eventually reunited with her soldier husband (*Reel America,* p. 168); and the *Hearst Pathé News* "including late war pictures."

These bookings suggest that both arguments in favor of Sunday movies had some validity: the Strand's bill might help to "keep the minds of the people off the horrors of the present conflict," and the Ben Ali's bill might help to "bring vividly before Sunday audiences the fact" of the war.

36. LH 17 July 1918, p. 10; LL 16 July 1918, p. 5. When a comparable trial took place in nearby Georgetown a month later, the theater owner was fined five dollars and court costs, another very modest penalty that does not seem to have been intended to halt Sunday screenings (LL 18 Aug. 1918. sec. 3, p. 6).

37. LH 23 July 1918, p. 2.

38. LL 22 July 1918, p. 5; LL 23 July 1918, p. 2.

39. LH 23 July 1918, p. 1.

40. LH 24 July 1918, pp. 1, 3.

41. LH 27 July 1918, p. 5.

42. LH 24 July 1918, p. 3.

43. LH 26 July 1918, p. 3.

44. LL 4 Aug. 1918, sec. 3, p. 6. An editorial in the *Leader* made a similar point, using Pittsburgh as its example of a city that benefited greatly from being "closed" on Sundays (LL 12 Aug. 1918, p. 4).

45. LH 30 July 1918, p. 8; LL 30 July 1918, p. 2.

46. LH 31 July 1918, p. 10.

47. LH 24 Aug. 1918, p. 2.

48. LL 18 Feb. 1919, p. 2.

49. LH 30 April 1918, p. 10; LL 29 April 1918, p. 10.

50. LL 12 Jan. 1918, p. 1.

51. LH 10 March 1918, pp. 1–2.

52. LL 16 March 1919, p. 1.

Chapter 9: Film Exhibition, 1919–1927

1. George T. Blakely, *Hard Times & New Deal in Kentucky, 1929–1939* (Lexington: University Press of Kentucky, 1986), pp. 7–9.

2. David Bordwell, Janet Staiger, and Kristin Thompson, *The Classical Hollywood Cinema: Film Style and Mode of Production to 1960* (New York: Columbia University Press, 1985), p. 231.

3. Garth Jowett, *Film: The Democratic Art* (Boston: Focal Press, 1976), pp. 139, 192–93.

4. David A. Cook, for example, states that these "exotic, 'atmospheric' theaters which could seat up to three thousand patrons spread to cities small and large across the country," as the audience for the movies became "increasingly middle class" (*A History of Narrative Film,* 2nd ed. [New York: Norton, 1990], p. 207). Benjamin B. Hampton drew a similar conclusion in 1931: "when features and fine theaters extended the movie habit into all classes, making it the universal American entertainment, the infection spread everywhere" (*A History of the Movies* [New York: Covici, Friede Publishers, 1931], p. 207). See also Robert Sklar, *Movie-Made America: A Cultural History of American*

Movies (New York: Vintage, 1975), p. 86; and David Robinson, for whom a description of how movies were shown and consumed in the 1920s becomes, in essence, the evocation in word and/or image of "the splendour and extravagance of the theatres that shot up at various times in the twenties" (*Hollywood in the Twenties* [New York: A. S. Barnes, 1968], p. 33).

5. Lary May, *Screening out the Past: The Birth of Mass Culture and the Motion Picture Industry* (New York: Oxford University Press, 1980), pp. 163, 157–58, 166.

6. May, *Screening out the Past*, p. 164.

7. David Naylor, *American Picture Palaces: The Architecture of Fantasy* (New York: Van Nostrand, 1981), p. 217. The only theater built in Kentucky in the 1920s mentioned by Naylor is the 3,273-seat Loew's United Artists Theater in Louisville, opened in 1928, a year that also saw 2,000-plus-seat theaters begin operation in Huntington, West Virginia, and Knoxville, Tennessee.

8. Gomery's relevant articles include: "The Picture Palace: Economic Sense or Hollywood Nonsense?" *Quarterly Review of Film Studies* 3, no. 1 (Winter 1978): 23–36; "The Growth of Movie Monopolies: The Case of Balaban & Katz," *Wide Angle* 3, no. 1 (1979): 44–63; "Saxe Amusement Enterprises: The Movies Come to Milwaukee," *Milwaukee History* 2, no. 1 (new series) (Spring 1979): 18–28; "The Movies Become Big Business: Publix Theatres and the Chain-Store Strategy," in *The American Movie Industry: The Business of Motion Pictures*, ed. Gorham Kindem (Carbondale: Southern Illinois University Press, 1982), pp. 104–16; "U.S. Film Exhibition: The Formation of a Big Business," in *The American Film Industry*, ed. Tino Balio (Madison: University of Wisconsin Press, 1985), pp. 218–28; "Movie-Going during Hollywood's Golden Age," *North Dakota Quarterly* 51, no. 3 (Summer 1983): 36–45; and "Film and Business History: The Development of an American Mass Entertainment Industry," *Journal of Contemporary History* 19 (1984): 89–103. His findings are summarized in *Shared Pleasures: A History of Movie Presentation in the United States* (Madison: University of Wisconsin Press, 1992), pp. 34–56.

Gomery's sense of the "business history" of exhibition in the 1920s differs appreciably from William Marston Seabury's *The Public and the Motion Picture Industry* (New York: Macmillan, 1926), p. 7, which also provides what could be called a business-oriented account of the period. For Seabury, the recent history of the motion picture industry was a veritable war between acquisitive production companies and beleaguered exhibitors, with the nation's movie theaters (and ultimately the future of the motion picture and the public's "vital interest") at stake. See also Hampton on "The Battle for the Theatres" (*A History of the Movies*, pp. 252–80).

9. Gomery, "The Picture Palace," p. 36. Charlotte Herzog, in contrast, identifies the "movie palace" as a "special type of big city movie theater" with certain "distinguishing characteristics," including "numerous appointments, lavish decorations, and enormous size." "A theater was not considered a palace," Herzog continues, "unless it had special services like ushers and doormen and elaborate interior decorations." But only if a "palace had a stage show, an orchestra, a pipe organ, plush ornamentation and a 'first-class' (not to be confused with first-run) film," could it be called "'de luxe'" ("The Movie Palace and the Theatrical Sources of Its Architectural Style," *Cinema Journal* 20, no. 2 [Spring 1981]: 15).

10. Richard Koszarski, *An Evening's Entertainment: The Age of the Silent Feature Picture, 1915–1928* (New York: Scribner's 1990), p. 13.

11. Craig W. Campbell, *Reel America and World War I* (Jefferson, N.C.: McFarland & Company, 1985), pp. 118–19, 125.

12. Thus for the week of 1 October 1920, the Orpheum offered episode 6 of *The Branded Four* (Select) on Friday, episode 12 of *The Vanishing Dagger* (Universal) on Saturday, episode 2 of *The Dragon's Net* (Universal) on Sunday, episode 3 of *The Lost City* (Warner Brothers) on Tuesday, and episode 2 of *The Tiger Band* (Warner Brothers) on Thursday. For information on serials during this period, see Kalton C. Lahue's two books: *Continued Next Week: A History of the Moving Picture Serial* (Norman: University of Oklahoma Press, 1964) and *Bound and Gagged: The Story of the Silent Serials*

(New York: Castle Books, 1968). Koszarski notes that by 1920 the firms producing serials were not "in the business of supplying the major downtown palaces; instead, their products went to small urban houses, country theaters, and other unaffiliated venues" (Koszarski, *An Evening's Entertainment*, p. 166).

13. LL 13 Feb. 1917, pp. 1, 5; LL 15 Feb. 1917, p. 1.

14. The MPTO was formed to resist what historian Benjamin B. Hampton called "the machinations of the ambitious, resourceful" head of Paramount, Adolf Zukor. Zukor's "agents," wrote Hampton, were using coercive tactics to acquire theaters in "small communities and thousands of independent exhibitors were fearful that they might be the next to fall" (*A History of the Movies*, pp. 263–64).

15. LH 16 March 1922, p. 3.

16. Koszarski, *An Evening's Entertainment*, p. 13.

17. The Shuberts were then in the midst of another war with Klaw & Erlanger for control of the legitimate theater in the United States. See Alfred Bernheim, *The Business of the Theatre: An Economic History of the American Theatre, 1750–1932* (1932, rpt. New York: Benjamin Blom, 1964), p. 71.

18. *Billboard* 28 June 1919. Clipping in Bowmar Collection, University of Kentucky Special Collections.

19. LH 22 Dec. 1919, p. 16.

20. Even though they shared films with the Phoenix Amusement Company's Lexington theaters, the theaters in outlying cities were run differently than the Ben Ali and the Strand. In Winchester, for example, films changed daily and each was shown twice: in the afternoon at the Colonial and in the evening at the Liberty. Only on Saturdays did both theaters operate full time. The same was true for the Phoenix Amusement Company's theaters in Paris and Richmond. Except for the Strand, all the theaters owned by this company were closed on Sundays (LH 19 Oct. 1919, sec. 3, p. 10).

A month after its purchase of the Ben Ali, the Phoenix Amusement Company ran a large Sunday advertisement in the *Herald* listing every feature film playing at all of its theaters for the coming week, as well as the bookings at the Lexington Opera House and the musicians who would be performing at the Strand and the Ben Ali (LH 1 Feb. 1920, sec. 3, p. 6). Aside from its practical function, this schedule effectively linked the Phoenix Amusement Company's small-town houses with its more lavish theaters in Lexington and suggested to would-be customers the sheer size and efficiency of this company's operations in the area. All the movies listed in this ad were identified by production company and star, but there was no corporate trademark or otherwise explicit reference to the Phoenix Amusement Company or to John Elliott, who rarely courted publicity.

21. Elliott's handling of his three Lexington theaters can be compared with the way Kunsky Enterprises in Detroit used stage shows as part of what Henry B. Aldridge calls a "strategy of product differentiation" ("The Role of the Stage Show in Film Exhibition: The Case of Detroit's Capitol Theatre," *Journal of Popular Film and Television* 10, no. 2 [Summer 1982]: 66–71).

22. LH 1 Feb. 1920, sec. 3, p. 6; LL 8 Oct. 1922, sec. 2, p. 9.

23. LH 6 Feb. 1921, sec. 2, p. 7. I do not know whether the orchestra, in addition to its concerts, also provided accompaniment for all or part of the film program. A few ads for the Ben Ali in the 1920s specifically announce that the orchestra will play "music especially suited to the picture" (see, for example, LH 17 Feb. 1924, sec. 3, p. 6).

24. Lawrence W. Levine in *Highbrow/Lowbrow: The Emergence of Cultural Hierarchy in America* (Cambridge: Harvard University Press, 1988), pp. 105–7, argues that "the nineteenth century's acceptance of musical eclecticism" and its "musical flexibility" was in the early years of the twentieth century overtaken by the larger "process of sacralization that was transforming the face of American culture" (p. 132). Perhaps one place where the sort of eclecticism that Levine describes flourished was in motion picture theater orchestras in the 1920s.

25. LH 4 April 1926, sec. 3, p. 9.

26. LH 4 June 1925, sec. 3, p. 6.

27. Paula S. Fass, *The Damned and the Beautiful: American Youth in the 1920's* (New York: Oxford University Press, 1977), pp. 300–301. By 1922 the University of Kentucky student newspaper was taking an editorial stance in favor of the "better side" of jazz music, though such music, the paper warned, also had its "dangerous and pernicious" side (*Kernel* 16 March 1923, p. 4; *Kernel* 23 Feb. 1923, p. 4). Four years earlier, however, the *Kernel* had sung a different tune, calling for the university to "expurgate the modern dance" and "jazz music," which it felt was inimical to any "dignified" dancing (*Kernel* 24 April 1919, p. 4).

28. Alfred L. Bernheim, "The Facts of Vaudeville" (1923) in *American Vaudeville as Seen by Its Contemporaries*, ed. Charles W. Stein (New York: Knopf, 1984), p. 129.

29. LL 16 Sept. 1923, p. 9.

30. LH 8 Aug. 1926, sec. 3, p. 6.

31. LH 8 July 1927, p. 8.

32. LH 4 Nov. 1921, pp. 1, 9.

33. LH 5 May 1922, p. 14.

34. May, *Screening out the Past*, p. 3.

35. LH 4 Feb. 1923, p. 1.

36. LH 24 May 1923, p. 1.

37. LH 20 Sept. 1923, p. 11.

38. LH 20 Oct. 1927, sec. 3, p. 7.

39. There was also a market, it seems, for exploitation films such as the "childbirth" movie, *Tell Me Why*, *The Red Kimono*, *The Road to Ruin* ("the vibrant life story of a delinquent girl"), and *The Street of Forgotten Women*, all shown at the Opera House in the late 1920s for two- or three-day engagements with no children admitted. In 1923 the Ada Meade had been rented by the Moral Uplift Film Producers for a two-day showing of *Are You Fit to Marry?* (graphically "laying bare" the "terrible result of unclean living"), with matinee shows for women and evening shows for men (LH 11 Feb. 1923, sec. 2, p. 9).

40. LH 20 April 1930, sec. 3, p. 1.

41. For a survey of the major Broadway productions during the 1920s, see Allen Churchill, *The Theatrical 20's* (New York: McGraw-Hill, 1975).

42. See Jack Poggi, *Theater in America: The Impact of Economic Forces, 1870–1967* (Ithaca: Cornell University Press, 1966), pp. 31–34.

43. See Poggi, *Theater in America*, pp. 28–45; Bernheim, *Business of the Theatre*, pp. 76–84; and Robert McLaughlin, *Broadway and Hollywood: A History of Economic Interaction* (New York: Arno, 1974), pp. 12–22.

44. Bernheim notes that by 1927 there were some 257 stock companies working in the United States, up approximately 80 percent from the year before (*Business of the Theatre*, pp. 92–97).

45. Poggi, *Theater in America*, p. 44.

46. The high social and financial status of these investors (as well as most members of the Phoenix Amusement Company's board of directors and the chief officers of the Lexington Opera House Company) are worth noting. For comparison's sake, see Robert S. Lynd and Helen Merrell Lynd, *Middletown: A Study in Contemporary American Culture* (New York: Harcourt, Brace, 1929), p. 268, in which the film exhibitors in Muncie, Indiana, are basically dismissed as a "group of men—an ex-peanut-stand proprietor, an ex-bicycle racer and race promoter, and so on—whose primary concern is making money." Even the sole "college-trained" exhibitor, the Lynds note, "is caught in the competitive game and matches his competitors' sensational advertisements."

47. LH 1 Oct. 1922, p. 2. Hampton mentions Levy as one of several men whose theater circuits were gaining power in the early 1920s. Levy's expansion "in Louisville and Kentucky" becomes for

Hampton part of a general trend away from "independent control of theaters, studios, and exchanges" (Hampton, *A History of the Movies,* p. 274). Koszarski notes that First National, which started "from an exhibition base," had by 1919 "successfully grown to include distribution and production as well." In 1921 First National merged with Associated Producers (distributor of films by Sennett, Ince, Allan Dwan, King Vidor, and others) to become Associated First National (*An Evening's Entertainment,* pp. 74–77).

48. See the promotional pamphlet, *Joseph & Joseph: Architects and Engineers* (Louisville: n.p., 1927).

49. LL 27 April 1922, p. 15.

50. The Kentucky is not mentioned in David Naylor's *American Picture Palaces,* but it is listed in Naylor's *Great American Movie Theaters* (Washington, D.C.: Preservation Press, 1987), which is not restricted to picture palaces. And by Gomery's criteria, the Kentucky would probably be termed a "mini-palace," for it sat fewer than fifteen hundred, had only a slightly fan-shaped auditorium, and did not regularly offer stage shows. It also seems to me doubtful whether the Kentucky had enough "nonfunctional decoration" (Gomery's phrase) or "elaborate interior decoration" (Herzog's phrase) to qualify as a picture palace.

51. See Naylor, *American Picture Palaces,* pp. 67–108; and Ben H. Hall, *The Best Remaining Seats* (New York: Bramhall House, 1961), pp. 93–102.

52. Walter Langsam, "Kentucky Historical Resources Inventory" (July 1979), p. 1. Lexington Historical Commission, Theater File. On the Adams style, see Joseph and Anne Rykwert, *The Brothers Adam: The Men and the Style* (London: Collins, 1985). Beaux Arts design, according to Robert T. Packard, is characterized by "symmetry, classical orders, emphasis on circulation and plan, the concept of axial organization and meaningful expression of function" (*Encyclopedia of Architecture, Design, Engineering, and Construction,* vol. 2 [New York: John Wiley, 1988], p. 271).

53. See Naylor, *American Picture Palaces,* p. 44; and Hall, *Best Remaining Seats,* pp. 104–19. Compare, for example, the Kentucky with the photographs of one of Lamb's smallest New York theaters, the Embassy, built in 1925, with seating for 598 (reproduced in R. W. Sexton, *American Theatres of Today* [New York: Architectural Book Publishing Company, 1930], vol. 1, p. 157). Both theaters have murals in the auditorium and a circular dome-shaped design on the ceiling, but there is much more decorative embellishment in the Embassy.

54. LH 1 Oct. 1922, p. 1.

55. LL 5 Oct. 1922, p. 11.

56. Koszarski, *An Evening's Entertainment,* p. 22. See also Hall, *Best Remaining Seats,* pp. 178–95.

57. LL 5 Oct. 1922, p. 11.

58. Identifying the Kentucky as a first-run theater would seem to be less problematic than calling it a "picture palace," but William Marston Seabury, writing in 1926, drew a distinction between the approximately 1,720 "first run" motion picture theaters in the United States and the two hundred or so "strictly first class first run" theaters in thirty major cities. The Kentucky and the Strand both differed from what Seabury calls the "first run" theater because they did not regularly schedule films for at least a week-long engagement, nor did they charge substantially higher admission prices than "lesser" theaters (Seabury, *Public and the Motion Picture Industry,* pp. 49–58).

59. LL 5 June 1924, p. 7.

60. LH 7 Feb. 1926, sec. 2, p. 1.

61. LL 28 Dec. 1924, sec. 2, p. 4.

62. LH 19 Sept. 1926, sec. 3, p. 5.

63. Koszarski, *An Evening's Entertainment,* p. 80.

64. Jowett, *Film: The Democratic Art,* pp. 202–3.

65. Koszarski, *An Evening's Entertainment,* pp. 54–61.

66. Gomery identifies three forms of live performance staged at picture palaces: the thematically organized "prologue" or "presentation" (which might or might not be consistent with the feature film); the "variety show" format with a series of acts; and the "headliner method," featuring one major performer ("Picture Palace," p. 25). See also Gomery, *Shared Pleasures*, pp. 216–17. Other scholars have examined how such strategies were employed in certain large downtown theaters in Detroit and Pittsburgh. See Aldridge, "Role of the Stage Show," and John L. Marsh, "Vaudefilm: Its Contribution to a Moviegoing America," *Journal of American Culture* 7, no. 3 (Fall 1984): 77–84.

67. Koszarski, *An Evening's Entertainment*, p. 41.

68. Whether this experience was somehow regionalized is another matter, which would require more extensive research into other locations in Kentucky and the South.

Chapter 10: Movies, Culture, and the "Jazz Environment"

1. LL 27 Oct. 1915, p. 12.

2. LH 14 July 1921, p. 6. That same year, according to one contemporary estimate, "nearly 100 circuits were reaching 9,597 communities in the United States and Canada" (quoted in Theodore Morrison, *Chautauqua: A Center for Education, Religion, and the Arts in America* [Chicago: University of Chicago Press, 1974], p. 181). Although Redpath's popularity nationwide dropped off substantially in 1927, tent Chautauqua continued to be held in Lexington, moving in 1927–30 to the grounds of the University of Kentucky, which co-sponsored sessions along with the local Kiwanis Club. On tent show Chautauqua, see Morrison, *Chautauqua*, pp. 173–92; and the anecdotal account by former circuit owner Harry P. Harrison, *Culture under Canvas: The Story of Tent Chautauqua* (New York: Hastings House, 1958).

3. According to promotional material, the seven-day 1927 Redpath program that stopped in Lexington was part of a circuit that reached 105 cities and towns from the deep South to Wisconsin during its eighteen-week season (*Kernel* 1 July 1927, p. 1).

4. LL 7 July 1923, p. 4.

5. LL 31 Jan. 1923, p. 4.

6. Lawrence W. Levine, *Highbrow/Lowbrow: The Emergence of Cultural Hierarchy in America* (Cambridge, Mass.: Harvard University Press, 1988), pp. 141 ff. "Art," declared a 1927 *Herald* editorial, is "coming into its own," because "the American people have an enlivened taste for the best things in theatricals, music and literature. There is observable a heightening morality and mentality" (LH 20 May 1927, p. 4).

7. The only noteworthy exception was the 1925–26 season, which, in addition to featuring the Cleveland Symphony Orchestra, a Russian pianist, and a Peruvian mezzo contralto, also included performances by Will Rogers and the Paul Whiteman Orchestra. It should be borne in mind, however, that Woodland Park Auditorium—home of the Artist Concert Series—was not an elegant temple dedicated solely to high culture. In the weeks after Paderewski's appearance, this unadorned, multi-purpose site was used for local charity events, a concert by the African-American Williams Jubilee Singers, a sermon by nationally known evangelist Billy Sunday, a road show motion picture, and a week-long indoor circus.

8. There were, according to Alfred L. Bernheim, 459 "little, experimental and community theaters" in the United States in 1922, and the number increased throughout the rest of the decade, as local organizations were inspired by the example of the Theater Guild (which had become all-professional) and the Provincetown Players (*The Business of the Theatre: An Economic History of the American Theatre, 1750–1932* [1932; rpt. New York: Benjamin Blom, 1964], 101–3).

9. LH 8 Jan. 1924, p. 2. The university's student newspaper was particularly enthusiastic about this new outlet for the "higher forms of dramatic art" (*Kernel* 11 Jan. 1924, p. 1). Subsequent editori-

als in the local press sounded the same note, praising the Romany Theater as a definite asset to the city's "cultural" life (LH 17 Jan. 1924, p. 4). In 1926 the *Kernel* boasted that "few plays of any real intellectual and artistic merit have been presented in Lexington in the last three years except at the Romany" (*Kernel* 8 Jan. 1926, p. 4).

10. *Kernel* 11 March 1927, p. 4.

11. *Kernel* 21 Sept. 1928, p. 4.

12. See Anthony Slide, *Before Video: A History of Non-Theatrical Film* (Westport, Conn.: Greenwood Press, 1992), pp. 59–74.

13. LL 28 March 1916, p. 8.

14. *Kernel* 6 April 1916, p. 5.

15. LH 20 Feb. 1929, p. 12.

16. LL 20 Nov. 1919, p. 4.

17. LL 26 Feb. 1920, p. 1. Other, more commercially minded nontheatrical uses of motion pictures during this period included, for example, the screening of films by a local auto company to promote Ford tractors (LH 17 Feb. 1923, p. 3) and by a traveling salesman, who promoted Florida land sales with motion pictures shown in a private Pullman car (LH 10 Sept. 1925, p. 5). Once or twice a year the American Legion sponsored an evening of World War I films at the Auditorium or a downtown theater.

18. LL 15 Nov. 1919, p. 4.

19. National Child Labor Committee, *Child Welfare in Kentucky* (New York: National Child Labor Committee, 1919), p. 123. This committee had the support of the Kentucky Federation of Women's Clubs and other private organizations and state agencies. Its report enumerated a long list of offenses that made carnivals "fitly described as traveling bawdy houses—unlicensed, unregulated, uncontrolled." In a most telling aside, the report noted that "the carnival, it may be added, is one place where whites and negroes freely mingle" (pp. 124–25).

20. LL 1 Nov. 1922, p. 1; LH 23 Jan. 1923, p. 10.

21. LH 27 May 1923, p. 4.

22. LH 30 July 1923, p. 5.

23. LH 27 May 1923, p. 4. This public declaration of principles is very much of a piece with a *Leader* editorial praising the way the 1923 state fair was run. Kentuckians, the *Leader* asserted, are "more interested in and moved by what is clean and elevating than by what is immoral and degrading . . . and are interested in preserving the highest standards for the sake of the youth in their homes and in the homes of their neighbors" (LL 30 Sept. 1923, p. 4). Implicit here is the notion that the diligent promotion of cleanliness and moral order is most crucial in those public sites where crowds (particularly youths) gather, separated from the workaday world, seeking fun, and thus ready prey to the unclean and debasing.

24. See the file on amusement parks in the Bowmar Collection, University of Kentucky Special Collections.

25. LH 1 Sept. 1927, p. 5. For 1923 figures, see LL 1 July 1923, p. 8.

26. LH 22 July 1923, sec. 2, p. 1.

27. LH 29 July 1927, p. 7.

28. See the case for playgrounds offered in *Child Welfare in Kentucky,* pp. 89–111.

29. LL 6 Oct. 1926, p. 4.

30. LL 22 June 1928, p. 4.

31. LH 27 May 1923, p. 4.

32. LH 15 July 1925, p. 12; LH 2 May 1926, sec. 3, p. 4.

33. LH 15 Sept. 1921, p. 4.

34. LL 3 Nov. 1924, p. 1.

35. LH 15 March 1925, sec. 3, p. 1.

36. LL 13 Oct. 1921, p. 8.

37. LH 18 Oct. 1920, p. 14.

38. LH 10 Feb. 1920, p. 3.

39. At this same period and throughout the 1920s—regardless of whatever scandals racked the film industry—moviegoing itself was still pictured in a host of syndicated cartoons and comic strips as an everyday occurrence for kids, dating couples, and families, an innocuous habit likely to bring out people's foibles and eccentricities. In Lexington newspapers during 1921–22, for example, these themes appeared in comic strips and cartoons such as "Everett True," "Doings of the Duffs," "Out Our Way," "Our Boarding House," and "Freckles and His Friends."

40. LH 15 Sept. 1921, p. 4.

41. LH 26 Sept. 1921, p. 4. The local chapter of the Anti-Blue Law League did little more than schedule a speech on "The Blueshiviskis [sic] and the Blue Laws" (LH 6 March 1922, p. 1).

42. LL 18 Sept. 1921, p. 4.

43. LH 20 July 1920, p. 3.

44. LL 8 Aug. 1927, p. 1. By the late 1920s, when Sunday movie screenings had long since ceased to be a pressing issue in Lexington, exhibitors' challenges to blue laws and sabbatarian efforts persisted in other parts of Kentucky, often with successful results for theater owners. In Mt. Sterling, Ashland, and Henderson, for example, theater operators disregarded church protests and initiated Sunday screenings; all were taken to court and were either acquitted or handed minimal fines by sympathetic juries. Fines up to $225 were assessed in Owensboro, where as many as nineteen theater employees were arrested for working on the Sabbath. After eleven weeks of arrests, a steady stream of trials, and a newspaper poll that showed Owensboro citizens favoring Sunday movies by a two-to-one margin, the presiding judge dismissed all charges against the theaters and declared that the court's time was too valuable to waste trying blue law cases (LL 5 Aug. 1930, p. 10). In central Kentucky, Lexington's relatively "open" Sunday policy remained the exception rather than the rule. Though the Phoenix Amusement Company had long operated a theater in nearby Richmond, for example, it was not until October 1930 that it began to offer Sunday screenings, and even then the action occasioned protest and arrests.

45. LH 9 Oct. 1921, p. 12.

46. LL 29 Oct. 1925, p. 1.

47. LH 13 June 1929, p. 2; LL 24 Nov. 1929, p. 1.

48. LH 22 Dec. 1920, pp. 1–2.

49. See Wid's Film Year Book, 1919–20, pp. 275–77. Garth Jowett notes that in 1922 censorship bills had been introduced in thirty-two states, with the crucial test case coming in Massachusetts, where the vote in a public referendum was over two-to-one against state censorship (Film: The Democratic Art [Boston: Focal Press, 1976], pp. 167–68).

50. Frankfort State Journal, 22 Feb. 1922, p. 1; LL 22 Feb. 1922, sec. 2, p. 2. The larger context for Brock's rationale was the entire discourse concerning children and the movies, which continued from the 1910s. See, for example, Jowett, Film: The Democratic Art, pp. 147–51, 215–17; and Alice Miller Mitchell, Children and the Movies (Chicago: University of Chicago Press, 1929), which was based on the study of schoolchildren and "juvenile delinquents" in Chicago. Local examples included a lecture delivered to the Women's Club of Central Kentucky on how the "ideals of young America" had "shifted from Washington to Hollywood" (LH 16 Dec. 1923, p. 1).

51. LH 31 Jan. 1922, pp. 1, 4.

52. LL 16 March 1922, p. 1.

53. Similarly, the University of Kentucky Kernel worried that a censorship board could easily become an "engine of oppression by hypercritical censorship and intolerance" (Kernel 3 March 1922, p. 4).

54. LH 1 March 1922, p. 9.

55. Frankfort *State Journal* 23 Feb. 1922, p. 4.

56. LL 27 Feb. 1922, p. 4.

57. On Hays, see Jowett, *Film: The Democratic Art*, pp. 164–76; Richard Koszarski, *An Evening's Entertainment: The Age of the Silent Feature Picture 1915–1928* (New York: Scribner's 1990), pp. 206–8; and Terry Ramsaye, *A Million and One Nights* (1926; rpt. New York: Simon and Schuster, 1986), pp. 803–21.

58. LL 16 Jan. 1921, p. 4. Thus the *Leader* promoted a contest sponsored by the Authors League in 1923 that gave cash prizes for the best suggestions on how to "improve the movies" (LL 3 June 1923, sec. 4, p. 1).

59. LL 23 Jan. 1922, p. 4. In an editorial in August 1922, the *Leader* explicitly spelled out why the motion picture industry needed to be "cleaned out": "the passion for romance and adventure are [sic] deeply rooted in man," thus the "lure of the film drama," from which people receive "by proxy, all the thrills they can stand." Since no substitute can be found for this pleasure, "so much more important, then, is it that life should be presented in its true colors and with some sense of proportion, and that the finer human qualities and nobler aspirations should be presented on the screen to which millions flock nightly" (LL 16 Aug. 1922, p. 4).

60. LL 6 April 1925, p. 4.

61. LL 23 Dec. 1923, p. 4.

62. LL 2 Aug. 1927, p. 4. On the reception of jazz, see Kathy J. Ogren, *The Jazz Revolution: Twenties America & the Meaning of Jazz* (New York: Oxford University Press, 1989).

63. LL 25 Feb. 1925, p. 4; LL 8 July 1925, p. 4; LL 25 July 1925, p. 4.

64. LL 29 July 1924, p. 4.

65. After 1925 the *Leader* was more inclined to find fault with a touring stage revue like *George White's Scandals*, with its "obtrusive and almost constant practical nudity" (LL 29 Sept. 1926, sec. 2, p. 4), and to endorse efforts to censor the New York theater, which had for too long sought to profit from "debauching the public mind" (LL 21 Feb. 1927, p. 4).

66. LL 17 April 1927, p. 5.

67. LL 12 Oct. 1927, p. 4.

68. LH 9 Sept. 1924, p. 4.

69. LH 16 July 1925, p. 4. In the same spirit, the *Herald* also applauded the motion picture industry's national "Greater Movie Season" advertising campaign in 1925. In Lexington this campaign included the publication of ads jointly promoting the Strand, Ben Ali, and the Kentucky theaters; a letter of endorsement from Mayor Hogan Yancey; and an article in which three Lexington pastors praised the efforts of the industry and local exhibitors and encouraged their parishioners to support the "better movies season" (LH 12 Aug. 1925, p. 7). Obviously, *local* legitimation was a crucial aspect of the "Greater Movie Season" campaign, which took its cue from Will Hays's well-publicized efforts to enlist the input and support of the Russell Sage Foundation, the Boy Scouts of America, the YMCA, and the General Federation of Women's Clubs (see Jowett, *Film: The Democratic Art*, pp. 173–76).

70. LH 14 Feb. 1926, sec. 3, p. 1.

71. LH 12 April 1927, p. 10.

72. On Arbuckle and the Hollywood scandals, see Jowett, *Film: The Democratic Art*, pp. 154–61. Two quite distinct early accounts are Ramsaye (*Million and One Nights*, pp. 806–9), who sees the Arbuckle affair as an episode in the saga of Will Hays, "the lone horseman and champion of the right"; and Benjamin B. Hampton (*A History of the Movies* [New York: Covici, Friede, 1931], pp. 281–99), who emphasizes the folly of the public, whose "extravagant" and "unreasoning" adulation so readily turned into a "barrage of suspicion and venom directed at yesterday's idols" (p. 288).

73. LL 16 Sept. 1921, p. 4.

74. LH 26 Sept. 1921, p. 4.

75. LH 10 Oct. 1921, p. 12.

76. Richard deCordova, *Picture Personalities: The Emergence of the Star System in America* (Urbana: University of Illinois Press, 1990), p. 129.

77. LH 6 Dec. 1921, p. 4.

78. LL 6 Dec. 1921, p. 4.

79. LL 29 Nov. 1922, p. 4.

80. LL 22 Dec. 1922, p. 1.

81. At first John Elliott said he would keep open the option of booking Arbuckle's films, depending on how successful they proved to be in the East and on how the "better class of people" reacted to the comic (LH 22 Dec. 1922, p. 2). He quickly bowed to public pressure.

82. LL 1 Feb. 1923, p. 4.

83. Harold Leonard, ed., *The Film Index: A Bibliography, Volume I, The Film as Art* (1941; rpt. New York: Arno Press, 1966) remains an indispensable source for this material. I survey a large number of magazine and journal articles in *The Stage/Screen Debate: A Study in Popular Aesthetics* (New York: Garland, 1983).

84. Weekly full-page spreads with promotional articles and photographs began to appear in 1913 in the *Leader* ("News of Photoplays and Photoplayers") and the *Herald* ("Gossip and Comment in the Realm of the Photoplay").

85. See Jane Gaines, "From Elephants to Lux Soap: The Programming and 'Flow' of Early Motion Picture Exploitation," *Velvet Light Trap* 25 (Spring 1990): 29–43.

86. LL 21 June 1927, p. 4.

87. Thomas Cripps, *Slow Fade to Black: The Negro in American Film, 1900–1942* (New York: Oxford University Press, 1977), pp. 115–49.

88. For an urban black situation at this time, see Mary Carbine, "'The Finest outside the Loop': Motion Picture Exhibition in Chicago's Black Metropolis, 1905–1928," *Camera Obscura* 23 (May 1990): 9–41. A broader interpretive framework for this period is offered by, among others, Houston A. Baker, *Modernism and the Harlem Renaissance* (Chicago: University of Chicago Press, 1987), who is concerned especially with "an emergent Afro-American *national* enterprise" (p. 71).

89. T. J. Woofter, Jr., *Negro Problems in Cities* (Garden City, N.Y.: Doubleday, Doran & Company, 1928), p. 263.

90. On the "patterns of segregation" for movie theaters in the 1920s, see Douglas Gomery, *Shared Pleasures: A History of Movie Presentation in the United States* (Madison: University of Wisconsin Press, 1992), pp. 158–60.

91. See the advertisements in the Louisville *Leader* during this period; and George C. Wright, *Life behind a Veil: Blacks in Louisville, Kentucky 1865–1930* (Baton Rouge: Louisiana State University Press, 1985), pp. 227–28.

92. George C. Wright, *A History of Blacks in Kentucky: In Pursuit of Equality, 1890–1980* (Frankfort: Kentucky Historical Society, 1992), p. 23.

93. LH 18 April 1921, p. 10.

94. LL 12 July 1925, sec. 2, p. 4.

95. Richard Koszarski writes that, during the silent period, the western "moved from the serious plateau of the early DeMille pictures to a genre clearly intended for children"; hence it became a "degraded" genre of decidedly "low status" (*An Evening's Entertainment*, p. 183). The Institute of Social and Religious Research concluded in its *Negro Problems in Cities* that "the fighting, shooting and stealing emphasized in western pictures is often found to be the basis of criminalistic imagery that affects young people" (p. 230).

96. LL 4 Oct. 1925, sec. 2, p. 5.

97. Miriam Hansen, *Babel and Babylon: Spectatorship in the American Silent Film* (Cambridge, Mass.: Harvard University Press, 1991), p. 100.

98. LH 22 June 1929, p. 1.

99. The justification for churches to promote such activities was ably set forth by a Sunday school teacher at the white Woodland Christian Church. When the Brotherhood Bible class at his church sponsored a free motion picture program (comprised of a one-reel comedy and a two-reel drama), the teacher justified the action by declaring: "my idea of a church is that it should be a real factor in the whole life of a community, ministering to the educational and entertainment features as well as to the spiritual welfare" (LL 25 July 1919, p. 8).

100. White Catholic churches, like St. Paul's, would occasionally sponsor screenings of films of the Knights of Columbus or the World Eucharist Congress. I found one example of a film program sponsored by a Catholic lay organization at St. Paul's that featured "wholesome entertainment" like *The Victim* and *The Eternal Light*, produced by the Catholic Art Association of New York (LH 10 Feb. 1920, p. 3).

101. LL 2 July 1930, p. 20.

102. LH 20 March 1921, p. 9. On these schools, see William Henry Fouse, "Educational History of the Negroes of Lexington," M.A. thesis (University of Cincinnati, 1937).

103. Lexington's parks and playgrounds occasionally made use of motion pictures during the 1920s, at one point screening a color travelogue on Hawaii (*The Paradise of the Pacific*), then in 1929 scheduling locally produced films of city events.

104. LL 11 Dec. 1921, p. 2.

105. Regardless of the protest against *The Birth of a Nation*, Griffith's Biograph films were frequently included in these programs, which leads me to wonder how much nontheatrical distribution may have contributed to the creation of a motion picture canon.

106. Ogren discusses the response to jazz within the black community, focusing almost exclusively on Chicago and New York City (*Jazz Revolution*, pp. 111–38).

107. LH 12 Jan. 1927, p. 2. See Fouse, "Educational History," pp. 57–71.

108. LL 15 July 1928, p. 15.

109. LL 15 June 1926, sec. 2, p. 1.

110. LH 21 Oct. 1925, p. 13.

111. *Negro Problems in Cities*, pp. 275, 281. The investigator was probably the principal of Lexington's new black high school. For a comparable assessment of dance halls, see William H. Jones, *Recreation and Amusements among Negroes in Washington, D.C.* (1927; rpt. Westport, Conn.: Negro Universities Press, 1970), pp. 121–34.

112. Some sense of the popularity of these events is suggested by the *Herald*'s Colored Notes' report that "Louis Armstrong's band created so much of a sensation that ministers in their pulpits preached about it"; and the Cab Calloway performance at the Palais Royale dance hall drew over fifteen hundred people, with "many white people as well as colored seen to pass the box office" (LH 31 July 1931, sec. 2, p. 6).

113. Roderick Nash, *The Nervous Generation: American Thought, 1917–1930* (Chicago: Rand McNally, 1970).

Chapter 11: The Coming of Sound and the Restructuring of Local Film Exhibition

1. LH 17 April 1927, sec. 3, p. 6.

2. Douglas Gomery, *Shared Pleasures: A History of Movie Presentation in the United States* (Madison: University of Wisconsin Press, 1992), p. 218.

3. Gomery, *Shared Pleasures*, pp. 224–26.

4. LH 4 Feb. 1928, p. 9.

5. LL 18 Nov. 1928, p. 32.

6. I will not trace the local "reception" of radio, but it is interesting to note that the *Leader,* precisely when it found much to complain about concerning the motion picture industry, praised radio in a 1925 editorial because the new medium "ought to be one aid to repose and contentment, since it influences so many families to stay closer by the hearthstone" (LL 15 March 1925, p. 4). Editorials on the subject from 1924 were apt to be entitled, "Possibilities of Radio" (LH 17 Dec. 1924, p. 4) and "The Wonder of Radio" (LL 7 April 1924, p. 4).

Television, which looked to be right over the horizon, also drew considerable attention. It seemed so imminent that the *Leader* was already worried that television programming would be dominated by prizefights and "bathing girl reviews" (LL 6 Aug. 1928, p. 4).

7. LH 16 Sept. 1927, p. 6. On the reaction to radio in this period, see Robert Edward Davis, *Response to Innovation: A Study of Popular Argument about New Mass Media* (New York: Arno Press, 1976).

8. Even the *Leader,* deeply suspicious of the motion picture industry for much of the 1920s, argued that the "talking motion picture would raise the movies to a higher plane," fulfilling the educational potential of the medium, which was—for better or worse—"a real element in the life of the nation" (LL 24 Feb. 1929, p. 4).

9. LL 20 April 1929, p. 10; LH 20 April 1929, pp. 9, 13.

10. Alexander Walker, *The Shattered Silents: How the Talkies Came to Stay* (New York: William Morrow, 1979), p. 193; see also, for example, Harry Geduld, *The Birth of the Talkies: From Edison to Jolson* (Bloomington: Indiana University Press, 1975), pp. 252–68. The way the motion picture industry converted to sound is covered by Douglas Gomery in "The Coming of Sound: Technological Change in the American Film Industry," in *The American Film Industry,* rev. ed., ed. Tino Balio (Madison: University of Wisconsin Press, 1985), pp. 229–51; and "'The Warner-Vitaphone Peril': The American Film Industry Reacts to the Innovation of Sound," in *The American Movie Industry: The Business of Motion Pictures,* ed. Gorham Kindem (Carbondale: Southern Illinois University Press, 1982), pp. 119–35.

11. LH 10 April 1931, p. 1.

12. LL 19 Jan. 1930, p. 1.

13. LL 14 March 1930, p. 8.

14. Other major changes in the ownership of Lexington's movie theaters during the 1930s only underscore how far commercial entertainment had altered since the Opera House was the city's sole permanent venue at the turn of the century. After Paramount was forced into receivership in 1933, Switow again took over the operation of the Kentucky and the State, only to lease the two theaters a month later to the Phoenix Amusement Company, meaning that as of April 1933, all four of Lexington's major movie houses were for the first time controlled by the same locally based company. In 1936 the Phoenix Amusement Company, in turn, was sold to the Schine Corporation, which added the Kentucky, Strand, Ben Ali, and State to its chain of sixty-five theaters in New York and twenty-five in Ohio.

15. Douglas Gomery, *The Hollywood Studio System* (New York: St. Martin's Press, 1986), p. 31. See also Douglas Gomery, "The Movies Become Big Business: Publix Theatres and the Chain Store Strategy," *Cinema Journal* 18 (Spring 1979): 29–40.

16. See several Publix-Kentucky documents on file in the Theatre Historical Society, Chicago: Analysis of Lease, Real Estate Tax Record, and General Property Information for the Kentucky and the State.

17. LL 13 Oct. 1929, p. 2.

18. LH 13 Oct. 1929, p. 6.

19. LL 11 April 1930, p. 31.

20. One extension of my research for this book is *At the Picture Show* (1993), a documentary I directed concerning moviegoing and film exhibition in the small Kentucky town of Campbellsville from the late 1920s to the early 1940s.

21. Bruce A. Austin, *Immediate Seating: A Look at Movie Audiences* (Belmont, Calif.: Wadsworth, 1989), p. 25.

22. Miriam Hansen, *Babel and Babylon: Spectatorship in American Silent Film* (Cambridge, Mass.: Harvard University Press, 1991), p. 99.

23. Mary Carbine, "'The Finest Outside the Loop': Motion Picture Exhibition in Chicago's Black Metropolis, 1905–1928," *Camera Obscura* 23 (May 1990): 9–41. This first-rate study suggests just how much Lexington differed from a "black metropolis" like Chicago.

24. Janet Staiger, *Interpreting Films: Studies in the Historical Reception of American Cinema* (Princeton: Princeton University Press, 1992), pp. 120, 104, 80–81.

25. Hansen, *Babel and Babylon*, p. 7.

26. Hansen, *Babel and Babylon*, p. 17.

INDEX

Unless otherwise indicated, all theaters, organizations, and institutions were based in Lexington, Kentucky.